The Strongest Link

The Strongest Link

An Oral History of Wartime Rape Survivors in Kosovo

ANNA DI LELLIO
and
GARENTINA KRAJA

OXFORD
UNIVERSITY PRESS

Oxford University Press is a department of the University of Oxford.
It furthers the University's objective of excellence in research, scholarship,
and education by publishing worldwide. Oxford is a registered trade mark of
Oxford University Press in the UK and in certain other countries.

Published in the United States of America by Oxford University Press
198 Madison Avenue, New York, NY 10016, United States of America.

© Oxford University Press 2025

All rights reserved. No part of this publication may be reproduced, stored in a retrieval system,
transmitted, used for text and data mining, or used for training artificial intelligence, in any form or
by any means, without the prior permission in writing of Oxford University Press, or as expressly
permitted by law, by license or under terms agreed with the appropriate reprographics rights
organization. Inquiries concerning reproduction outside the scope of the above should be sent
to the Rights Department, Oxford University Press, at the address above.

You must not circulate this work in any other form
and you must impose this same condition on any acquirer.

CIP data is on file at the Library of Congress.

ISBN 9780197699294

DOI: 10.1093/9780197699324.001.0001

Printed by Marquis, Canada

The manufacturer's authorized representative in the EU for product safety is
Oxford University Press España S.A., Parque Empresarial San Fernando de Henares,
Avenida de Castilla, 2 – 28830 Madrid (www.oup.es/en).

Contents

Introduction: Narrating Their Lives	1
1. A War Against Women	19
2. Families	40
3. A New Home	56
4. Insecurity	73
5. War	95
6. They Would Not Touch Women and Children	122
7. Silences	146
8. Justice	169
9. What Remains	189
10. The Strength Inside	215
Appendix	227
Notes	231
Bibliography	251
Index	267

Introduction

Narrating Their Lives

Rape is always present in times of conflict, universally condemned as one of the most heinous crimes. Yet, it is neglected in historical narratives, often appearing as a mere footnote or not at all. Stories of wartime sexual violence, challenging to document, distressing to hear, and unsettling to describe, remain muted; this silence further silences survivors, who carry physical and emotional scars without feeling able—or allowed—to talk about their ordeals. We experienced the burden of their silence while working closely with survivors of wartime rape in Kosovo, whether we were reporting on the conflict, shaping policy, researching transitional justice, or producing the artist Alketa Xhafa-Mripa's installation "Thinking of You." In this participatory art project, involving the collection of dresses across Kosovo, we met scores of women, all publicly silent about their stories and their identities. Some whispered to us, "I am one of them," before retreating to their anonymity. Some took us aside to talk about the war and "what happened" in hushed, tearful voices. Downcast eyes and pained faces spoke for the rest.

As we got to know those women, we understood that their silence was not an absence but a presence wanting to be revealed.[1] We began to feel shame for the indifference of others, and that shame turned into indignation, a feeling we thought we should share through action, as inaction became unbearable.[2] And so, we opened a dialogue with survivors that also could be written and communicated to readers in Kosovo and beyond, in an effort to rescue their stories from suppression.

The Kosovo War began in March 1998 as a counterinsurgency that pitted the Serbian state against the Albanian separatist guerrilla Kosovo Liberation Army (KLA), but quickly turned into a campaign of ethnic cleansing and an international conflict after NATO intervention at the end of March 1999. Albanian civilians bore the brunt of the conflict, with hundreds of thousands expelled from their homes, and thousands killed, tortured, or raped.

Hostilities ceased in June 1999 with the withdrawal of Serbia from Kosovo and the establishment of a United Nations–led international administration that lasted until 2008, when Kosovo declared independence. For almost two decades since the end of the war, Kosovo's society did not acknowledge the existence of survivors of sexual violence. To quote a Kosovo diplomat who prefers to maintain anonymity, "We knew what happened, but nobody talked about it, so I was able to think that it did not happen, that we were not like Bosnia," a theater of wartime systematic rape occurring a few years prior; "I did and did not want to see it. I knew it all along but my brain was my last defense."[3]

We heard the same admission of denial, perhaps not so clearly self-aware, from several people in Kosovo, and always proffered in deeply apologetic, even anguished tones. It sounded as if they "sort of knew it," but had to disassociate themselves from their memories to avoid acknowledging their own wounds, losses, and failures.[4]

Denial does not happen just in Kosovo. It has been an effective defensive mechanism against the collective trauma of wartime rape in many countries throughout history. It took decades after the Second World War to recognize the systematic rape of women in Nanqjing, Berlin, and Montecassino, while sex slaves, euphemistically called "comfort women" by their Japanese traffickers, were almost all dead before receiving their first public acknowledgment. In Kosovo, Martë Tunaj became the first woman to testify against a Serb police officer in a rape trial one year after the war.[5] She was the only witness until a handful of survivors testified as protected witnesses at the International Criminal Tribunal for the Former Yugoslavia (ICTY) against the president of Serbia, Slobodan Milošević, and other Serbian military and political leaders. For years after that, both the society and the victims kept silent.

More recently, this silence has been broken in Kosovo thanks to the lobbying of women's rights and survivors' advocates for justice and public recognition.[6] Since 2017, advocates and journalists have been collecting and publishing wrenching personal accounts of sexual violence, all anonymous.[7] A woman lent her own story to the journalist Murtezi-Shala to produce a fictionalized account, *Unë e përdhunuara* (I, the Raped), in 2018. That same year, Vasfije Krasniqi-Goodman publicly acknowledged her experience as a survivor, giving the first visible face to a collective trauma.[8] Shyhrete Tahiri-Sylejmani followed suit, making public her deposition to Kosovo's Special Prosecutor's office against members of the Serb paramilitaries who raped her in 1999.[9] Since 2018, no one else has stepped forward.

In Their Own Words

Despite this slow and limited emergence of the issue of sexual violence in public, we learned that just breaking silence is not enough. When Kadire Tahiraj, one of the survivors' leading advocates, told us, "We cannot write the history of the Kosovo War without including sexual violence," we heard this as a call to overcome survivors' marginality not only in society but also in history.[10] This recognition opened new questions.

The history of the 1998–1999 war began to be written before the war itself had ended. The world media moved into Kosovo only two years after having left Bosnia and Herzegovina, bringing set patterns of analysis; they replayed the scenarios of the war against civilians they had observed in Bosnia.[11] Later, scholars and policymakers wrote about the eventful NATO intervention, employing different frames—whether they saw it as a humanitarian operation to stop Milošević's ethnic cleansing campaign against Albanian civilians, or as the last imperialist interference in a pocket of resistance against the new post–Cold War world order.[12] The widespread and systematic sexual violence perpetrated by Serbian security forces emerged in the media coverage of the war and was specifically investigated by Human Rights Watch, the Organization for the Security and Cooperation in Europe (OSCE), the United Nations Population Fund (UNFPA), and the United Nations Development Fund for Women (UNIFEM).[13] Yet it found no place in the epic history that KLA fighters and their supporters were writing within Kosovo, focusing on the heroic rebellion against Serbian oppression as the culmination of a national tradition of struggle for freedom.[14] In the postwar period, while political and social actors hailing from the war built their legitimation on this tradition, the memory of the crimes against civilians has been curiously marginalized in public discussions, and so has the memory of sexual violence.

We found the same failure to recognize the importance of sexual violence in the Kosovo War among the broader community of scholars, as well as in the work of international and domestic justice and international organizations. The Kosovo case has been systematically overlooked in social science essays dealing with wartime sexual violence, and more general treatments of the Kosovo War are silent about this crime. A notable exception is the work of human rights organizations such as Human Rights Watch and Amnesty International, among others, which addressed and continue to address the issue of justice for all survivors, including Serbian and Roma women, targeted during the war but also in the interethnic violence that broke out in the immediate aftermath.[15]

As for the courts, the ICTY delivered only one guilty verdict against Serbian leaders indicted for sexual violence as a crime against humanity, before reversing on appeal in 2014 the acquittals of the other defendants in the case against Milošević. At the same tribunal, a KLA fighter was charged with the rape of a Roma woman and was acquitted.[16] In the hybrid Kosovo courts under supervision by the European Union Rule of Law Mission (EULEX), only two cases have been prosecuted with no conviction. The first and only conviction for wartime rape was handed down to a Serbian ex-policeman by Prishtina Basic Court at the end of 2022.[17] Finally, the United Nations Special Representative on Conflict-Related Sexual Violence annual report has consistently omitted Kosovo, despite protests. Testimonies from the survivors of rape of the Kosovo War were published only in 2021 in a United Nations anthology published under the auspices of the UN Secretary General's Representative on Sexual Violence in Conflict.[18]

Whether individually or in collaboration, the authors of this book have tried to close this knowledge gap by writing journal articles that analyze the survivors' search for justice, or that map sexual violence against Albanian women as one of the weapons of ethnic cleansing.[19] By focusing on such a criminal campaign, we are not diminishing the gravity of sexual violence committed against women of other ethnic groups by Serbian forces, KLA soldiers, or Albanian civilians, or the violence committed against Albanian men, the latter reporting their experience only since 2019 and in very low numbers. On the contrary—we have been investigating the long-term consequences of sexual violence for all victims, no matter their gender or their national belonging, in the context of a study commissioned by the women's rights and health organizations Medica Gjakova and medica mondiale.[20] We hope that other researchers take on the important task of examining all episodes of interethnic sexual violence that occurred during or after the Kosovo War, following the lead of Olivera Simić in Republika Srpska.[21] It is thanks to her work that we can better understand the double victimization of Bosnian Serb survivors, who have been severely marginalized and silenced by their own society's refusal to acknowledge them, and have unfairly received the same treatment from scholars, feminists, and human rights activists for belonging to the main perpetrators' group in the Yugoslav wars. As for men, survivors' reticence to come forward has made them almost invisible in Kosovo and has made it easier to neglect them until now.[22] This should change. Understanding the victimization of men and boys would help in understanding the system of power embedded in the patriarchate that hurt men as well as women.[23]

Our book is just about Albanian women. It was born from personal interaction with those who were targeted by the Milošević regime's campaign of ethnic cleansing, and along with Kadire Tahiraj we felt that their history deserved its own chapter. This particular frame may find criticism even within their own society, because it complicates a dominant Albanian national narrative limited to the opposition of victimization to heroism, in itself a gendered contrast between the passive, the weak—in a word, the feminine and feminized—and the strong, active males. Here we are paying attention to the lives of individual women who should never be defined just by their traumatic experience. We were guided by the thought of the unbearable elision of women's subjectivity in classic narratives of rape, beginning with those biblical stories in which women are completely absent from the narrative except for their defilement, echoing a larger silence that extends across time, space, and cultures.[24]

Ordinary people's private lives are usually not interesting for history, but in the history we wanted to write, they are the focus of research and narration, no matter how difficult those lives are to tell and hear. When Feride Rushiti, a veteran survivors' advocate, recalled that one survivor once compared herself to a sack of garbage that everyone wants to put away, we felt that woman's dejection and the injustice of it.[25] In our encounters with survivors, we never shied away from the grim stories of violence, but we knew that there was so much more to hear and learn from them. We were struck by other messages, both explicit and implicit: "I wasn't always like this"; "My dreams were shattered"; "Why should I be ashamed? I am not guilty of anything." We witnessed the pain and shame, but also the anger and the pride, and the enormous strength of all the women we met. Looking at them as survivors, a respectful label that nevertheless cannot contain a person's full humanity and continues to sexualize her, felt wrong. It also felt incomplete. We realized that besides learning how to understand women's silence, we had to learn how to hear them when they spoke.

We thought about how to fulfill our goals of uncovering stories of ethnic conflict and wartime violence and still present the comprehensive range of human experiences that can never be contained in ethnic, national, or gender groupings, even when ethnicity and gender are so salient. We did not want to lose the subjectivity of the extraordinary women we had met, while still maintaining the anonymity of those who would accept to speak to us. It was clear from the beginning that the answer was to work in the tradition of oral history, a discipline born in the 1970s with the explicit political objective of democratizing history because it did gather neglected voices, the voices from below, but quickly moved beyond the simple, though commendable, archival production of testimonies. Our inspiration has been the teaching of the great scholars who critically built oral history as a different way of interpreting sources: Ron Grele's conversational narrative approach, Alessandro Portelli's reading of interviews as producers of meaning, and Luisa Passerini's uncovering of subjectivity as it emerges from several dimensions, including memory and ideology.[26] Using an oral history approach has allowed us to build a thread connecting a plurality of life stories as they are remembered by the tellers. Sexual violence, albeit devastatingly dominant, is one among other experiences.

The Researchers

This book is, first of all, about the women who told us their life stories. The researchers are responsible for conducting the interviews and for presenting them in ways that would be intelligible to the tellers and the readers. Conscious of the ethical issues concerning outsiders' research on wartime rape survivors, we begin by first reviewing our roles.

As women, we felt close to survivors, but none of us ever experienced anything similar to what they did. Indeed, we wore different shades of the outsider's position. Anna Di Lellio was born in Italy and spent more than half of her life in the United States, the country most loved by Albanians, and her association with America made her a sympathetic foreigner. Having resided and worked in Kosovo with international organizations and education institutions for long periods since 1999, she is no stranger to Kosovo, but rather a person who is near although not belonging.[27] She has written extensively on Kosovo culture and politics, including sexual violence during the war. Even when she was not known personally by the interviewees, her collaboration on some projects with advocates of survivors' rights and her working knowledge of Albanian were pivotal in establishing a relationship of trust. Garentina Kraja, a Kosovo Albanian born in Kosovo, was educated in the United States, and after residing in Israel for seven years, is now living and working in Washington, D.C. As a reporter for the Kosovo daily

Koha Ditore, she covered the front lines during the conflict, knew intimately most of the villages that the survivors came from, and witnessed the aftermath of the fighting that left their villages razed. She later covered the refugee crisis in Macedonia, including stories of deportation, assassinations, and rape, after being herself expelled from Kosovo with hundreds of thousands of Albanians. Her work as an adviser to President Atifete Jahjaga, who spearheaded some of the policy efforts to aid survivors, involved her in policies regarding survivors.

We have been talking about our positionality for a while. In our two-decades-long friendship, we have had many conversations about everything, but work, war, politics, and justice for survivors of sexual violence have consistently been the topics that most interested us and fired our passion. We also knew by experience that any researcher—always an expert of sorts, whether a journalist, a member of a nongovernmental organization (NGO), an investigator, or a social scientist—would necessarily find themselves in an asymmetric power relationship with the people they interview and write about. We experienced that power gap throughout our careers. We then focused first on what was more ethically crucial: to ensure that the women who would be willing to tell us their life stories would do so of their own free will, that the telling would not retraumatize them, and that we would represent them respectfully and truthfully.

These self-imposed guidelines are only apparently straightforward. We understood that a woman's desire to speak up about her experience of sexual violence may change and even fade, depending on a broad set of individual and social circumstances that are not always under her control.[28] From oral historians of wartime sexual violence in different contexts, we were alerted of the risks of imposing a professional agenda even on willing participants. As Naynika Mookherjee shows in her critical assessment of an activist oral history of the *birangona*, survivors of the 1971 war that led to the partition of Pakistan, the researchers' intent of documenting crimes, educating the larger public, and seeking justice led them to change the survivors' narratives to make them fit the conversational structure of human rights and feminism; in doing so, they erased the complexity of individual lives.[29] We tried not to do so.

It would have been very difficult, if not impossible, to confront these issues without the crucial support of the leading organizations that provide services to survivors and advocate for their rights, on whose expertise and knowledge we fully relied. Feride Rushiti, the director of the Kosovo

Rehabilitation Centre for Torture Victims Center (KRTC) in Prishtina, was critical in selecting the majority of the interviewees. We first contacted her because we knew her well. She has been involved with survivors for the past twenty-five years as a doctor, an advocate, and the founder/director of the largest service providers for victims of torture in Kosovo. She knows her clients and their condition firsthand. In consultation with the in-house psychologists, she helped select the women who would accept to be interviewed and who would likely not be retraumatized in the process. All interviews were conducted on the premises of the Center, a place where women felt safe, where they knew their anonymity would be shielded, and support would be at hand if necessary. We spoke over the internet only with one because she no longer lives in Kosovo. The rest of the interviews were also conducted at the offices of other organizations that facilitated their selection: Medica Gjakova in Gjakova and the Center for the Promotion of Women's Rights in Drenas, both organizations that play an important role in the lives of survivors.

As for our potential bias in favor of this book's subjects, we found no fault in standing by, feeling sympathy, and advocating for wartime rape survivors, who are struggling to achieve recognition and rights. Our standing is consistent with the condemnation of war crimes and crimes against humanity and the will to contribute to justice for their victims. Oral historians' commitment to furthering social justice is often apparent, and is facilitated by the main attributes of oral history itself:[30] a particular narrative form that is richer than other forms of autobiography and storytelling because of the flexible and expansive character of the interviews and the active intervention of the historian; the affective engagement of the interviewers with the narrators and subsequently the larger audience; and the historical content of the narration that connects biography and history.

With other oral historians of survivors in different contexts, we agreed that making the suffering of an individual a social experience would be one form of justice.[31] We did consider whether that notion would hold true in contemporary Kosovo and whether it would lead to a good outcome for the survivors themselves. We were satisfied by the knowledge gathered from our previous work and the reactions to the 2015 installation "Thinking of You," which consisted in a grassroots, country-wide collection of dresses that were hung on clotheslines in the football stadium of Prishtina to honor survivors of sexual violence. The installation made use of art's symbolic imagination to make anonymous survivors publicly visible and bring a private trauma to the public sphere.[32] By breaking the silence around sexual violence, the installation also intervened in the power dynamics characterizing public secrets, which stigmatize and subordinate survivors; as a result, survivors and their representatives felt empowered. Finally, the installation expanded social and institutional recognition, which pressured the state to implement the law that provides a pension to survivors.[33]

We now know that achieving social recognition and implementing a reparation policy are a step in the right direction. Still, it is just a "thin" acknowledgment that does not go beyond formal acceptance and is not enough for survivors. They long for "thick" acknowledgment, which can be described as empathetic acceptance by everyone, not just sympathetic listeners, everywhere—in the family, the neighborhood, the village, the town, and the country. What would it take to fulfill their desire? Perhaps nothing short of a moral revolution similar to the one Dom Lush Gjergji, the Catholic Bishop Vicar of Kosovo, saw happening during the mass campaign for the reconciliation of blood feuds in 1990.[34] To paraphrase what he said on the occasion of the twenty-seventh anniversary of the event, the campaign leadership managed to persuade individuals and families to renounce vengeance by replacing honor with love as a key principle of the society.[35] They did not visit the victims just to ask them to forgive the blood of their loved ones, but to share their grief. They put themselves in their shoes, as survivors of sexual violence would like us to do.

The Narrators

We interviewed a total of twenty women in 2015 and 2018. Garentina Kraja conducted thirteen interviews alone and three with Anna Di Lellio. Kadire Tahiraj conducted four on her own. The interviews lasted for a little more than one hour on average. We spoke more than once with three participants. All the interviews were conducted by native speakers, without an interpreter present. The participants signed consent forms which stated the use of the interviews and the commitment of the researchers to guarantee the anonymity of the interviewees. One gave her assent verbally, through the phone, allowing its recording, since she lives in a third country. Another survivor did not want her story to be recorded, but accepted notes to be taken as she spoke. We already discussed the positionality of the researchers. Here, it is important to highlight that although Garentina Kraja is a Kosovo native and deeply knowledgeable of the war, which she experienced as a journalist and a refugee, the fact that she belongs to the urban elites and no longer lives in Kosovo created a gap between her life experience and the tellers that worked in unexpected ways. As we constantly interrogated ourselves about our condition as outsiders, we realized that rather than hindering communication, the distance between us and the narrators facilitated it. They knew we would not and could not breach our commitment to keeping the interviews confidential because we do not belong to their social circle and the community that matters to them. Of the interviewers, Kadire Tahiraj, director of the Drenas Center, is the only insider, insofar as she shares a rural background and now works closely with survivors. She has been in close contact over the years with the individuals she interviewed and enjoys their complete trust. We did not share the transcripts or the draft of the book with participants. However, when asked by some of them, we explained how we chose to present their stories and showed them their quotations.

In agreement with the professionals who help to care for the survivors, the main criterion to select the interviewees was their willingness to speak to us. The majority come from rural Kosovo, especially the regions of Drenica and Dukagjin, which were targeted for greater and more brutal violence than other parts of Kosovo because they were less ethnically mixed and were more prominent centers of armed resistance against Milošević's Serbia. The higher number of interviews from those areas reflects the reality of the war. The rest are from the northern and northeastern regions and from Prishtina. The age of the women at the time of the interviews varies from early thirties to early sixties. Most were in their twenties during the war, some were older, and a few were minors. This range reflects that women of all ages were targeted, as we confirmed by looking at a database of about four hundred survivors of sexual violence provided by Medica Gjakova, which was the base of our research on rape as a weapon of war in Kosovo and other campaigns of ethnic cleansing.[36]

The language of those interviews is the vernacular of the women and varies according to their region of origin. They were later expertly transcribed with seed funds made available by the Kosovo Oral History Initiative by Arzana Kraja—a film director, a writer, a sister, and a friend who experienced the apartheid and the war of the 1990s and was among those deported from Kosovo in 1999. We lost her unexpectedly on November 13, 2019. Her sister Garentina, one of the coauthors, dedicates her work in this book to her memory, a beautiful soul who cared deeply about telling the stories of the unsung heroes. In the transcripts, Arzana tried to maintain the cadence of each woman's speech, and to use punctuation to reflect the flow of the speech as much as possible, although assigning punctuation to spoken words is inevitably arbitrary.

In the final English translation of the quotations, all done by the authors, we omitted the repetitive saying that frequently occurs in the spoken language but did not change the idioms and the expressions that might be typical of a region, a generation, or an individual. We changed all the narrators' names, and chose the names that were more frequently given in the generation to which the woman belonged, based on information retrieved from the Kosovo Statistics Agency records. We were careful to not include any information which would reveal their identities, including their town or village, the number of their siblings, or any other unique identifiers.

We conducted the interviews as conversations about the lives of the participants. There was no list of questions prepared by interviewers. Interventions were kept at a minimum and were targeted to explain or clarify points made by the tellers. All participants were aware that they had been asked to be interviewed as rape survivors. However, the interviewers made it clear that the tellers should feel free to talk about anything they thought was important to them and that they were not required to recount the violence they experienced in detail because the focus of the research was not sexual violence per se, but their life stories. How they spoke about the rape and torture they endured during the war was surprisingly vivid at times and different in each case, but did not take the greatest part of the telling.

We did not face any tension in conducting interviews about life stories with a group identified primarily for the violence they experienced and potentially reduced to that violence, a possibility which Anna Sheftel addresses in her oral history of Bosnian and Holocaust survivors.[37] As we showed genuine interest in hearing stories from the beginning of their lives, we found that participants opened up to us beyond the recounting of violence. Mary Marshall Clark, who writes from the perspective of an oral historian interested in narratives of trauma, has suggested an intriguing connection between narrative and medicine: "Beginning with a laundry list of symptoms shifts the attention away from the life story, or the story of the person, and that shift can slow down the process of telling the story of the body and of reaching a diagnosis that by necessity may require the history of a person as talking about symptoms shifts away the attention from the life story."[38] Knowing that the beginning is the most important element of a story, we did not begin with the history of violence but by asking about childhood memories, and from there many other memories emerged. And while we cannot claim that we now know the whole life of participants, we gathered a complex collection of poignant memories of the past and representations of the present.

The interviews were psychologically draining for all involved. On many occasions, both the interviewers and the women cried and had to stop for a few minutes to regain their composure. However, there was never a moment when they showed an intention to withdraw their participation in the interview. They were all interested in telling their story. Some were accustomed to talking about themselves, having done it with investigators, prosecutors, and psychologists. Others were less forthcoming but always willing participants. At times, the narrators changed the tone or the volume of their voices. Several of them spoke more softly when they talked about being pulled out of school to get married. Their voices went even lower, down to a whisper, when recounting the war and the violence. Those who talked about feeling disappointed at meeting their groom on the wedding day raised their voice as they forcefully stated their dislike. In other instances, they spoke firmly and louder, as when they talked about their anger at the social pressure that contributed to stigmatizing them and their resentment at society's neglect, or when they stated what they want now for themselves and their children. All those emotions cannot be fully transposed into the written text. Our efforts, inevitably, are based on the written transcript. Body language and intonation are lacking, but we did our best to communicate through the text the women's forceful and expressive testimonies.

Finally, a word on the terms used. We followed Portelli in his preference for "narrative" and "narrators," rather than "testimony" and "informants." This, however, does not mean that the women who agreed to speak to us are less credible than witnesses, but reveals a different emphasis in the research: "'Narrative' implies an awareness of the role of verbal organization and of the inherent ambiguity and connotative aura of language, which can be rendered less ambiguous only at the price of heavy loss of information. 'Narrator,' on the other hand, spotlights the speaker's subjective presence."[39]

Women's Lives—A Map

Once we had recorded the interviews, we discussed how to present them to the reader. We decided that the book's structure would be influenced by the choice of collecting life stories, and we followed in part a chronological approach intertwining individual experiences and broader historical events. The chronology, however, is not an orderly series of events; it provides context while also evoking themes. The emerging narrative places episodes, moods and feelings—in sum, the humanity of the tellers—within time frames that are established through individual recollection of a shared history.

In composing the narrative, we were primarily inspired by Alessandro Portelli's approach in *The Order Has Been Carried Out*, in which he edited the collected stories to produce a choral narration.[40] By choral, we do not mean homogeneous. We attempted a polyphonic narration, as Portelli calls it. We did not present the interviews as monologues or as evidence to back up our arguments on the subject, but used fragments of interviews in parallel or counterpoint. In this regard, our book substantially differs from other oral history accounts of survivors' experiences, for example those of neighboring Bosnia, from the heart-wrenching testimonies collected by journalist Seada Vranić and the Center for Investigation and Documentation in Sarajevo, to Selma Leydesdorff's work on the women of Srebrenica and Inger Skjelsbæk's narrative analysis of interviews with survivors.[41] The voice of the tellers dominates the narration, and only when the flow of their speech was too halted and difficult to comprehend did we paraphrase it.

The narration has a choral quality because of the overrepresentation of women from rural Kosovo, where traditional mores and customs were still much alive in prewar years and continue to exert a significant influence in the postwar period. Most of the narrators share this traditionalist social and cultural background, which differs from urban life, especially in contemporary Kosovo. While the book is primarily based on the interviews with survivors, we also used interviews conducted by the Kosovo Oral History Initiative; they are mostly but not exclusively interviews with women active as rights' advocates or as politicians, and their identity is public. Other interviews cited in the book were conducted over the years with a range of individuals, from former KLA commanders to journalists who covered the war. To complement oral sources, we included written sources, such as books, articles, reports, and ICTY documents and transcripts. All those sources are necessary to provide a context for the tellers' narrations, which are truthful testimonies but speak to what the subjects remember they did, wanted to do, felt, and thought about events unfolding around them, perhaps even more than to the events themselves.

This is an oral history. We invite readers to look at the narrative we present as the product of the communication that we, as the authors, had with both the tellers and their texts. We wrote what we heard from them and what we read in their words, adding context based on what we know about their world and the history of Kosovo. As the tellers allowed us to see them from the inside, we tried to capture their thoughts and feelings. Throughout, they answer with great clarity the question which haunts them and us, listeners and readers, often explicitly and always implicitly: "How is it possible to go on living after what happened?"

The individual answers to such a question naturally vary, although there are inevitably patterns because the experience of trauma was collective. The Kosovo War, the last European war of the past century, was not about religion but about territory; nevertheless, it was permeated by gendered ethno-religious ideologies that were crucial to "othering" Albanians, dehumanizing them, and defining Kosovo as an ethnically charged borderscape to be cleansed. The political use of "our" women as signifiers of the nation that must be defended, and "their" women, especially their bodies, as symbolic of the enemy nation that must be humiliated, repressed, and excluded, dominated the language used before the war. Within the context of Milošević's Serbia, a state-run propaganda targeted Albanian men as rapists and demeaned Albanian women as reproductive machines, the instrument of an inferior oriental culture for a demographic domination of Kosovo. Such propaganda had already seeped into local communities, fueling rumors and fears when the security forces previously active in Bosnia, and responsible there for widespread, systematic sexual violence against Muslim women, moved into Kosovo. This weaving of nationalism, religious hatred, and hyper-masculinity is not unique to Kosovo, and has been comprehensively discussed in the context of all the Yugoslav wars.[42] We found echoes of a similar dynamic and its weaponization in the campaign of ethnic cleansing waged by the state of Myanmar against its Rohingya population, and in several other similar cases.[43]

Since most of our narrators hail from rural Kosovo, their early lives are rich with stories of the shared memories of time spent among extended, farming families. In remembering that past, the adult women weave a complex narrative that includes feelings and knowledge, moving from nostalgia and happiness to sadness and anger. They reveal a warm, communal family environment defined by traditionalist customs and ordered by patriarchal rules. In remembering, they also approach the submission to those rules critically, highlighting the consequences of communal order for individual freedom, and in particular for women. They all remember the poverty.

Listening to their memories of childhood brought to mind the stories of peasant women interviewed by oral historian Nuto Revelli during the late 1970s in the Langhe, the mountainous region of the Italian Piedmont bordering France.[44] Though they referred mostly to life before the Second World War, the Italian women talked of families as small communities that pulled resources together to survive off the very poor economy of small, mountainous landholdings, a way of life that was destroyed by industrialization in the 1950s and 1960s. Here is Maria: "We were three sisters, had only a little land, very little, one cow....I sold my hair, I must have been eight years old, in exchange for a little dress." Another Maria: "My mother was carrying a bundle of hay on her head when she started labor and she was about to lose me, she carried me in her apron." Caterina: "How did we live? Bread and milk were our basic food, but I was never hungry, more or less everyone was like us, nobody went hungry....I began to work as a child, as a shepherd. I would leave at eight in the morning and come back at nine in the evening, all day with one piece of bread." And Marianna: "In the winter we children slept in the stable, on top of the hay for the goats, in the summer in the barn or on the floor, where they kept the tools and sacks of wheat." We could replace their names with the names of our narrators and the stories could stay the same. Revelli titled his book *L'anello più forte* [The strongest link], turning upside down the stereotypical classification of women as the weaker sex, and we titled ours *The Strongest Link* to echo his sentiment.

The constraints on the lives of our narrators were not just cultural and social. In prewar rural Kosovo, long-standing political isolation from the central government, especially for families whose members had been involved in movements promoting a republican status for Kosovo within Yugoslavia or even a secession, meant no access to resources and power. In that context, it was impossible for girls to continue their education after the state-mandated eight years for a variety of reasons that have to do with lack of means, the difficulty of reaching schools that were few and distant, and the fact that education served little purpose for a life destined to focus on home and children. Out of school and obligated to accept arranged marriages, young women entered new families where they were supposed to assume the roles that they had seen their mothers play. As they talk about that transformation, they recognize that it was then that they first learned and practiced how to be silent about their aspirations, desires, and thoughts—an awareness that later moved them to make a different life possible for their daughters. The contrast with life in the cities could not be starker, as Yugoslav cities have been places of rapid growth and social and cultural modernization in the post–Second World War period.

Building on the feelings of greater insecurity that the narrators developed throughout the 1980s and 1990s, we mapped their experience of danger even before the war. They became acquainted with what was happening in the Yugoslav army, where suddenly a large number of young Albanian conscripts began dying, officially classified as suicides, and shipped home in sealed coffins. They saw relatives being beaten in their homes by police and came to know how prisoners of conscience, as Amnesty International called the Albanians crowding Yugoslav detention centers, were tortured by investigators and guards. The youngest among the women interviewed were still of school age when Milošević ascended to power, and they could not continue schooling because it became simply too dangerous to cross checkpoints on the way to class. In a foreshadowing of what was yet to come, streets, schools, hospitals, and even homes felt increasingly unsafe.

Perhaps the most difficult to write and read is the narration of memories of displacement and violence. We discussed at length the problem of wearing down the reader with repetitions because, especially in rural Kosovo, everybody lived through the same terrifying and tiring sieges, flights, displacements, forced marches, and violence. We ultimately decided to present most of the stories, to convey the narrators' fear and exhaustion. These are vivid recollections of how, suddenly, the houses that in childhood memories were happily packed with family became infernal shelters crowded with crying children and cantankerous older people. We heard, time and time again, of lack of food, water, and privacy, and no hope to escape unscathed. On their own, as the men fled to escape certain beating or death, the women were terrified and daring at the same time. They stayed behind to guard the house, the older people, and their children. They went out of hiding in search of food, carrying clothes and provisions to the underground fighters, or trying to protect more vulnerable members of their family, taking the active roles thus far played by men. They perhaps knew the risks but still thought that women and children would be spared, and if they feared mal-treatment, they certainly could not imagine that sexual violence would be one of the Serb security forces' weapons against Albanian civilians. They were proven wrong.

Telling stories of violence was not the primary motivation to write this book. Rather, we felt the pull exerted by the survivors' eloquent silence. Because we began from silence, we felt the need to define it by deciphering what silence meant to the individuals as they understood it: self-imposed silence, whether by shock, shame, and circumstances; other-imposed by social pressure, whether implicitly or explicitly, a learned silence since adolescence; and silence that is both assumed on themselves and reinforced by stigma. It is from the tellers' stories that we drew a wealth of signs, information, and feelings. The narrators' self-understanding of how silence is required from women in a patriarchal culture echoed what we knew about silence as evidence of feminine virtue in any culture and since time immemorial.

Those who directly confronted Milošević at the ICTY broke their silence in unique ways that can be best understood by their willingness to speak to power. In the semi-public context of a court of law, they found the courage to do what had been denied to them, that is, tell the truth about their experience to the man who had so much power over them once, and now refused to relinquish it, by manipulating their vulnerability. Although Milošević no longer had any capacity to hurt them from his seat at the criminal defendants' table, he still embodied the evil power that had turned their lives upside down. Nevertheless, they spoke to that power, taking the significant risk of being retraumatized, understanding their duty to the law's normative order.

When we listened to narrators discuss the "afterward," we were overwhelmed by the complex array of feelings and circumstances. They told us about the lingering trauma, the nightmares, the suicidal thoughts, the difficult relationships with equally traumatized families, and the relentless power of stigma that keeps them "in" and "down," pressuring to conform to the normative and social order of their society and always in a degraded position.[45] We recognized that all those psychological and social responses to trauma can be best explained as complex post-traumatic stress disorder (CPTSD), which describes severe distress in survivors of prolonged trauma.[46] But we also heard the will to live, testify, and publicly redeem their lives. NGOs and activists who have worked with survivors since the end of the war have been pivotal in enabling them to regain some self-confidence by tapping into their inner resources. Just the beginning of teaching them to recognize and name their feelings, one advocate told us, was itself a long journey. As psychologists converse with survivors about their whole life, they help understand the shame at having survived a terrible ordeal, an understanding that can change the trajectory of their identity.

Our hope is that our compassionate listening strengthened the narrators' narrative agency, that our encounter with them made possible the re-emergence of suppressed truth.[47] In their telling, alternative stories emerge of courage, endurance, and strength, not simply victimization. To use the symbolic narrative of the stories of rapes in Ovid's *Metamorphoses*, ancient tales that still speak to us because sexual violence has been experienced by women through centuries, Kosovo survivors show that they can escape from their destiny of silence.

What the women we interviewed do is weave their traumatic experience into the tapestry of their lives, like Ovid's Philomena. Philomena's brother-in-law rapes her, then cuts out her tongue and locks her away in order to prevent any accusation. She nevertheless refuses to be a passive victim and "writes" the story of her rape on a tapestry she weaves for everyone to see. It is telling that this archetypal character continues to inspire action, such as the U.S.-based Common Thread, an NGO of psychologists and other trauma experts who have revived the ancient practice of weaving as a healing method: they gather women to sew their stories onto cloth and find support in each other. In Kosovo, the weaving is metaphorical but equally powerful.

The Strongest Link: An Oral History of Wartime Rape Survivors in Kosovo. Anna Di Lellio and Garentina Kraja, Oxford University Press. © Oxford University Press 2025. DOI: 10.1093/9780197699324.003.0001

1

A War Against Women

The Yugoslav army tanks began to roll through the crossing of Merdare at Kosovo's northeastern border on March 3, 1989, and with them, trucks loaded with soldiers ordered to quell a "counter-revolution" that was threatening, according to state authorities, the very existence of the country.[1] Kosovo was paralyzed by a general strike against the revocation of provincial autonomy within the Yugoslav Federation; from the top leadership to students and workers, all Albanians had rebelled against the return of Kosovo under the rule of the Republic of Serbia. By engaging the army, the state's reaction went beyond ordinary repression to establish a military occupation, with martial law, curfew, checkpoints, and unbridled army and police violence.

"It's going to be a war against women," predicted Sevdije Ahmeti, a librarian from Pristina who shortly thereafter organized the Albanian women's resistance with a handful of other professionals.[2] It was not an unfounded premonition; for a decade, public conversations had been saturated with a language that sexualized and dehumanized Albanians, as Serbian nationalist groups blanketed the state media with a nasty propaganda that depicted Albanian men as rapists of Serbian women, and Albanian women as breeders. Yet nobody acknowledged Sevdije's foreboding. The political leadership that monopolized, unopposed, the Albanian mass resistance to Belgrade told her to drop that kind of talk because "it might give some ideas to the enemy."[3] At any rate, the nation was under attack, not the women: focusing on women's issues was a distraction from the national cause. The leadership could not see that there was a connection between gender and nationalism and never understood the profound influence of this connection on the patterns of sexual violence immediately deployed under martial law and later, in the war.

A Modern Form of Hatred

The hostility between Albanians and Serbs in Kosovo did not begin in 1989. It was not the product of ancient hatreds,[4] but dates back to the early twentieth century, the time of the formation of the Serbian and Albanian states from the ashes of the Ottoman Empire. This epochal process failed to align statehood with nation, setting the stage for an enduring interethnic conflict that began with the 1912 Serbian Kingdom's annexation of Kosovo.[5] Serbs thought that the annexation was a liberation, the reconquest of a Christian land that belonged to them, but found few Serbs left among a predominantly Albanian and Muslim population.[6] Albanians experienced the annexation as a violent occupation, and became a hostile minority for the ruling elites of Serbia, later Yugoslavia.[7] If Albanians until then had built their claims to nationhood in relation to the Ottomans, they now developed anti-Slavic sentiments as the new rulers crushed their aspirations to either unite with the just born Albanian Republic, or enjoy autonomy within the Ottoman Empire.[8] Nationalist circles, whether Albanian or Serbian, have argued about who owns Kosovo ever since, by framing the issue of "ownership" in terms of historical rights and conflicting narratives of Kosovo as their ancestral land. Serbs went back hundreds of years, to the fourteenth century, focusing on their medieval kings, the warrior-saints who built churches and fought against Islam. Albanians went back much earlier, to their pre-Roman Illyrian forefathers as the original inhabitants of Kosovo and all the neighboring territory populated by Albanians in modern times.[9]

Kosovo was the site of the 1389 battle at the field of blackbirds that pitted a coalition of regional forces against the advancing Ottomans and became a foundational myth for the Serbian nation.[10] It took other clashes and several more decades for the Balkans to finally be subjected to Ottoman rule, but the 1389 battle acquired unique meaning thanks to a well-known epic tradition that emerged as a literary phenomenon in the late nineteenth century.[11] The leaders of both camps perished in Kosovo: the Serbian prince Lazar Hrebeljanović in battle and Sultan Murat I assassinated by a knight from the opposing camp in a suicide mission. By celebrating the first death as a model sacrifice for Christianity and the nation, the second as a testimony of Serbian valor and loyalty through the deed of the legendary killer of the sultan, Miloš Obilić, the Serbian epic fed a narrative of the subsequent loss of sovereignty to the Ottomans as a tale of victimization and redemption. Albanians do not feature at all in this narrative.[12] Writers and diplomats who engaged in forming the modern Serbian nation in the early twentieth century assumed that Albanians were latecomers and that they were replacing the "original" Serbian population of Kosovo. Those Serbian elites transferred to Albanians the most damning features of primitivism expurgated from the ambivalent figure of the "wild man" that had come to represent the Balkan people in the Western Europeans' intellectual construction of the East.[13] In his typology of Balkan psychological types, which he pitched to the Great Powers as an expert at the 1919 Paris Peace Conference, the geographer and ethnologist Jovan Cvijić depicted Serbs as strong highlanders who could unify the South Slavs, and Albanians as a population without history and civilization, an undeserving criminal group.[14] Throughout the twentieth century, Serbian nationalists explicitly laid out a series of policies toward Albanians ranging from assimilation to deportation in documents of the Orthodox Church, intellectuals' manifestos, and political programs.[15]

Kosovo's place as the Albanians' ancestral home from time immemorial is key to defining the "Albanian question," a dominant theme in the pan-Albanian national movement. It is best illustrated by the diplomat Mehmet bey Konitza in 1918 as the claim that "the restoration of the Albanian state within her ethnographical limits" was crucial for peace in the Balkans.[16] That question was not settled at the 1912 Conference of London, when an independent Albania was carved out of the Ottoman Empire, though its borders remained unsettled for several years among the wrangling of Western powers over the Balkans. By 1918, Kosovo was part of the Kingdom of Serbs, Croats, and Slovenes. Among other punishing policies, an agrarian reform dispossessed Albanian peasants while favoring both Serbian elites and war veterans, and pushed thousands to emigrate to Turkey in the attempt to change the ethnic composition of Kosovo.[17] None of the repressive policies implemented by the kingdom completely succeeded in "pacifying" Kosovo, where *kaçak*, Albanian outlaws, roamed through the countryside. The Drenica native Grigorije Božović was a seminarian, a journalist, and a Serbian ministry inspector, who described them as being "not plain criminal, political and social brigands, as such, but a particular type of Albanian outlaws...who have become a revolting sickness, nowadays assuming a new, nationalist, and consequently anti-state form, and thereby becoming our great problem."[18]

The Second World War began in the Kingdom of Yugoslavia in April 1941 with the invasion of the country by the Axis and the flight of King Petar II to London.[19] The kingdom was split between Germany, Italy, Hungary, and Bulgaria. Germany established a quisling government in Belgrade and ruled over Serbia and northern Kosovo. Italy occupied the Adriatic coastline of Croatia, including Montenegro, and joined the majority of Kosovo to Albania, annexed two years earlier, to create Greater Albania.

Despite its imposing name, Greater Albania was nothing more than a protectorate of the Italian Fascist empire, which kept the local leadership and the people subjugated and under control through important concessions.[20] The right to schooling in the Albanian language, prohibited in the Yugoslav Kingdom, was a key one; another was the license to expel the very Serbian colonists who had been settled in Kosovo during the interwar period.[21] The memory of those violent expulsions is still kept alive in Serbian historiography and popular culture as genocidal violence.[22]

In Kosovo, it is the memory of wartime Greater Albania and the "good" Italian occupation that the people still cherish, the subordination to the Axis occupiers justified by the freedom gained from Serbia.[23] Not surprisingly, many more Serbs and Montenegrins than Albanians joined the ranks of the anti-Fascist insurgency of Tito's partisans who freed most of Yugoslavia of the Italians and Germans. The occupation ended by the late fall of 1944, the war in the spring of 1945, but peace did not immediately follow. Civil conflicts continued, as the newly installed Communist government gained control over the territory by violently suppressing the ideological and national opposition. Those conflicts disappeared from Communist official historiography, but also were often ignored or forgotten by Western scholars because they did not fit easily into historical narratives about the Second World War and its aftermath.[24] Locally, they were never forgotten, even when they only lived in the subterranean memory of survivors, and the memory of the violence embedded in civil conflicts was elaborated on all sides as the memory of genocidal violence, feeding deep hostilities across Yugoslavia.[25] In Kosovo, an Albanian armed resistance in Drenica to the mass conscription called by Tito to fight the retreating Wehrmacht in the north and push toward Trieste was suppressed by Yugoslav partisans. The crackdown on the rebellion, including notable episodes of violence against civilians, crushed any possibility of a new beginning for Albanians and Serbs in Kosovo after the collapse of "Old Yugoslavia."[26]

The New Yugoslavia

The advent of socialism in 1945 had theoretically ushered in the era of a Yugoslav supranationalism, classically represented by the slogan "brotherhood and unity" among different national groups. However, Albanians were not included in the scheme that recognized six constituent peoples of Yugoslavia—Bosnians (categorized as Muslim from 1971), Croats, Montenegrins, Macedonians, Serbs, and Slovenes—each endowed with an autonomous republic. Kosovo was annexed to the Republic of Serbia. For Albanian Communists, who believed in the promises of a new society that would either allow national self-determination or make borders insignificant, at least within the socialist world, Kosovo's status should not have constituted an unsurpassable obstacle to independent life. Events proved the opposite. Three years later, Kosovo was still under martial law. Yugoslav authorities framed any manifestation of rebellion or even dissent as the product of lingering fascist sympathies; even the Albanian Communist leadership was suspected of Anti-Yugoslavism in the aftermath of the war, a suspicion that was revived any time ethnic or political tensions escalated.[27]

In June 1948, all ties with neighboring Communist Albania were severed, as Stalin broke with Yugoslavia's president Tito, and Albanian leader Enver Hoxha sided with the Soviet Union. The split was due to Stalin's anger at Tito's expansionist foreign policy that planned to "swallow" Albania into Yugoslavia while stirring the Greek civil war and disturbing the balance of power with the West.[28] On this occasion, Hoxha, who had been very close to Tito during the war and in the immediate aftermath, behaved as he consistently did over the years: he waited until he could postpone a decision, and then took the side that was more convenient to him, claiming that he stood up to Tito, while in reality he wanted to save his position.[29] Albanians in both countries were hit hard by this historical event: families who were used to freely crossing the borders between the two countries found themselves suddenly divided, and many were not able to meet again for decades.[30] The history of Serbian-Albanian hostilities has since developed as a conflict between the centralizing Serbian Republic and its Kosovo periphery, with Albanians a minority in the Republic but the province's demographic majority, too close for comfort to their kin state next door.[31]

The slow opening of Yugoslavia, which coincided with the sacking of Tito's closest collaborator Aleksandar Ranković in 1966, offered a window of opportunity for better relationships between Serbs and Albanians. Sometimes known as *palach* (the executioner), Ranković was in charge of internal affairs and since 1948 had vigorously pursued pro-Stalin "Cominformists," from the Communist Information Bureau that banded together all the European parties under Moscow's guidance. With the Cominformists, other types of troublemakers were constructed as "enemy of the state," among them unloyal Albanians, who became targets of state repression.[32] Police sweeps of rural Kosovo in search for weapons became routine, as well as the purchase of weapons to hand over in order to avoid torture. With the demise of Ranković, the police state that ruled Kosovo also relaxed.[33] However, a fundamental change arrived only a few years later.

The Constitutional reform of 1974 granted Kosovo the status of an autonomous province of the Republic of Serbia and a degree of independence that came closer to the status enjoyed by the other Yugoslav republics. A regional Communist League and government elite could thus emerge, for the first time reflecting the demographic makeup of Kosovo more than the traditional Yugoslav power structure. In the three decades following the war and so long as federalism was substantially weakened by Yugoslavia's initial preference for Stalin's centralized economic and political model, Communist leaders dependent on Belgrade held a disproportionate role in local power structures. In Kosovo, this meant that the Serbian and Montenegrin minority was overrepresented in the leadership: a quarter of the province population, they accounted for 50 percent of party membership and 68 percent of leading positions.[34]

With the 1974 Constitution, the self-governing power granted to Kosovo and further decentralizing reforms allowed the largely Albanian society of Kosovo to acquire the basic features of the Yugoslav system. A new political elite emerged within the frame of the party: by the late 1970s, Albanians were two-thirds of the League of Communists in Kosovo, reversing the postwar trend.[35] Blue-collar workers grew in number and status due to state-directed industrialization, and so did white-collar workers, with the expansion of the public sector and a burgeoning education system that allowed the Albanian language for the first time in the history of Yugoslavia. Organizations of neighborhoods, workers, professionals, women, students and youth—the Socialist Alliance of Working People (SAWP)—facilitated the capillary penetration of the state in the society. It promoted participation through grassroots consultation on leadership selection, policy proposal, and implementation. At its peak, in the early 1970s, the Yugoslav self-management system involved about 800,000 persons out of a workforce of 4 millions, and that made participation firmly rooted.[36]

What this change did not do was socialize dissenting groups to the core value of multinational Yugoslavia. Instead, it created a uniquely pluralistic socialist system, opening up opportunities for mobilization, especially in urban centers, at the same time that the legitimacy of the Yugoslav economic and political system was beginning to show the first signs of erosion.[37] In

Kosovo, educators who were able for the first time to express themselves in Albanian and teach Albanian history and culture provided an appealing alternative national frame. In particular, the University of Prishtina, founded in 1970, played a crucial role in building an Albanian national consciousness, and the student movements of 1968, 1981, and 1997 became the main engines of mass mobilization demanding a republic status for Kosovo.[38] The local Serbian minority, anxious about losing long-held privileges, began to complain of threats posed by an alleged untenable blackmail: either "forced Albanianization" or migration. Those who left Kosovo for Serbia claimed to have been forced to do so, feeding a public discourse of Serbian victimization and displacement that was never confirmed by any evidence. Serbian emigration from poor regions of Yugoslavia in the 1970s and 1980s was not unique to Kosovo, was never as high as nationalist propaganda held, and was largely for economic or family reasons, with a few cases of intimidation or pressure.[39]

On their part, supporters of Pan-Albanianism thought that the autonomy achieved so far was just another form of subordination to Serbia. They were never allowed to develop a national mass movement, as the efficient Yugoslav secret service, capable of infiltrating even the most secret groups, managed to identify their members, who were incarcerated, tortured, and sometimes killed in prison. Illegality was the normal condition of this loose network of militants known by the collective name of *Ilegalja*, organized in small clandestine groups that constantly renewed their membership after arrests or migration through recruits made in family circles, prisons, universities, and the diaspora. Perhaps it was this cycle of destruction and rebirth that gave *Ilegalja* the appearance of continuity throughout the postwar period.

In reality, it was never a cohesive and homogeneous organization, however ideologically united the different *Ilegalja* groups seemed in their proclaimed greater affinity for the Marxism-Leninism of Enver Hoxha than for the brand of Communism practiced in Tito's Yugoslavia. They simply fought for the liberation of Kosovo from Serbia and unification with Albania.[40] The target of state repression of *Ilegalja* was vast, including all members of a subversive family. Even when not directly involved in actions deemed subversive, one could be banned from school or denied a job, guilty by association. On the opposite spectrum there was another Albanian society, integrated and sharing in the relative comfort of Yugoslavia, where the early separation from Stalin had facilitated more collaborative relationships with the West and freedom of movement across Europe unparalleled in the Eastern bloc.

Under a Police State

President Tito ruled over Yugoslavia from 1945 until his death in 1980 using a successful mix of repressive policies, his own charisma, and conflict-management abilities. With Tito gone, the federal center weakened, and demands for more decentralization from the wealthiest republics such as Slovenia and Croatia, the latter still recovering from the 1971 mass arrests and purges of reformists, collided with centralizing and hegemonic pulls from Serbia.[41] A new period of unrest and instability began. In March 1981, for the first time since the end of the Second World War, the Yugoslav army was employed in Kosovo to quash a student protest that quickly grew into a national mobilization for Kosovo's status as a republic.[42] From the point of view of state authorities, this was not a legitimate demand, given that the six constituent Yugoslav republics were built on nations, and according to the Orwellian language of the Constitution, Albanians, which made the majority of Kosovo's population, were not a nation, but a "nationality." The demand for a republic was indeed dangerous, because it foreshadowed the long-held aspiration of *Ilegalja*'s fight for unification with the Republic of Albania. Facing popular unrest, the Yugoslav leadership did not split along ethnic lines in their reaction. Both Serbian and Albanian Communists agreed that Kosovo had to remain part of the Republic of Serbia, enjoying only as much autonomy as could be granted to a province.

Throughout the 1980s, ethnic hostilities increasingly worsened. Activists who pursued their national aspirations in clandestine groups had always been hunted down by an overpowering secret police, the infamous UDB-a,[43] but after 1981 state repression cast a wider net to silence any potential supporter of a republic of Kosovo. The army and police showed no restraint against the rebels. They beat and killed scores of protesters, arrested and tortured hundreds more, while the courts delivered long jail sentences to prisoners of conscience.[44] The Communist League purged its elites of less conformist individuals. Gone was its top leader Mahmut Bakalli, guilty of providing a Marxist-style sociopolitical analysis of the unrest, but mostly for not having prevented it. For cadres in state institutions, the liberal professions, and even the arts, the mere suspicion of sympathies for the protesters or any show of interest for anything Albanian became grounds for firing and ostracism, a process of purges euphemistically called *diferencimi* (differentiation).[45] Through a combination of selected targeting and mass violence, within a few months, order had been restored.

Still, in ways that the Yugoslav security apparatus had not been able to foresee, the repression enlarged and empowered the Albanian movement for national independence. Mass arrests and long sentences for prisoners of conscience turned prisons into schools of rebellion. Emigration was the other training ground for political activists. Since the 1950s, Albanians in Kosovo had considered the West a refuge, whether for economic reasons or to escape political persecution, but in the 1960s and 1970s the Yugoslav government actively encouraged migration. It was a move that had two goals: to transfer abroad the problem of political dissent, and to maintain the mirage of Yugoslav consumerism that was not available to all, certainly not to the Albanian minority. Inequality and poverty were guaranteed for them by the stifling impact of state repression on structural obstacles to development, such as their rural economy and society.[46] In the 1980s, the many Albanian migrants found in the West the place not only where they could work to support their families at home, but also where they could organize, far from the control of a repressive state.

It was different in 1989, because national differences split the unity of the Communist leadership of Kosovo and the federal system was also showing serious signs of crisis. The president of the Communist League of Serbia, Slobodan Milošević, was a ruthless apparatchik who had climbed to the top post by navigating the party's corridors of power and exploiting both the nationalist inclinations of intellectual, religious, and military elites, and a growing popular unrest. By then, everywhere throughout Yugoslavia the streets were full of workers who felt aggrieved by decreasing salaries and a mismanaged economy that was entering the seventh straight year of recession. That was not supposed to happen in a socialist country whose legitimacy rested on making workers happy. It was a risky time for the Communist leadership, who needed only to look East to see Communist states collapse one by one. For Milošević, workers' discontent was an opportunity to strengthen his power, especially as mass protest against the underperforming ruling bureaucracies of the Yugoslav republics began to be expressed in nationalist terms.[47] He rode the unrest in the northern Serbian province of Vojvodina and replaced the local leadership with men loyal to him, then reshaped the Montenegrin leadership in a similar fashion.

When Milošević turned to Kosovo, he felt supported by a mass movement of local Serbs who resented even the small economic and political gains made by Albanians in the previous decade and demanded a return to their lost privileges. Milošević satisfied their demands by revoking the autonomy enjoyed by the province since 1974. The entire Albanian population of Kosovo protested, from the top Communist leadership to the students, the workers, and especially the miners, with a heroic week-long hunger strike in the pits.[48] He framed the unrest as a "counter-revolution" in the making and persuaded the Yugoslav federal presidency to send in the tanks. A counter-revolution it was not. Begun as a protest against re-centralization of power, the strikes had dramatized the birth of "Albanians as a political subject in Yugoslavia," in the words of political analyst Shkëlzen Maliqi.[49] Maliqi thought that Albanians had broken the "psychological barrier" dating from the bloody repression of 1981, which had disciplined them to refrain from any public demonstration of national identity.

The writer Mehmet Kraja also concluded that the Albanian national identity had made a quantum leap and had eroded internal differences, but went further, understanding the strike as a rupture that had exposed the futility of believing that one could be both Albanian and Yugoslav.[50] The disintegration of Yugoslavia began right then, when it became evident that the Communist elite in Belgrade and the top army brass would not concede any terrain to federalist aspirations. As Slovenia and Croatia prepared to secede, Kosovo saw police and army shoot on demonstrators in the streets, a growing wave of arrests, a series of legal and administrative decisions restricting civil liberties, and scores of trials on charges of sedition, as well as the purging of all Albanians from state institutions and workplaces. The first to be let go were the Albanian police and the territorial defense that was a sort of national guard—in other words, all Albanians who could legitimately hold weapons. In their stead, new police forces were sent directly from Serbia, and local Serb civilians began to arm as a citizens' militia.[51]

The reaction of Albanians was to organize province-wide civil resistance, which throughout the 1990s gained respect internationally for its alignment with the pacifist movement and its ability for self-government.[52] In quick succession, from 1990 to 1992, the dissolved Provincial Assembly declared the independence of the Republic of Kosova and drafted a constitution, a popular referendum overwhelmingly confirmed that decision, and elections held in private homes as polling stations created the republican assembly and the government.[53] The resetting of Kosovo as an alternative state was the result of a culture of resilience and peace as much as of structural circumstances. It was made possible by the extensive Yugoslav social organization of the Workers' Alliance (SAWP), whose Albanian members joined en bloc the party-movement of the *Lidhja Demokratike e Kosovës*

(Democratic League of Kosovo, LDK), providing the structure and the cadres to the self-styled state of Kosovo.[54] At the helm of the new party were the intellectual circles less organic to the old Communist apparatchik, organized in the Association of Philosophers and Sociologists and the Association of Writers.[55] Albanians and Serbs began to live in two "separate worlds."[56] Serbs kept the administrative buildings and Albanians organized their own, literally underground. They attended separate schools, went to separate hospitals, patronized different shops and restaurants, and even walked on different and separate sides of the *korzo*, the main pedestrian street in the capital Pristina, during their daily promenades.

Those two worlds were so starkly different, and their access to government resources and power so lopsided, that the label of apartheid-system began to be widely used to describe Kosovo. With virtually no support from the state, Albanians' quality of life was greatly diminished. Their schools were makeshift classrooms in private homes and basements, their hospitals were small, ill-equipped clinics. A region-wide welfare association called Nënë Tereza (Mother Theresa), organized with the support of the Catholic clergy but not confessional in structure or mission, presided over a mutual-help national community, which got by on remittances from families abroad, a scheme of self-taxation adopted by the diaspora in the West, and thousands of volunteers. The self-styled Kosovo state led by Ibrahim Rugova, the head of the Association of Writers of Kosovo, who was voted president in unofficial elections, existed only in name. However, it made the decisive choice to not engage the Serbian state militarily, since the terrifying news of carnage and destruction coming from the Bosnian front showed the directions that events would take in Kosovo if war broke out.

Gendered Nations

Throughout the 1990s, as Serbia became embroiled in bloody conflicts elsewhere, from Slovenia to Croatia and Bosnia, a relative truce reigned over Kosovo—a temporary truce, rife with ethnic tensions and low-intensity violence. Fear and hatred against Albanians had found fertile terrain during the previous decade in Serbian nationalists' racist propaganda that exploited and manipulated gender as the enemy's weapon. In the narrative thus conjured, Serbs had lost Kosovo to Albanians by failing to keep their birth rate higher, and through the rape of their women by Albanians. Though there was no evidence on which to base such an accusation, the idea of Serbian masculinity diminished by an alleged Albanian animal sexuality worked well to stir up both ethnic hostilities and individual insecurities.[57]

This highly symbolic conflict revolving around sexual imagery turned into grotesque reality in 1985, when Djordje Martinović, a Serbian clerk at the military garrison of Gjilan, reported an injury caused by a broken bottle in his backside.[58] Martinović initially said that two—or more—Albanian men had been his torturers, but quickly recanted that version of the incident to admit that he was the one who placed the bottle in his rectum. All the possibilities played in public discourse: that Albanians had attacked Martinović, that Serbs had done it instead but only to blame Albanians, that Martinović had done it to himself, and even that he had jumped from a tree onto the bottle, given the seriousness of his injury. What is important is that the incident had a significant impact on an impressionable audience that was riveted by this sordid story and was fed by state media with an abundance of lies and manipulative versions of the event. Months later, the courts and medical examiners concluded that the injury was self-inflicted, but the consequences of the sentiments aroused by the incident were fatal for Yugoslavia.

In 1986, a petition to the assembly of Yugoslavia by 216 Serbian intellectuals called this case of "rape" a symbol of "the predicament of all Serbs in Kosovo," charging that even "old women and nuns" were being raped by Albanians.[59] The petition called Martinović "the new deacon Avakum," after an eighteenth-century Serbian Orthodox clergyman condemned by the Ottomans to be impaled. The notorious Memorandum of the Serbian Academy of Sciences and Arts suggested a connection of the Martinović case to "the darkest days of the Turkish practice of impalement."[60] "Impalement by a beer bottle" came to signify the historical violent subjugation of Serbs by the Turks, and by extension their Albanian allies, as sexual humiliation.[61] In her indictment of nationalist propaganda, writer Dubravka Ugrešić said that the war in Yugoslavia began precisely in 1985, "with the posterior of a completely innocent Serb peasant."[62]

Throughout the last years of the 1980s, an unrelenting campaign conducted through all Serbian media presented the rape of Serb women by Albanian men as a common crime. In a 1987 special issue of the journal of philosophy *Theoria* devoted to the Kosovo problem, a well-known psychologist, Djordje Vuković, wrote that Albanians "rape whomever they can, married women and girls, old women, as well as ten-years olds. They rape them everywhere: in public places, at bus stops, in ambulance cars."[63] No evidence ever confirmed the reality of such crimes, but the report nevertheless produced mass anxiety and generalized condemnation.[64] The Serbian Criminal Code was amended in 1986 to punish sexual assault across national lines more severely than other rapes. In 1988, the newspaper *Politika* was saturated with reports of rapes or attempted rapes of Serbian women within the context of Albanian separatism. Among other sensationalist titles, "Rapes are the main means by which Albanian separatists' plan of an ethnically pure Kosovo will be realized," and "Women want to know whether they will be protected or whether we are going to emigrate from Kosovo collectively."[65] The Serbian media publicly threatened Albanians: "Let them rape; we can rape too."[66] There was no official criticism or condemnation following that extraordinary statement.

The intensity of this media attack pushed Albanians as a group into a defensive position, from which they rallied around their denigrated traditionalist society and morals by upholding them against corrupting outside influence. One might read in this context the curious—and extreme—case of the Albanian Communist leader Fadil Hoxha, who reportedly proposed importing prostitutes from Serbia or other parts of Yugoslavia to perform functions that the notoriously modest Albanian women could not possibly perform, thus solving the so-called epidemic of rapes.[67] This flippant and insulting statement, allegedly proffered in a private meeting and always categorically denied by Hoxha as hostile propaganda,[68] brought thousands of Serbian women and children into the streets under banners reading, "We are not whores, we are mothers" and "We are the mothers of the sons of Serbia."[69] Building on a strong connection between gender, sexuality, and the ethno-nation, each group deployed stereotypes of their own women as mothers and those of the enemy as whores.

Bahtije Abrashi, the president of the Kosovo Women's Conference, a socialist mass organization of women, met the brunt of the sexualized ethnic hatred for Albanians in a rally of Serbs in Fushë Kosova, a town outside Prishtina: "When I went inside the hall, I saw that there were probably 300 people. Milošević was there as well and they were all for Milošević.... They said, 'You know nothing, you only know how to give birth...we will rape you all.' They had it in their plans, because they said, 'First we will rape Fadil Hoxha, he insulted us.' I said, 'Why are you attributing that insult to Fadil Hoxha? He already apologized for what he never said.' The hall fired up even more at that moment. 'We will rape Fadil Hoxha's wife...his wife, his daughter, his daughter in law,' they called them by their names, 'we will rape all Albanians, and you too.' They almost beat me up. This was the mood that reigned at the time."[70]

In 1990, as insecurity and violence became the norm for Albanians, the newly formed Council for the Defense of Human Rights and Freedom (KMLDNJ) began to collect cases of human rights violation in Kosovo. There was no Albanian presence in the police or the courts, because these institutions had been the first to be ethnically purged. Martial law conferred enormous power on law enforcement, in particular the license to invade houses without any warrant. As a young human rights field researcher, Nazlie Bala quickly became aware that rapes of Albanian women by the police were becoming a frequent occurrence from 1990. Armed with a notebook and a pencil, Nazlie took down the story of two housewives, in Vushtrri and Gjilan, who had been raped by the police.[71] The reporting followed a well-worn script: police broke into houses late at night or very early in the morning in search for weapons, and they beat up and arrested the men, who were later tortured in jail, some of them killed at the police station, while the women were taken to a separate room and raped. In rural areas, where Albanians lived in isolated family compounds, police separated the men from the women and gang-raped the latter with total impunity.

The Council's leadership preferred to record the incidents as the ill-treatment of someone's wife, sister, or cousin. Human rights activists understood that they had to straddle the line between denouncing this heinous crime and protecting the privacy of the victims, but women's rights activists such as Sevdije Ahmeti began to resent the fact that victims lost their identity in the process: their identity would be subsumed in the identity of their male relatives. Vjosa Dobruna, a friend and a doctor, felt the same: "In the reports, they always wrote that the women were collateral damage, and that the damage and the violations didn't really affect the women, but the men. I had a very difficult time with that, and on the days I was assigned a case, I would go and get the testimony and write the woman's name, but when I went to the office I saw that they had erased that name."[72] Vjosa looked for support elsewhere. A loose transnational network of feminists were quickly coming together to respond to the Bosnian crisis, as a stream of Muslim women refugees were flooding into neighboring countries carrying horrific stories of gang rapes and rape camps. Vjosa established contact with Raffaella Lamberti and the other women at the Casa delle Donne of Bologna, Italy, at a gathering of Western European and Yugoslav women's rights activists.

She obtained the first funds and much needed logistical as well as moral support.[73]

Sevdije and Vjosa left their work at the council to focus on the violence against women. This is how the Center for the Protection of Women and Children in Pristina came about in 1993. It was a hard decision, because it went against the wishes of the political leadership. Vjosa remembers a talk she had with the much respected President Ibrahim Rugova, who told her, "What are you doing? You are dividing the society. Instead of us making a common front against Serbia, you are talking about women's rights." There simply was no room for any public opposition to the violence against women in the national strategy of civil resistance against Serbia. On February 12, 1995, a nineteen-year-old Albanian girl reported that she had been raped by police in a village near Gjilan. After wrangling for days over the propriety of publicizing the incident, the village women stood together in the street in silent protest, only to be quickly dispersed and sent home by Albanian leaders.[74] By then, the women working at the center had understood that Sevdije's initial intuition was right: the war was a war against women.

In 1995, any hope for a negotiated solution to the crisis in Kosovo was crushed. The Contact Group, the steering group on Balkan issues that included the United States, Great Britain, France, Germany, Italy, and Russia, excluded the Kosovo delegation from the Dayton Peace Conference, which put an end to the Bosnian conflict. Hundreds of Albanian Americans rallied at the gate of the U.S. air base where the peace talks were held, demanding to meet chief negotiator Richard Holbrooke. As a prominent member of the Albanian diaspora, Bruno Selimaj, remembers it, it was Rudolph Perina, the chargé d'affaires at the U.S. embassy in Belgrade, who met with them and destroyed all their hopes for an internationalization of their cause: "There would be a future conference on Kosovo, but now it is not the time."[75] The time for a diplomatic solution of the Kosovo crisis did not come fast enough.

Clearing Operations

Three years later, in March 1998, the Kosovo war began in earnest when Serbian security forces came head to head with the Kosovo Liberation Army (KLA). An armed group of Albanian independentists had been training since the beginning of 1991, but later was conducting small acts of sabotage and then attacks against Serbian police and military.[76] The brutality of Serbian counterinsurgency, which disproportionately killed civilians as it targeted insurgents, made international headlines. Most importantly, it energized the Albanian diaspora, which contributed funds and fighters to the KLA, until then a small and underprepared network of friends and members of the nationalist underground.[77] As the war intensified, the violence against women also escalated as part of what armies tasked with ethnic cleansing across countries and times like to call "clearing operations"—a deployment of troops engaged in violent campaigns against civilians that are intended to cut insurgents from their communities.[78] By the end of the year, almost half a million civilians were displaced from their homes and lived in camps hastily set up in the valleys or the mountains, or were taking shelter in neighboring villages, drawn for protection to areas where the KLA showed more strength. Refugees lived precariously, crammed into the homes of relatives or camping in the mountains.

With the humanitarian emergency, the specter of Bosnia came back to haunt Western countries. In July 1995, Srebrenica, a small town in eastern Bosnia that had been declared a "safe area" after growing fourfold with the arrival of Bosniaks (Muslim civilians) displaced from its surroundings, had fallen to the Bosnian Serbian army. In the days immediately following the surrender, that same army killed 8,000 Bosniak men, raped the women, and expelled the rest to make the population purely Serbian.[79] In the case of Kosovo, NATO countries came together and decided that a repeat of the Srebrenica genocide had to be avoided at all costs. Several attempts at deescalating the situation, from establishing international monitors to verify negotiated truces to the peace conference at Rambouillet, near Paris, in February 1999, had all been unsuccessful. As diplomacy failed, NATO decided to go to war against Serbia to stop the crackdown on Kosovo. Lacking authorization of the Security Council, the war violated international law and was illegal, but a broad agreement formed on its legitimacy, since its primary stated goal was a "humanitarian intervention."[80]

On March 24, 1999, a NATO bombing campaign against Serbia began. What happened next was Milošević's intensification of an ethnic cleansing campaign of Albanians, whose memory should not be lost nor sanitized. While Western planes flew from 15,000 feet above the ground, Serbian security forces unleashed their vengeful rage on civilians with renewed fury and no real opposition on the ground.[81] They were not defending their country from NATO, since they flew no planes, and with paramilitary formations under their command, they certainly did not defend Kosovo, but destroyed a large part of it. Serbia has never acknowledged its responsibility in the war. Instead, revisionist accounts of the war continue to deny ethnic cleansing, always referred to it in quotation marks, and attribute the human losses to "intertwined war scenarios," including NATO and the Serbian army and paramilitaries.[82] Within a little more than two months, half the Albanian population of Kosovo, about 800,000 in total, had been expelled; Albanians did not flee the bombing, as Serbia always maintained. The war came to a conclusion with the Military Technical Agreement between KFOR and Serbia, also known as the "Kumanovo Agreement," signed on June 9, 1999, that ordered the withdrawal of Yugoslav and Serbian armed forces. The bombing was responsible for 453 civilian casualties, including 220 Albanians, 205 Serbs, and 28 Roma. The count of civilian casualties, whether killed or missing, from January 1, 1998, through June 14, 1999 was 7,903, including 7,346 Albanians, 385 Serbs, and 172 Roma and others.[83]

Wartime Sexual Violence

The survivors of sexual violence during the conflict are not as precisely accounted for as the dead, but their number is high, even according to the U.S.-based Centers for Disease Control, which put the figure at about 20,000.[84] Plenty of evidence, collected during and immediately after the war by transnational human rights investigators, confirms widespread and systematic sexual violence.[85] Kosovo thus remains inexplicably absent from current global surveys, such as the United Nations Annual Report on Conflict-Related Sexual Violence, especially because it is a key case to understanding the dynamics of sexual violence as a "weapon of war."

Scholarly research has criticized the categorization of sexual violence as a "weapon of war," despite its being almost a commonplace in policy debates, for failing a test of verifiability.[86] For sexual violence to be a weapon of war, as the argument goes, there must be evidence of explicit orders issued by commanders, evidence that is typically very hard to obtain and was not found in the Kosovo case either. However, we came to the conclusion that indeed Kosovo is emblematic of the use of sexual violence as a weapon of war based on our analysis of oral history interviews and ethnographic observations, ICTY documents, and the mapping of war violence, cross-referencing a large subset of cases of sexual violence (388) with the

Humanitarian Law Center database of mass killing.[87] We could verify the key dimensions of frequency and geographical diffusion of sexual violence and determined that it was perpetrated on a scale too great to suggest randomness; it targeted victims of all ages; it occurred countrywide to accompany other manifestations of violence; and it was part of a military strategy.

Although there are survivors among women belonging to other ethnic groups, sexual violence was directed against Albanian women and men because of who they were. As they were raped, they were cursed and dehumanized for being Albanian "breeders," "washing machines," and othered as aliens to the "Serbian" land of Kosovo. They were often gang-raped, detained for days as sex slaves in private and public buildings. They were beaten, bruised, burned, cut, branded, and in many instances, assaulted in public. In the cities, Serbian forces raped women at home, in hotels, in police stations or administrative buildings, and during the mass deportations of Albanians during the NATO war, pulled from refugee columns, train wagons, and bus stations. In rural areas, it occurred concurrently with other crimes, such as mass killing, property destruction, and forced expulsion, during highly controlled and coordinated military operations, with the political objective of persecuting and expelling Albanians.

Seen in context, the collective targeting and persecution of Albanians was enough for the ICTY to conclude that sexual violence was indeed systematic, that is, planned, without further evidence of explicit orders.[88] The law is clear in this matter, as the commentary to the Rome Statute clarifies regarding widespread and systematic rape: "proof that the perpetrator had knowledge of all characteristics of the attack or the precise details of the plan or policy of the State or organization" is not necessary; it's enough that "the perpetrator intended to further such an attack."[89] The ICTY judged four Serbian military and political leaders responsible for having committed the crime against humanity of persecution through sexual assault in Kosovo; one was convicted by the Trial Chamber, the rest on appeal.[90] In the trial, the judges had initially found that too few instances of rape had been brought to their attention to convict the defendants. Few witnesses, a total of five, had testified as protected witnesses, and as the identity of some of them was revealed, other potential witnesses were discouraged from coming forward. But on appeal, the judges determined that "relevant legal standards" allowed them to infer discriminatory intent even in a handful of cases, because the crimes of sexual violence occurred during a planned mass expulsion of Albanian civilians that employed a systematic campaign of terror and violence.[91] The intent to discriminate, the judges concluded, could not be contradicted by the randomness suggested by the low number of cases under review.[92]

The ICTY trials provide a wealth of publicly available documentation that does not contain orders to commit sexual violence or reveal the motivations of perpetrators. What it does reveal is a context of a highly organized and disciplined structure which was the Serbian security system, including army, police, special forces, and paramilitaries. In court documents, we found evidence of several forms of implied orders that strategically incited subordinates to commit violence.[93] Military leaders chose euphemisms and code language when giving orders. Some "acted" criminal orders rather than gave them. They decriminalized criminal behavior of which they were aware by not punishing it. They gave vague, fragmented orders that would be known and understood differently by different subgroups under their command. Finally, they outsourced violence to paramilitary groups that appeared independent and uncontrollable, but were branches of their organizations. The main goal of the military operation in Kosovo was to execute an ethnic cleansing campaign, and the Serbian security forces used sexual violence, in combination with other forms of violence, to terrorize communities and force them to leave.

In this book we focus on Albanian women, but we are aware of other groups that were victimized, including Albanian men. In Kosovo, only a few male survivors are known to psychosocial services providers. The sexual violence perpetrated on them remains grossly underreported and underresearched. This is not unusual across conflicts. In Bosnia, evidence of sexual violence against men in detention has been documented at the ICTY and investigated in domestic war trials, but nothing is known about violence outside prisons and camps. From our interviews with five male survivors while researching the long-term consequences of sexual violence, we began to understand that they were assaulted in police stations or detention centers, at home, and at check points; that they were targeted because they were Albanians and were told so; and that the intent to terrorize was manifest in indiscriminate rape of men and boys of all ages. The pattern of this crime was similar to the pattern of sexual violence perpetrated against women.

That the entire population of Albanians was targeted for sexual violence does not surprise if enough attention is paid to how gender played a key role in a range of institutional efforts to subordinate, exclude, and repress. In the prewar period, the mobilization of ethnic, religious, and gendered ideologies incited a conflict in which masculine ideas of domination and honor came to define the nation.[94] Serbia was defined as a strong nation engaged in the defense of Serbian women from Albanian sexual predators, whose nation was turned into a weak and feminized target of sexual violence.[95] State policies of the expulsion of Albanians from all institutions and workplaces configured them as virtually stateless and powerless.

Sexual violence targeted also Roma, a diverse group that used to include Albanian and Serbian speakers and both Muslims and Orthodox Christians. Estimated at just under 10 percent of the overall population of Kosovo, in the early 1990s this group was divided into three: Roma, Ashkali, and Egyptians.[96] Why and when the women of these groups were targeted, and by whom, can be explained by the dynamics of the Kosovo conflict.[97] As Milošević consolidated his grip on Kosovo, Serbian authorities used these marginal minorities as the pretext to engineer a more "ethnically diverse" political representation and dilute the demographic prominence of Albanians. Many were forced to emigrate by the deterioration of the security situation. Of those who stayed, some were invited to take the jobs from which Albanians had been fired, only to be fired in turn when Serbian refugees from Croatia and Bosnia were shipped to Kosovo and took their place. With the war, the Serbian military and political authorities treated Roma, Ashkali, and Egyptians erratically. At times they victimized them; other times they used them as subordinated "allies," often forcing them to perform loathsome jobs—such as grave-digging—or to join Serbian security forces.

Albanian-speaking Roma, Ashkali, and Egyptians shared the fate of Albanians. During the NATO intervention, the Serbian army and police tortured, raped, killed, and expelled Roma families, along with Albanians.[98] After the NATO deployment in the region in June 1999, and the establishment of a UN-led international administration, UNMIK, a security vacuum made Kosovo very dangerous for Roma, Ashkali, and Egyptians, all lumped together as collaborationists with the Serbian regime. Sexual violence against these groups by the KLA during or immediately after the war was documented by the European Roma Rights Center, Human Rights Watch, and the OSCE.[99] In one case tried at the ICTY, although the defenders were acquitted in the first instance, on appeal, and in a retrial, the court was satisfied that one KLA soldier had raped the Roma witness.[100]

Postwar Kosovo was an international trusteeship from 1999 until February 17, 2008, when the Assembly declared independence. The

Republic of Kosovo has been recognized by all G7 states and 101 members of the United Nations, but not by Serbia and its most important ally, Russia. Kosovo functions as a liberal democracy with a constitution that guarantees special rights to minorities, Serbs in the first place, who have large margins of autonomy in the municipalities where they are the majority and in the northern part of the country, contiguous with Serbia. In the aftermath of the war, Serbs who stayed in Kosovo were targeted with violence, notably in the summer of 1999 and later in 2004. Still, while there are accounts of people killed or disappeared, little or nothing is known about sexual violence perpetrated on them.

On the occasion of a study commissioned by the women's rights organizations medica mondiale and Medica Gjakova, we interviewed a Serbian woman married to an Albanian who was raped twice, during the war and immediately after, by the same Kosovo Liberation Army (KLA) who killed her husband, while her teenage son had been murdered earlier by unknown perpetrators. Such instances could have been motivated by revenge and reprisal, or the desire to terrorize and remove minorities from Kosovo, and deserve further investigation by both scholars and the courts. They belong, however, to the same logic of collective targeting that dominated the broader campaign of ethnic cleansing of Albanians by the Serbian state.

Since the end of the Kosovo war, thousands of women have sought help from organizations providing medical and psychological help, and they are slowly and painfully coming to terms with what happened to them. They have begun to "come out of their cave," as one survivor put it,[101] though they still prefer to maintain anonymity. As we listened to their stories, we realized that they were speaking about traumatic experiences, utter lack of solace, isolation and stigma, but also much more, since their lives did not begin or end with the war.

The Strongest Link: An Oral History of Wartime Rape Survivors in Kosovo. Anna Di Lellio and Garentina Kraja, Oxford University Press. © Oxford University Press 2025. DOI: 10.1093/9780197699324.003.0002

2
Families

Merita's father was the youngest of his brothers, and all their families lived with the grandparents, thirty people in all. The adult couples each occupied one room of the big house, but the children slept together: "We were many and happy. Back then maybe we didn't have money, didn't have food and all that, but there was a sort of spiritual happiness, there was no worry, care or concern." Born in the early seventies, Merita grew up in the central, rural area of Kosovo that is only a few kilometers from Pristina but remained a very isolated and poor region until the war. "I had a normal life, you know, the same life as all of our people, a normal farmer's life."

That was life in the Albanian "joint family," made up of a number of different nuclei from the same lineage cohabiting in an egalitarian relationship to each other. Better known by the Slavic name *zadruga*, this household structure is common to the entire western Balkans region and beyond. More precisely, it is both common to cultures with a certain kind of agriculture and herding activities, and unique to different national contexts. As Margaret Mead explained, "Table and chairs are remarkably similar in form and function: the way in which different people sit on them, or at them, varies enormously."[1]

The joint family lasted longest in Kosovo, much to the dismay of the authors of *Косово/Kosova*, an ambitious bilingual monograph published in 1973 by the regional Communist leaders, who followed Engels's evolutionary theory of the family and considered the *zadruga* as *mbeturina* (left over, relic) of the past, destined to disappear with economic development.[2] Although they were not the norm, very large families were still found in the mountainous western region of Dukagjin or the central area of Drenica in 1971, where more than half of the active households of Kosovo lived off sustenance farming.[3]

What had remained unchanged since the 1950s was the traditional social structure and culture of the family, as the American anthropologist Janet Reineck found in the late 1980s when she conducted fieldwork in western Kosovo.[4] Reineck's research provides an excellent guide to understanding the Albanian traditional household as it was structured and functioned, with the extended family and the nuclear family at the bottom of a stratified social structure, in which each level refers to some criterion of inclusiveness:[5] the *fis*, or clan, group (whose members believe themselves to be descended from a founding ancestor along patrilineal lines), the village, the *farefis* (known patrilineal descent group, or widest group of relatives, defined by exogamy), the network of cousins, and the father's brothers. Those groupings are determined by the "tree of blood" (*gjaku*), the generations descending from the father, which is separate from the "tree of milk" (*gjini*), or relations linked to the mother—a categorization still very meaningful in all the contemporary Albanian-speaking world.[6] Knowledge of the male ancestors is fundamental in this lineage organization that is common to Serbia, Montenegro, and Herzegovina.[7] In Albanian society, the *fis* is identified with the clan, where a common ancestry also shares a territory and enjoys a certain autonomy and should not be confused with a tribe, a political entity with the authority to arbitrate disputes, nor does it translate into a clannish social structure.[8]

The individual becomes a person in this context. The basic unit of the family is the house, a social group with multiple functions—economic, political, juridical, and customary.[9] An Albanian child's world comprises the *oda*, or the men's room where the guests are received; the communal kitchen, where women and children congregate; the bedrooms for the married couples; and the rooms where all the children sleep together. Although contacts with the outside world are reserved to men, all the other activities, such as housework, work in the fields, care of animals, and trade, are distributed among the members of the family. Children are perceived and treated like small adults; they work daily in some capacity and quickly grow in their future roles.

Në Baqillak (Living Together)

Coming of age not far from Merita in rural Drenica, other narrators, such as Shpresa, Edona, and Shkurta, belonged to the same world. Their stories intersect. As we listened to their childhood stories, we realized that each of them could pick up where another left off.

Shpresa too was born in a joint family: "We were *në baqillak*, do you know what that means? We lived all packed together, all thirty-two of us." In her house there were so many children sleeping in one small bedroom, lying on mattresses that covered the entire floor, that only a small space remained for a tiny heater, "a crumb of a heater," and that was not enough. Shpresa did not like the cold or the idea of sleeping with her older brothers, but, "Where else could I have gone?"

Edona and her sisters huddled together "under one quilted blanket, on top of one foam mat. Today if you brush against another, they yell, 'Why are you pulling my blanket?' But we could do it, all of us sisters, we slept under one blanket, on one foam mat. That blanket was pulled here and there, our feet all uncovered. This was our life, I'm not lying." As for the comfort of indoor plumbing, the only bathroom in Edona's house did not have a toilet; it was just a room with a hole in the ground, a place to bathe known by the Turkish word *hamamgjik:* "I didn't find a bathroom even at my husband's family, I'll be honest, because at my husband's I met the same poverty. We didn't have a toilet to sit on. Now we often say, 'At night, our back hurts, all our spine hurts.' And one of my sisters says, 'How could they not hurt?' Because back then, we would slip out from under the blanket at night and go to the outhouse, freeze, and then get back into bed, shaking from the cold."

During the day there was much work to be done. As the oldest of a large family, Shkurta learned how to cook at the age of five: "I helped my mother at home with all the housework. I also did crochet and knitted; in short, I did all the handiwork, I was practically a housekeeper." Edona and her sisters contributed to building their house, preparing the mud that their father used to plaster the bricks, since no mortar was available: "At night we lit a lamp and held it so he could work. We built one room, then another one, and then another one, till we made three rooms. We tilled every palm of the one hectare of cornfield we had. We set the alarm clock, but we woke up on our own at 4 a.m., alarm or no alarm. Dad never had to come to knock on the door and call, 'Wake up!' We got up and went to the field to plow the soil until 10 a.m., then we went home to eat, and Dad would say, 'Now sleep and rest until the afternoon, when it's cooler.'"

Edona's father had been married before, but his first wife died without giving birth. "The real wealth arrived when he had us. My uncle, I swear on these two eyes, would come and tell dad, 'You are greedy, you filled the entire field with your girls, while we are left with unused tools.'" This is how the girls handled the plowing tool: two of them grabbed it, one on each side, because they were so young and small that they would not have been able to move it otherwise.

When she was not busy in the fields, Merita tended the livestock. She was not even twelve when she learned to milk the cows. Yet, she remembers never complaining or feeling the need to stop doing what she was doing and rest. On the contrary, grown up and strong as she was, she was very proud of being able to do the work of the adults, and especially of making her mother smile as she looked at her hard-working child. Shpresa milked cows until she turned fourteen, "then I began the handiwork. My first job was to make socks which I took to the city to sell. I made a bridal trousseau for myself, to bring with me when I got married. I made those linens by myself. I made them to be like all my friends. You know, the custom was for the family of the bride to give money or other things to the groom, but my family didn't have anything, and I took it upon myself to bring something to the groom, and did everything on my own, with my hands. That's it. Life wasn't good at all then: food, everything was worse."

Come Bajram, the holiday which concludes the month-long fasting of Ramadan, it was time to rest. Edona's father would say, "Today I am selling a lamb," to raise cash and buy presents for his daughters, and that memory brings a smile to her face: "We were happy, young, I could go back even now to those days and to that life." She and her sisters could not sleep all night on the eve of Bajram; they stayed awake in feverish anticipation of the treats that were coming. Maybe some new shoes? A shirt? It did not matter really; everything was wonderful during Bajram. It was a holiday, and holidays were also devoted to family reunions.

For Merita, the best time was when relatives came to visit from Pristina and stayed overnight in the extra room kept for such occasions. They were her mother's sisters and brothers with their families, more doting adults, more cousins to play with. The days before their arrival were full of excitement as the women prepared *flija*, a pie of layered dough baked for hours, that was everyone's favorite. They would squat by a campfire and lay the thin flour pancakes one by one on a lid resting on the burning charcoal. The layers got browner as they continued to cook and turned into a delicious meal for everybody gathered in the barn just next to the house. Those are the happiest memories of her childhood, not as fun as weddings, but almost. Like all children, Merita loved weddings. When else could all the relatives come together, even the uncles and aunts on her mother's side? Everybody loved the music of the tambourines and the laughter of the women dancing. For Merita, happiness meant realizing that everyone at the party looked at her mother, the most beautiful woman there. Her father was also very handsome but not as tall as his wife. To her daughter, she looked like a real lady, an artist, because she had so much grace and style.

Maybe parties were so special because everyday life was so hard for mothers. Edona's mother would bring mugs full of milk, coffee, and juice to restore her husband and daughters when they were busy in the fields; she made lunch, but also worked alongside them. She worked through all her many pregnancies, up to when she was in labor. "She worked for seven men, she was that strong. We could be in the field, by the horse cart, perhaps you cannot understand, you know? My mother would tell us, 'You rest,' and she would carry on her back the bundles of corn to my dad."

Not far from Edona's village, Shkurta's mother Ardita carried roof tiles on a cart during a rainy day, while her husband had gone to a wedding party: "It was all done when the sun came out." That's how they managed to put a roof on the poor shack they called home. Ardita used the same cart to carry laundry; because she had no diapers for her many children and the only available substitutes were some cloths, she always had piles of them to wash and there was no source of water right where she lived. "Whenever I went to a nearby well, they came out and said, 'Why are you coming to do your laundry in my well?' I would then push the cart, crying, to the creek, which was farther away."

Hailing from the mountains in the West, Fitore also lived in a self-contained world that managed its own poor economy. She appeared so embarrassed by her poor childhood as she was recounting it, that she was very reluctant to give any detail, and she needed reassurance from the interviewers that they too had somehow shared the experience of village life, or at least had memories of it through visits to older relatives. She also never had a bedroom of her own, or a bed for that matter, but always slept on the floor. For Valbona, from central Kosovo, not even Bajram was ever joyous, nor was New Year's Eve. On these holidays the children expect presents, but Valbona's father, a poor farmer who almost killed himself working yet could never make ends meet, had no money for any extra expense. "Sometimes we had shoes, sometimes we didn't, and sometimes.... Sometimes I cannot think about my childhood because I cry. Who could go to school? Now that I have grown up children, and they are university students, sometimes I worry about them, but then I say, 'They are doing well, we are doing well, we have some means, it's not that bad.' And sometimes I think about all that, and can't let it go."

Poverty is a painful recollection, mixed with memories of a family that at times is seen as a sort of a paradise lost through the eyes of the adult women those girls have become. What remains salient is the togetherness, both physical and prescriptive, experienced in the bosom of the father's relations, the large house.

Troubles in Paradise

For Merita, "Going to school was an indescribable happiness. We did not even think of going out with boys, we only wanted to do better in school. I wanted to register at the university and there was an issue of money, but we said that we would manage somehow. But I had an aunt who was a matchmaker and one day she came to mediate for this boy…and I got married."

In western Kosovo, Ganimete's parents and their many girls and boys lived with the family of her father's brother, all sixty of them together. Ganimete's family had always experienced trying times. Her parents had lost two infant sons, and her father could not work because of a disability. Though her mother did more than her share of the work, from taking care of the children and the home to tending the livestock and harvesting the fields, she had little voice in the family's affairs because her husband was not physically or economically powerful. Her eldest son was the first to get an education, but the second did not. "My uncle did not let him go to school, he sent him to the mountain during the summer, to take care of the livestock. We had about one hundred sheep, and at the time livestock was more important than the education of the children." The eldest daughter was kept at home too: "she was born at a time when girls were not sent to school, but were married as soon as they grew up."

Troubles started when her mother registered her second daughter in middle school. "We are talking about sometime in the seventies, it was 1970 in fact." Ganimete was just a child then but remembers well what happened. Her uncle was adamant that nobody would be allowed to go to school, not even the boys, let alone the girls, and not just because the family needed hands in the fields. He also hated the state and its schools, the regime of the *Shki*, as he called the Serbs, a crude name for Slavs that is commonly used among Albanians. There were no arguments or fights, and nobody in the family made a comment about the girl going to school, but Ganimete's uncle became estranged from her father. Not only the family, but also the relatives and even the neighbors—in short, all the people composing the *rrethi*—began to shun Ganimete's mother. The *rrethi* (literally, the immediate social circle) is a powerful social group in Albanian society. It is not just where most of the daily interactions take place; it is where reputations are made and unmade. With a silent protest, all the people in the *rrethi* blamed Ganimete's mother for a decision that was out of bounds, disrespectful of traditional customs. "That was when I began to understand life. I remember as if it was today when we had that wedding. How many times did we have parties? My mother always wore the national costume and always was a leading figure in these events. But after my sister finished her first year of high school—I belonged to a younger generation, I was in primary school—I saw, I noticed that many women would not talk to my mother. When she came home she gathered all the boys and the girls, also the girls, and said, 'Swear on the breast from which I fed you! Don't do anything that will shame me, because I broke the ice in this village, when I sent you to school.' I will always remember her words, 'Did you see what I had to go through today? I always held a handkerchief and danced in front of the women, today I felt very bad: women didn't talk to me because I have a daughter who goes to school.'"

Sending a daughter to school against the will of the head of the household was good enough cause for splitting the big family, a traumatic process called *nda buka*, "breaking the bread," or "the separation of brothers."[10] All of a sudden, Ganimete's parents lost the support of the corporate structure of their rural family and had to find new ways to earn a living. "We children were sent to gather cranberries and wheat sheaves that summer, and we sold them at the market. We bought a shop near the house, it was a sort of depot, and with the money we made, we went to school, we sent my brother and my sister to school. And somehow, we managed our own livelihood because we had cows, livestock, we had a garden, we didn't need to buy all the things that others were buying." Ganimete's sister was sent to live with relatives in the city and attended school there. The eldest son became a teacher.

If the *rrethi* had thought that ostracism would deter Ganimete's mother from "being different," they were mistaken. She was indeed a trailblazer. Only six years after she was ignored at a wedding for wanting to give her daughter an education, all the girls from the village began to go to school. The three-kilometer walk to the school in a village nearby was a long trek by city's standards, but in rural Kosovo, which did not know of school buses, it was the norm. It was not the length of the walk that worried parents; rather, it was the danger that unescorted girls could face along the way. Every day, Ganimete's mother walked her and her friends to the high school, which was located in the city, "but it wasn't a city, there was only the school, the post office, and a clinic, I mean, there was nothing, but it was the largest town in the area." With short hair, dressed like boys and mixed with the boys from the family, the girls walked to school camouflaged for protection.

Ten years later than Ganimete, Hava Shala, who ended up in jail as an adolescent for her political activities after 1981, was walking to school on the same mountains, also dressed like a boy. "Maybe it was a way of dressing instinctively chosen to defend myself from the mindset that prejudiced girls if they typically dressed like girls. I am mainly talking about the village mindset. But it was also because we had to travel for twelve–thirteen kilometers in both directions to go to school, and on top of that, thirteen kilometers in the cold."[11] Not surprisingly, parents were full of trepidation for those long trips across the Kosovo rural landscape, trips often taken in the dark of winter evenings and early mornings. Young children felt no different, as we learned from childhood scares that are notable in many present recollections of earlier times across generations and genders.

The general structural lack of opportunities for education in rural areas was the same in the 1980s as in the 1960s, when Dom Lush Gjergji, the current Catholic bishop vicar of Kosovo, was a child.[12] Born and raised in the mountains of Karadak in southeastern Kosovo, he still remembers the four-hour-long trek to his middle school as the crossing of a fabulistic landscape full of treacherous passages: mountain paths good only for goats, small rivers with no bridge and frozen in the winter, tilled fields and villages protected by ogre-like farmers and Serbs, and dark woods resonant with the howling of wolves. In Dom Lush's memory, a friendly nature comes to his rescue from this hostile environment in the guise of human-like dogs that become his "guardian angels." One dog in particular is musical, and barks an accompaniment to Lush's flute-playing, like an animal in the stories of St. Francis.

In the telling of a narrator, childhood memories take a different salience. Thus, a little episode looms larger in Ganimete's story, retrospectively shadowing the terror of loneliness and vulnerability. It happened that as a child she had to walk three or four kilometers to meet the bus for school, leaving home when the sun was not up yet. She was afraid of the dogs in a stockyard along the way and their deafening barks any time she passed by. She was afraid of the sound of footsteps in the dark once she left the safety of her house, and she needed reassurance. Her mother escorted her from their *lagje* (the extended family compound) to the next one, where she joined other students for the long walk to the bus station.

One day, after school, a failure of the transformer's box provoked a blackout and the students took the bus to go back home earlier than usual. "We didn't know how to call home to tell them the time of our arrival because back then there was no telephone, and they couldn't come for us, so I got off the bus and walked home alone from the station. It was winter, oh my God! It was so cold and I was so afraid! I had a kind of bag, it was a round bag with a flap and as I ran home, that bag made a tak-tak-tak. I thought that someone was running behind me, so I ran and ran. I took a shortcut through the woods, and I felt that someone had caught me, he was behind me and when I went uphill, he came uphill.... We did not have flashlights, we didn't have anything, and when I stopped, he stopped."

Ganimete decided to quit school: she never wanted to walk that walk again. One week later, her mother figured out what had really happened, and when the girl went back to school, she confessed that she had not been ill, just scared: "There was nobody after me, it was just the flap of the bag, it was loose and made a noise. As I was running on the mountain, I fell and because of the strong wind a piece of wood, an oak branch, caught my *opanga* (rubber shoes common in the countryside) and I ran, ran...the oak was behind me and it seemed that someone was following me. I realized later that there was nobody. The students laughed but then they hugged me, 'Don't be afraid, if you need us to come to the village uphill to pick you up, we will come to your village, just don't drop out of school.'"

Shkurta's family was so poor, that among all the children in her family they had just one notebook and one pencil, but never a book: nobody in her nuclear family had any education beyond the mandatory eighth grade, and nobody in her extended family either. In her case, nobody could complain of unequal treatment because the conditions for sending the children to school were simply not there. In other cases, if the choice of who would continue to study could be made, boys were given precedence—except that if quitting school to lend a hand in the fields was for boys a necessity dictated by specific economic circumstances, for girls it was routine. The adults justified the different treatment of boys and girls as tradition, one of those rules of the *kanun*, the unwritten law of the mountains, which relegates women to an exclusively domestic role.

The Unwritten Law on Women

In the region that comprises contemporary Kosovo, northern Albania, and southern Montenegro, the *kanun*, from the Greek "canon," is the unwritten, customary law that informs family and social life. It is a body of rules distinct from the Revealed Law (Shari'a) and not to be confused with the Turkish Kanuni, established in the sixteenth century by Syleiman al Kanuni.[13] In the Albanian context, it is also called, more poetically, the "law of the mountain."[14]

These days, the *kanun* is more easily explained by referring to its written codification.[15] One can find a coffee table edition of *The Code of Lekë Dukagjin* in the bookstores, or online, and read it as a book of law, with chapters and articles on specific subjects, covering all aspects of family and social life. It is perhaps because of this book that outsiders have come to see the Albanian traditional social structure as an ordered universe that can be objectively understood and interpreted thanks to a body of scholarly knowledge, as if every practical behavior followed predetermined rules. They are helped in this belief by those informants in the field who often refer to the *kanun* as a key organizing principle of their society, the mark of Albanianness. Reality is much more complicated than that: the order that the unwritten law purports to uphold is not fixed but has variations in practice, and more often than not, practices are ideologically invoked to justify and legitimize existing power relations.

Neither the women we interviewed nor most ordinary Albanians have read the book, although many do commonly refer to the *kanun* as the rules of behavior regulating intra- and inter-family relations. It is about "the ways things used to be,"[16] or *ashtu e kemi ligji* (these are our customs), *tradita*, *doket* (synonyms for customs),[17] as people tell anthropologists who ask for explanations, or simply, "our mentality."[18] It worked, and still works, as a self-regulating social mechanism that is effective, in Pierre Bourdieu's words, only insofar as talks of customary rules find a good reception in "the schemes of perception and appreciation deposited...in every member of the group, i.e., the disposition of the habitus."[19]

The *kanun* prescribes a subordinate role for women in the family and in society, as Margaret Hasluck elaborates: "In the words of the Unwritten Law, 'a man has blood, and a woman kin,' i.e. a man has a pedigree, and a woman has her own relatives, and a 'woman is anybody's daughter,' i.e. comes from anywhere and has no pedigree." [...] The Unwritten Law states further that a 'wife is a sack for carrying things,' i.e. she was in her husband's house to bear his children."[20]

However, the answer to why girls must drop out of school to marry cannot be found in any chapter of the *kanun*. Yet the *kanun* is often invoked when girls reach puberty and are considered ready to fulfill their assigned role of ensuring the continuation and the integrity of a family other than theirs. Education is not necessary to this end, nor is it desirable. Being ready for marriage is. Given the future roles of girls in the new families, their chastity and moral reputation are paramount. Protecting girls from the danger of interaction with the outside world is one of the reasons for pulling them out of school as soon as they reach puberty. A girl who spends her adolescence at home, preparing her bridal trousseau (*çejz* or *paja*) rather than going to school, shows that she is capable of working and at the same time pure. A girl who has a secondary education might disrupt the family order, as she might be less willing to submit.[21]

There are a variety of practices that provide answers as to whom and why girls marry.[22] The composition of the family is often an important factor, for example, when grown daughters are seen as vulnerable as long as they are unmarried because they cannot be protected by a brother or by an aging father. Poor economic conditions accelerate the decision to marry a daughter "up." Finally, the pursuit of a strategy of alliances suggests that one's daughters should be married to another family's brothers. No matter the circumstances, girls are never asked for their opinion, though more often than not boys too have no say in the matter. How much of that tradition is still alive today is a matter of circumstance. Before the war, it was the rule.

If promising a girl in marriage at a very early age, and years before the wedding, makes sense for a family as it plans its own longer-term survival, expansion, or strengthening, it does not always make sense for the girl. Xhejrane Lokaj, a nurse who became a strong feminist advocate, was a precocious and independent girl from the same mountainous region as Ganimete, and only a few years older, when she learned that men would be coming for her as soon as she grew up a little.[23] She found that distasteful, because at twelve or thirteen, the girls were still too young and too tiny. By then, none in her cohort had reached puberty yet. Later, after she became a nurse, she knew why: they were not growing fast enough because of lack of good nutrition. She could never understand how those childlike girls could be seen as potential brides.

Shpresa was engaged when she turned twelve to a man who lived in a distant village, but she was allowed to complete her mandatory education until eighth grade. That time in school was not easy, with her friends taunting her, "'When will you go there?' 'Who is going to pick you up in school now?' 'Your father sent you away!' I did not like it when my father said, 'You are getting engaged.' But I did what I was told. I was nineteen years old when I got married." Blerta was ten when her father got her engaged, "like that, without asking me at all. And I didn't even know what an engagement was. My goal was to study medicine, had they let me. I wanted it with all my heart. I was still a child in seventh grade when the other kids heard of my engagement and began to call me, 'Bride! Bride! Bride!' At the time, who would want to go to school as a bride? I quit."

Valbona was engaged at sixteen, after quitting school six months before graduation. "It was because of a Serbian book we had to buy. My father did not want to buy it; he said, 'Do without it.' I did not understand that at the time ethnic hostility was so strong. Any time I went to school without that book the teacher kicked me out. Still, my father would not buy the book. I got tired of this situation because it kind of seemed that I was being played, I could not face the stress. The director of the school called my father, 'Why is she leaving? Why is such a good student leaving? You must support her. Let her continue.' I don't know how many times they summoned my father to the school. 'Why are you stopping her? Why are you stopping this girl who is doing so well?'"

She cannot blame her father, because he supported her in school even though the family did not have the means for such a luxury. "He would say, 'Because with education you will get ahead.' My father told me words that I can't get out of my mind because they are true. When he saw that I wasn't going to school anymore, he said, 'Gosh! Fine, my daughter, just go ahead, make the end of that broomstick as clean as a whistle.' What? But that's what he really said, he said that. But now that I'm stuck with housework all day long, the whole day, I understand what he meant, I realize that it's truly a thankless job, especially sweeping the floor. Maybe I would have achieved something more, I would have had a status of my own. But my time came, he got me engaged at sixteen, I was so young!"

Ganimete's mother defied her family's ostracism to educate her daughters. Yes, she was a trailblazer, but she was also in tune with the policies of the time. In the early 1970s, education had become a top priority for the regional

Communist leadership, by that time largely composed of Albanians.[24] At the end of the Second World War, when schools in the Albanian language opened for the first time, two-thirds of Albanian women were illiterate. By 1981, that number was down to 26.3 percent, a substantial progress that touched mostly the cities and was characterized by an enduring gender gap, as the illiteracy rate for men went down to 9.3 percent.[25] However, despite the relaxation of the pressure on curricula and language instructions to assimilate Albanians to Yugoslavia, many families discontinued girls' education for fear of a possible "contamination" with Serbian culture.[26] Ganimete's uncle and Valbona's father did not want to take that risk.

Especially in rural families, there was a strong resistance to change. Not even a teenager, Xhejrane Lokaj defied her family: "My mother didn't have the power to protect me, because as a mother without a son she was in a lower position in the eyes of the women of the *rrethi*, but also of the men, and of the entire family." Xhejrane wondered, "Oh God, when I grow up, do I really have to get married? Should I do nothing else with my life?" It was a cousin who helped. Heteme Lokaj Kastrati was the head of the Socialist Youth in Deçan and Xhejrane's secret correspondent. Xhejrane confided in her through messages carried by her younger sister, and together they found a solution to her problem. The newspaper had reported that some girls, one from Podujevo, another from Pristina, had run away from home because they did not want to be pulled out of school; they had gone to the police seeking support for completing the mandatory eight years of school, which they also understood as their right to an education.

The movement of girls demanding an education was to be reckoned with. Vjosa Dobruna's parents were both educators. Hers was a well-established family in the capital, known for its activism. They were a reasonable choice as a safe haven for runaway girls, and in fact they sheltered a few. Dobruna remembers the case of another teenage girl: "Her father came to see us; it was a very tense situation, but he calmed down when he saw that we were five girls in my family and he felt comfortable about leaving his daughter with us."[27]

Xhejrane, too, planned an escape. One night, while all her family was sleeping, she grabbed her school report card and with no money in her pockets—there was no money around the house anyway—she sneaked out of the house. It took a six-kilometer march in the dark to reach the police station of Deçan from the village of Pobergjë. Now protected by the state, she registered for school, was given a scholarship, and settled in the students' dorm. "What I had done was a disgrace at that time. My father felt very bad, he felt threatened by tradition and by other family members. Someone would come and tell me, 'A war is going on back home.' Someone else would come and say, 'They have decided to murder you.' Someone else would say, 'They have completely ostracized your father.' I lived with these stories. Someone else would come and bring me the news, 'Today they arrived in Prizren,' because then Prizren was far from Pobergjë, not very close, not every family had cars, you know, they came by bus. Traveling was so difficult, they would have come only for something big, and something big, I thought, would be killing me to avenge the shame I had brought upon them."

Edona, by contrast, left school without protesting. "I didn't want to destroy my home, so I did what I was told." And as told, she got married very young, like all her sisters. It all began when her grandfather noticed that his granddaughters, the babies he had taken care of when they were still in the cradle while their mother was pregnant again and again, the same girls he had played with until then, had become little women. That thought came to him as a sudden realization, though they had been growing up for a while, and their forms had already begun to change. And when he said, "You grew up quickly, vuuuu!" everything changed. Grandpa became their escort along the trip through the fields to the school. The walk was too much for him, so he sat in the school courtyard for the entire morning, waiting for the bell to signal the end of the last period, and for them to come out and make the trip back home under his supervision.

"How can they let you go home from school alone!" He disapproved of what he thought was the parents' indifference to the girls' safety. He disapproved of many things, but mostly of the pants and dresses the girls would have loved to buy. They should wear only *dimja*, he thought, the willowy Turkish-style pants, neither skirt nor pants really, but a combination of the two. Those were the same forms-hiding *dimja* that older women continued to wear as Western fashion was becoming popular among the Yugoslav youth. His refusal to buy "modern" clothes had nothing to do with money, and he promised to sell one sheep to buy new *dimja*, but jeans? Never. And so the girls wore *dimja* in school, the only ones in class keeping with the tradition. It was embarrassing, but disobeying Grandpa was not an option. Fortunately, Edona's schoolmates never teased her, never objected to her outdated and style-less look, so "grannie-like." Nor did the teachers make any comment, and Edona is still grateful to this day for their discretion and understanding.

She loved school and her classmates. She never owned a textbook, and instead used a book that a girl with more means had bought. They shipped the book back and forth between their two houses: she borrowed it, did her homework quickly, and returned it in time for the friend to do her own. She would have loved to hang out with kids her age, or better, to go on school trips that took the young students to some faraway place in Yugoslavia, maybe the coast, or just camping somewhere. She never did. "Grandpa would say, 'I will give you money to buy something but why do you ask me to go on a trip?' 'But Grandpa, everyone is going, everyone.' Oh, and we begged him so much, one would say we were asking for blood. He always said, 'No.' He would say, adamantly, 'No, no.'" Had she insisted, would she have been able to break his stubborn refusal to let her go? Perhaps, but she chose not to. "I wouldn't have enjoyed that trip." She and her sisters loved their grandfather, whom in their own way they tried to protect because he had been a political prisoner for six or seven years, she could not quite remember how long, and he had been released as a broken man, as he said, "They subtracted twenty years from my life!"

Edona submitted to her grandfather's authority, Merita to her father's. Merita was proud because she was the best student in history and geography. The history of the Illyrians and the wars of ancient Greece impressed her young mind. She reveled in the approval of the teachers, who were so much more sophisticated than the villagers and also made her feel a bit more sophisticated. Focused as she was on studying and learning, she did not even think of boys. Yet, continuing her studies was not in the cards, even if they had found the means to pay for it. Whether it was the fault of the *kanun*, she does not say. It was just that she was expected to do something else with her life, and her aunt, who was a marriage broker, had plans for her.

It was much easier to break the accepted pattern of behavior when the girls could count on the support of male members of the family. That becomes apparent in stories such as the one of Marta Prekpalaj, who struggled well into the late 1970s in rural Kosovo to get an education, but became a literacy activist and a teacher against all odds: "the problem was to continue high school. Relatives said that I shouldn't go to school, that girls had to stay home, be engaged to marry, work on the bride's trousseau, and so on. I was persistent, but also very importantly, I had my father's support, my late father, who didn't have an education. It's not that my mother didn't want me to go to school, but the *rrethi* had a greater influence on my mother and they said that a girl shouldn't go to school alone, also because nobody knew what a girl who went to school alone did, or what happened in school. From that *rrethi*, only three girls of my generation continued their schooling. Because of all that, it was difficult at the time to persuade my *rrethi* to let me go to school, but thanks to my persistence and the support of my father, later also of my big brother, I managed to finish high school."[28]

Hava Shala, who became a social worker, completed her schooling roughly at the same time as Marta, thanks to her father's support. He had a more modern view of women, perhaps acquired as an immigrant in Germany, and whatever the people of the village of Tushec thought about girls' education, he defied them.

3
A New Home

When they get married, girls come into a new family from the outside, mostly from different villages, according to rules of exogamy that are stricter than both the Koranic and Christian law.[1] Valbona's marriage was arranged. "Going out by ourselves? No way! I never saw him in person until the night of the wedding. No, I didn't choose him, but I tell you, sometimes this is better, you know, when you get married. There is no miracle, no one hundred percent success, there isn't. Besides, where would I have gone?" The marriage broker came with the boy to ask for Valbona's hand, not the usual way of dealing with a marriage mediation, which excludes the two main subjects of the negotiation. The problem was that already in the mid-1980s the number and frequency of police patrols in rural areas had increased, and traveling parties made fewer and more efficient trips. Thus the broker brought the bridegroom as well. For the adolescent Valbona, the sudden realization that she was about to leave home and move far away, to someone else's house, was traumatic. The wedding was something to remember, though. No bus was going to her village, but it did come for her, and it was a good-looking car, carrying the wedding party that would take her to her new home. As the only son, the groom did not have many male relatives who could escort her, but still, it was a big party.

Blerta married at seventeen. "My older brother got married but there were demonstrations and things were happening, so he moved to Germany, and my father was getting older, thus I got married. My father was not educated, neither was my mother, but I don't begrudge my father, rather I begrudge my mother, even today I hate that they didn't ask me. Why? I am a mother today. I wouldn't let my daughter marry someone she doesn't love, someone she doesn't know, and create a family with him." Blerta met her betrothed only at the wedding. She knew his family name, but not what he looked like. She spent the day before celebrating in the *kanagjegj*, from the Turkish *kina gecesi*, or the night of the henna, which is the ritual bachelorette party, in which friends and female relatives celebrate the young bride, singing, dancing, and painting their skin with henna. It's a mix of joyful and sorrowful time, as all attention is focused on the young bride, but also on her departure from her family to join a new home. During this time, Blerta felt the anxious anticipation of what was expected her, of which she had little or no idea. Then the wedding party came to pick her up.

She sat on the couch of her groom's house for the wedding pictures. "Nowadays girls are happy at their weddings, back then the custom was different, I was very composed, looking down...yes, looking down under the *duvak*, the bridal veil. And when they brought in the groom to take the photo with the bride, it was the first time in my life that I saw him. I turned and saw him, I said to myself, 'Maybe, inshallah, it's not that one.' But it was that one. That was it. What could I have done? No, I don't know whether he knew me. Of course he looked at me, but I was so unhappy that I didn't have the courage to say anything. I didn't like him because he was too short, no, I didn't like him. But at the time, you had to do what the family said, like it or not, so my father wouldn't lose his face."

Unhappy with the choice made for her, Blerta did not expect she would dislike everything, even her new family; she thought that it was too small and too poor. Thus, when three days after the wedding she went back to her paternal house to visit her family, as tradition dictates, she begged them, "'Please, don't let me go back, I am so unhappy!' But they sent me back: there was no support, in short, your mother and father did not support you, and nobody else supported you, not at all, at that time."

In the traditional context, as a girl joins the husband's family, she becomes a subjugated member of this new community, and she has to accept that the ties with her original family were loosened. There is a crucial social exchange in this process. The bride's side loses a member, but it is free from the responsibility of controlling the girl's reproductive activity and/or protecting her, and it might gain either financially or politically through an alliance with the new family. Marriages are forever, and not only because breaking one means much more than splitting a couple. With the arrival of the young bride, the bridegroom's side acquires more than a new addition: given the young bride's fertility potential, it gains all her offspring, according to patrilinear patterns of kinship. Thus if the mother dies or leaves, the children stay with the father.

As in other comparable cultures, the value of a woman depends on her capacity to have boys, an outcome that increases the family's capital in the absence of mechanization of farming. As an old folk saying goes, "*nuk është zot-shtëpie ai që ka qe, apo ai që ka djem*" (the lord of the household is not the one who has oxens, but the one who has boys). The birth of a daughter is not an occasion for rejoicing, as she is a potential mother of descendants belonging to a foreign lineage. As a matter of fact, women do not belong to any genealogy, as Margaret Hasluck explains: "The society of the Albanian mountains was patrilineal, and took so little account of women that whereas the names of the ancestors in the male line might be known for as many as twenty generations, those in the female line were forgotten after two or three."[2]

Berit Backer called being a woman in the traditional Albanian family an "occupational status" which includes the smooth management of the household, and centers on the ability to produce the male lineage.[3] A barren woman is seen as lacking, and she could be replaced by a second wife. A woman has no right to her own children, nor to inheritance.[4] The value of a woman is inferior to that of a man; in the regulation of blood feuds according to customary law, the price to be paid for killing a woman is the same as that for wounding a man, about half the price for the killing of a man, and a pregnant woman victim is worth double, but the gender of the baby determines the total price.[5] A common name for women as well as small children is *robët*, which means subordinated members of the household, but is also an archaic word for household slaves or prisoners.[6]

The family structure is the context in which, from an early age, Albanians learn submission to parental authority and to a double relation of domination: domination of men over women and older people over younger.[7] Upon entering into a new house, a *nusja*, the young bride, is fundamentally "on trial."[8] She must prove her beauty, reserve, industriousness, and abilities in the care of the household. Older women, especially the mother-in-law, establish from the outset the expectations to which she must conform; their relationship can be tense but also close and almost filial.[9] The relationship with the sisters-in-law is commonly competitive over reputation and favor, for example, to establish who works harder or behaves better, or who can get away with working less.[10] Overall, a woman learns how to accept the life in which she finds herself in the new family because she has no other choice: the rhetorical question that our narrators repeated most commonly was, "*Çka me bo?*" (What could I do?).

Blerta was eighteen when she was pregnant with her oldest daughter, but her marriage was already over. "I didn't have the courage to leave my child, to have them take her, raise her. I thought, 'What would happen to this child?' In short, I decided to sacrifice my life and devote it to my children." Thus life went on, in relative poverty. Only her brother-in-law had a job, while her husband, a high school graduate, never did, and her father-in-law had retired. "We had land, but I can't say that we worked the land and lived from the land, absolutely not. We kept a cow, we made things for ourselves."

There was very little money at home, yet the very first months of married life were good for Afërdita. After that, violence, humiliation, and a general hostility within the family made it very difficult to keep the marriage together. Her husband began to drink, she suspects under the influence of his friends, and came home late at night, inebriated. "As time passed, he punched me and kicked me with some leather belt that he had, a thick one. When he later sobered up, he apologized. 'I am sorry that I spend so much money on drinks.' I'd say to myself, 'It's just because he is drunk.'" Five years passed before her first girl was born, in 1995. Before then, she had been pregnant twice but miscarried because of the beating. Yet, his family blamed her. "'Leave her,' his mother said, 'she is not able to give birth.' 'No,' he said, 'I will keep her. I will not get another wife.'" Afërdita tried to understand her mother-in-law's dismissive attitude. The older woman had been abandoned by her husband and had raised her sons with the in-laws, forced to live far from home and without a husband who would enhance her role in the family. It was her time now, as the mother-in-law, the *plaka* (old lady) of the house, to exert the authority she never had, certainly not to challenge her son's authority which was paramount, but to decide about what was proper and acceptable in the family, and especially regarding Afërdita. And Afërdita had not even been her first choice to marry her son.

An old custom allows a man to take home, without scandal, another woman who could have his children in order to circumvent the problem of a barren wife. Afërdita felt caught in a paradoxical situation. "It was he who wanted to marry me. He said to my maternal uncle's son, 'Find me a bride.' My uncle's son told him, 'What kind of wife shall I get for you, bro?' 'That very one who is passing by.' I was just passing by with my mother and father to go to my sister's. 'That very one who is passing by shall be my bride.'" She puzzled over the question: Why did her father accept that boy's marriage proposal? She does not understand it to this day, because everybody knew that the young man was poor; he did not even have a home of his own. Yet, Afërdita said nothing to her family about her ordeal at home not to cause pain to her father, not to make him think he was the cause of her suffering for having given her away to a man without a prospect.

With the birth of the first daughter, a miracle happened. Afërdita's husband, who used to go to sleep right as his family woke up, stopped coming home late and drunk. It was the three of them now, and she felt the marriage had a second chance. But then "he began to hit us both, my daughter and me. My girl was only nine months old. And he made me all blue here in the face, because that metal belt of his, when it hits you, affects the eye. I took my daughter and went to my mother's. He said, 'Don't dare.' I said, 'It's over. Everything is over between you and me,' and left. My mom, 'What do you have in your eye?' 'Mom, I was hit by wood, I was chopping wood, and the wood hit my eye.' 'Really? But you also have it here, and there.' 'Mom, it hit me only here, and don't ask me again.' 'And what does the girl have?' 'Wood,' I said, 'it went from me to the girl.' 'Eeee,' said my dad, 'She is lying and by much. Come on, show me your body.' He had just heard from the son of his brother who lived near us that my husband came home late, and maltreated me…. 'Tell us all, Afërdita,' he said, 'we can bring to an end the good relationships we have with your husband.' 'Oh dad, five years have passed. Never again I want to go through what I went through in those five years.' Anyway, dad called on them. And my husband promised, 'I won't beat her, I won't do it, alcohol makes me do it.' My father told him, 'Drop the alcohol. What is dearer to you? Your child or alcohol?' Three, four months passed and he did not drink. Later, I got pregnant again, and again with another girl."

It was so much different for Merita. She was so crushed when they pulled her out of school to get married to a young man in Pristina, that she sobs remembering that time. She moved to the city from her village to find, unexpectedly, such great happiness in her marriage that the memory of it changes her mood and makes her smile: "I didn't know him. He was the neighbor of my mother's sister, you know? Maybe I went to my aunt as a child to spend the night or to be there for the day and he saw me, but at the time I didn't have any idea that something was happening. I never saw this boy. I just knew his sister, but it never occurred to me that this could happen. He came to my house twice, three times. 'Come inside,' said dad, 'let's take care of this and get engaged, whether you like it or not. You are not going to date him.' This is how things were before. Inside the house there was his mother, with relatives, with the sister I knew, and like that, we got engaged."

They were married within three months. "To tell you the truth, to me he seemed the handsomest of men. I cannot describe how much I liked him at the time. Now we are old, it's not like that. What do they say? 'Don't get old!'"

The groom's family was very friendly to her, especially his mother, a woman of very little schooling but with an open mind, who never ordered her around but respected her and, in short, never behaved like the negative stereotype of a mother-in-law. Merita did call her "mom". "I had a life that nobody had. I went out wearing pants, short skirts.... My husband never stopped me. 'Pants are better,' mom said, 'and so are tighter clothes because they envelop the whole body, because in the strong wind, and in the rain, a dress lets the cold in, and at the same time the wind raises the dress, and what happens? Everyone might see underneath. So, pants are better, go where you want and don't be afraid.' Pants and short skirts in the summer. When there were guests, she helped me. It was rare for someone to be able to go out the way I did."

Merita cannot remember any jealousy or bad feelings in her husband's family. Her brothers-in-law living abroad helped as they could, and they managed to build a new house. When she had two children, her life felt complete.

Shpresa too never saw her husband before the wedding, never even talked to him on the phone—nobody had a phone—and they never even exchanged a letter. Yet it all went well with him from the beginning. "Just his village was a disaster. It had absolutely nothing. It did not have food, it was a completely underdeveloped village. And I did suffer. Believe it or not, I raised all my children by myself, more or less. My family also helped me a little, and with their help I was able to raise my children."

Edona, like all her sisters, married when she turned eighteen. One year earlier, a neighbor had thought she would be a good match for his best friend from school and that boy came to her village to check her out. "Shortly after, the marriage broker came. At the time we had no telephone, nothing. I was very upset, I ran away from dad because I felt so embarrassed! My father told me, 'A good boy is coming, you will marry him but we will remain close,' because my village was near. But I felt bad because I was leaving my family and there was so much work to be done at home!" However, life turned out to be good for her in the new family and she felt no nostalgia for home, because her husband became the head of the family after his father's death, six months after the wedding. As a result, she also occupied a position of relative privilege in the household. She was spared much of the work in the fields and was well loved. "I will never forget a Bajram, I bought a dress to look different from the other young brides in the family."

Her husband and his mother had worked in the fields all day, harvesting more than usual. "I asked them, 'Is all that for the cows or what is it for?' My husband got on the tractor and went to sell it in the city and we got the money for the dress. My dress is purple, I still have it, I never lost it, it has three roses, one purple and two white on the shoulder. During the war I bought a big white plastic bucket with a cover and hid the dress inside because I thought, 'Maybe they won't kill us, I'll be back home and I won't have to buy it again because I have no money.' And my husband dug a hole, it took two days to dig it and I put that bucket with all the clothes, the vests, the *dimja*, everything."

There is more than the primary reproductive function to the role of women in the family. In a crowded household, they become both the source and the shock absorbers of inevitable communal conflicts, only apparently suppressed by the absolute equality which is the rule among the men; inequality strikes the wrong note in the mythical unity of the family. Valbona's uncle was better off than her father because he had a job and did not rely only on farming: "We were together, but we were not together with him, he used his salary only for his family. We saw that they had clothes, they had shoes, we saw it, you know, they bought things and we saw them, we did not have food and they did." It fell on her watchful mother to hide the all too evident inequality. She did not let Valbona play with her cousin so that her daughter, equal in age to the other, would not feel the gap between them when the children were handed a snack: sometimes it was just the difference between eating a piece of bread or a biscuit.

Shpresa observed her mother's dealing with her two sisters-in-law. "One of them said she was too sick to work in the fields, and never did. Can you believe she stayed inside the house for twenty years and made babies? She just made babies. And my mother had the task of both making the bread and bringing it uphill. Now, my father told his own brother, 'Hey, who made the bread they brought us? Let her bring it to us.' 'Never mind, she is sick,' he said. She never lent a hand, she was like that non-stop."

It was even worse with the other sister-in-law. "In the whole *fis*, they never fought about nonsense, they did not fight about anything. My father had some words with someone from a nearby *mahalla*,[11] and this latter planned to kill someone in our *mahalla*, but he killed my uncle, not my father. My uncle's boys remained orphans. Now, his wife said to my mother, 'They killed my husband because of your husband.' She said, 'Oj, what do I have to do with it? Did I tell the murderer to kill him? He planned the killing.' Quarrels...non-stop. She did as she liked, and especially for my mother it was a catastrophe. My mother did not have any pleasure in life, nor did her children. Back then they didn't know how to be careful. Now, if you don't want to have children, you do something, you are careful. My mother had up to eleven children. My uncle's wife said, 'You are having children because of the violence I suffered. They killed my husband and I can no longer have children, while you are having children with your husband. You have a child a day.' We always argued, all of us, because when my mother wasn't well, we all felt it in our body, we all grieved, we were oppressed by everything. I wasn't happy one day in my life, my life is a catastrophe. Seeing my family unhappy was a catastrophe."

Shpresa's uncle had fallen victim to a blood feud. Regulated by norms believed to date back to the Middle Ages and known through oral transmission in the local communities of Kosovo and northern Albania, blood feuds and their management are not just an Albanian custom, but a shared tradition in nearly every continent, and particularly in the neighboring Slavic societies of Montenegro.[12] Perhaps uniquely in Kosovo because of a combination of traditionalism and deep mistrust of law enforcement, blood feuds were common in the 1970s, so much so that Communist Yugoslavia had tried to eradicate this kind of communal justice by appropriating the traditional norms of the *kanun* to create "reconciliation councils" that would mediate feuding as self-management organs.[13] Those efforts never succeeded. If there was to be reconciliation between parties (*pajtimi*), the community elders (*pleqnia*) would be the mediators. It took a popular movement for mass reconciliation in 1991 to put a stop to the escalation of extra-judicial killing, but that came much later and owed its success to a growing sentiment of national unity in the face of external threats.[14]

In the 1970s, the enduring legitimacy of revenge killing was still rooted in its strong identification with the "essence" of what it means to be Albanian, more precisely, an Albanian man: honorable and egalitarian. This idea is a construction created early on by the Franciscan fathers from Shkodra, engaged in building an Albanian national identity in the early twentieth century, who turned on its head the negative image that blood feuds had in Western Europe. To paraphrase Father Gjergj Fishta, the *kanun*, which regulates blood feuds, is an originally democratic law because it does not recognize any sovereignty but the will of the people.[15] The other side of that ideal equality of the society of men is the reality of hierarchies of power in the private sphere, in which women and the young are subordinated to the privileged male elders. This contrast is rationalized and dignified as deference to an accepted moral code.

All the women we interviewed, who had to struggle with the challenges that the tradition presents to their personhood, were always forced to reconcile with a tradition transgenerationally transmitted, as in the case of Valbona, that embeds inequality in the good functioning of the family, and rewards voluntary subjection by calling it virtue.[16] Valbona experienced conflict in her new home as well. "There are those sisters-in-law who want to be on their own and lead, dominate you. And I have one sister-in-law…what she did traumatized me. It got to me. And I couldn't tell anyone. You know, when one gets married, what do they call it? Honeymoon? Let me tell you what my family said, all of them said, my mother said on my honeymoon, 'Have a good trip my girl, this and that, and don't talk. Don't talk. Don't talk.' Her *amanet*[17] was exactly this, 'Don't talk because you mustn't talk.' Yes, in the sense of 'Don't talk back, do what they say.' You know, I never talked, I just cried, I cried all night, I tell you, even my husband didn't know what to do. Even our children say, 'Don't get mixed up.' That's it."

The City Is Another World

Urban societies built on nuclear families, in which adults are employed in government, trade, or the professions, had been developing in all the major centers of Kosovo since the end of the Second World War. In Mitrovica, the industrial and mining town in the north, postwar socialist Yugoslavia had created a managerial and workers' aristocracy. Culture, crafts, and trade flourished in Peja and Prizren, a legacy of their economies in the Middle Ages or of their administrative role under the Ottomans. In Gjakova, where the anti-Fascist resistance had been stronger and supplied more cadres to the new socialist state, there were plenty of employment opportunities in the state-run factories. The capital, Pristina, naturally concentrated power and wealth, with its elite that ran the state business and its institutions, from the courts to the police and the media. For Albanians, social and economic conditions improved significantly in the 1970s, when further decentralization of government functions allowed a better alignment of demographic and leadership positions, favoring Albanians.

Families were much smaller in towns, but our narrators describe them as being just as warm as the large households in the countryside. Or perhaps it is natural that childhood is universally remembered as a time of love, if not happiness. As a child growing up in a mid-size town during the 1970s, Afërdita was the youngest, and that, she always thought, made her special. She remembers her sister lovingly braiding her hair with flowers, but especially her father's present, a brand new purple bicycle, which forever endeared her to that color. More than a decade younger than Afërdita and living in a nearby town, Vlora had siblings also from her father's previous marriage, but she was happy with "the older children who lived in our family; we never knew 'us and them,' because our parents taught us all to love each other very much, to be close to each other." As for Ajshe, any time she experienced a loss, someone was there to pick up the pieces. She never knew her mother, who died giving birth to her, but she was lovingly raised by the wives of her paternal uncles until she was a toddler. When her father remarried, she found in her stepmother, who could not bear children, an extraordinary love. Ajshe was only a pre-teen when she lost her stepmother as well, but she got back on her feet once again with the help of her family. It was only when her father died, on the day she received her high school diploma, that she felt irreparably lonely.

The Kosovo towns were stratified and diverse, as all urban socialist societies were, with elites that had benefited under successive regimes by filling the ranks of the economic, political, and cultural establishment. Even with many children and a stay-at-home wife, Kimete's father was able to guarantee a good life to his family thanks to his position as a civil servant in the capital. They lived in an apartment on the outskirts of the central city, which was rapidly developing in the early 1970s. The apartment had central heating and all the basic comforts that houses in the countryside lacked. There was no work to be done for Kimete as a child, who was growing up in the 1970s, a decade that is widely considered the most prosperous for Kosovo and Yugoslavia as well. She had homework, but that was often sweetened by field trips. On holidays, like all the other families of the provincial nomenklatura, Kimete's family traveled to the Dalmatian coast.

For girls coming of age in the 1970s and living in Pristina, the opportunity to complete high school and even attend the newly established university were much higher, especially if their families were part of the state bureaucracy. It did not go all that smoothly. Socialist Yugoslavia had its internal hierarchies and systemic inequality. Nazlie Bala, who grew up to be a human rights activist and leading member of the political party *Vetëvendosjë*, was an A student, and was encouraged to apply to the Sami Frashëri gymnasium, "but the only kids allowed to attend these schools were the children whose parents held high positions, such as the children of company directors, of leaders of the Communist Party, the Socialist Party, whatever, those who were the state's leaders. If you came from a middle class family, you were directed to other schools, which were also good, but this was an obvious division. At the gymnasium there were only the 'Buxhovanë children,' as we called those who owned rich houses in the new neighborhoods of Taslixhe, Dragodan, and Bregu i Diellit. These were children who had everything. If you weren't one of them, you were directed to the vocational high schools: the teachers' training Normale School, the Agriculture High School, the Economics High School, and the Technical High School. There were often advantages depending on where you came from. If you came from Prizren or Gjakova, you had a lot of advantages, if you came from Podujevo, Vushtrri, or Mitrovica, you had very few advantages. Sometimes you could get in because they needed you to fill the quotas, so that they could maintain that they had students from other areas."[18]

Kimete attended all the top schools in Prishtina, first the Branislav Nušić elementary school, now renamed Gjergj Fishta, and then Ivo Lola Ibar gymnasium, now Sami Frashëri.[19] It is hard even for locals to keep straight all the name changes—of streets, buildings, and schools—depending on who is governing and their respective rosters of heroes. Her teacher, Nadire Dida, was one of the first Albanian teachers after the Second World War, and a beloved fixture in the educational elite of the capital. Kimete has the fondest memory of filling out the grade book that Ms. Dida entrusted to her because she had such good handwriting. Three years into high school, she fell in love with a boy her age from a similar background. The young couple continued their studies, he in Belgrade, she in Pristina, dating any time he came back home on breaks. Following a very different script from tradition, they got married after they both had finished their studies and had found employment.

Ajshe was the daughter of a municipal civil servant and living comfortably in her town, but she fell in love with a boy from the surroundings of a nearby town who had studied law: "Meeting my husband was my *kismet*.[20]

We dated for two years, we got engaged, we got married. We were very happy in our marriage, in our engagement, and while dating. We both worked in the same company."

Though they were ten years apart and grew up in the 1970s and 1980s, Ajshe and Kimete had a life that was not very different from the life of the urban youth of Yugoslavia, or Western Europe, for that matter. School was key for the emancipation of young women who could afford it. Ola Syla, a few years older than Ganimete and from the same provincial region, was the daughter of a Montenegrin woman and an Albanian Communist partisan fighter who had become a judge after the war.[21] Despite the early death of her father, her family background offered her a wider range of opportunities. Still hyper-protected by her only brother, who never allowed her to go to a high school dance, or study medicine because night shifts would be too risky for a woman, she enrolled in law school in the newly established University of Pristina. She met her future husband in front of the women's dorm, where she had secured a bed. He had parked his FICA, the small FIAT car made in Yugoslavia that had become the symbol of well-being and modernity, in front of her window, claiming a flat tire. She thought he was Serbian, given his "modern look," and he thought she was Serbian as well. As a flirtatious banter ensued, they quickly discovered that they were both Albanian, and soon after they became engaged.

They met on campus, but they could easily have met on the tree-lined, central pedestrian street, known as *korzo*, where strolling has been taking place daily in Pristina, and still takes place, since the end of the Second World War. Moving the capital of Kosovo from Prizren in 1947 was the most revolutionary transformation of Pristina since the Ottomans. The old city had grown around the large but small-scale covered *çarshia* (market) and was served by two axial roads, the most important of them the east-west axis *Divanjolli*, or *Divan Yolu* in Turkish, literally the Road to the Imperial Council, linking Constantinople to Rome. Narrow and winding streets followed the contours of families' residences and *mahalla*. Teams of volunteers drafted by the Communist Party of Yugoslavia dismantled the lively market and the adjacent *hamam* (public baths), synagogue, church, and mosque, at the sound of the "Internationale."[22] It took three days to finish the job, with no second thought about destroying the city's cultural heritage. When reconstruction started in earnest, the song's lyric, "We must destroy the old world, and build a new one," ruled the day. Thus was built the new main street, the *korzo*, with its modernist-style buildings of the Regional

Parliament, the National Theatre, the Municipality, and the Monument to Brotherhood and Unity. These public buildings were the right scale to blend in with the older Ottoman sites of the fifteenth-century Bazaar (Tas) Mosque and the Big Mosque, but they stood out among the smaller residential buildings of the center.

The *korzo* became the social center of the city from the beginning, and every generation has a story to tell about it. Nadire Dida, Kimete's beloved teacher in primary school, and the beloved teacher of many generations, met her future husband in the *korzo* of Pristina in 1948, when the street was brand new. The young man had seen her pass by from a distance and dared to send her a card to the school. "It was a photograph of the very first flowers that bloom in the spring with a note on the back, 'I finally decided to write you, and to tell you that I sincerely love you.'" Shortly after, as she walked along the *korzo* with a classmate, the young man began to walk behind them. "He said, 'May I accompany you?' Very embarrassing. But the girl who was with me walked away. While we were walking, he said, 'I wrote you [using the formal address] a card, I don't know whether you received it. Did you receive it?' I said, 'Yes, I received it.' And he kept walking with me. And the other girl, she walked away! It was just the two of us."[23]

Years later, not much had changed. In the 1960s, Safete Rogova was still a young, aspiring actress and not yet the beloved star of Kosovo theater. "In those days there were no cafes or bars in Pristina, the only recreational activity was found in the *korzo*. We, young women in the gymnasium, dressed up to go to the *korzo* and look at a boy, at someone we liked, someone we had sympathy for. However, we were under strict discipline in the family, my friends and I, and my dad would say, 'Go out but come back by 18:30, or 19:00, or 20:00.' Sometimes we stayed out until 5 minutes to 20:00, so we took our shoes off and ran to get home as quickly as we could, because at 20:00 the door would be locked. The rules were very strict, and I sometimes asked, 'Why?' Maybe it shouldn't have been that way, maybe it was because there were such large families with many children, that sort of discipline was needed."[24]

In the early 1970s, the *korzo* in Pristina acquired an even greater socializing role, a sort of Facebook of the time, in the words of Ola Syla: "Each group of friends had their own tree where they stopped, so if you were looking for someone, you knew which tree to stop at and you could find them at eight o'clock in the evening. There, like on Facebook, we all knew who was dating whom, who broke up, and who went to the seaside because we could see their suntan. Simple as that. When we came back from the seaside we would say, 'Let's go out to the *korzo* and show off our tan.'"

The impact that the relaxation of state repression and government decentralization had on Albanians coming of age in the 1970s cannot be overestimated. Albanian youth from the urban middle class, especially Pristina, really were "a blessed generation."[25] In a moving memory of that time, writer and musician Migjen Kelmendi recalls when, one day, the one-liter bottle of Coca-Cola arrived in the Prishtina shops and everyone was amazed. People who went to look at this extraordinary artifact in the store windows made him think of Gabriel García Márquez's Macondo residents, gathered to marvel at ice. Coca-Cola replaced the popular rose tea as the drink to serve house guests, but also caused anguish among impressionable Albanian youth. The pull of the civilization able to produce Coca-Cola, the Beatles, and Hollywood became irresistible, and they ached to be part of it. It was almost impossible to forget their Albanianness, however, and not just because their fathers kept hammering into them the importance of being Albanian. Yugoslavia never let them forget it. From Serbs' pejorative pronunciation of the word for Albanian *šiptar*, sometimes *šiftar* (intentional mispronunciation of *shqiptar*, Albanian), it was clear that to be an Albanian meant one was backward. The question was how to remain Albanian while at the same time becoming part of the Coca-Cola civilization.

Girls began to go to parties and to be freer to engage with boys who were not their brothers. Kosovo had gained new institutions, such as the University of Prishtina, Prishtina Radio and Television, the five-star hotel Grand, and the spectacular sports center Boro & Ramiz, named after the partisans who had died together and had come to symbolize the friendship between Albanians and Serbs. Most importantly, favorable loans became available. By paying 1 Deutsche mark, one would receive 3 marks, with a deadline of twenty years for repayment in Yugoslav dinars. Inflation further improved these already good conditions. Albanians became free to consume as never before. They built new homes in the hills around the center of Pristina, on the hilly neighborhoods of Dragodan, Taslixhe, and Velania, furnishing them with imported appliances. They bought foreign cars and spent their summers in Greece and Turkey. As the prohibition to emigrate relaxed, the unemployed from the rural world left for Germany and Switzerland, bringing back crucial resources. Villagers too were able to buy foreign vehicles. From the time the British Ferguson tractors made their first appearance, they quickly became a status symbol.

Some things were not changing, however. There were not many other opportunities for youth socialization without adult supervision well into the late 1980s, when Nazlie Bala came of age. "Everything I experienced as a young person I experienced in the *korzo*. At the end of the school day, depending on the season, we went out from 18:00 until 22:00. We walked in four walking lanes, two in each direction. Back then there were no coffee shops like now. There were restaurants, however as a young woman you could not go to a restaurant. Going to a restaurant and drinking something, a Coca-Cola or a coffee, going to a restaurant to rest, which is a basic human need, was considered immoral...you were always afraid that a relative could see you. And what did you do in the *korzo*? You bought some sunflower seeds and sat in what we call the circle, which is where the Zahir Pajaziti statue is now, and ate sunflower seeds. At that time, if you had long nails it was considered immoral, if you wore nail polish, that was considered immoral, or if you put makeup on, or lipstick, or eyeliner. Dying your hair was considered inappropriate, 'Why would a young girl dye her hair?' Wearing a mini-skirt was considered immoral. High heels were also considered immoral. There were two or three coffee shops at that time, and especially Xheni café. It was the dream of all my peers at that time to sit there and drink a long espresso, but we only heard about it and never got to try the espresso."[26]

As privileged as urban life was in socialist Yugoslavia, compared to rural society, it was obviously still a society in transition. Urban families were often splinter groups from larger rural families, which ended for various reasons. As conditions were significantly improving throughout Kosovo during the 1970s, drawing people from rural communities to better jobs and living conditions in town, families became smaller. They brought with them traditional mores.

At the age of five, Blerta moved from a village to a western town. "We were a small family. I was still a child and can't remember very well when we separated from my uncles and came to the city. I grew up only with my mother, my father, and my brothers." Although she remembers neither the exact date of their departure from the village nor how they left, she believes it must have been at the beginning of the 1980s, when her father split from his extended family of farmers and began to work as a craftsman. Fatime came to the city from a nearby village in the late 1970s, when she was three; she has no memory whatsoever of village life. With her father's salary from good employment, the eight children in her family had "a middle-class life."

Qëndresa, who moved to a bigger city but after the war, experienced the separation as a trauma: "the war destroyed us, when my father split from his brothers." She remembers very well how all her uncles, their wives, and her grandparents doted on her, because she was the eldest child, born after so many years, that her parents were beginning to despair. Even today she misses that sustaining togetherness.

Families that were new in town had to adjust to the relatively freer environment in which the girls lived. That brought problems. In Pristina, Fatime did not mind the long walk to school from her suburban home, even though she carried a school bag that was so big, it came down to her knee. She loved school, even though she was not the best student, and with all her older sisters successfully attending high school or universities, she never thought she would be kept home. One summer day, just after she finished seventh grade, one of her older sisters did not come home. "They said that she had left, she had gotten married. Now, my father feared that I too would do the same and did not let me go to school anymore." Fatime lobbied her eldest sister and got assurance from her that she could complete high school. "I picked up the documents and took them to the Technical School, I took them there secretly, so that now she would not change her mind. After some days I went to see whether my name was there. It was there! I went once more and saw and read it again, letter by letter. I was enrolled. I told my mother, I told my father, 'So, will you let me go?' He said, 'No, we won't let you go.' I suffered because of this, I suffered a lot."

Fatime's father, lured from a village to the capital by a good job, struggled with the transition. After his teenage daughter eloped with a boy she had met independently from her family, he reverted to the comforting tradition of arranging an early marriage for Fatime, who was just reaching puberty. More than thirty years later, she cannot reminisce about that time without sobbing: "They came and asked for my hand and my father wanted to get me engaged. I did not know that boy, and he did not know me, we did not know each other. And they decided to get me engaged. It was December, the end of December '92. And I got engaged, I got married in June. And that night, when the bridegroom entered the room, I said, 'Who? Oh!' I was disappointed, you know, when he entered the room, when I saw him, because I had never seen him before and I did not like him, but he locked the door and I knew it was him. And I did not like him at all, not even a crumb of him, I didn't like him. But with the passing of time, it went well and everything was OK. The families liked each other a lot and they treated me well there. Soon after I gave birth to a girl."

Something else was happening at the time. By the end of the 1980s, police violence was already on the rise with Milošević at the helm of Serbia. Then, the war broke out in the rest of Yugoslavia. The more unsafe families felt, the more inclined they were to shift the responsibility of protecting their girls to someone else, the bridegroom's family for example. Sevdije Ahmeti had taken for granted the freedom gained as a professional woman. When she saw that state repression, including the firing of all Albanians from their jobs, was bringing back traditionalism to the city, Sevdije rebelled against what she called a sort of conspiracy of "the forces of tradition and of the police" to control women.[27] "I became a feminist before I knew what feminism was. Before, women like me had no problem going out, but now we had joined the army of women who had always stayed home. That changed things. Take my husband as an example: all of a sudden, when he saw me going out, he asked me, 'Where are you going?' He never did that before."[28]

The Strongest Link: An Oral History of Wartime Rape Survivors in Kosovo. Anna Di Lellio and Garentina Kraja, Oxford University Press. © Oxford University Press 2025. DOI: 10.1093/9780197699324.003.0004

4

Insecurity

A feeling of greater insecurity characterized the "situation," as people commonly refer to life in Kosovo during the 1990s. But when did it really begin? Was it in 1989, with Milošević's ascent to power, inaugurating a period of state repression and organized violence? Or was it earlier, in 1981, after the widespread popular protests calling for the change of Kosovo's status from a province of Serbia to a republic of Yugoslavia? The answer to these questions depends on places and people. The 1990s began with martial law, but the 1980s were also trying times, with mass purges in the Communist League and government institutions, as well as mass incarcerations. It's certain that the notable improvement that Kosovo had achieved in the 1970s, with greater provincial autonomy and freedoms, the expansion of the educational system, and the increased standard of living, began to crumble in 1981. It was just one year after the death of Marshall Tito.

The 1981 unrest began on March 11 at the University of Pristina. The story, as commonly told, maintains that students rebelled against the poor conditions of the university canteen, and their protest sparked a wider mobilization, ending with political demands that Kosovo be recognized as a republic. Offering a sociologically more nuanced interpretation, the provincial leadership of the Communist League, and in particular, Kosovo's secretary Mahmut Bakalli, interpreted the unrest as the result of the economic slowdown across the whole of Kosovo, and consequently the loss of hope for continuing progress. The reason for the student protest was the gap between the growing number of graduates from the University of Pristina and their narrowing chances of finding suitable employment.

Bakalli lost his position for appearing too understanding of what the other top party brass saw instead as a conspiracy to create havoc by local nationalist groups sponsored by neighboring Communist Albanians. Seeing anti-Yugoslav spies everywhere, Kosovo's and Serbia's leadership reacted by implementing a Stalinist policy of purges. However, as paranoid as they were, they were right about one thing. The rebellion that began in the university mess hall was not exactly spontaneous. It had been planned beforehand by Pan-Albanian underground groups, among them several women activists. It was Bahrije Kastrati who sparked the protest.[1] She did indeed throw her plate on the floor of the canteen in protest against the substandard food served there. The next morning, undetected by the police who were looking for agitators, she traveled to Prizren to print political tracts and spread the protest in the province. With her was a future KLA fighter, Xheva Krasniqi Ladrovci, who became famous during the war after she died together with her husband in a shootout with Serbian forces. But in 1981, she was with her friend Bahrije distributing hundreds of flyers during the night, going from place to place, camouflaged as men.

By April 1, the student demonstrations had become daily mass protests of people from all walks of life that brought to the fore national demands for more provincial autonomy.[2] They were met with brutal force by the police and army units which were moved into Kosovo from other Yugoslav republics. By the end of April, a number of protesters had been killed, ranging from twelve according to official sources to three hundred in the estimates of Amnesty International.[3] The dynamic of demonstrations in the streets and violent crackdown rapidly took the shape of a confrontation between a national uprising that was nurtured by the underground groups of *Ilegalja* and the Communist League's and central government's insistence on unity. Because protesters were asking for the Kosovo Republic, a demand that raised the specter of secession and unification with Albania, they were accused of reviving the national question—anathema in Communist ideology. Though the Albanian Communist leadership managed the conflict with unflinching loyalty to Yugoslavia, the confrontation immediately took the shape of an ethnic conflict, and the ensuing witch hunt cast a wide net on the Albanian population.

All "counter-revolutionaries," often also called *ballist*, the name of the Albanian non-Communist resistance during the Second World War, became targets of purges—in the political jargon of the time euphemistically called *diferencimi* (differentiation).[4] That meant mass layoffs from the workplace and expulsions from the party. A rigorous, Stalinist censorship stifled all manifestations of public life. Just to give an example, at Radio TV Prishtina a metal box called "Embargo" became the repository of all creative works deemed unpublishable by the censor. That's where *Malësore*,[5] a song composed by Shaqir Hoti, a musician in the Radio orchestra, ended up after playing only once.[6] The song's opening lyrics went like this: "Oh my mountain girl, oh Albanian, shining like a fiery star on the mountains."

Hoti was interrogated: "Whom are you singing to? What does 'mountain girl' mean? A brave Albanian from.... You want to hide something." Fortunately, he had only written the melody, not the lyrics, but for a while he had problems with the management. The suspicions that state authorities felt about a language they did not understand and found dissembling turned into a self-fulfilling prophecy. In the 1980s, the persecutory workings of censorship, says the writer Mehmet Kraja, deepened changes that were already happening to the Albanian language, which fully became a language of metaphors to disguise patriotic feelings for Albania.[7]

The courts handed down long jail sentences to activists for sedition or complicity in seditious acts.[8] Those suspected sympathizers were targeted for "isolation," a form of ostracism that was both institutional and social, as neighbors and even friends halted all interactions with "counter-revolutionaries," for fear of being considered guilty by association. Sevdije Ahmeti recalls that an acquaintance, who had spent two years in jail for political activity in *Ilegalja*, looked very surprised when she invited her over for coffee.[9] Nobody else except the activist's close family had talked to her since her release. Isolation was liberally applied to children or close relatives of suspects: scholarships, admission to the dorms, and jobs could be withdrawn from individuals who belonged to "unreliable" families, in the language of the state.

For Albanians—first and primarily the militants of nationalist groups, but then eventually most of the people—places previously deemed safe became unsafe across Kosovo. Throughout the next ten years, until war broke out in 1998, they had to learn how to live in places of higher insecurity. As Merita recalls, "Fear was a normal feeling for us, we have always been afraid. All the protests, all the violence, were normal. We felt those painful feelings, we were afraid, and we all went through that."

Protests and Militance

In 1981, Ganimete was in her first year of her town's gymnasium. She was a spirited young woman who joined the first demonstration in March with her entire class and helped organize the participation of younger students. In town visiting a relative's house, she was on the balcony when she saw people flooding the streets and ran downstairs to catch up with them. She did not heed her older relatives' plea to stay home. They felt apprehensive about possible repercussions, had she been identified as a militant. She felt emboldened by the freedom of action that the protest allowed and feared the police less than her family: "When they used teargas to disperse us, I did not have the courage to go back home or to my relatives' house."

Her brother was with her, the one whose hope for education had been curtailed by the family and who had become a militant of the Albanian underground. He was in all the protests. It was under his guidance, later that spring, that Ganimete and her classmates from high school, defying bans on public gatherings, made the trek across the mountains to attend the burial of a man they considered a martyr to the national cause, Tahir Meha.[10] Meha was a villager from a nationalist family whose different generations had always joined armed rebellions against the Serbian state, from the interwar outlaws to the resisters against the Yugoslav partisans. His own older brother Beqir had been sentenced to Goli Otok, a barren Croatian island that from 1949 until 1989 was Yugoslavia's own gulag. Not surprisingly, Tahir had always been under some form of surveillance and had recently been released from short but brutal detention. In May 1981, at the end of a day-long siege of his compound in the hills of Drenica, after he refused to report to the police station as ordered, he was killed, along with his father Nebih. They had engaged the police in a shootout, breaking with the choice of nonviolence made by Albanian nationalist groups after the end of the Second World War, and in the charged atmosphere of the time, they became a symbol of resistance. The ban on a public funeral was designed to preempt mass rallies; challenging the ban was an act of resistance.

The decade of the 1980s was bookended by mass protests. The 1981 protests spread through all the schools like wildfire. Hatmone Haradinaj was in her dorm at the University of Prishtina, listening to a newly acquired cassette of Albanians songs with other freshmen, when she heard the noise of the crowd in the streets and joined them with her group.[11] Naime Maçastena Sherifi was in primary school when, with all her classmates, she was drawn to the windows by the cries of the high school students who had entered the school yard waving an Albanian flag.[12] The principal had issued an order to lock the young students in, fearing for their safety, so the kids just jumped out the window and joined the demonstrators.

Afërdita too was just a child when the demonstrations began in her town in 1981. "My mother went to the demonstrations, my father went, even my grandmother who was eighty years old went. My brother got me ready and took me by the hand, 'Come on, let's go to the demonstrations.' My father encouraged us, 'Go, because they are asking Kosova to be a Republic, to be independent of the *Shki*.'" Her mother tried to stop them, fearing police violence, but had no such worry later, after Milošević established martial law in Kosovo in 1989, provoking a new wave of mass street protests. "Everyone took to the streets. It was then that they jailed dad. At the time he was about 61 years old. And they beat him, they beat him so much that from that day on, dad was never really well. He was always losing blood from the colon or the kidney. Now we were always afraid, '*Ku ku*,[13] *Shki, kuku*, they are going to beat us!' He was persecuted by *Shki*.... We had chaos in the streets, but it was not like today, now the men go out on their own and the women too, no, back then the men finished their work, and the women stayed at home, and we went out as families. I was hit, the police hit and arrested people even at the market. But we were young and wanted to be free from the occupiers. The situation was really bad, it was a catastrophe."

For Merita, in rural Kosovo, "the situation began in 1989." She remembers how everyone was involved in the protests against Milošević, including the children and the women. What followed the protests against the Milošević regime in 1989 was a period of enforced calm, partly because Kosovo had become a veritable police state, partly because the Albanian leadership, under the guidance of President Ibrahim Rugova, maintained an uncompromising refusal to encourage any active resistance against the regime. By the mid-1990s, that principled stand had taken a severe hit by the failure of reaching any negotiated agreement, including participating in the Dayton Accords, which ended the Bosnian war in 1995. For Albanians, Dayton was a "trauma."[14]

When a new generation of students took to the streets on October 1, 1997, to demand the return of the Albanians to the university buildings from which they had been barred since 1991, their action came as a shock to the political leadership.[15] In 1996, there had been an "education agreement," brokered by the Italian Catholic organization Sant Egidio and signed by Rugova and Milošević, to end the ban of Albanian students from school facilities, but it was never implemented.[16] The students' active demand to return to the university was an unprecedented show of defiance against not only Serbian state authorities but also President Ibrahim Rugova, who refused to support them despite their peaceful protests. The movement met a violent police crackdown and a wall of opposition. On April 30, 1998, the deadline set for reopening the Faculty of Engineering, Serbian students stood their ground; they left the building only two weeks later, after completely destroying the school to the last piece of furniture.[17]

Arrests, Detentions, and Interrogations

More than six thousand Albanians have confirmed that they were detained as political prisoners during the 1990s, but the Kosovo Association of Political Prisoners numbers many more members, as police repression stepped up after the demonstrations of 1981.[18] They arrested known leaders of the *Ilegalja* such as Metush Krasniqi, who had been sentenced to eighteen years for the first time in 1958, and released him after eight years in 1966, as a result of the fall of Ranković. In 1981, they kept him in jail for four months as a preventive measure to separate him from the protests, but in 1985 they arrested him again, and when he returned one year later, his health was so compromised that he died immediately after.[19] Hydajet Hyseni, returned from self-imposed exile in Switzerland to escape arrest, and photographed as he addressed the protesters from a tree, spent the entire decade (1981–1991) in jail, and his memory of constant torture is still very vivid.[20]

Beside known militants, high school seniors were arrested for shouting slogans in the school yard, like Enver Dugolli in Drenas, an offense that cost him six years of prison and marked him as a terrorist until he was arrested again in 1997, to be released only in 2001, two years after the end of the war.[21] In Prizen, Nait Hasani was a sixteen-year-old who was found guilty of treason for trying to flush a photo of Tito down the toilet in the school restrooms and went straight to jail, where he served time in four different stints for a total of ten years; after he was released he became one of the founders of the KLA.[22] In jail, they were all tortured almost nightly.[23]

Individuals were arrested as they shouted slogans, during street rallies, during weapons searches, for handing out political pamphlets, because they wore black and red clothes (the colors of the Albanian flag), or for carrying the Albanian flag. Afërdita's father was arrested four times because when men in his extended family got married, he always showed up at their wedding parties, as per tradition, carrying not only the Yugoslav flag, the "flag of the *Shki*," but also the flag of the Republic of Albania, which Albanians everywhere consider their national flag. Yugoslav authorities had temporarily authorized the display of that flag between 1974 and 1981, but after that they began to see it as a rallying cry for separatist activities. During the 1990s, carrying an Albanian flag in public became a good reason to detain people and later implement surveillance and harassment of suspects.

Afërdita: "In '96 they took my father to jail. Someone said that at 3 p.m. on that Saturday—Saturday was market day—some fifteen minutes previous, he had bought a weapon from my father and gave the caliber and the number and everything. Or maybe the *Shki* made up the report to catch my dad, to arrest him on weapon possession charges. They came, took him inside the house, beat him up, and arrested him. We were visiting relatives, and someone called on those fixed telephones we had back then to tell us what was happening. They told me to go home and tell the police that dad was ill. I ran home, but dad wasn't there anymore, he was already in prison. My mother said, 'They took dad to jail because of weapons,' but he never had weapons. They came to pick him up and kill him. They held dad in jail for three weeks, and for those three weeks we stayed by the entrance of the jail—my mother, my brothers, everybody. I was pregnant with my second daughter, it was the beginning of my pregnancy, the third or fourth month. I did not realize that I was pregnant because I was so upset! I was in so much distress! We took my father from jail to the hospital. In three weeks he had lost much blood from the mouth, from the nose, that we all gave blood for him, he needed four kilos of it. That time they killed my father. Dad died on the 30th of the twelfth month of '96. We held a wake for three weeks, then I went back home. Later, a certain worry seized me, and my stomach began to hurt a lot. Because somehow I lost a person who was not just a parent, he was a pillar of the house."

Political prisoners left prison as broken men, like Edona's grandfather, who was always sick in his stomach after spending six or seven years in detention; she cannot remember precisely how long. He used to tell his granddaughters how he survived torture thanks to a chunk of salt, small rocks of salt that people used to buy in lieu of packaged salt, "For nine or ten days, when I licked it, I found the strength to go and drink water."

Several women also were arrested for their participation in the clandestine Albanian national movement which the protest had re-energized. In 1984, on the day their class celebrated high school graduation, Hava Shala and her friend Myrvete Dreshaj were served a harsh prison sentence. They had been arrested in Peja with a group of six girls for distributing nationalist tracts and spent the following four years in detention, where they were beaten and subjected to sleep and food deprivation and electroshocks.[24] Shukrije Gashi, detained and tried in 1983, was a university student who had spent nights writing fliers by hand. Like others, during the pretrial phase she was interrogated daily, asked to name names, or sign lists of suspected terrorists. "I never talked.... We had pledged an oath as women that we would rather die than talk. Because there was also another side to our movement, which was to make the men understand that we were as strong as them." That's when the torture began. "Zoran stepped in. He was smoking a cigarette, and since I didn't speak, he took the cigarette and stubbed it on my eyebrow, and my forehead, so I would speak. I fainted from the pain.... And then, after I came to my senses, they started questioning me again. Fortunately, I have low blood pressure, and this helped me to get weak quickly, so they couldn't continue.... They even used a stimulating injection. I did some research on this stimulating injection, which has a weakening effect on people with low blood pressure. And as soon as I got the injection, I totally collapsed."

The same fear of surrendering to torture and betraying her friends, but mostly her brothers, who trusted her, overwhelmed Zyrafete Berisha Lushaj, arrested as she met with other university students to celebrate the anniversary of the 1981 protests.[25]

Shukrije and other women prisoners thought that the men were subjected to worse treatment in jail. "And we were going mad! They continued the tortures nonstop the whole time. We decided to protest. And we did that. We protested. We started by banging on doors. Our doors were made of steel. And the knocking sounded loud. [...] The reason was to make a huge noise in order to attract the attention of the guards and stop the beating of men and boys. They rushed furiously to the floor where women and girls were, and what a sight! It was a dreadful sight. They were in rolled-up sleeves and all across their faces and on their hands there was blood."

In the 1980s, Kosovo was under the Yugoslav regime which included all ethnic groups. Shukrije and her friends remarked with considerable revulsion that the torturing guards were all Albanian.

A regular practice of the police, which increased during the 1990s, was to temporarily hold suspects arrested for political activities in the police stations for "informative interrogations," in the jargon of the time, which could result in beating and torture. The police blacklist also included individuals who were not associated with the underground groups but were involved in social activism, such as women's groups. For women, the specter of the threat of sexual violence always loomed large, and avoidance of such violence was a matter of sheer luck.

Vjosa Dobruna: "During these years, I have been to the police station eleven times. I was questioned eleven times, as they say. I was beaten up eleven times. Many times they came to take me at night. After the war, for a long time, I could not hear someone walking on the stairs by night, I could not.... For many years I had many fears, and many traumas that were not only mine.... We all tried to pretend that we were stronger so we could help others but not because we were strong, the fear existed, and it was terrible. For example, I had a pair of shoes, I will never forget, from a brand...I always wanted to buy expensive shoes, I had dark blue Bruno Magli shoes. Everyone said that when they were questioned in the police station, besides being beaten, they also were sexually abused. The first time they sent me to the police station I was wearing those shoes, and when I left the police station in the center of Prishtina I walked, looking at my shoes the whole time saying, 'Oh, these shoes brought me luck. I will never stop wearing them.' And many times, Bajram Kelmendi,[26] when I talked with the late, told me 'Vjosa, tell me immediately when they call you, don't go to the police without me.' And we always laughed with Bajram when he said, 'Are you wearing your Bruno Magli shoes?' I would say, 'Yes.' 'Did they beat you?'... 'No, no, I passed this time without sexual abuse, the shoes are bringing me luck.' Even when they deported me from Kosovo, I wore the same shoes. Those shoes lasted for a long time, and I kept them since I had this fixation that they protected me. One creates any kind of mechanism to protect oneself from fear."

Conscript Suicides

After the outbreak of war in Croatia in 1991, and one year later in Bosnia-Herzegovina, the Yugoslav People's Army (*Jugoslavenska Narodna Armija*, *JNA*) had become entirely Serbian and Montenegrin. In 1991, Helsinki Watch began to receive several reports that non-Serbian minorities were beaten or even killed after being recruited, and information gathered in Kosovo pointed to a number of deaths of Albanian conscripts, all listed as suicides by the military authorities.[27] The human rights group listed the names of eight victims, deceased between September 1989 and November

1991, but was never able to confirm what families in Kosovo were certain about: that their young men had been killed, execution style. For a society where suicide was almost unheard of at the time, that it would happen at all, let alone at such a rate, was unthinkable. To be sure, the evidence in support of the hypothesis of murder was mostly circumstantial. It was the handling of the incidents by the military authorities that raised doubts about the cause of those deaths and thus the suspicion of a cover-up. There was no hint of any official investigation of this rather unusual occurrence, nor were the families ever allowed to know what had happened; there were no autopsies. All the bodies were shipped back home in sealed coffins.

Nobody could inspect the body of Afërdita's cousin, the son of her paternal uncle, who returned in a coffin from the military barracks close to the border between Slovenia and Austria. "My aunt said that they could see how he looked only a little, they saw a little of his face, and saw that blood was streaming down his face." Afërdita's own brother had a brush with death when he was drafted in 1986: "My brother said, 'When I was in the army I wasn't killed by a hair by Serbs with mines.'"

Ganimete saw her neighbor come back in a coffin from his military service. He was a twenty-two-year-old recruit, a close friend of her brother. They said he had committed suicide, but everyone believed it was a lie.

Dom Lush Gjergji was escorting a crew of the Italian *TV Rai Uno* on a visit to Kodra e Trimave, a poor neighborhood of Prishtina, when they met a large gathering of people mourning one of these young recruits: "The man of the house came out when someone recognized me and called, 'Dom Lush Gjergji!' And he said to me, 'It's good that God brought you here.' I said, 'I know that it's not good, but thanks to God it will be better! They killed your son, and they closed the coffin, they sealed it. Would you do me a favor, a courageous act? Open the coffin, and we will film it with the camera of the Italian television *Rai Uno*.' He dispersed the people, and he also dispersed the members of the Yugoslav army who were there by telling them, 'We have our own ritual, we have to mourn the victim.' We entered the room, and he opened the coffin. The body had five bullets in the back. And we filmed it. And this was the first evidence that was given to the world through *Rai Uno*, that these were not suicides, but murders. They were represented as such only to destroy the morale and the will of the people."[28]

The army had become a very hostile environment for Albanian conscripts, following the mass shooting at the barracks of the Serbian town of Paraćin in September 1987, in which a young Albanian soldier from Kosovo, Aziz Kelmendi, killed four other soldiers and wounded five. The incident was immediately constructed by the state media as a "shot against Yugoslavia," and a planned attack against Serbs, even though there was only one Serb among the victims; to confirm this accusatory information campaign, eight Albanians co-conspirators were convicted in a show trial on the basis of confessions extorted under torture.[29] Kelmendi's father was charged with unlawful weapon possession, and the media sensationalized the arrest. alleging that he had hidden the weapon in his wife's peasant-like large pants, the *dimja*, highlighting at once women's subordination and backwardness as well as men's cowardice.[30]

As violence against Albanian businesses was unleashed in the streets of Serbia following the mass shooting in Paraćin, Milošević triumphed, only two weeks later, at the Eighth Plenum of the Communist League of Serbia on a platform of aggressive defense of the Serbian nation. Until then, the draft was seen as a rite of passage from boyhood to adulthood and was celebrated accordingly. That was no longer the case. Thinking back about those times, oral historian Arbnora Dushi told us that in her social circle, when young men were drafted, families stood in front of a photographer to have their portrait taken, not as an occasion to rejoice, but to dread.[31]

The war increased this already deep anxiety about the draft. The Kosovo leadership struck an agreement with Croatia to let several thousand Albanians stationed there leave the army without repercussions.[32] Families helped their youth desert the army. Ganimete's youngest brother was eighteen in 1993 when he was called up. She went to see him in the barracks with her father; cunningly, they managed to take her brother out of his cantonment, and from the city, through a travel agency, they sent him abroad illegally. Blerta's brother migrated rather than answering the call to serve in the Yugoslav army to be deployed by Serbia to fight in Croatia and Bosnia. He left his wife and children in the care of his family. At the end of 1989, Adelina's brother, slightly older than her and the only one to go to school in their family, enlisted. "He had gotten the call to go to the army. He stayed for twelve months, and then the war began. So he left Yugoslavia and sought asylum abroad. The first time he came back to Kosovo was when the demonstrations started again in 1998."

The Hospitals

After the police detained and beat Ganimete's youngest brother, leaving him to bleed on the ground, she picked him up to take him to the hospital, but his condition deteriorated along the way, and he lost consciousness.

Desperately looking for help, she approached a man tending some sheep and carrying a flask of water from a nearby spring. He gave her water, and when he understood that the young man was in that state because of being beaten by the police, "he said, 'Don't take him to the hospital in the city because they are worse there.'" Instead, he took a sheepskin he had in the house and wrapped her brother in it, resorting to a traditional remedy for the relief of aches and wounds. In the meanwhile, Ganimete's other brother had been taken to the hospital, where journalists came to interview him and the family. "But we didn't dare leave my brother alone for a moment there, because there was a certain doctor there, who said to my brother, 'Nothing is the matter with you.' Another doctor, an Albanian, told us, 'Leave immediately because tonight they will come and you know what they do when they come.'" That was a decisive warning, and they immediately left because they knew that when the police were in pursuit of "irredentists," they searched everywhere and did not stop at the door of an emergency room.

After Serbia revoked Kosovo's autonomy, ethnic conflict was explicitly transferred to the heart of the hospitals. First came the firings of the Albanian medical personnel. Dobruna, a pediatrician, was fired on August 15, 1990. She remembers the date very well because it was her parents' anniversary and she had organized a surprise party at night. "At 8:20 a.m., at least fifteen policemen came and surrounded the hospital. I was on the first floor then, I led the department of developmental and neurological disorders of children from birth to one year, and I was checking a child because work began at 7 a.m. A few weeks earlier all the Serbian doctors and nurses had quit, and when I came to work that day, I saw a Serbian nurse, whose husband was the director of the police station near the hospital. And I was surprised, 'Did you talk to the director?' Because if you didn't come to work for three days, you would lose your job. She said, 'That rule is only valid for you Albanians'—she said it in Serbian, *za vas Šiptari* (for you Albanians)—'not for us.' I didn't say anything. I'll fix it later, I'll take care of this later, I thought, and went in because there were so many patients! And they brought me a patient, he was a former political prisoner from Gjilan who brought in his nephew to have him checked. And while I was checking him, the police came and said, 'Leave the kid, get out of here.' 'Why?' We argued. The Serbian nurse, Zorica, said to the police, 'What did I tell you? The Albanians who work here are all like this one.' She was cursing, something. Samka, the other nurse, said, standing by the door, 'She won't get out, it won't work.'"

Vjosa Dobruna refused to leave the hospital until 2 p.m., completing her shift. "In the meantime, they brought me the official papers, which said that I got fired because I missed three days of work, but actually I had been at work. Until then they had only fired people from RTP [Radio and Television Prishtina], not doctors. But in the evening we heard that I wasn't the first one, even in the surgery department they had fired people. The next day I got ready and went to work again. Three or four policemen chased me out. I went in even the day after that, I made it like a routine, and now, it was kinda fun to do that. Every day at 7 a.m., I got dressed, I got ready, and I went to work. The police stood in front of the door, they said, 'We'll beat you,' to the point that my colleagues, the ones who were still working, said, 'Don't come here to provoke them.' When there were the union protests of September 3, that's when they all got fired."

The Albanian doctors and nurses forced to leave the hospitals converged into the self-help organization *Nënë Tereza*, to set up makeshift clinics. Dom Lush Gjiergji was part of its leadership. The brothers Sedaj, one of them a doctor, had talked to the late Bishop Nikë Prela about creating a humanitarian, charitable association, and the bishop had appointed Dom Lush to help them. And Dom Lush got down to work. "We made the preparation for May 10 of 1991. We founded it here in Prishtina. We wrote a statute, we did everything that needed to be done, and we registered. It was our luck, it was God's providence."[33] *Nënë Tereza* was not a confessional organization and involved a large variety of volunteers, including Doctor Dobruna: "I talked with Dom Lush and *bac*[34] Jak [Mita], and I went to work there, but one day I worked as a pediatrician, and three days I worked with logistics. I collected equipment, wrote applications for funds, and wrote some reports that I still have with me, I did everything. I got in touch with the Caritas of Vienna, the Caritas of Firenze, the whole world."[35]

Fatime had her first daughter one year after she got married. Three years later, she was pregnant with another one, and there was no other place for her to give birth but a makeshift *Nënë Tereza* clinic. "The case was complicated, and they had to call the doctor. The doctor came, and he turned my child around, he put his hand like this and went, 'Oh...' I hurt very badly, I don't know what he said at that moment, I don't know, he said words like, 'I cannot see the head at all.' 'Oh doctor,' I said, 'I went for a check-up two weeks ago, and they told me it was all OK.' Now, he got something. 'I found her,' he said. He brought out her head like this, you know, she had the umbilical cord wrapped around her like a bottle of a liter and a half of that water of Kllokot, she was tied up like that. I had died, but I felt liberated at once. That baby was born, and afterward, they called home, and said, 'We are keeping her here to rest.' And when I picked up that baby, her mouth was open and round like a twenty cent, because the umbilical cord was wrongly wrapped around. I was so worried about that child."

Fatime was lucky, because the *Nënë Tereza* clinics lacked so many things that some people avoided them. Instead, they took the risk and chose to go to a difficult-to-reach and hostile hospital which was staffed with Serbian personnel but was also better equipped than the friendly Albanian clinics. In the capital, Kimete's mother decided her daughter would go to the hospital to give birth. She said that much to her husband since her son-in-law had repaired abroad to safety. It was 1997, and the situation had become critical, with the country on the verge of war. Kimete found herself in a hostile Serbian hospital: "When I went into labor we decided I would go to the hospital, but by then only Serbs were working there; we gave them 10 Deutsche marks so they would not kill me. I also gave money to a nurse so she would look after me. As I was in labor, she screamed at me in Serbian, '*Sramota!*' (Shame on you!), for giving birth. In the end, she said, 'Your daughter is alive, you see, nobody died!'

At about the same time, Edona was also admitted to the hospital of Prishtina. "In my husband's family, there had not been a child for twenty years and change. And my father-in-law had had barely these two boys, many others had died, and only these two had grown up. My husband said, 'Even the oaks in the mountain are happy.' I just wanted to know that this pregnancy would go well, a birth with no problem. They put me in a room, and I was in pain, and they left me there shouting and wailing. At the time they spoke only Serbian, and I did not understand what the nurse said, and now, she grabbed my hands, I'll never forget, she grabbed my hands and held them hard. My mother-in-law, who knew Serbian, told me that the doctors and the nurses were saying to me, 'You are too young. Did you want to give birth? Now, put up with it!'"

The day after giving birth, Edona was told to leave, and she found herself both anxious about her own health and relieved. Everything in the hospital was foreign to her and frightful, even the other patients. An encounter with two Serb women in the elevator made her shake with fear, "I can still see the dress, a *saballëk*, a dowry robe as we used to call them, a thick one, only that, no trousers nor sweatpants, nothing." Edona received nothing to eat or drink at the hospital, nor could she see her child. Her savvy mother-in-law bribed a nurse to let her check on the baby. When a nephew came to pick her up by car, "it seemed that the whole hospital had opened up."

A trip to the hospital could be objectively dangerous, along roads with multiple checkpoints. Many years later, for Doctor Dobruna there is still no relief from the painful memory of a woman who could not reach the clinic in time to save her baby. The woman had been deported back to Kosovo from Germany because she lacked legal residence, while her husband stayed behind. "She had a beautiful daughter, but the girl got sick. Her parents-in-law didn't allow her to leave the village because 'the Serbian military might rape you.' Serbian violence manifested itself as one more reason to limit freedom of movement for women, although women kept the place together, they kept Kosovo together, because the husbands were abroad. So she brought her child to me at the edge of death, the girl died in my arms. I was horrified when she told me why she had not brought her child to the clinic until then. I asked her, 'Why didn't you bring her earlier?' 'My parents-in-law wouldn't allow me to go out.' I was so horrified, I even cried more than the woman whose child died. I couldn't let go of that child."

Vlora's father accompanied his wife to Pristina already well into the war, in late 1998, because the local hospital was not well equipped and her mother had a difficult pregnancy. On the road, they were stopped by Serbian police. "They said, 'Hajde inshallah you will have a boy!' Yes, they said, 'Inshallah you will have a boy.' My mother said, 'With all that pain and the problems I had, when they said, 'Inshallah you will have a boy,' I said, 'Ooo, kuku, inshallah I will have a boy but not, inshallah, to leave him in your hands!'"

In School

In 1990, the Milošević regime made teaching and learning in the Albanian language institutionally impossible, by establishing Serbian as the only official language and requesting an oath of loyalty to Serbia from all teachers. With Albanians kicked out of state schools, a veritable system of apartheid along ethnic lines was established, where schools became the scene of a low-intensity ethnic conflict. The children understood only partially the sudden changes that erected barriers, both physical and social, between Albanians and Serbs.

In Prishtina, Jehona Gjurgjeala was eleven in 1990: "I went to Dardania elementary school. I returned after winter break—I can't remember what grade I was in, but I knew the school very well—and now, you run upstairs and want to turn right to go to the other corridor, and suddenly see a wall that has been built during the break. And that was kind of the beginning of the separation between Serbs and Albanians. The Serbs had taken half of the school and left us the other half. We were three times as many students. They had one shift. They had taken all the best chairs, desks, and everything else, while we, on the other side, had to manage somehow. When you are so young, that doesn't impress you that much. OK, the wall! But you keep going."[36]

Stefan Surlić attended the same school two years later: "What I actually remember, the school was divided exactly like that: there was a Serbian and an Albanian part, so to speak, they had different entrances. And that was the case until the beginning of the war. We had this central courtyard actually, and I will never forget that image: we could see one another from the window, we were on one side, they were on the other, and I know that all of us kids raised three fingers, and they two. We just looked at one another, and there was stillness, there were no threats nor anything else, just stillness, through that glass. And that is one of the images that will stay with me forever, that stillness, no emotional response, just the fingers raised and a line, which seemed at the time, and as time passes seems insurmountable, and which was passed down to the younger generations."[37]

Perhaps the kids did experience the hostility among adults that was growing into an open conflict as a competition between two teams: one team holding the nationalist Serbian symbol of the three raised fingers, originally representing the Trinity and a symbol of Serbian Orthodoxy, and the other, the Albanian, making the V sign of victory. More likely, even the schoolchildren had become politicized.

High school and university classes were held in private homes, but the youngest students could still go to segregated primary and middle schools in most cities. But why the separating wall? Conspiracy theories proliferated when hundreds of Albanian students all across Kosovo began to show signs of poisoning. The walls were seen as protection for Serbian children from the state's murderous attack on Albanian children. It was the end of March, beginning of April 1990, when reports of mass poisoning in schools transpired in the Yugoslav media.[38] In Peja, two of Xhejrane's sisters suddenly fell prey to convulsions caused by acute stomach cramps. In Mitrovica, three of Valdete Idrizi's classmates and her sister Linda, all in middle school, got very sick at the same time, with no previous symptoms of illness. That terrified families and spread panic throughout the schools. Valdete remembers that "[w]e didn't even know how to behave with Linda. She had cramps. Our grandmother told us to put a stick in her mouth because she would bite her tongue, which happened when she had a seizure. And you didn't know when she would have another attack. And once, we lived on the third floor, and she was looking outside the window, and she was struck like that. Fortunately, someone in the family grabbed her because she could have fallen and died."

Although a UN toxicologist concluded that sarin had been found in a blood sample taken from Kosovo children, and Serbia had sarin in the inventory of chemical weapons it was producing, the phenomenon of mass poisoning was never officially resolved.[39] The Serbian government blocked any independent investigation of the incident, and the media explained it as mass hysteria, while also claiming that, on the contrary, Albanians were plotting the poisoning of Serbian and Montenegrin schoolchildren.[40]

When Albanians remember their time in high school or university during the 1990s, they speak, more often than not, about discomfort and fear. They had to take the teacher's dictation sitting on the floor and balancing their notebooks on their lap. And for those who lived in rural areas, there was the trauma of having to walk miles to reach a place called school, which frequently was a private house. With the establishment of martial law after 1989, the long walks through the countryside to reach makeshift classrooms became even more treacherous than usual. As a high-school student, a man who is now a teacher told us how the police once stopped him, manhandled him, called him "irredentist," and finally took away from him the history book he had just bought; when he reached home, he cried more because of losing that book than for the physical abuse suffered at the checkpoint.[41] With some luck, lessons lasted as long as twenty minutes, if the teachers managed to pass checkpoints without being held. When the police stopped a group of teachers in a car, Shukrije Tahiraj was hectored, "You should not teach Albanian, if you want Albanian schools, go to Albania."[42] She thought that, as a woman, she got better treatment: while her male colleagues were severely beaten, she was hit "only" on her hands with a stick until they became very swollen.

Not having a school near the house, for Teuta the risks were too high. "I only have eight years of school, because when it was time for me to go to high school, there was no school, you could not study in schools, only in homes. My parents did not want me to go, and neither did I. And I stayed at home. I only did housework. We worked the land, we worked at home. The conditions were so bad that you couldn't do what you wanted." The effort to educate their youth became one of the main goals of the parallel society that Albanians built. It involved all the teachers previously employed by the state system, but also scores of volunteers. Ajshe was older and already married when she answered the call to help. "I put my name down at the center, and I told them to bring three–four girls so that I could support them with food and clothes and other needs, they would be all my charges. They brought four girls. One of them stayed with us for three years, and the other three stayed for four years. And I supported generation after generation of relatives because in my town there was a school of medicine. We were able to help."

At Home

The Serbian police made the house the most unsafe place throughout the 1990s. If they could not find their target there, they could always punish a member of the family, and terrorize the others. Police operations seemed to follow a script. Afërdita cannot even remember how many times they came to her house searching for weapons. Her father was selling cigarettes in the market, not a legal activity at the time, but not considered seditious either. "They would search through all the clothes, the armoire, and the couch, and throw everything on the floor. They would go to the yard because there was a big yard at my mother's and a hen's house and ask where my father had hidden weapons. They would say, 'Hey! Vraćemo opet,' we will be back again, you know? They said, 'We will come back, we are not joking.' This went on until '97."

Police came to the house looking for young men of military age who were avoiding the draft, such as Blerta's brother, who in 1992 illegally crossed the border to reach Germany. Informants had perhaps revealed the escape, but it's certain that the police knew he had just left. "I remember it as if it were today: three military vehicles, we called them Pinzgauers, arrived, and police filled up the entire yard of my father's house, they were everywhere, they also went up to the attic. And I was pregnant, I had one more month to go before having my girl. I remember that I said, 'Dad, the police are here.' It was horrible, they filled up the whole house. They surrounded us. They wanted my brother. They said, 'Young bride, where is your husband?' My sister-in-law said, 'He is not here. He is out.' 'You lie.' So, they took my father and maltreated him, beat him up. Almost for an entire year and longer they came and beat my father. He hid in the fields, in the mountains, still, we did not have any peace from them. The other brother was sixteen and a half, and he was also forced to leave illegally."

In 1991, an extraordinary grassroots mobilization, orchestrated by the unofficial leadership of Kosovo—a collection of former unions and party leaders, former political prisoners, intellectuals, and students—organized the first free elections independently from the socialist state. It was an informal affair, albeit incredibly complex in its realization. Polling stations were set up in private houses, and Ganimete's home was one of them. Following tradition, men and women occupied separate spaces: there was the *oda e burrave* (men's room), where only men were allowed unless a woman was let in to serve meals, though it is more likely a young man who transported food from the kitchen and the quarter where women prepare the meals and live. The women's quarter was full of women who had come to cast their vote, and with them was Ganimete's brother. Informants, once again, told the police about what was happening there and they promptly arrived. Ganimete and her brother grabbed all the political pamphlets that were on the table and fled outside, to the barn. "We had cows, and by the cows, there was a trough full of husk, and there were also other sacks of husk, about five–six sacks that had not been put in that trough. So, we got into that trough, and we got those sacks—I was very young and weak yet with my brother I emptied fifty kilograms of husk to cover ourselves. They all came, the police did not leave any place unsearched, but could not find us, they even took a knife and stuck it in. But I came out when I thought that they had not found us in their hunt and they caught us. And later they took my brother for interrogation, they kept him for twenty-four hours."

The police returned to Ganimete's house in 1995, searching for weapons. About thirty agents rounded up the family and interrogated even her old mother because as a descendant of famous outlaws who were active between the two world wars, she was still a suspect by association. "Mehmet Gradica and Ibrahim Rugova left automatic weapons with you!,"[43] they shouted at her. "Only a boy, my brother's newly born girl, and I were left in the house, the others were not there. We were all pulled outside, they tied us with wire. And they climbed upstairs, we had a two-story house and went everywhere, raided the rooms of the young brides and my room where I had a trousseau, a trunk. They messed everything up, and took my brothers' passports and all the money that was there. At the time I had a shop, I had just begun to come back to life a little, but they took all the money. That day they also took my two brothers and held them at the police station for twenty-four hours. When they came and said, 'Where is your brother?' I went to the neighbor's, where my younger brother was attending the wake for the man's son, the one killed as a conscript. I have been feeling guilty about that since then. He had told me, over and over again, 'When someone comes and asks for me, call me wherever I am, so they will not mistreat you.' And I did, and the police took him, and they beat him as they tugged him into their car. They took my other brother too. They were in the car, and I, running after them with my brother's daughter.... That brother had registered me as a baby when I was born."

The police constantly tailed Ganimete's activist brother, and their house searches were very predictable. It was an obvious strategy of harassment and thievery, methodically implemented with the goal of terrorizing. In 1996 they came to summon his son because they could not find him. They would have taken the eight-year-old boy to blackmail the family into revealing where the father was hiding. Ganimete intervened in his defense. "I said, 'This is not his boy, this is my son.' The police said, 'This cannot be your son because you are fair, and this one has a dark face.' I said, 'The boy looks like his father.' I was not married then, but I took that boy and left." The reaction of the police was swift: they gave Ganimete's family an ultimatum to leave the village, all of them. Only her brother took the road to the mountains, like many men. He reached Albania and from there Western Europe.

House searches often included abuse against women, yet another terrorizing practice of Serbian police. Afërdita's father was worried about what could happen to her and her sisters after news of sexual violence and its consequences had traveled across Kosovo. It was 1987 when he heard that a young girl had jumped off the third floor of her apartment building in Skënderaj after a visit from the police and swore to himself his daughters would not have the same fate. "My father said, 'I am marrying you young, and I am sending you away because they are targeting us with dishonor.' It had never occurred to us that someone could rape you; they could kill you, yes, but never rape. I got married when I wasn't yet fifteen, I was fourteen and a half, just that the *Shki* wouldn't take me. Such beasts! 'Hey, dad,' we said, 'explain what happened.' 'Come on, hey, listen to your dad,' he said, 'dad knows better, and you, my daughters, must listen to me, must do what dad says.'" Afërdita got engaged in June 1989 to a man who was twelve years older and unknown to her. They married in December. "On the day they got me engaged, I went to the hospital for an infusion because I was very upset. I said, 'Why do they take me away from playing and other things? I am only fourteen years old!' I asked my mother, 'What do I have to do?' because I didn't even know anything. 'Make food, work, do those things.' My father said, 'I don't know what they did, those who went into that house.'"

On November 26, 1997, Merita read in the newspaper that a teacher, Halit Geci, had been killed in a police drive-by shooting during a sweeping counterinsurgency operation in Drenica. He was inside his school, guarding his students, a bystander caught in the indiscriminate violence that the Milošević police exercised, as they attempted to capture or kill known KLA fighters.[44] "Was it *Rilindja*? Was it *Koha Ditore*? Now I can't remember which paper, but I read it in the paper, and I don't know how much I cried about that." The Yugoslav daily *Rilindja* (Renaissance), founded in 1945 and the first Kosovo-wide newspaper in the Albanian language, had been closed by Milošević in 1993, but resurrected by some of its former staff and LDK's Information Office as a daily under the name of the specialized newspaper *Bujku* (The Farmer). Merita may have confused it with the old newspaper. *Bujku* became the mouthpiece of the self-styled Kosovo state led by Rugova. In 1997, the newspaper *Koha Ditore* (Daily Times) was emerging as an independent media with the look of a Western newspaper, thanks to Western funds.

It was *Koha Ditore* that reported more extensively from the front line with its team of cub reporters, students just out of high school.[45] They covered Geci's funeral, set two days after the incident, and thus on November 28, the Day of the Flag, the main Albanian national holiday. They saw how three KLA fighters, two of them unmasked, arrived in a black car, suddenly materializing among the twenty thousand people who had gathered for the occasion on the hills of Llausha, in central Kosovo. The insurgents read a war statement,[46] showing to the Albanians in Kosovo, and the world, that indeed there was an independent guerrilla, which was not a creation of the Serbian Secret Services, as argued by President Rugova, who was adamantly opposed to starting an armed insurrection. The crowd approached the guerrillas, trying to touch them, as if to test whether they were real, and broke into chants, "KLA! KLA!"[47]

After that episode, police and army surveillance increased, and so did the number of checkpoints along the roads and streets of Kosovo, making traveling a dangerous activity. *The Guardian* correspondent Jonathan Steele remembers traveling across Kosovo as a surreal experience: "we went from one checkpoint to another and they just asked us whether we had seen terrorists."[48] Less than two months later from the first public apparition of the KLA, *Koha Ditore* journalists driving across Drenica met no checkpoints after Skënderaj, saw no traffic, as buses were no longer circulating, and after 2 p.m. plunged into the dark like everybody else, because the electricity had been cut off—a sign that more attacks were imminent.[49]

The Strongest Link: An Oral History of Wartime Rape Survivors in Kosovo. Anna Di Lellio and Garentina Kraja, Oxford University Press. © Oxford University Press 2025. DOI: 10.1093/9780197699324.003.0005

5
War

The war began in March 1998 in the central region of Drenica. With 94 percent of the population registered as Albanian, Drenica was the poorest part of Kosovo, which was the poorest province of Yugoslavia. Predominantly devoted to farming, except for a roof tiles factory in Skënderaj and the metallurgic complex of Feronikel in Drenas, it remained locked in a subsistence economy. In the 1970s, when the socioeconomic situation was improving across Kosovo, Drenica was still underperforming economically, remaining a world apart from urban Albanian society. Still, it held historical significance because of the richness of its oral tradition and the general acknowledgment of its past as a continuous struggle for independence from foreign oppressors.[1] For Yugoslavia's eternal capital Belgrade, Drenica was, and had always been, a territory to be tamed, a Vandée. It was the home of bandits under the kingdom of Serbia in the 1920s and of anti-Yugoslav insurgents during the Second World War. When Slobodan Milošević rose to power in the late 1980s, Drenica had become an early incubator of the KLA, the hotbed of Albanian terrorism for Belgrade, and thus the focus of Serbian police surveillance and repression.

In 1998, the memory of the last mass rebellion and its bloody suppression during the war that led to the birth of socialist Yugoslavia in 1945 still loomed large. Milošević was inspired by it, as he explained during a meeting with NATO Commander, General Wesley Clark: "[Milošević] turned to me and said, 'General Clark,' he said, 'We know how to handle these murderers, these rapists, these criminals.' He said, 'We've done this before.' I said, 'Well, when?' He said, 'In Drenica in 1946.' And I said, 'What did you do?' He said, 'We killed all of them.' He said, 'We killed them all.'"[2]

Counterinsurgency

At the end of February 1998, Slobodan Milošević unleashed a counterinsurgency against the villages of the high plateau of Drenica. Serbian security forces had gone in as a reprisal for the ambush and killing of two Serbian policemen by KLA insurgents. In the villages of Likoshan and Qirez, they targeted civilians, murdering ten unarmed men of the Ahmeti family and a pregnant woman, among others.[3] A few days later, believing they would eliminate the leadership of the KLA by capturing or killing its reputed commander, Adem Jashari, they besieged his family's compound in Prekaz, moving in both on the ground with artillery and encircling helicopter gunships.[4] This operation of combined police and army troops took eighty-three victims, among them the entire Jashari family, including the children; only Besarta, an eleven-year-old girl, survived.[5] A month earlier, an attempt to do away with Adem Jashari had encountered strong resistance, as many armed villagers had gathered on the hills above the compound and opened fire on the police; a major confrontation was avoided only through the mediation of the Albanian civilian leadership, who rushed in from Prishtina in the afternoon. The Serbian Interior Ministry described the event as a "clash between Albanian gangs over their loot," and quickly covered up the news to avoid embarrassment.[6]

On that occasion, Adem's teenage daughter Iliriana and his niece Selvete were wounded.[7] The two girls were awakened in the pre-dawn hours by the first shots coming from the besieging Serbian forces, just as the house turned quiet after the excitement of *syfyr*, the meal consumed during Ramadan before fasting.[8] Weeks later, Hamëz Jashari, Adem's older brother, re-enacted the attack for a group of reporters from *Koha Ditore*, pointing at the water tower of the nearby ammunition factory where Serb snipers had positioned themselves for years to terrorize the family.[9] Once again, Adem had escaped arrest, helped by armed relatives, friends, and villagers who gathered in the woody hill near the house and engaged the Serbian forces in a shootout. "They treated us like dirt, they shot us without giving any notice. Had they not come from the mountain...," said the patriarch Shaban Jashari to visiting journalists, who were stunned by the presence of so many armed young men, dressed in uniform with KLA insignia, crowding the Jashari *oda*.[10] The second time around, in March, Milošević did not take any chances, sealed a large area around Prekaz to impede any rescue operation, and sent in special "anti-terrorist" units to complete the job. And they did.

The Prekaz massacre was readily defined at the time as a victory of the state over terrorists in all official statements coming out of the government offices in Prishtina and Belgrade. With detached, bureaucratic language, Serbian authorities announced to Western media the success of a police operation against the KLA: "We have struck at their heart and we have dealt terrorists a lethal blow."[11] In the official records published by the Serbian Ministry of Foreign Affairs in English for an international audience, it was the KLA that attacked Serb police, not vice versa, killing one agent; it was the KLA that did not allow civilians to leave the premises despite the effort by the police to guarantee their personal safety, and in the "crushing of the resistance...when police officers put their lives at risk, 51 persons perished."[12]

Serbian state television showed the ruins of the Jashari compound and the bodies of two "terrorists," one of them a chief KLA commander, and state media reported that the civilian victims had been killed by terrorists to prevent them from surrendering, who then blamed Serbian forces for the massacre.[13] General Nebošja Pavković, commander of the Yugoslav 3rd Army in Kosovo and later convicted for crimes of war and crimes against humanity at the ICTY, told the American news media *PBS* that he knew the region was a nest of terrorists: "one particular family was up to no good in the region, and one action was about capturing their leader, which was a successful action. That followed with the liquidation of a few members, a consequence."[14]

Though international media filmed the attack on Prekaz from the hilltops nearby, showing the deployment of Serbian armored vehicles and heavy artillery in the attack on rural houses, it was only days later—and after rumors that Adem Jashari had escaped alive—that the Serbian authorities allowed international media to a depot where the corpses of the Jashari family, draped in white sheets, were lined up. The Belgrade district prosecutor was encouraged to initiate prosecution of media that would use the term "Albanians," rather than "*šiptar* terrorist gangs."[15] The consistent use of the term "terrorist" for any Albanian casualty served two purposes: to deny the KLA the status of combatants and dehumanize the victims, whether civilian or not, and also to depoliticize the rebellion. Serbian forces laid the Jasharis in unmarked graves in a field near their compound without care for the bodies or the local death rituals. Shortly afterward, a handful of villagers exhumed the bodies, identified them, and gave them a proper burial according to Muslim tradition, orienting the graves toward Mecca.[16]

Unbeknownst to both international observers and the Milošević government, the myth of the "legendary commander" Adem Jashari was born from the ashes of Prekaz, and with it, the construction of a narrative centered on the Albanian heroic rebels to Serbian occupation, which changed the dynamic of the conflict.[17] The Albanian diaspora moved from supporting the peaceful resistance to the KLA's side. This meant a substantial flow of funds to purchase weapons, the development of successful lobbies of foreign governments, and a surge of volunteers.[18] Until March 1998, only a handful of fighters had joined the KLA, which gained the bulk of its effective strength following the events at Prekaz. Seeking protection from the Serbian destructive offensive, more Albanians joined the KLA than would have otherwise, as a comprehensive study on recruitment found, matching "the intensity of recruits' participation, the reported period of enlistment and the place of origin" with "the pattern of Serbian government counterinsurgency."[19] This was when the war began in earnest.

The chief prosecutor at the ICTY, Louise Arbour, took notice. On March 8, she declared the territorial and temporal jurisdiction of the Court over violations of international humanitarian law and the law of war in Kosovo, evoking the notions of crimes against humanity in line with the UN Declaration of Human Rights (Art. 3 and 5) and the Geneva Convention for civilians targeted in war.[20]

Milošević was undeterred by the decision of the ICTY. His forces continued their operations in Drenica, unleashing violence against civilians that culminated in what Human Rights Watch called a "week of terror" in September 1998.[21] Then he focused on the western mountains of Kosovo. That is the region which Albanians call *Rrafsh i Dukagjinit* (Dukagjin Plateau), perhaps after the medieval lord *duka Gjin* (duke John), who also ruled over parts of neighboring Albania and is reputed to have canonized the unwritten law of the mountains.[22] Serbs call the same region Metohija, which literally means "domain of the church," after the rich endowments that medieval Serbian rulers gave to Orthodox monasteries.[23] Gjakova and Peja, important market and trade centers on the axis of communication with Albania and Montenegro, are the main regional centers. Peja is the seat of the Serbian Orthodox Patriarchate, whose beautiful churches are rivaled only by the fourteenth-century monastery in nearby Deçan, the burial ground of the medieval king Stefan of the Nemanjić dynasty, who is also a saint with miraculous powers.

In 1998, the KLA had a stronghold in the surroundings of the overwhelmingly Albanian-populated Deçan, an expanse of mountains and pasture dotted with farmhouses, among them the compound of the Haradinaj, a family that was emerging as the local leadership of the Albanian insurgents. For Ramush Haradinaj, who became one of the KLA top commanders, it was evident that popular support for an insurrection was growing after his brother Luan was killed by the Serbian forces in an ambush in the late spring of 1997. As Haradinaj remembers, on the occasion of his brother's funeral, "Thousands of men came to visit, some out of curiosity, but everyone who came to offer condolences felt brave and offered to arm. They would come by our house, have a cup of coffee, tell us where they were from, how many supplies they had, and ask whether we needed them."[24]

Milošević had set his eyes on the Haradinaj and besieged their compound in Gllogjan on March 24, 1998. Unlike the Jashari, the Haradinaj managed to escape: "Our aim was to fight and to survive, not to get killed in the house."[25] Serbian forces repeated the same pattern of wanton destruction shown in Drenica. At first, as troops shelled villages they thought were harboring the KLA, people left their homes to avoid being caught in the conflict. They made quick decisions, out of fear, or to follow instructions by the KLA, who were their relatives or neighbors. But Serbian troops' search for the insurgents proceeded village to village and house to house, turning rather quickly into a hunt for Albanian civilians everywhere: fellow travelers, family relations, and even individuals with no connection with the KLA. Many were beaten, detained, tortured, raped, and killed. Throughout 1998, a total war played out in the villages, the forests, the hills, and the mountains across Kosovo, alternatively used as sheltering and hiding havens or detention camps and places of horror.

At the Heart of Kosovo

Villages in the hills around Drenica are small hamlets, each a cluster of homes gathering extended family groups, surrounded by land that is lusciously green in the summer, heavily snowed during winter. The recent war has produced a small revolution. As the largest electoral base of the *Partia Demokratike e Kosovës* (PDK, Democratic Party of Kosovo), the party that emerged from the war and remained in power almost continuously for twenty years until 2020, Drenica has clearly benefited from a closer relationship with central power. More roads have been enlarged and paved, and if walking in the streets of central Skënderaj, its major town, was still a hazardous wade through mud in the immediate aftermath of the war, ten years later the joke was that an old car would look like new if it only had been driven in Drenica. This is an exaggeration, since government neglect and poverty still afflict the area, but it reflects widespread perception.

Back in 1998, only one narrow two-lane road was paved, the main artery connecting Komoran to Drenas and Skënderaj, and from there, to Mitrovica. Unpaved roads, dusty in summer, were viscous from mud or covered by snow and ice in winter. In March, as the counterinsurgency raged, caravans of tractors and people were obliged to play a cat-and-mouse game with Serbian security forces, using these roads or even more perilous paths through the woods to avoid detection. Drita moved from place to place with her seven children tagging along, "I lived outdoors for two years, surviving on whatever food we could find." Thousands shared her experience, and largely because of this, individual stories convey a chorus of confusion, hunger, thirst, fear, pain, and horror, through the voices of the protagonists. Memories are muddled: at times, places and dates come sharply into focus, but more often, time lengthens or compresses.

Edona: "It was not spring, it was cold, I don't know whether it was winter, which month it was, but it was cold. We knew that the army had come, many troops had come to Kosovo, and they were moving on us. We had an electricity transmitter near us, and they said that the army was positioned there. In short, we went to sleep with that worry, because that transmitter was really close to our house and they were coming and going. We were still asleep when my brother-in-law knocked on the door in the very early morning, 'Move, they are coming!' I grabbed my baby, my mother-in-law grabbed a large basket with a few provisions, and we both got on a tractor. As all the tractors lined up on the road, we could not even get out of our yard because of the traffic. There was the whole village out there and the other surrounding villages too. We went to a mosque and stayed there for two days and two nights, two days and two nights without putting anything in our mouths. Nothing, nothing, nothing!"

The mosque was "chockablock" with people of all ages, except the adult men, most of whom had withdrawn into the neighboring woods. Edona had enough milk to breastfeed her baby, but, "you could have killed him, he would not take the milk." There was shooting and burning outside, but she really panicked only when she thought the baby might die of starvation. She spotted, at the front of the mosque, a group of women who were busy working around a cooker to make some sort of bread. Edona approached them. "Sister, please give me just a crumb of bread, I don't want my son to die. He is not even two years old." What they had was just some mush made of flour, but it was food that she put in her pocket. With that, and a small bottle filled with *sherbet*, a mix of water and sugar that mothers used to give their babies for lack of better nutrition, she felt temporarily reassured, though her baby would drink or eat only "a bit of food as small as a crumb, one crumb. I said to myself, 'Who knows when we'll get back home."

At the end of two days, the police kicked the group of displaced civilians out of the mosque, forcing them to move to another village and find shelter in a school. A massacre had just happened there, and the school was cold and dark, as the electricity had been cut. There were only wooden desks to sit on. Exhausted, Edona laid her son on one of them. Twenty-four hours later, she was again on the move, this time on foot because the police had burned the tractors. Back to the mosque. It was not just the children's cries that filled the room; several wounded, one hit in the leg by a grenade, were brought in for treatment and they lay on the cold floor, howling. When night fell, it began to snow.

Edona's family and her neighbors were forced out of the mosque a second time. "We walked to a village along the road which they once called a goat path, because only the goats could walk there. Believe me: thorns caught us, brambles caught us, we walked all night, all night. In the morning, the police separated the men from women and children, and they took us to some unfinished house, one of those houses made with concrete blocks, you know, without doors, without windows, only the roof was done. They said, 'Get inside!' The wind blew in. We just put some hay to lie on. Everywhere there were members of my family lying down." That is when she realized she could no longer see her husband. Her brother-in-law volunteered to go out looking for him but never came back, and only later Edona heard that he had joined the KLA and subsequently had been captured. That day, anxiously waiting for news, she heard shooting outside and a neighbor brought the news that two men had been killed. Could they have been her husband and his paternal uncle? Nobody could confirm the identity of the people who had been executed.

A woman from that village took a peek at the house full of displaced people and saw the desperate conditions in which they were living. "She invited me to her house. I said, 'No, I don't want to be separated from them.' She said, 'You will not be separated from them because they will take you too where they'll go and because we cannot keep you with us, we can only clean you up.' She gave me clothes. She had a curved sofa there, with a white sheep skin all around, I fell on it and went to sleep like a dead person, oh God, I was so tired!" Her hostess was not afraid of harboring a crying child even when her family protested, lest he attracted the attention of the Serbian police. When Edona left, two days later, she gave her a package of food. Edona's mother-in-law rolled the goods in a sweater which she then tied into a bundle. "When we returned home, we found that they had burnt our house, there were flames, smoke. We went to a relative's house and stayed there, I don't know how many days." Edona heard that her husband was alive. He had repaired to the mountains and had joined the KLA, more because he had nowhere else to go, than out of a commitment to fight. "One evening he came to the house and said, 'Don't wait for me. Go in the direction of all the columns of refugees and stay with them. I don't dare go with you. I leave you in the hands of God, I must go to the mountains."

Chased once more, the three close families that constituted Edona's group moved nearer the smoldering ruins of her own house. The men hid in the fields behind the house, among the willows by the river, and stayed there until the movement of troops subsided. There were only two old men left and a teenage boy with women and children, all with intestinal illnesses. Finally, Serbian troops gathered the whole village, including Edona's family. "They kept us there, on that meadow, for say, three–four hours. Believe me, they were firing, fiuuuu fiuuu fiuuu.... There were twenty-four men from our village. They lined them up in front of us, oooh, they were not ten meters from us, and they executed them. Then, they said to us, 'Move!' They sent us all to the next bigger village. Believe me, we walked over the bodies of the twenty-four men. All the women my age are left without a husband. There are also those who are younger than I am, whose husbands were killed there. We cried, we yelled. I was tired. Hungry. Afraid. But what could I do? The people in the column walked as fast as they could. I will not forget this ordeal, I had my boy on my back and a bag with some clothes with something for my child, some cloths, because there were no diapers there. A policeman, a soldier, stopped me, in Serbian, 'What are you doing? Move quicker!' He was behind me, 'Move!' We ran and ran, and we got to a village. They kept us there for the whole war, we did not move from there."

Edona settled in a house left empty by her parents' neighbor. In that mayhem, there was no sense of ownership, and after each house was burned, exhausted and frightened civilians moved into the next one. For a few days, she thought they had found a good shelter after almost one year of peregrination. They were still chockablock in the house, but importantly, they had managed to bring some flour with them and were not feeling hungry.

The war began the same day for Valbona, who lived nearby and was just a few years older than Edona. "The war began the day that my son was five weeks old." She too got on a tractor and left her house, as Serbian troops killed people and burned property, terrifying the civilian population. She got back home only after the Jashari massacre. "Somehow I cannot remember that night, you know, because I was sick, anxious, what we experienced was like a dream but I wasn't dreaming." The summer of 1998 passed without another massive offensive, until September. "We heard a 'bum bum bum,' from Vushtrri in the direction of Drenica and we went to our friends' house. We went to many places actually, two nights here, three nights there, three weeks somewhere else until we went back home." Valbona's house became a temporary shelter, hosting as many as forty refugees at a time: all the women were in one room, the men in another. "I was pregnant again, six months after I had my oldest son. They told me, 'Why so quickly?' But my husband was *hasret*,[26] the war broke out, one didn't know who and what but when, and we knew that the men had to go, the war is for men. I said, 'If I am left on my own, at least I will have two children.' I was six months pregnant with my son, now, what to do? I was pregnant through the fall. When I was getting close to my due time and was running here and there, I told my mother-in-law, 'I want to go out and be killed, surrender. I cannot stand this anymore.' But when they came close to the village we left, we went to my mother's family. They said that they were burning villages, but we didn't know whether it was our village. I took my sixty-year-old mother-in-law with me. The sister-in-law I told you about? The mean girl? She was four years older than me, she did not come, she stayed with her sister, whose family too had taken refuge there. Her own mother told her, 'Let's go, can't you see me? I cannot take care of myself, I cannot move, when this boy is on the ground I cannot pick him up. Come with us.' She did not come, she stayed with her sister and the other refugees."

Valbona felt safer at her parents' house. She felt the love of her mother and her younger sister, who helped with the baby. That place too was full of refugees, mostly women and children, and plenty of babies. "My father had brought a cow, it was good he did that, because in the evening everyone had run out of milk." In such close quarters, tempers began to fray, and fear drew the best and the worst from people. "I will never forget what my mother said. She went, 'Take the baby and leave,' he was five weeks, 'the baby cries in the house, go back.' How could my mother? 'Get out,' she said, 'go, take your child to your home. Get out, leave.' I did not move. I said, 'Here, I am staying here with you.' We went straight into the war."

Shpresa: "My daughter was one year old, one year and two–three months old and she became very hungry, and she cried. My husband's uncle said, 'Shut her mouth.' I said, 'Uncle, with what do I shut her mouth?' 'Shut her mouth, otherwise they will come, don't you hear the grenades? They will hear us.'" Shpresa was young, inexperienced, and caught in the same offensive as the one that had surprised Valbona's family. With other villagers, she had fled to the mountains, where they stayed for ten days, sleeping on nylon tarps, under the continuous shelling of Serbian troops. Her husband had gone into hiding. Like Valbona's husband, he was not a soldier; he just hid in the mountain with his younger brother and other men, scavenging for food any time there was a lull in the fighting. At one point, he managed to escape abroad and lost contact with his family; Shpresa found out that he was alive only after the war.

For a month, Shpresa's family lived like nomads, moving from the camp in the mountains to a relative's village downhill, then back to their house, when they discovered that three neighbors had been killed. "After two weeks we had to leave again. My brother came. 'Hey, Shpresa, are you coming?' He came with a tractor, 'I guess the war is finished in our village. Let's go, let's go, that now nothing will happen.'" Shpresa loaded the tractor with one bag of her baby daughter's clothes, and a trunk with all her family pictures and a crib. "I said to myself, 'If she cries in the mountain, I will calm her down in the crib.'" But that night another offensive began and the deafening shelling sounded like a thunderstorm. In their anxious search for safer places, Shpresa's family and neighbors often trailed behind troops, barely escaping massacres. "We had some women among us whose fathers had been killed." Shpresa was never able to reach her paternal house, but had to stop for a few days in a valley, trying to avoid army convoys that swarmed the roads, only to return to the place from which they had started.

In the Western Mountains

Teuta was twenty-one years old and lived in the middle of a war zone, but with no direct connection to the insurgency. "The war began in '98 for us, the main front was there, in the village where we lived. And what we didn't go through! Now in one village, then in another. How many times did we leave and then come back to the house in 1998! At times we had moments of danger, at times moments of peace, and thus the year passed." In September 1998, Serbian troops rounded up all the villages as far as she could see and chased people out of their homes without giving them the time to grab even a bag. They put her family on a bus and barked, "Scrum to Peja! Then go where you like." She hardly remembers where and when she went after that in her nomadic search for safety, moving from village to village. "There is actually nothing to remember, only the shelling. They shot from above and shot on the house, on the yard, everywhere." Three months later, they went back to their own house and found it completely destroyed by fire. "Because there were no windows or anything else left, my dad made some windows from wood and used a nylon tarp to make a room for us to live in. We stayed there, I mean, in our house, until March '99."

That is the same village that Blerta reached with her two toddlers, an infant who was born during the war, and other women from her extended family. They stayed in a house whose owner was unknown to them, but that was not new, they had found people ready to take them in as they had crossed the hills. They thought they could sit out the fighting there, all the thirty people who crowded the house. Blerta had spent the spring of 1998 not far from there with the other women of her family, washing and cooking for KLA fighters—not only her husband and the younger men who had come back from Western Europe to fight, but also those who were streaming from Drenica after the first Serbian offensive. Her house became a base on the way to the border with Albania: fighters came, spent the night, then left and others came. With all the men in her family engaged in the war, she was the only protector of her young children. On August 1, 1998, KLA fighters told the villagers they were no longer safe there as Serbian troops were approaching. They gathered them in a group and led them away, some to neighboring villages, others to the mountains. Blerta and her children stayed at her maternal aunt's house. The next day, in the early morning, the Serbian army took the village and captured all the men. "They killed my paternal uncle, they killed something like seventeen members of my family, on my father's side." For women and children, that meant yet another displacement.

By 1998, there was no refuge left in the western mountains of Kosovo, not in the villages and not in town. A year earlier, Ganimete had married someone she had never met before and who had fled abroad to avoid arrest, leaving her alone at home with his aging and ailing mother. In November she began to have problems with her pregnancy and shortly after, she can't remember precisely when, on the advice of the doctor she ventured to the hospital in the nearest town for some checkups. One day there was a shoot-out. Mervete Maksutaj, a KLA fighter, had come to free some comrades who were detained as patients at the hospital. According to the official account of the events that followed, she broke into the main entrance of the hospital with hand grenades, and engaged with the Serbian police who were on the second floor.[27] It was chaos. When silence set on the hospital, some Serbian officers lay dead, including a doctor in the maternity ward. Mervete was killed as she was retreating.

The hospital staff took their rage out on the maternity patients. "We were four women in that room, one was with twins. And they hit the babies, they hit us, they beat us as they could with kicks and punches and we suddenly aborted our children. And when they took the baby I aborted, they brought him to me and said, 'A boy!' At the time I was five months pregnant and I didn't know what the baby was going to be." Ganimete's family promptly organized a rescue mission, but she and the other women were so afraid that they refused to follow the Bosniak man who had been sent to pick them up. They needed further reassurance. Only after Ganimete's brother called the hospital and gave her new instructions, they resolved to leave. They bribed a Serbian janitor, who hid them in the basement until they made contact with the Bosniak driver. When he called, the four of them quickly left the hospital and got in the car.

"At the first checkpoint past the town, soldiers stopped the car and took us all to a sort of house...was it a restaurant? A hotel? Honestly we couldn't say, we had never been to a restaurant before the war. That place just looked like a house like ours, it was two-story high. We had just aborted, were smeared with blood, had had no food or drinks, but they took us inside and kept us there for four days. Five of them gang-raped us all." Unbeknownst to Ganimete, the driver who had been paid to take her back home had gone to her family and told them that the women never left the hospital. Thus nobody was looking for them, while they were tortured in the anonymity of a rural house very near the same town. The Serbian men wore ribbons over their uniforms and masks on their faces. They shouted all the time, while the women, ill and very tired, couldn't even cry. They each saw what was happening but could not help one another, knowing their torturers were in total control. "When they took us, I never thought they would rape us.

Today I know. Had there been a stronger woman with a revolver in her hands!..."

As 1998 came to a close, Milošević had lost control of almost half of Kosovo's territory, especially the region of Drenica, where the war escalated against both armed formations and civilians. A November survey of the areas most touched by the war registered 210 out of 258 villages severely damaged; almost a third of all houses had been completely destroyed.[28] A total of 2,156 people were killed or disappeared in 1998 across Kosovo. Of them, 1,804 were Albanians: 1,100 civilians, 703 KLA, and 1 MUP (*Ministarstvo unutrašnjih poslova*, Ministry of Internal Affairs). Serbian casualties were 289, including 132 civilians and 157 VJ (*Vojska Jugoslavije*, Yugoslav Army ND MUP). Roma and other minorities were 63: 46 civilians and 17 VJ/MUP.[29]

Under NATO's Planes

NATO intervention against the Federal Republic of Yugoslavia (FRY) began on March 24, 1999. The bombing campaign was supposed to last only a few days, but ended seventy-eight days later, on June 12, when a ceasefire was signed in Kumanovo. During that period, NATO planes, flying more than 15,000 feet above ground, targeted military objectives, including infrastructure, in Serbia and Kosovo. No NATO soldier set foot on the ground, but after the bombing campaign began, more Serbian troops arrived in Kosovo. Incapable of countering NATO's planes, Serbian forces focused on Albanian civilians, both as revenge for having asked for Western intervention, and as a deliberate strategy of ethnic cleansing.[30]

Edona: "They came one morning, they put us in the yard and kept us there standing all day. We wanted to sit down, but they didn't let us. Oh, that day! It would have been better had they executed everybody. They pretended to shoot us, with their finger, 'You! You! You! You!' They came in my direction too. I don't know what time it was, it was the afternoon. They took the young boys, they took the men and undressed them as God made them, and then they forced them to dance in front of us. As they came close to us we felt so scared! There was a truck with a yellow tarp, they took them away as naked as God made them. Mothers saw their children and husbands taken on that truck. There was an old man, my mother's uncle, who said to us, 'I am with you, don't be scared.' He was the only man they left with us, just him, the old man. They took my younger sister, they called her by her name, 'Let's go.' They grabbed her and made their way towards the house, my mother and I screamed. My sister fainted by the entrance door and they left her there. They told me in Serbian, 'Go get water from the well!' I thought they said they were going to kill me in the well. My mother's uncle, who knew Serbian, said 'No! Water! Niece, he is saying water, get the water.' I got water for my sister, and immediately she came back to life."

Edona saw Serbian forces getting busy, moving in and out, looting what they could and scattering everything else. When they brought food and drinks, and made the women serve them, Edona understood they were going to make the house their temporary base. The popular local brandy *raki* began to flow and the group became more boisterous. None of the Albanians slept that night. Normally, they would have retired to the bedrooms upstairs, but nobody moved from the kitchen. It was a small room for the thirty-odd people who had found shelter there, and there was no adjacent living room. They just crammed inside the kitchen, in an anxious state of suspension. All of a sudden the Serbian soldiers burst in. "When they took my son from my arms, I screamed to high heaven. They dragged me, they pushed me upstairs to the second floor, the three of them. As they pushed me upstairs, I cried only God knows how. They left my mom and an older woman downstairs. She said, 'Don't worry about your son, I'll hold him.'"

The house had one of those solid, wooden staircases that local craftsmen used to make. Edona tried to resist by holding on tight to the balustrade as a soldier kicked her and dragged her to the second floor. At one point she stopped resisting since no resistance would have obtained any result, but at least she could avoid the blows. A man moved past her and wrested her away. Behind her, the other women were pushed one by one to the second floor, crying and screaming. "When I entered that room, I saw a wooden trunk behind the door. I sat there, I tried to defend myself. They tore my clothes. I cried, I screamed. They raped me. I lost consciousness, I fainted." As the night progressed, more soldiers came to torture them, she can't tell how many. "The first, the ones who took us upstairs, wore black uniforms. And ribbons, they wore red ribbons, I don't know whether they were chetniks or any other soldier, but they all had beards. They just said, *'Jebem ti majku!'* (I fuck your mother!) They never stopped shoving us and kicking us. They finished by putting out cigarettes…on our breasts."

When she came back to her senses, Edona realized the men had left and she wanted to leave but couldn't think about where to go. She had no clothes, she felt lost. Then the old neighbor came in. "She closed the door slowly and called, 'Are you alive?' She wore a brown sweater with a collar, an old-style sweater for old people, and she gave it to me, 'Get dressed daughter, that this is nothing. It's the war, it is nothing.'" Edona was not the only one to be assaulted that night. There were three other women of her family in the same room with her and many more in the house, in her recollection a total of fifteen to twenty women. She knows the names of them all.

A few hills away, near Ardita's village, there were Serbian troops stationed. "I left with my whole family, but we soon split from my husband and my boys because there was an offensive and I told them, 'Go, go, because tomorrow those Serb barbarians will come and if they find the men they will kill them.' Only my youngest son stayed with me and all the others went with their father and their uncles. They never came back. They took all of them, lined them up, beat them, then sent them to another town, where they put them in a school. Then they said, 'Go wherever you want, nobody will hurt you, you will not be hurt by *Shki*.'[31] But they stopped them again, took them to a meadow, beat them again, then they fired on them."

Serbian troops took the women back and forth to different villages. "Finally, they said, 'Go, the war is over now, go back to your homes. Cook and eat something.' Back home, we had some corn flour and we made some food when two people arrived. The *Shki* had sent them. Bam, bam, bam, they knocked on our doors, 'Come to the school of the village, the *Shki* are calling you, if you don't come they will come here to kill you.' We left all we had, we ran faster and faster to go to the *Shki*. They were not all lodging in the school. They slept in private houses too. We stayed there in the school for three nights with the *Shki*. They came to the door and urinated in front of us, brandishing their guns and their knives.... We slept in the basement. My daughters were shaking from fear. I tried to hide them behind me however I could. At one point, a *Shki* came in, I was lying down, he poked me, he did, 'tup,' on the blanket and left. My sister-in-law said, 'For the love of God, go to my children, because now that Serb is coming here.' And I left my daughters, I went to the children of my in-law and hid them. I was in the middle, one daughter here, a boy here. And they came again and poked me. They didn't kill me there."

They came again later. "They took us to a big field by the school and there they tied us up with tape. And I didn't know anything, only when they came and grabbed my daughters I cried. They said, 'We will kill you all!' They took my girls and I no longer saw where they were taking them. They said, 'Go back to the building if you don't want to be killed.' I didn't go back. I didn't understand anything from fear. I said to myself, let them do what they want. They hit me three times, bap, bap, bap. I thought, are they going to kill me? From there, they took me by force to the school. They said, 'Undress.' I defended myself, 'No, I will never undress, never.' They took my clothes off by force, the two of them. One hit me. One slapped me, vup, vup, vup, and made my face all red. They did what they wanted with me. When I returned to the group, the people there thought they had killed me, but they saw that I was alive and were surprised, but nobody dared to raise their heads. Maybe they had killed their children, maybe they had taken them away, but they didn't dare look at anybody, just head down. You had no courage to look up. After that, they put us on two trucks and took us elsewhere. We didn't look at each other during that trip. They kept us there for three weeks. How shall I put it, it was ten meters deep of *Shki* out there. One night my sister-in-law said that the *Shki* had told her, 'Find us some girls because the army is bored.' Oj, that night how miserable we were! They ate and drank and came to us every night."

They came also for Ardita's daughter, Shkurta. "They wore masks and just gestured, get up! with their fingers. No, you didn't have the courage to speak or look up. You didn't want to open your mouth. You couldn't say anything. I had my child with me, he is the only one I have. Since that day I haven't been able to have any more children."

Drita too became a prisoner, along with two friends and her adolescent daughter. Before being captured, they had been camping outdoors for months, deprived of even the smallest comfort, as they were moved around by the Serbian army or fled on their own, seeking reprieve from the fighting. Even as displaced civilians, they had been fired on, and several in their company had been wounded by grenades dropped on their makeshift encampment. The women were locked in a house for twenty-two days, which they spent under the constant assault of Serbian forces until one morning, after waking up from an unusually quiet night, they understood that the soldiers had left and had abandoned their prison.

Serbian troops descended upon Valbona's village shortly after the beginning of the NATO bombing, apparently looking for KLA insurgents. They rounded up all the one hundred people who were there.

"They said, 'You help them.' Ah, you did not dare say, 'No.' We were paralyzed, didn't even dare say, 'No,' or cry because they got worse." The soldiers separated the men from the women and pushed the terrified captives to begin a new march through the fields and across the hills. A visibly pregnant Valbona carried her baby in her arms and a bundle of clothes on her back, pushing her kid brother ahead of her. She noticed that her younger sister carried all of her baby's clothes, she loved him so. All along the march they heard shouts, "'Let's go, hey!' '*U redu, da*' (In line, yes). Sometimes the soldiers took care of us, they let us stop to drink water, but very little. Sometimes it happened that some of them felt compassion for us, but it happened very little, because usually they rather maltreated us, and now, they took care of us, 'Rest a little, drink water!' And they carried my son, they took him from my arms because we were tired and I was sneezing and they carried him. Some young soldiers held him, I don't know, maybe they were married, maybe not, young soldiers. They played with him and cuddled him. This child did, like children do, 'Ta ta ta.' They began that baby talk, 'Ta ta ta.' 'Tata,' in Serbian, is 'dad.' They said, 'Dad,' you know, and cuddled him. They played with him as we rested and they held him, they gave the child some meat and then gave him back to us."

The soldiers led them to a mosque and left them there. At night, men in uniform came in. Some were the same soldiers who had played with her son in the morning, others were new faces. "Kuku, when they came in, they entered as if hunting, they were wild. They at once asked for gold, money, they asked at knife point, they had two–three knives in their hands. Whoever was not quiet, immediately, knives to their neck! They took me and put me in line, 'You, you, you!' I was pregnant, I wore a black coat, my hair was tied up like this, like today, I was young at the time, they didn't know I was a married woman and I was in line with the girls. My son used to cry and wail any time I left him. So, when I was put in the line and my mother took him in her arms, he squirmed, trying to grab me, and cried and cried. In the yard, a *magjup*,[32] I will never forget him, he guarded all the doors, turned to me, 'Baby, baby, baby. Go back!' I was eight months pregnant, they said that I had life, 'She has life!' Everybody said, 'This one stays,' and 'You rest, go back.' They took some of the women away, but sent me back. They kept the door locked, and someone guarded us. The women said, 'They will burn us, they will pour fuel, I saw hay outside.' Everyone was afraid."

They stayed there until they were kicked out again, and they were ordered to walk without turning back even just to look, or they would be killed. New troops caught up with them shortly after. "We were prisoners there, I don't know how many weeks. How did I sleep? I didn't, I just lay down on a little bit of hay, because they were sloshing around, they entered and left, sloshing in the corridor. I lay down like this, because my child did not want to sleep, he wanted to be only with me at night, in my arms here, until the morning." Valbona's mother-in-law and younger sister, the eighteen-year-old girl who doted on her nephew, were among the women who were taken away and were never to be seen again. They were found in a well, three months after the war, with six other women's bodies.[33] Valbona's family had hoped that somehow they had survived the war. "Once they told us, 'They went to Macedonia.' It wasn't neighbors who said this and that, but people closer to us, you know. They said, 'They saw your sister with your mother-in-law in Macedonia.' And this gave us some joy, we waited, but they were not found at all, that's it."

Serbian soldiers surrounded Shpresa's hideout "just before Saint George, was it April?[34] I forget now. We were so crowded there, about sixty people in that house. We didn't go hungry there because my nephew got hold of a calf and killed it." The soldiers called everybody out. They made the remaining men in her family, her teenage nephew, the old father-in-law, and her brother-in-law, lie face down on the meadow in front of the house. All the others had to stand in line without moving.

Valbona: "One or two soldiers wore a bandanna. Now, they grabbed me by the hair, two people grabbed me and took me to a house, you know. I lost consciousness, I passed out, I lost consciousness. I am telling you, when that gang left, I saw I was naked, I am not lying. When that gang left I was completely naked, I could not find my shoes, I was so ashamed of returning to my family like that! They kept me for hours. It wasn't days, why lie? When I went out of there—it was like an old house where they put me, an old house—oh my! when I went out, there was nobody. Eh, I had not walked so far that I saw a tracksuit and I put it on. When I went in, all the women said, 'Eh Shpresa, eh?' I said, 'Nothing.' I didn't talk to my father-in-law, my mother-in-law, or my sister-in-law. What to say? That I had gone out to exercise?"

Her torturers had put out their cigarettes on Shpresa's legs, making her skin a geography of burning blisters. Clad in her tracksuit, her legs burning, she found some cloths to cover her wounds. "I had marks from here to here. I was the only one to know, until the legs healed." Her brother-in-law, father-in-law, and nephew had been spared, and they guided a column of refugees first to Prizren, then toward the border with Albania, less than twenty miles away, trying to cross over. It took one more month to leave Kosovo, as Serbian troops turned them back to Prizren twice before they reached the border.

Qëndresa, a frightened teenager from an ethnically and religiously mixed village with a large extended family including great-grandparents, was also ordered to leave and then was sent back to Prizren once she reached the border. After two days, as nothing happened, they returned home. From then on, the war played out all types of horror in the confinement of their village, where Albanians became virtual prisoners of the army and of their Serb neighbors, who registered all their names, keeping score of how many members were in each family. "There was a sort of shop, we all had to go in and release a signed statement because they thought that we knew about the KLA, you know."

The problem was that Qëndresa's uncle had kept a diary since the very beginning of the war, where he wrote everything he could observe, including the day the war began, or the day the KLA had formed locally. "There was an Albanian neighbor, who was a bit too talkative. When the *Shki* arrived, when they came to the village, they came to search the house. They found my uncle's notebook, and since that day we don't know his fate. His sixteen-year-old son went with his father, they took him too. Nothing is known about them, nothing." Qëndresa's own father, another uncle, and the grandfather, who had no connection with the insurgency, were also picked up and tied up outside their homes as hostages. Soldiers and police piled hay around them and threatened to set them on fire. They were now going for her uncle's other son. "'Tell us about him, when did he take weapons?' You know, because my uncle had written that down. They didn't talk. They hit them on their hands. 'We will burn you!' We were in the yard and saw everything." Qëndresa was very close to her father, and terribly worried that with his heart problems he could not survive standing outdoors all night, being punched and hit. "I brought him some water and the police grabbed me and tied my hands with a belt. When my brother, who was with a cow, saw me tied up, he ran, ran to me, he wanted to untie me." The resolution of this ordeal came from where they least expected. "It was our good fortune that in the village there was a *Shka*, who recognized us and said, 'Don't! This is a good family.'" During the next two months, Serbian troops came and went, and ordered the Albanian villagers around: "Hey, bring me water! Move! Bring me coffee!" Nobody could complain or refuse to comply.

It quickly became clear that being in the streets was very risky, and women felt both vulnerable and untouchable. It was a contradiction that tragically played everywhere, as men caught in the street risked getting killed and women went out in their stead, fearful but somehow hoping to avoid detection. Her grandmother disguised thirteen-year-old Qëndresa as a grown-up, married woman. She made her wear a scarf and take a child with her whenever she left the house, thinking that the status of mother would grant her protection. It looked like a successful ruse, because Qëndresa was already well developed and could easily pass for an adult. "If my family did not dare go out, my great-grandfather, may his soul rest in peace, could come with me. And he did. He said, 'They should kill me before I leave her.' When they stopped us, oh my, how they hit him! But what could he have done? You couldn't have done anything to them, you couldn't push them back. I knew I had fallen in their hands. They, all of them tattooed, with masks, immediately made the gesture of slitting throats with their knives, shouting 'Massacre! Massacre!' You see, I was still a child and didn't know what they wanted to do, I said to myself, 'They want to hit me, to kill me.' There were four people at one point, I know. I lost consciousness, I couldn't tell what happened to my body. I know that I was cut here, here in my hand, I have many marks, you see, they hurt me with cigarettes, they put out cigarettes on my body and what didn't they do! The *Shki*, what can they do to a body!"

The kidnappers held Qëndresa captive together with four other women, all members of her extended family, she the youngest of them. She did not see the other women, they were immediately separated, and only later she learned that they had been released not long after. She was not as lucky. "I was in a sort of room, it was like a stable and it was locked. I never knew whether it was day or night, never, they just told me later that I was there for two weeks. I did not know anything about my family, nothing. And my family did not know any of that, where I was, where they took me, whether I was alive or dead." Except that her father found out where she was and begged a friendly Serb from the village to help him rescue her. "When that Serb picked me up, I was completely naked. He wrapped me in his own jacket to take me to my family, so my family would not see me in the condition I was in. My father welcomed me home, and at that precise moment I thought it would have been better not to have been alive at all, better not to have been let go, better to have been killed there, than go back to my family like that."

Serbian forces came to Teuta's village on March 30. "They rounded us up and sent us to a house, to the basement. 'We only want to keep you here to shelter you,' they said, explaining that they were fighting with the KLA stationed in another village. 'We just want to keep you here now and then you go back again.' They put us in a basement and they were firing from the second floor of the house. They had all sorts of weapons—tanks, armored cars, and so on. During the day we were all together, men and women, from about six in the morning till evening, until night fell. At midday, they took us to a meadow, and took some people away. Then they took us back to their tanks and said, 'Do we kill you or don't we kill you? Do we leave it here or don't we?' They talked among themselves. They sometimes took some people and said, 'We will pour fuel on you and we'll set you in flames.' Then they returned us to the basement but we saw how they burnt the houses because they were shooting and saying, 'Look how we'll burn you!'"

Soldiers waited for night to fall to get into the basement and pull everyone out. "'We want to separate women from men,' they said. 'Women and children! Come on girls!' I remember I was with my brother, a child, and when he saw them he began to shake, he was so afraid of them. And I took my brother and went forward when they said, 'Let's go,' and they took us to a house. And they kept us all night in that house. The living room was full and it was so full that I could not breathe, it was so full of people, all women and children. Soldiers came back at around midnight. 'We are looking for some girls to do some house cleaning.' I didn't even have a place to sit or stand, I was behind a sofa. I didn't know then that it was nighttime because there was no light or anything, we were always in the dark. And they entered with a flashlight and I just lifted my head when one of them said, 'What are you standing there for? Come on, get out.' He took me outside and to another house, me and two other girls."

Once in the house, they separated Teuta from the other two girls and raped her. "And afterwards, after they had done their job, they said, 'Now take your clothes and go wherever you want.' How I begged them! 'I am begging you to kill me, give me one bullet!' 'Why? Are you with the KLA? They did worse to you.' 'I have nothing to do with the KLA. Kill me!' 'No, I will not kill you!' They spoke Serbian and I didn't understand them. There was one policeman who knew Albanian, he translated for them and stood guard at the door, put them on line and let them in, one by one."

It was at the same time and in the same area, also in some sort of basement, that Blerta was held with many other women and children. She was also taken to a meadow with other villagers, and saw soldiers take some men away; to this day she doesn't know their fate. What she can never forget is the soldiers' greed. "They took my gold, a two-meter-long chain, and everything else we had hidden in the bags with the clothes. We didn't hide anything on ourselves because they body searched us, and if you resisted they slapped you." It was the night of March 31. They heard the soldiers laugh and shout as they were getting drunk. The women were put in separate rooms, beaten and gang-raped all night. "They saw that I had a sort of laissez passer, and said, 'You are KLA, where is your husband?' 'Where are they?' Everyone knows they would ask this. But you lied and said, 'My husband is not here, he is abroad.' And they cursed me, knocked me down on the floor. In the morning they ordered everybody out, 'Go to Albania!'" And the villagers did; they climbed on tractors and trucks and left in the direction of Albania. A group of about forty men were stopped and pulled out of the convoy. Nothing has been heard about them since. Both Teuta and Blerta reached the refugee camps across the border after a two-day trip, Teuta with her parents and siblings, Blerta with her own children.

Like Blerta, Fitore had connections with the KLA from the same region through her older brother, who had joined a nearby base just to work in logistics. "The war was terrible for everybody, but was even more terrible for us. For twelve months my father was forced to work, to dig trenches.... His son was a soldier of our army, and he was a soldier for *Shki*." There is clear evidence that during the NATO bombing campaign, Serbian security forces detained men and forced them to dig trenches, clear bunkers, and perform any other manual work which was deemed necessary for the army's strategic objectives.[35] "When our *Shki* began to kill Albanians and burn our houses, we all got on tractors and left. We went up the mountain, and reached this hollow which is between two villages and is very deep, but they found us because they knew that place." Surrounded by soldiers, the villagers were pushed out of the hollow and to the road, where tanks were waiting for them. They watched as their tractors were burned with all the clothes and everything else they had managed to bring with them. From the hill, they could also see all the other villages on the plateau burning. Left without transport, the villagers were forced to walk in a line ahead of the tanks and flanked by soldiers until they reached their burned homes. Both soldiers and refugees camped there.

Fitore was mostly anxious about her brother, because she had heard that he had been wounded. The next day she decided to brave the treacherous trek to the mountain to reach the KLA base where she thought he might be staying. She took her little sister with her. But they could get only as far as the village school before Serbian soldiers caught up with them. "About this I cannot talk any further. I didn't see my brother. They let us go after a few days. It was the army, like our army, but they were all tattooed, with a black bandana on their head. My sister fortunately was not raped, and I even have a document by a doctor stating that. But my fate was different."

On the opposite side of Kosovo, in the northeast, there was no KLA fighter in the village of seventeen-year-old Liridona. She never saw an Albanian insurgent or heard about them during the whole duration of the war. In the village, everyone stayed put behind locked doors, afraid of Serbian soldiers, of KLA fighters, of anyone carrying weapons. Liridona's stepfather was convinced that the war would be short and at first refused to leave the house, but when he saw the Serbian army enter Kosovo on the first day of the NATO intervention, he gathered his family, including his wife, Liridona and her little sister, locked the door, and walked out.

He thought it was a temporary retreat and they would be back soon—after all, he was not involved in any hostile activity. They had not packed anything, not even a change of clothes. Instead, they were almost immediately captured and sent to a military base in a nearby Serbian village. "They asked us whether we had the names of those who had joined the KLA, until a commander came and from there they took us to the upper part of the village. We filled a room there, it was night, it was icy cold there, the room was as cold as ice. There were also two or three neighbors from our village. In those moments I thought of nothing actually, a person cannot think anymore, I mean, you are paralyzed, you don't know what will happen, everyone for himself, because we knew nothing, we just heard that they were shooting outside. They said, 'We are going to kill you! We are going to throw a bomb in there!' They scared us until the morning."

The following morning, the soldiers gathered them all and escorted them to their homes to pick up some clothes, "and right then they burned everything. Our houses were shacks but they were good because we lived there. They were ours." Back on the road, Liridona, her family, and their neighbors were taken back to another village in Serbia and from there to a military barrack. "The men were separated from the women and beaten to a pulp until the evening, I don't know how long, two nights maybe? I actually don't know when they reunited us." The women were left alone, but shaken by cold, hunger, and fear. Called by the women's cries, doctors came to check on the men, who had been taken back to the room semi-conscious and covered in blood. More interrogations followed after they were taken to a police station in Serbia, and always without any food or drink. "'What is your name?' 'Do you have any family abroad?' 'Did you take weapons?' Questions like that."

When they were finally released in the evening, they had to sign letters that stated they had not been beaten or abused in detention. "Soldiers escorted us to the bus station and told us, 'Wait till six in the morning when the bus comes and return to Merdare,' which meant the border. We stayed at the station all night, because we didn't have anywhere else to stay. We sat there, without food or drinks. At around four or five in the morning, I don't know, it was still dark, a jeep came, a big jeep which was bigger than others, carrying special forces and they took me. Just, *'Dodji ovamo!'* (Come here!). I looked older, like a woman. And they took me. One person, a policeman, like a gendarme, how to say, a special force, grabbed me and drove me to the mountain. It seemed to me that the trip lasted one hundred years. There was like a small creek there and I will never forget, he raped me there, in the jeep. I immediately started to cry, it's normal, and I wasn't feeling good and he held me down and immediately after he finished, I began to bleed, you know, I felt so bad! Before he released me, he raised his gun. I thought that he was going to kill me. What could I have done? When you are in those hands you cannot do anything, you cannot pray, nothing. He said, 'Hey, go there in the water.' There was like a small creek there, I don't know what that place was, the water was as cold as ice, and I was also cold. He said, 'Get in the water, wash up and go.' I asked, 'Are you going to kill me or not?' ' No, I am not going to kill you, but get in and I'll take you back.' And he took me back. It would have been better to be buried, you know, to be killed, than be seen by all those neighbors. It was not my neighbors' business, because I didn't go voluntarily, but it was so difficult! I said, 'It would have been better if he left me there, better had I been lost, you know.' My stomach was tearing. Even today I lose blood from my colon."

Why did Liridona's family go back home, after all that? The neighbors thought better than that. Too scared of being picked up again, they escaped across the mountains. For Liridona that was not an option. Her mother was ill, her sister still a child, and her brother had left much earlier, at the age of eleven, to escape their stepfather's abuse. Her stepfather, a violent man, made all the decisions for the family. He held her tightly by the arm and dragged her back to the house. They had nowhere else to go. Besides, there was that letter they had gotten from the police, a sort of release paper. Guards had told them, "Go back to your house, don't go anywhere because they will shoot you, just go, they will shoot if you go to the mountains."

Two or three days had not passed from their return, when the army established a base near their house; it was a base of reservists, as they were called. It is not that Liridona's family had a house. They had made their way back on two tractors, to find the house burned and everything gone. Their only shelter was a sort of basement. Soldiers had given them some food and told them to stay put. But from time to time they visited them. They did not bother Liridona's younger sister because they thought she was a boy. They threatened them with knives to their throat, "Do you want Rugova?" "Do you want NATO?" "None of us spoke Serbian, only dad. We slept on some planks in the basement. We did what we could, mom baked something with flour on a black stove we had recovered from the old burnt house, it was molden corn flour, while we used to have cows and chickens before."

Anytime Serbian forces came to the village, firing their automatic weapons to call the attention of those who were locked inside their homes, Liridona was the first to go out. She moved slowly, crying: "'I am a woman, I have no weapon, I am in my house.' The soldiers changed every day, they were never the same. It was almost the end of May when they began to come and rape me almost every day. Not the same soldiers but others, some young, some drunk and others high on drugs, there were all kinds of them. From the end of the month almost all who came raped me. They wanted to take my sister too, but I told them, 'She is too young, I am here!' It pained me so much to see her cry, she was so young! We had cut her hair, you know, so they would not take her because she was so beautiful. I did what I could."

This went on until June 5, a week before NATO entered Kosovo. That day a civilian and a soldier came, her stepfather did not hear them, as he was a bit deaf. Since Serbian forces had begun to round up Albanians again, he went to the back of the house, where they had a dog, because he thought that maybe some displaced Albanian was there and he wanted to check whether he knew them. Instead, he found the two Serbs. "The civilian shouted to my father, 'Do you like NATO? Do you like Rugova?' He beat my father, then he focused on my sister. I went up to him twice, three times, 'Leave my sister alone, let her go.' He shouted, '*Jebem ti mater*' (fuck your mother) and grabbed me. He slapped me three times, then pointed his gun at me but didn't kill me. I said to myself, 'If they see she is a child they will leave her alone.' But no! I went up to him three times, and I didn't think at all about being killed. This civilian wore a light gray jacket, black pants, a black shirt, while the soldiers were like regular soldiers with uniforms and automatic weapons. He had a revolver, I will never forget. I remember it as if it was today that he had a big stomach like a *magjup*, because he was a *magjup*. He threw my sister to the ground and pointed his gun to her ear. I did not see what happened to my father because when I saw that, I ran to my mother and told her, 'Oj mom, they killed her!' She froze, you know, 'No! Go take her!' I saw everything. They killed her and then left to go to a neighbor's house, the house of an old woman, because they saw she had some money. I ran to my sister, I thought she would survive, I gave her mouth-to-mouth respiration, you know, but she had lost too much blood. One, two minutes and her heart did not make it. She died. It was 8:30 on the Voice of America when they were killed, I know that because we listened to a small radio. I had to drag myself out of there."

Liridona walked to the nearest town with her mother. The town was nearby, but they had never been there and everything looked unfamiliar. They were in a daze, and could not see what was around them. Serbian forces were rounding up Albanians there too, because it was curfew time, and the two women, feeling trapped, began to cry. They thus drew the attention of soldiers in dark brown uniforms, who arrested them and took them to a house. One told them, "You violated the quiet by crying, he doesn't care about what you do but don't make the mistake of crying." The two women had no idea who "he" was or what the problem was. Then "he" arrived and reproached them for crying for no reason. "Mom was sick, I was very scalding from the worry, from the tears, I was red in the face. And I grabbed him, you know, begged him not to kill us." The man handed his gun to another soldier, "Take this gun and kill her," but the soldier did not move. Everyone was telling him, "Take it, take it!" because they were afraid of that man. Still, nobody moved. "He" hit the soldier for not obeying the order, then left, saying, "OK, now wait until morning and let them go, let them go wherever they want to go." Liridona was gang-raped all night in that house. In the morning they told her, "Take your clothes and get dressed, now you can go wherever you want."

The Strongest Link: An Oral History of Wartime Rape Survivors in Kosovo. Anna Di Lellio and Garentina Kraja, Oxford University Press. © Oxford University Press 2025. DOI: 10.1093/9780197699324.003.0006

6

They Would Not Touch Women and Children

In the beginning, for most people in the cities the war was something that happened far away, even though its epicenter was less than thirty miles from the capital Prishtina and just at the outskirts of Gjakova and Peja. They read about it in the media. So great was the disconnection between the city and the countryside that Albanian journalists who ventured out of town were ironically greeted at KLA checkpoints with the salutation, "Life is good there in Prishtina, isn'it? Like in Switzerland?"[1] While the independent newspaper *Koha Ditore* also reported on skirmishes with the KLA, the organ of the national Albanian leadership *Bujku* focused exclusively on the victimization of civilians. But no matter the spin, all media extensively covered the massive counterinsurgency operations.

Cities were not exactly peaceful. Xheraldina Vula, a journalist for RTV2, remembers that in Prishtina, "after 3 or 4 p.m. not a single soul was in the streets. It smelled of war.... It was scary; in the streets you only saw young Serbs with guns."[2] Nevertheless, there were protests, and when they started, women were at the forefront. Flora Brovina, of the League of Women, was attending a meeting of the LDK on the afternoon of February 28, 1998:[3] "During a break from the meeting we heard of Likoshan and Qirez, where planes were involved, and helicopters and the police had killed many people. I didn't go back to the meeting but told Shukrie Rexha, a former political prisoner, to go inside and tell the men that the women were leaving to go to the U.S. Office. I didn't have a phone, it didn't work, I don't know whether I had paid the bill or not, but I went to the neighbor's and called another activist and told her to call her friends and tell her friends to call others. We snowballed the information that at the appointed time we would meet at the U.S. Office."

Three thousand women gathered there. "Among the twenty people killed there was a pregnant woman of the Nehbiu family. Then the war started, with the killing of that woman and the baby in her womb."[4]

An even more impressive gathering of women took place a week later, after the March massacre of Prekaz, when thousands of them, brandishing loaves of bread, tried to force their way past the cordon of army and police blocking all access to Drenica. Edita Tahiri, then minister of foreign affairs of the self-styled Kosovo Republic, was among the organizers.[5] They had come up with the idea of staging a protest that would have a strong visual impact, since the international media were converging on Kosovo. The bread powerfully symbolized the needs of the Drenica population, which had been besieged by the army for days. Bakers mobilized by the LDK provided the loaves. Predictably, the women were stopped just outside Prishtina by an impressive deployment of troops, but they made their point. Edita Tahiri, who spoke English, addressed the troops and the cameras of the Associated Press. Unable to go further, demonstrators turned around and returned the bread to the bakeries. Years later, U.S. General Wesley Clark remembered how the protest with women holding loaves of bread had been the most impressive visual statement of the Kosovo crisis.[6]

Vjosa Dobruna was also there. "There were other protests later in front of the international organizations that worked in Kosovo, mainly the High Commission for Refugees, which did not help Kosovo people, even though they were displaced from their houses, because they were dealing only with Serbian refugees from Croatia who had been brought by train by Serbs after Operation Storm in Croatia.[7] We, women groups, went to the mountains of Berisha, to Pagarusha, and other places, to Dragobil, and offered help as much as we could. I cannot say that it was difficult, not even now when I think about it, because at that moment it was a very natural part of our work. We were part of that population and we took the courage to do something. It was our obligation."[8]

For doctors such as Flora Brovina and Vjosa Dobruna, or human rights activists such as Nazlie Bala, Sevdije Ahmeti, and the sisters Igballe and Safete Rogova, traveling in the rural areas of Kosovo was not a novelty. They had been doing it through the 1990s. However, 1998 was a turning point. Demonstrations to denounce the violence in Drenica took place in all the cities.

In Peja, Lumka (Lumturije) Krasniqi was a young woman who had been active in the blood feud reconciliation movement back in 1990 and had taken a leadership position in organizing cultural groups in town.[9] On March 18, 1998, she participated in the mass rally in support of Drenica, and when with other friends she heard of the beating and killing of some protesters who were stopped from joining the demonstrators, she set out to take action. "We decided to establish the Council for Emergencies on March 18 to give aid to people, to be more united, because the protest showed lack of organization, of leadership.... We were divided in several groups, and I was in charge of medicine and food for the displaced. We went to the war zones as well, I mean, inside the war, so our activity expanded. I remember that we sent first aid to the village of Vojnik, in Drenica. We sent it with a big truck, it was full of stuff, we knocked on every door to ask every manufacturer, organization, drugstore to give us whatever they had. In the beginning people in Peja didn't know that we were with the Council for Emergencies, they only knew that we were helping with refugees in the city. We would settle them with family, in some houses, we would find them a place to stay.... I remember filling the truck with things to send to Vojnik. We didn't even know where it was nor where its entrance was. There were police checkpoints everywhere back then. We sent first aid with a truck full of food there, we sent medicines, clothes. Half of it was dedicated to that zone, to the people who were isolated, but another part of it went to the headquarters of the KLA, which was just established there."

That was the activity of a number of daring individuals. More in general, life in the cities continued within the usual constraints of state repression but in relative peace, because of their sharp separation from the countryside.

All that began to change with the very first day of NATO bombing, March 24, 1999. A few days earlier, all the international peacekeeping monitors of the OSCE, foreign media, and diplomatic personnel were ordered out. Military checkpoints quickly multiplied in different neighborhoods, while men in uniform—Serbian soldiers, police, special forces, and civilians—roamed the streets, smashing windows, looting stores, and establishing a regime of total terror. As elsewhere, in Prishtina too, Albanians stayed inside their homes, with doors locked and curtains drawn. All the activities that had sprung up in the tense period before NATO's intervention came to a halt, as foreign nationals—from aid workers to diplomats and journalists—were evacuated.

That was the time when even contacting the Red Cross, which Beti Muharremi had been doing regularly as a volunteer, was impossible:[10] "Some relatives who for some reason thought that they would be safer in Pristina came and stayed in our apartment. People began to stay locked up in their homes, the stores began to get broken into, the windows were broken, Serbs started to take things from the stores, because Albanians did not dare go outside. My apartment was in the center of the city but we didn't dare leave the house. Even our telephone lines, all the telephone lines of Albanians, were cut off, while those of the Serbs remained functional. It seemed interesting but also impossible to me, but it turns out it was possible. I noticed that our close neighbor, who had bought the apartment from a Serb, had a functioning phone because the apartment was still under the name of a Serb. I thought that the phone didn't work because of the situation, but no, Serbs had telephone service, while we couldn't communicate with anyone. And without a way to communicate, I didn't know where my father was, where my brother was, where his children were. One day, our closest Serbian neighbor knocked on my door and asked to talk to my husband. He said, 'Can we please agree that if you are in danger, I will protect your family, but if it will be our turn to be in danger, you will protect us?' 'Yes,' we said, 'But can you please let us use your phone to call our relatives and check where they are?' And he said, 'OK, take the key to my apartment, you can use the phone.' And when I went in there, when I looked at his balcony, I saw a sniper gun and a bag filled with bullets, I mean, that neighbor was a sniper."

By March 25, uniformed and armed Serbian civilians were standing by the main entrance of the apartment building where Vjosa Dobruna, who was well-known as an activist both in Kosovo and abroad, lived:[11] "But on the ground floor we had a basement through which one could enter the building, so all the Albanians used the basement to get in. And I did too. At three o'clock, they called me on the phone, I had a mobile with a foreign number, and they told me that they had set the *Çarshia e Madhe* (Big Market) in Gjakova on fire, they had killed an OSCE employee in Gjakova, they had killed doctor Izet and an activist, actually an OSCE employee, and they had taken Bajram Kelmendi and his two sons. A friend of mine from Belgrade, Nataša Kandić, called me.[12] So, I left through the basement and went to the next building where my parents lived, to see if I could send text messages with my phone, when a neighbor came and said, 'Vjosa, you are jeopardizing the whole building, the police are coming to get you.' They wanted to break the door, but I had enough time to run out before they came in. I escaped from the balcony of the living room, in the back of the building."

After hiding in different apartments, Dobruna was caught a few days later in the street, as she was going to check on her parents. "They beat all of us who were in the car, my sister, her husband with their child, and me; they stole everything we had, gold and money, and kicked us out of Kosovo."

Ola Syla stayed put in her apartment with her family.[13] "Someone had to go out to get supplies and it was I who went out for my husband and sons. I bought bread, flour, oil, sugar, thinking that if we had to stay home, because we didn't dare go out, the children would at least have something to eat. We filled the freezer to the brim, there was no more room for bread or anything else. My sister-in-law, who had left a couple of days earlier, phoned me from Macedonia and told me, 'Ola please, dress up well! Dress well, tidy yourself up, put make-up on and put on your best-looking clothes. Because if you are well dressed and if you look good, it will be easier to cross through checkpoints.' You know, they said that if you were a woman from the village, ignorant, or uneducated, they would mistreat you to the max. While they had some consideration for a woman who is, or looks, more emancipated."

Pranvera Musa, twenty-one at the time, had been left without a job when the staff of the UN World Food Programme, where she was an administrator, was evacuated:[14] "Of course I went out to look for milk or bread, but never alone, always with my mother and her cousin. At checkpoints they would point a gun to my head, shouting, 'Where are your brothers?' 'They are not here, they are in Germany.' 'You are lying, they are in the mountains, fighting.' I just stared at them, I didn't care. If they didn't see fear in you, they wouldn't dare touch you, it would be boring for them. But I always carried a knife with me, if they touched me, I figured it would be either me or them."

Inverting the stereotype of the vulnerable, fearful woman was a trick that some women played. Igo (Igballe) Rogova drove everywhere to bring drugs and various supplies. Her sister Safete remembers that anytime Igo was stopped at checkpoints and was asked, roughly,[15] "*'Gdje ideš?'* (Where are you going?), she would not answer in a low voice, *'Idem'* but instead she would shout, louder than they, *'Idem tamo'* (I am going there), so the soldiers would say, 'She is not OK' and let her pass." To be persuasive in their act, urban women had to speak fluent Serbian and they did, having learned it in school or interacting with Serbs. Rural women had only met Serbs in law enforcement and spoke their own Albanian dialect.

The War Comes Inside the Apartments

"We didn't have money, where to go, where to flee. I stayed home until the end of the war." Kimete lived in a middle-class neighborhood of Pristina with its ethnically mixed residents. She was left with her parents and young children, while her husband fled to safety abroad. What her family did was get ready for police raids. "People said, 'Set up the coffee table because if they find it all laid out they will not mistreat you.'" Such was the conventional wisdom at the time. It was a strategy of defense founded on hospitality, a key trait among Albanians, which extends the obligation of a generous reception even to uninvited guests. It did not work. "Two Serbs came to our apartment and the first thing they did was kick the coffee table upside down. They took dad to another room and hit him very hard; he screamed. One grabbed my mother and hit her with a metal chain, shoved her to one side, and left her there to bleed. My daughters began to cry and scream and one pulled out a knife. They took my dad back to another room. He said, 'Don't say anything, I will survive it, we cannot do anything.' They took my mom to the room. Dad repeated, 'Don't say anything.' They put my sister-in-law and me in a car and drove out of town."

There is little that escapes the vigilant watch of the neighbors in the apartment blocks of Kosovo towns, and even if everybody was hiding inside, they could not avoid hearing the commotion in the hall and the screeching tires of the police car as it sped away. Everyone knew that the two women had been taken away. Kimete's father had noticed that the men who had come to his apartment were not wearing regular army uniforms, and as soon as he could compose himself he went to complain to the army. Kimete, with her sister-in-law, had been taken to a house whose floor and walls were full of blood. We could only say, "Just don't cut us up, because we left children at home," as the men staged a mock interrogation, "Where is your husband, he is with the KLA, ah?" before assaulting them. They were released when the Serbian army came to free them, as they had promised to her father.

Merita's family thought they should not leave their home, at the outskirts of Pristina. Even when on the first night of NATO intervention the shelling woke everybody up, her husband remained calm under the comforter, because he thought that nobody would bother them, as they had not joined any armed or political group. But she and her mother-in-law could not sleep. Frightened but also curious, they went to the balcony and saw that shelling had lit up the whole city. The older woman, who had survived the Second World War, wiped out her mouth that had suddenly become very dry. "'Oh mom, what's up? Whatever happens, we will go with all the other people wherever they go.' 'Oh my daughter,' she said, 'you don't know what war is!'" Merita didn't quite get that warning. She had a different understanding of the war. She thought of it as a war of liberation from what she saw as Serbian oppression, a war that might require spilling blood, but would end with freedom. She thought about the possibility of dying, but nothing else.

The following morning, Serbian troops came into her neighborhood. There was great confusion, there was so much to think about, and in a hurry. What should they take with them? Where should they go? There was no plan for that. They ended up in the neighbor's basement, a big one, with hundreds of people inside. It was chaos. There were babies, kids, and sick old people walking with canes. Merita was holding her one-year-old son and her two-year-old daughter, both crying in the noisy confusion of the moment. She didn't notice when her girl slipped from her hand and tried to make for the door, just as the snipers began to shoot. She could hear the bullets against the wall and ran after her daughter in a panic. With her mother-in-law, she weighed the option of staying inside and risking being killed versus the option of leaving, but to go where? The dilemma was soon solved by a kid who called them out: the whole neighborhood was in the street, and troops were rounding everybody up on the main road.

The basement emptied out quickly, only a girl with a sick old man stayed behind. Soldiers turned to the old man, and hit him. "They shouted, 'You can walk because you are not blind!' He was blind in two eyes, but they beat him and hit his legs. He was both invalid and blind. Who knows what they did to the girl there! It was the army. They were all in different brown and green uniforms and with masks. All wore masks that day, you could not see anyone's face. They said, 'Don't you love Serbia?' This and that, in Serbian. 'Stand up, I am going to show you what Serbia is.' They took three thousand people that day, they said, and put us all in the sports hall Boro-Ramiz. We were there with all our neighbors, until the evening."

In the evening, the same crowd was again shoved into trucks and cars. The panic spread that all the men would be killed, that they must disguise themselves as women to avoid execution. Would that have done the trick? Fehmi Agani, a well-known intellectual and a key leader of the self-styled Kosovo Republic, tried to leave by train dressed as an old woman, but he was recognized, pulled out of the train car, and shot on the station platform.[16]

When Merita's convoy suddenly stopped, they feared the worst, but it was just that the road was blocked and nothing moved. Merita's family and many others got off the truck and went home. That night, Merita and three other women baked bread for as many people as they could; she remembers dozens of people at her house. But in the morning, nobody had any more doubts about what to do; they all left for the mountains. She carried her son on her back, her husband took the girl, and the others followed, a large group of people of all ages and carts with a few belongings and some food. It was a convoy of thirty-two people, the whole family of Merita's husband, among them a seventy-year-old man who walked for hours without ever stopping. For the following month they moved from one village to another, finding refuge at relatives' homes but also helped by random strangers.

At one point, Merita's group reached a village where a massacre had just been perpetrated. "We felt a sort of smell, but I didn't know where it was coming from. My mother-in-law said, 'It's that smell. Be quiet, don't talk,' because soldiers were all around. It was full of dead people. My daughter went, 'Oj mom, the heads are gone!' Blood up to here. We walked and the smell, the smell! Dead cows, people who had been killed in their homes. We knew that one week earlier they had hit the area but we did not know what happened. When an armored car passed we immediately crouched and hid until it went away." Some students who were hiding nearby crossed their path. "They went like, 'Where are you going?' 'Prishtina.' 'What? Prishtina? They were shooting just outside the city today, in Kolovica. It isn't over.' We walked very slowly and sat in the fields on that hill for two nights. We got back home at around 5 in the morning."

Their watchdog had been killed. Inside the house, they found mayhem: all the doors had been shattered, and the long hallway was covered with shards of glass; everything had been stolen, with the exception of a few food supplies hidden in the attic. Still, it felt good that they were all together, in one piece, safe at home.

It was the very beginning of May, and the days were getting warmer. For one week nothing happened. A sudden offensive in the neighborhood broke the peace. There was a house nearby sheltering about sixty people. Merita heard the noise of shooting, the crying and wailing of women and children, the shouting in Serbian ordering an execution, but could not see what was happening. When the noise subsided a little, her mother-in-law decided to go out and check by herself. It was right when she reached the door and was about to pick up the keys that Merita, who was out in the yard, saw the soldiers closing in and called her back. "They kicked the door open, '*Gazda,*

gazda!' (The head of the house!) And before they reached us, I jumped through the window into the house, found my passport and hid under the bed." But there was no place to hide. The six uniformed men who came in, with automatic weapons leveled at all the people inside the house, first found her. "They asked, 'Where is the landlord? '*Gde je gazda?*' I said, '*Ide te kmoshija* (*sic*, broken Serbian), he is at the neighbor's.'" Then, they found her husband. They took all the money he had on him before beating him senseless in front of everybody, in a widespread practice of robbery and extortion that accompanied the violence against civilians.[17]

One of the soldiers approached Merita, ordering her to show an ID. After a perfunctory check of the document he said, "*Ti lepotica*" (You are beautiful), took her baby son from her arms and shoved him in the cradle, and then grabbed her by the hair. She was gang-raped by all of the six men in front of her husband as they kept kicking him. "I remember as if it were today how strongly I held onto my shirt. They tore my hair, they punched me and dragged me. 'Let them kill me,' I said to myself, 'Better dead than what they are doing to me.' I lost consciousness, I only came back to my senses once and I saw my husband and my son on the floor, the cradle overturned. I didn't see my daughter because she was in the other room with my mother-in-law. They made me black and blue." Merita woke up after they had gone and the first thing she saw was the sad but hopeful face of her mother-in-law, "Thank God you are alive!" The sister of the old woman came by and helped wash the blood that covered her bruised body. She was two months pregnant at the time, and everyone was crying around her. She heard her husband, who had been taken outside the house and beaten more, screaming to high heaven.

Afërdita too had thought that her mother's apartment in the city would be safer than the village where she lived with her husband. After an anxious trip on a bus fully loaded with her family and all the cousins from the village, a place where she has never returned since, Afërdita felt good when she saw her mother's smiling face at the bus station. Only a few days earlier, Afërdita's mind was somewhere else. Her husband was behaving much better since he had stopped drinking and had accompanied her to the doctor because her pregnancy was not going well. Back at the house, they found a cousin waiting for them, anxious to hear what the doctor said. It was nothing serious, rather a sort of heartache due to grief for the recent death of her father. There was the usual chit-chat with her cousin's wife, but Afërdita had just put the coffee pot on the stove when the normality of the day was interrupted by the noise of shooting. At first, she thought it might be the neighbors celebrating. "'Who is getting married?' I asked my cousin. 'Inshallah it was a wedding! This isn't the wedding season.' We all ducked, because the shooting felt very near. 'Be careful,' he said, 'take the children, take some clothes and come to us,' because he had a basement." From the second floor, they peeked through the window curtains and saw Serbian forces everywhere on the hill.

The next morning, they waited for the first moment of quiet. "To tell you the truth, we didn't know what was happening. My husband carried one girl, I did the other, the little one, and we went to our cousin's. One, two, three days, and we ran out of diapers." They ran out of milk too: she first, from stress, and the cow later. The children did not stop crying from hunger. One night, Afërdita ran to her home to grab some food and sheets to make desperately needed diapers. She got lucky, because she managed to avoid a volley of bullets shot by snipers from the police station uphill. By then, it was clear what was happening, as dozens of tanks appeared from all sides and the news reported nonstop about the offensive nearby. Her mother was constantly on the phone from the city, crazy with fear for Afërdita's life, and at the same time afraid that their conversations could be tapped by the police.

When the NATO bombing began, Afërdita was already at her mother's, living in very cramped quarters with her nuclear family, her two cousins, and a dozen children, though in relative quiet. Within a few days, Serbian forces emptied the city of its Albanian population and burned their homes. "The terror began on the night of Bajram, I don't know the exact date but I know it was Bajram. *Shki* expelled us from our homes and took us to a nearby village. When we got there, the head of the house where we were staying said, 'Have a good Bajram, tonight it's Bajram.'" In 1999, Kurban Bajram or Eid al-Adha[18] was on March 28. After a while, Afërdita and her family went back home. They found their house ransacked and looted, and cleaned it up as best they could.

Uniformed men barged in at 5 a.m. when everyone was still asleep and gave the order to immediately vacate the house. "They all wore masks. Maybe they were the same police who had come to search our house when my father was still alive, maybe they were others. They said, 'This is the neighborhood of pretty women.' And it was really true. There were many beautiful women in that part of town. They beat my brother and my husband and took them outside, but I don't know where they took them from there. My mom could not defend us: me, my sister, and the wife of my brother. They grabbed my mom, one man threatened her with a knife, he was fat, fat and tall. One took me, another grabbed my brother's wife, and another my sister. Around maybe fifteen men came inside. The children cried and screamed. My brother's son screamed, 'You killed them! You killed them!' The children didn't know what was happening because they were very young, but they suspected it was something bad because we were screaming."

The Serbian police gang-raped all the women in the house that day. When the men of the family came back, they asked to describe what happened. "My brother's son said, 'They danced, a man danced with auntie.' He didn't know what he was saying. 'What is that? Dancing with auntie? He danced like this?' 'No, he danced with his legs.' I said, 'It's enough that we are back together.' My husband said, 'From today on you are not my wife anymore.'" Afërdita could not find the strength to talk back, she had no voice, she could speak only with gestures, while she felt her body was drained of all blood. Her husband said he would decide later, when things calmed down, where they would go. Afërdita heard his brother's conversation with their mother. "He asked, 'Mom, what shall I do with my wife?' 'Just shut your mouth, see what her husband did to your sister? Do you want to do the same as that soulless man? Why didn't he defend us? Why didn't you fight the police to defend your wife?' My brother did not make a sound."

A week later, troops came back to the apartment and drove everybody out. All the men were picked up by the army, put on trucks, and locked in the prison of Smrekovica. The women and the children were put on trucks going in a different direction. At first, Afërdita did not know where they were being taken. She noticed there were many Roma in the streets, and noticed their freedom of movement among Serbian troops, for whom they played music in exchange for food. She did not know that her truck was heading to Studime, to the town's school.[19] All the women on the trucks were locked in the school by soldiers wearing different uniforms—some were in blue, others in gray, some had painted faces, it was difficult to discern who they were. "Those who raped me wore masks. They had blue uniforms, but wore masks. They called them paramilitaries. For three days and three nights they never left us. I don't know how many men raped us in one day. There were seventeen women. I was cut here, in my forehead, with a knife, here and also in two places on my knee, but they are much better healed. And this is a stigma for my entire life. They kept us there, in that school, for three days and three nights. It was a school, a house, there was a sort of cooking space and rooms after rooms, I don't know what it was. For precisely six hours they put us in one room, after six hours they took us to another. One raped me, one, two, someone liked me and kept me for himself. All of those who were there, the police, played with our bodies as it pleased them. We were conscious, unconscious."

For the whole time that Aferdita was the target of humiliating physical violations, she heard one of her torturers say, "'You are Albanian, you can endure this. Come on, you can tolerate this. Albanians have endurance, they are very resistant.' It was cold, but they said, 'Don't get dressed, because you are expected to be killed' and 'Arkan has asked for women. Let's go, be ready that we are taking you to Arkan.' How could we get ready? They beat us up, they used us. I put a t-shirt on, one of those t-shirts they gave us. They loaded us on a truck. We went to a village near Smrekovica." Along the trip, the twelve women on the truck managed to untie themselves. They jumped off the truck. "First one, then two and all the others after me. I don't know who all those women were. I knew the ones who were my neighbors, though I never knew their fate, and I don't feel good asking them. We entered a village and a woman gave us some clothes and we got dressed. She asked, 'Do you want bread?' But what bread? Who had thought about bread? We had been three days and three nights without eating and drinking, only rape, with them drinking raki."

Afërdita and her sister managed to make their way back home and find their mother with all the children, twelve of them. "Mom was so happy! She cried and screamed and, 'It's so good that you are alive!' She kissed our hands, she kissed our eyes, she kissed our feet." As warm and welcoming as the house was, it was not safe. That night in April when the husband and the mother-in-law of Afërdita's sister came to pick her up, Serbian troops also showed up at the door. "'Where are you hiding? Whom are you hiding?' My sister said, 'I am not hiding anybody, here is my husband.' And they took him and killed him and their daughter. She was a toddler. They did not let us bury them, that day there was no burial, and only fifteen years after the war my sister found out where they had been buried."

Terror in the City Streets

At the very outskirts of Prishtina, Fatime had not been able to stay in her house, which had been a safe haven for the refugees who began to stream into the city as early as the fall of 1997. When the NATO intervention began, and Serbian forces swarmed the city, she repaired with her daughter, a toddler, and a crowd of about three hundred women and children to a large basement nearby. She was six months pregnant. A week later, after a shootout erupted just outside their refuge, they were shepherded in the middle of the night to some houses uphill by KLA fighters. Fatime could not see her husband among them, only some other younger relatives. In the morning, it became clear that there was no food left because Serbian forces had taken all the bread the women had baked the night before and left behind. Hungry and scared, the civilians discussed among themselves what to do. Where could they find food and who would go out to fetch it? The best option was a house uphill, but that meant getting closer to an area where there had been police action, and many buildings had been burned. The group's decision coalesced on Fatime. "You go! You'll have a child with you," meaning, nothing will happen to you.

Fatime was not the type who refused to do her share of work. Since the beginning of the war she had baked and cooked all day long, or tended the cows, ready on a moment's notice to feed fighters who stopped by to refuel on food or brought with them streams of hungry and terrified displaced women and children. However, she knew the danger of going outside. In the bunker, she had heard the shooting, the firing of tear gas, and the shouts of soldiers. She knew that six or seven KLA fighters had been killed nearby, and two neighbors, civilians, had been the collateral damage of that particular operation. Serbian forces had shelled the nearby school, then burned what was left, and had stolen all the animals in the stable: she knew, because she heard the *tak tak tak* of the hooves on the asphalt as the cows were led away. When her family told her that she had to go out and fetch food, she felt vulnerable and exposed as never before. Pregnant and without her husband, she had been relying on her father-in-law and his brother, older men who could not join the fighting and had stayed behind with women and children. But just a few hours earlier, her husband's uncle had told her to leave the shelter with her daughter and relieve their crowd from the two extra mouths that needed feeding: "Go find your husband, we are full here!"

When she was told that she was the best option they had to find food, she said, "OK, I will go if I have to, but there are other four or five who can go out looking for food, I cannot, I am pregnant." Then she turned to her father-in-law. "Can you come with me? I am afraid, I don't have the guts to go alone, will you come with me?" It was March 30, the day that Serbian forces began to empty out Prishtina. Fatime held her daughter by the hand, the older man walked in front of them, "because men always walk faster." They found themselves in a Roma neighborhood, nobody else in the narrow and winding streets but Roma. It was only when they reached the crossroad with the main street that she saw a group of paramilitaries. The main street was full of people, all lined up in a column. It was six days after the start of bombing, and Serbian forces had begun to systematically empty Prishtina of Albanian residents.

Fatime and her small group turned uphill, "and there they stopped us. I was carrying a bag and I could not run, I was so afraid that I couldn't move. I was completely blocked and I leaned on some door that was on the left. I said, 'Open the door,' because I thought I could get inside and maybe if someone had locked the door they could open it now. I leaned on that door and waited. The door was locked. I pushed. It did not open, but some sort of sound came, and the sky turned into another color. They were coming uphill shooting. There were two men wearing masks and gloves up to here and they were shooting. Now, what to do? I left my bag there on the ground with the girl, and the bag hid the girl and they thought that I was hiding something. And my girl said, 'Who is that mom?' 'He is your uncle, be quiet, nothing happened.'"

Fatime held her daughter tight and moved in the direction where all the people were, trying to reach the front of the column, but the two soldiers turned to her. "And I raised my hands, 'Don't kill me, don't you see I have a child with me?' One of them went, 'Where are you going? Where have you gone?' He spoke Serbian, sometimes Serbian, some other times Albanian. 'Oh, I said, I went home, my home is here.' I didn't dare say that my home was uphill, where there was fighting. And one came closer, 'Where is your husband? In the KLA?' 'No, he is in Germany. I am married, and I am here only with my child.' 'Ah! I saw you before.' 'It wasn't me.' And he came closer, held my hands and moved to kiss me. The other soldier approached the walls of the house, 'What do you have in the bag?' 'Nothing, just my daughter's clothes and an apple.' And truly that's what I had in the bag, an apple. And he began to kiss me and I moved away from them. And when he said,

'*Dodji ovamo!*' (Come here!) I moved away, but he came closer. I was holding my daughter by the hand and he fired his automatic weapon. I turned back and looked at my daughter, but I almost didn't recognize her. She was shaking as if she had been electrocuted, that girl was all shaken, she went, '*ovovovov!*' I got closer to her and said, 'I am here, I am here.' To them, I said, 'Do what you wish.'"

At that moment, Fatime's father-in-law, who was walking ahead of her, turned back, raised his hands, and shouted, "Come on, don't do it!" He started to walk uphill toward her. The Serbs fired their automatic weapons at him and she saw him fall in a volley of bullets. "He is dead, I thought, it's over, but felt nothing, my spirit was dead too. I turned and said, 'I am here, just don't kill us.' I accepted everything, though I knew that it was nothing good, but in that moment the spirit is weak, and in that moment the spirit is in charge. And when they returned, he removed his mask, the first one had a black mask, and he grabbed me by the hair, he shook my head down and kicked those big doors open. And he dragged me there, pulled my clothes and came closer. He took off his clothes, came forward and forced himself on me. He slapped me with such force! I remember how he slapped me. The others undressed me, and they also began and I don't know when they were done with it. May God kill them! May they never find peace in their souls! And he hurt me so much when he did that, because I was pregnant and he hit me with such slaps! Tak! He made me deaf in my two ears. I could no longer hear. And I never saw what they did to me, I only felt that terror. When they were done, 'Go now, go, go,' they said, 'you asked for NATO, and NATO killed you.'"

When they let go of her, Fatime realized that her daughter was still near her. "My daughter, four and a half years old, saw everything. After that, they kicked me in the back, they knocked me down, until I fell on my knees, I have marks here. Someone said that NATO was bombing us and the affair ended there. And they took me in the direction of the railroad, 'Go, continue with them.' My legs were not working, I couldn't walk. And when I finally reached the column of people, I got in at the end of it. I said to myself, 'If they begin to kill us, I will be behind,' again, with the hope to live. I said to myself, 'How could they kill a woman with a child?'"

That is what Ajshe thought too. "I took my son with me, thinking that if they saw me with a child they wouldn't hurt me. I also took some money, as we did anytime we went out to buy food or something else, in case that something bad would happen and we thought that with some money we could find more tolerance and would be let go. That day I had one thousand German marks with me." All the men in Ajshe's family were fighting with the KLA. They had left their town and had gone into hiding throughout the whole war, moving from place to place to avoid detection. They communicated with their family via radio, as the phone line was either not working or under police surveillance.

One day, Ajshe's brother-in-law made a special request for some warm clothes they desperately needed and she did as told: she went to the town market, filled some bags with wool socks, sweaters, and whatever she could find there, and prepared for her trip. She got off the bus, traveling in the direction of Pristina until the bridge of Rokovina, on the road for Kralan. Kralan is a tragic landmark, because Serbian forces massacred ninety Albanian civilians there in April 1999.[20] But that day, Ajshe had not gone much farther than the bridge when she heard the approach of police sirens, "*'Viu viu viu!'...'Gde ideš gospodjo?'* (Where are you going, miss?) 'Home, my home is in Kralan, and I am going home now.' 'What do you have there?' 'I live in another town and half of my family is here and here are their clothes.'"

The police began to curse her and her family, using such filthy language that she does not want to repeat any words they said. There were three men in that car, they squeezed her, her son and her bags, inside the car and drove to the police station of Gjakova. "Listening to their accent I can say they were local police. The newcomers all had another accent, from Belgrade, I mean from Serbia, while those who took me there were local." They pushed her into a room full of blood, but someone objected to the presence of the child, thus they separated them and moved her to another room, which looked to her like a room in one of those interrogation scenes in old movies: there were some wooden chairs and not much else. "There they began, 'Where were you going?' 'Why were you going there?' 'What were you looking for?' 'We will do this and that to you if you don't talk!' I was raped. I defended myself as best as I could. They ripped my clothes, the first went, then the second, the third... I know that they gave me some water. Their looks were different because some faces were painted, others weren't, and I didn't know anything anymore until around, maybe it was midnight, I don't precisely know what time it was. They had taken me at around six. The team that took me came in, surely to change shifts. One said, 'Are you still here?' 'What can you give us so we can let you go?' I had hidden some money. He said, 'Yyyyyyh! We have plenty of money and gold!' One of them was saying, 'If you don't have what can release you... I had it up to here with you!"'

Ajshe's son began to scream. "He cried, 'Mom, did they hit you a lot?' My clothes were all ripped, my clothes were torn. I have photographs to prove this. At one point they also brought in an Albanian young man to rape me, they said he was with them. He said, 'No, I cannot do that to my sister.' Sister in what sense? They thought in the real sense of sister. He said, 'No, she is my sister as an Albanian.' And they beat him. 'Oh sister,' he said, 'I am *hasret*, in case they kill me, I'll tell you where my house is, go tell them.' They beat him so hard, he was covered in blood, they hit him in the head, in the stomach.... When they let me go. I was soaked, without underpants. I found only one thing to cover myself, something like a tablecloth, because my clothes... absolutely not. My son told me, 'Where are your clothes, mom, aren't you cold?' I said, 'No, mami, I am not, I got so hot because they hit me a lot.' It occurred to me that I could use the story that they hit me a lot as a cover. As we approached a house, a woman peeked through the door, 'Oj sister, what happened there? I don't dare open the door, I will just give you some clothes.' She handed me something. I put on a sweater and a jacket, and began to walk. She did say, 'I don't dare let you in.' I didn't say yes nor no, I didn't talk, I couldn't talk, but my son did: 'Come on mom, let's go. Oh mom, she doesn't dare let us in.'"

Ajshe kept walking with her son in tow, without knowing where she was heading. "I was like a mad person. Then, another police car came. 'Where are you going?' 'Here and there,' I explained the case, 'this, this, and this.' The police verified whether it was true through a radio link and they said, 'Yes, she surely knows something.' 'Get in the car!' Oh God! In the car again! They drove me across Gjakova until they found an empty house, a completely demolished house. One of them found the money and called the others, 'We are going to finish the job here and get paid too.' The other said, 'No, don't you see the condition in which she is?'"

She was raped again.

After she was released, Ajshe knocked on another door for help. This time it opened. Luckily, the woman of the house was a nurse, who could treat her wounds. "In the morning, 'Oh sister,' she said, 'go to your family, go, because if they find you here, they will burn the house and kill us.' I went to the bus station. When I got on the bus the conductor recognized me and said, 'What happened to you?' 'The police came and hit us.' He said, 'But what did they want?' 'You know, I got married in this area.' And I went home. My husband was holding his head in his hands. He had driven around looking for us. He cried and cried. How many times had I gone in the direction of Prishtina, and nothing happened? But that time..."

Vlora thought they would not do anything to a child, and though she looked well-developed she was still a child at thirteen. In fact, at first she could not really fathom the war. She kept hearing the adults talking about the NATO military intervention, about Serbian forces approaching her town in northern Kosovo, and who was killed and who was spared, but mostly she heard the noise of Serbian mortars shelling nearby villages. Her extended family, chased out of their homes, had gathered at her place, with uncles and aunts and crying children. They stayed there for a whole month. Then, the noise got closer. Frightened, they moved to the elementary school's basement, hoping to find a safe haven there. There were who knows how many people in that basement, the entire neighborhood and the refugees who had joined them from villages nearby. Outside, Serbian troops swarmed all over town, expelling civilians, looting and then burning their homes. They also came to their basement and ordered everybody to line up in the street. Vlora remembers how soldiers shouted in Serbian, "Sit down!" "Stand up!" She still sees the buses, which, they were told, would take them to Albania or Macedonia. "We said, 'Who knows where they are taking us! Are they taking us to Serbia? Who knows what they will do.'" It was chaos, and in the confusion the family got separated: she, her mother, and the baby on one side, finding refuge with some close relatives nearby, and her father with the rest of the family on the other side, in the refugee column.

For days, the only news reaching Vlora was of a big massacre nearby. Nothing from her father, who had been seen in the same locality. From the time she was a small child, she had been proud of taking initiatives and contributing to the family. Now, she felt she was in charge, especially because her mother was so distraught that she had run out of milk for the baby, and there was no other milk around. "Occasionally we could smash an apple and give it to him, a potato, but my brother didn't eat it and he was losing weight, did not have the strength to swallow." By the time her father showed up, having survived the massacre by hiding in a stream all night, she had already made up her mind. "I said to my mother, 'I know where we keep the milk at home, shall I go and get it?' Because at that time they said they wouldn't round up women, while men didn't dare go out." At first her mother refused to let her go, but she insisted. "'Mom, I am going today because they say that nothing is going to happen.' 'Ok, go but be careful. If you see danger in the street or something, come back.' That was my mother's instruction. And I went, my father and all the others knew that I was going."

And off Vlora went, wearing her best clothes. She thought she was ready to face anything. "I wore black pants and a red sweater with some sort of black stripes, one of those sweaters that were popular at the time. I got it as a present for Bajram from my father. It felt heavy because the weather was beginning to be warmer, it was the beginning of spring. I will never forget that sweater, it is always in front of my eyes." It was not easy to reach her house but she managed, summoning all the courage she had to cross the streets full of looters, soldiers, and tanks, her heart beating faster and faster, with a voice inside her that said, "Something will happen to me, something will happen to me." She found her home ransacked and robbed of most things, but the milk was there, and so were some baby clothes.

It was on the way back that three men in a white car, two of them masked, stopped her. "They might have said something but I didn't understand it and they asked me again, gesturing, how old I was, and I did thirteen with my fingers. They spoke among each other as I began to walk and the car approached me again. They looked at each other, said something and one came out and pushed me into the car. From that moment I began to cry and scream and they lowered my head, so nobody would see me. I don't know why they did that, they were not afraid of anybody!"

They took Vlora to one of the houses they had emptied out of people and ransacked. They beat her up until she stopped fighting back. "Somehow I grew weaker, you know, I had no more strength, I know that they hit me in the face. I remember everything, I remember the wall they pushed me against, I remember how they pulled their knife to massacre me, how they pointed their automatic weapon to kill me. I fainted, I don't even know what happened, I know I was raped, I felt pain in my body. When I opened my eyes they had left the house and I saw only myself, naked, you know, I was bloody below and I knew what had happened to me but I managed only to get up very quickly and think about my family, I knew they were worried about me. And I got up and left. It didn't occur to me to pick up some milk, nothing, I just left."

Walking in a daze, Vlora got lost in the streets that she knew so well, until she suddenly remembered her way. It was getting dark and everyone at her relatives' house was outside in the yard, anxiously waiting for her return. When they spotted her, they quickly approached her and began to stare. All she said was that she had gotten lost, but could not explain much more. Her parents took her to a room, followed by all the women in the house, at which point her father left. Vlora, who was only able to cry, but could not talk to answer her mother's questions, found the strength to say, "I love you very much, dad!"

Mass Exodus

The house sounded with the cries of the children were the only people left with Afërdita and her mother, when Serbian troops once again barged in, rounded them up, and ordered, "You! on the bus! Go in the direction you wish.'" But where to go? She was on one bus with her daughters and the children of her younger brother, who had been forcibly recruited in the army years earlier but had defected and fled. The buses traveled to Macedonia in the direction of the refugee camp of Stankovec at the border, through the Preshevo Valley in Serbia. They traveled through checkpoints manned by soldiers, "all as big as doors, and all with their faces painted." Those soldiers robbed the refugees at knifepoint of all the money they had; they even robbed the drivers, who had extorted money from refugees at the beginning of the trip. In Preshevo, they were all told to get off the bus and walk. Afërdita was bleeding, worried sick about her sister, whom she had left with the bodies of her husband and daughter in the street, but she shepherded the children to the village of Miratovc, where they managed to get some food and drink. She had been a heavy woman before the war, but she was down to one hundred pounds. Three days later they were in Stankovec. Two nurses checked her, "You must be stitched, you have a gash of six centimeters in your colon, and it needs to be stitched."

Merita and her husband spent the day trying to pull themselves together, comforted by their closest relatives. That did not last long. The soldiers came back, this time with the order to clear the premises before 9 a.m. the next day if they did not want to be killed. Merita could not walk and could hardly sit, but they managed to put her in a neighbor's car while the rest walked to the bus station, even her daughter, a toddler. Her brother-in-law did not make it. They killed him when they reached the Grand Hotel.

It was a sad company of exhausted old people, crying children, and distraught women that climbed onto buses in the direction of Macedonia. To secure seats and perhaps hoping for protection as well, Merita's family had given the Serb driver all the money and objects of value they had. They had traveled less than an hour from Prishtina when at a checkpoint Serbian soldiers pulled out her other brother-in-law and a neighbor, waited for three hours for an order to come, and then executed them. The buses were stopped once again a few kilometers from the border. This time it was like a stakeout of a stagecoach in a western film: armed men wearing bandannas came down the mountains. Everyone was searched for valuables and robbed, including the driver, before driving away and leaving the passengers stranded in no man's land. Again, the Serbian soldiers chose a few men from the group, and held them there for hours, seemingly waiting for an order. In the end, they executed them. The living were left with the concerns of the moment: How to reach the camps? How to feed the kids? Merita: "For me it was all the same, nothing seemed interesting anymore, not at all. I just cried."

The mass expulsion of Albanians from Prishtina was in full swing, and fear, pain, and exhaustion were about to overwhelm Fatime, as she joined the column of refugees. Soldiers continued to shout, "Move!" but she could barely hear them. They didn't let anyone step out of the column, and she had to grab her daughter without much gentility when the girl sat down, refusing to walk any further. Merita watched in silence as the soldiers pulled all the young men out of the column and beat them. At the train station, she met an old aunt and her father-in-law. It was the first time she saw him, after he had fallen under a volley of bullets. They were both incredulous to find each other still alive. It was a happy and brief reunion, as he headed back to pick up other children who had been left alone, as the men ran away. After the first moments of exhilaration, she realized that it was the apocalypse all around her. There were thousands of people around the small building of the station, across the streets and the rails, with no shelter, no bathroom, and no food. Someone gave birth to a child, you could hear the Serbian soldiers ask for a doctor or a midwife. Merita left her daughter with the old aunt, hoping to find someone else from her family who could travel with them. "We were there until the morning. In the morning the train was filled with people, the buses were filled with people, I did not dare go anywhere, I was waiting for someone to come with me somewhere."

The mass expulsion of Albanians had just begun. Nobody knew where they were going, but everyone wanted to leave the hell that Prishtina had become. The soldiers called for women and children to get on the buses first. "When I got closer to the bus, one woman saw me and said, in Serbian, 'Come! Come and I will take the child.' The door of the bus was closing. Now, I had the outstretched hands of that woman here, and the bus was full. Did I dare to leave my daughter with her? I didn't." Merita looked for another bus and spotted one at the other end of the station. She held tight to her child and her bag, trying to also keep the old aunt close to her. She shouted to a soldier, "'I have a child.' He pointed his weapon at me and I pulled that aunt toward me because she was crying, she was more afraid than I was. As I pulled her, a man, an Albanian, said, 'No, no, no! Not you! You cannot get on this bus.' 'Why?' 'Because this is a bus for families, I must take my family.' It was a Barileva Tours bus, or what is now called Barileva Tours. He said, 'This is for families, when another bus comes, you'll take that.' There was a big *Shka* there, he knocked the Albanian to the ground and to me, 'Up!' I was stunned by what he had done and immediately got on the bus and said to myself, 'Now he will kill us.' But when I got on the bus, one from that same family said to me, 'Out! Get out! This is only for families.' 'I am not getting out. That *Shka* got me up here.' Then I saw that there were enough seats at the end of the bus. My aunt wanted to get off, but I said, 'Come with me!' And I dragged her. And the bus left the train station in the direction of Bllace."

When the bus got to the Macedonian border, the soldiers made it take another route through Tetovo. Merita had no food, while the others on the bus were better prepared, they were eating hamburgers, drinking water, but offered nothing to the child, who was crying from hunger. The aunt came to the rescue, she shamed the passengers into sharing some of their food. "And they gave her a Plazma biscuit. When she took it, and she put it closer to her mouth, she vomited until it seemed she had nothing more inside. That hit me too and I vomited my entire stomach. When we entered a neutral zone, Albanians from Macedonia arrived, some with cakes, some with bread, you know, with milk, with something and they gave me the first cake. Actually, they fed the children first, they thought that the adults could endure more. A child is 'greater than the king,' or so they say."

At the border, it was still chaotic, and accommodation was to be found only in tents, but Merita remembered there was an uncle nearby and she could find shelter there, but she did not exactly know where he lived. Finally, a compassionate bus conductor took her to his house. "I said, 'I am not getting inside, maybe I will just clean up, please find me some clothes.' And they found some clothes and I cleaned up. Until the morning I did not know where I was, where I slept. When I woke up, the woman of the house had made some bread, it was the best in the world, and she brought some more. I don't know how long I stayed there, I just stayed there, with that family."

Adelina, who had just become an adult in 1999, never made it to Macedonia. She and her large family had been refugees in Prishtina, in their own country, since 1998. With their house burned in the village and Serbian forces swarming the entire rural region of central Kosovo, there was no place they could call home anymore. Prishtina had been a safe haven for a while. Even on the first night of the NATO bombing, as her parents listened to the news, she and one of her sisters found comfort in playing their favorite song on the recorder, the song they used to listen to when they fell asleep. Their generous host, a man who had no children but some extra room and money to spare, figured out rather quickly the risks this family would encounter. He took Adelina's father aside and said, "I don't have anybody, but you have many daughters. Look at all those people going to Albania and Macedonia, why aren't you going with them?" Her father had thought of it, of course, but where to find the money for the trip? Left penniless by the war that had displaced him from his home and his land, he had only a precious coin, saved for the dowry of one of his girls who was engaged. The host understood and offered to give him some money. "My father did not feel good about taking money without giving anything in exchange." He offered the precious coin to their host, who said, "If we stay alive and come back safe, you will give me my marks back and I will return you the coin."

Three times they set out to go to Macedonia. Three times they were stopped and sent back by Serbian forces who alternately pushed refugees out of the country or held them back as human shields, a strategy to protect their army from NATO and KLA attacks.[21] Adelina's family felt stuck. They first tried private transportation, then they traveled by bus, having spent all the little money they had, but once again they were ordered to get off and walk. They ended up in a column of displaced people outside Prishtina, all walking in the direction of the border with Macedonia, some eighty kilometers away. They were stopped again. It was her father's white *plis*, the traditional conic felt hat, that betrayed their rural origin and triggered the interest of the soldiers. They stopped them, took all their documents, and shouted, "'You are from Drenica!' They separated us, hit us, maltreated us, then made us walk for some hours. My father knew something bad would happen because he said, 'Not all of us are coming back, we made a mistake.' He knew."

When they reached the post office at the center of Pristina, four guards pushed all the women into the building. Adelina remembers their faces, but especially the one of a Roma among them, as he was shorter and heavier than the Serbs. At the post office there were several telephone booths, those old-style wooden cabins where people could use public phones in privacy. It was almost noon when the women of Adelina's family, tired and scared and still unsuspecting of the full extent of what would happen to them, got pushed, each into one cabin. When Adelina tells her story, she gets agitated from that moment on: she tries to re-enact what she could not see, trapped in the phone booth, but could somehow hear, "My ears were ringing. I heard like a person who had an accident that hurt her ears, I heard but could hear very little." As she recounts what happened then, she bangs her head against the wall as she did back then, hoping to numb the pain in her head. "I heard my mother, 'Why are you doing this to us?' I heard her say, 'Do what you want with me, but leave them.' These words stayed with me for many years. You know, I heard that she grabbed a weapon from a guard. In the booth, I heard everything my sister said, in the booth you could hear but you did not know what was happening."

Adelina felt paralyzed with fear. "There were some shelves in that phone booth but I didn't dare touch them, and there was a very small window, what to call it, a sort of hole. I could see from that sort of window, though it was very small. I thought that maybe I would get lucky and recognize someone who worked at the post office. I am telling you, I didn't stop crying, 'What do you want with me?' And I thought, 'Dad will never see us,' because I knew that he was looking for us but I was completely hidden from sight." Five or six hours later, it was evening, and they let them go. Adelina has never gone back to Prishtina. Even when invited to meetings of women rights' organizations, she doesn't go. She knows the post office is no longer there, razed to the ground by NATO bombs a few days later, "But if I see even a single *magjup*, I need a long time to pull myself together."

The Strongest Link: An Oral History of Wartime Rape Survivors in Kosovo. Anna Di Lellio and Garentina Kraja, Oxford University Press. © Oxford University Press 2025. DOI: 10.1093/9780197699324.003.0007

7
Silences

On the fifth day of her captivity, Ganimete heard that the shooting had subsided. There had been an exchange of fire between her Serbian kidnappers and the KLA not too far from the house, but now there was silence inside and outside. A man from the village came in to check whether the Serbs were still there, but they had all left. Ganimete knew him and trusted him, so when he invited her and the other women to his tractor, they piled up on it and drove toward Montenegro. "We didn't have a thing with us, and we were all bloody. They didn't know that we were wounded, had been raped, and just had an abortion. They just said, 'We will bandage you because you are losing blood.' We didn't dare say what happened to us. We said nothing."

On the other side of the border, they were met by a different crowd. Journalists from all over the world had gathered there and at all other border crossings with Kosovo, reporting on the story of the mass expulsion of Albanians.[1] A woman journalist approached Ganimete. "I spoke only Albanian, I didn't even know what questions she asked. I wore a tracksuit with stripes, I had long black hair, and I was completely covered in blood. 'What happened in Kosovo?' she asked, and I told her my story, I told her my name and that I had been...actually, I can't remember what I told her."

The refugees spent the night in a factory, where Ganimete and her friends were given first aid, enough to stem the flow of blood. The following day they traveled again, this time across the mountains toward Albania. Ganimete spotted a hospital that did not look very promising but went in anyway. She was used to the relative development of Yugoslavia; northern Albania, with its abysmal poverty, did not compare well. The conditions of the gynecological ward were terrible, but there was something comforting in the sound of the doctor's voice, especially his dialect, so similar to the *Ghegnisht* variant of Albanian that is spoken in Kosovo. He told her that something was still in her womb after the miscarriage, it had stayed there for the whole time she had been captive of Serbian troops, five days in all. The doctor and the nurses were mystified by her condition, and asked questions. "I told them my story. They asked me, 'What happened? Don't you see how damaged you are?' I said, 'This and that happened.' And they wrote it down. I gave them my name because at that moment I didn't know how to hide my story, and I didn't think that I had to hide it. Now I am going to tell you why I kept silent later. In Albania, I learned that my husband had been killed. After the war, life was much harder for those who were looking for the missing, for the dead. We too had members of our family killed, missing, and somehow I was alive and nobody would talk about me, nor would I talk. I survived and it was very hard, but those who had not gone through the same experience as I, said, 'Others suffered more, someone lost a leg, someone part of their family, they were hit much harder.'"

Ganimete spent the first year of peacetime in the solitary and sad confines of her village, where her brother had told her to stay put. She had no company other than her sister: her mother was still abroad with the rest of the family. Any contact with the outside was very complicated, as there was no functioning phone or mail. She had to take a van, the only public transport available at the time, and travel somewhere else just to find a phone line. When her family returned home, her mother, who was mourning her own brother, killed in the war, took the situation head-on. "Listen to me, I know what happened to you, everything, all. You must be strong after all that happened! It would have been better had they killed you than left you in this condition, because you will suffer all your life. Just listen to me, daughter, take everything and go. You cannot stay here, a little move would do you better, it will be good for your health."

Ganimete wondered why her family was always forced to leave home. As political activists, her brothers had constantly been under police surveillance, and they had to go abroad to escape threats and violence. Now it was she who had to flee. "I made the big mistake of giving an interview to the foreign media. I didn't know that I had to keep it a secret, I didn't know that it was shameful, do you understand? And in the region where I lived, my whole family would be stigmatized by the *rrethi*." She got married and again took the road of exile, chased out not by the Serbian police, but by her closest community.

Like all the other survivors, Ganimete had to live with a paradox, which made their experience unspeakable, not in the sense of indescribable, but in the sense of nasty, as Paul Fussell wrote about the experience of soldiers.[2] They felt the impulse and the need to speak as an act of denunciation of what had happened to them, but they were crushed by overwhelming shame, and by the understanding that nobody was willing to listen.[3] While they were assaulted, they had to be silent, as Shkurta recalled: "They did what they wanted to us and we never dared talk. This is the worst: you didn't dare say anything to Serbs, you didn't even dare say 'Ah!'" Afterward, the first instruction they received from the people closest to them was not to talk. They quickly turned inward, conscious of being marked as different—and stained. They were only capable of inner monologues, like the literary characters that Pat Barker created after the captive women turned into sex slaves by the Greeks in the Trojan war.[4]

We learn from the trauma literature that survivors' silence is internal at first. It is caused by the necessity not to relive a past horrific experience, which may be a subjective choice, though most often is repressed memory, outside the control of the individual's will. Then again, denouncing a suffered violation is what survivors might desire to do, especially if that exposes the perpetrators to condemnation and punishment, and thus transfers onto them the humiliation and powerlessness felt by their victims. This desire to talk finds powerful obstacles in cultural myths and social conventions, which have muted and continue to mute survivors of sexual violence. The silence they keep is not just a complete absence of speech or an imposed ban on communication. Survivors keep silent and talk at different times, for different reasons, with different people, moved by internal urges or stopped by external constraints. They are constantly engaged in managing information about themselves in order to "pass," in Erving Goffman's words, deciding whether "to tell or not to tell; to let on or not to let on: to lie or not to lie; and in each case, to whom, how, when and where."[5]

The Shattering of Language

In the immediate aftermath of their release from their captors, the women were invariably in shock. The end of violence implied a violent return to their senses, which many had lost during the ordeal. They woke up to a naked body that was burned, cut, and bloody. Covering their wounds and their nudity was their first and main concern, and as they felt the presence of their body, they also felt the absence of their voice.[6] They were terrified and in pain, and talking would have meant making an impossible leap to words, which is precisely what Virginia Woolf meant when she wrote that pain resists language.[7] A "speechless terror" grows with pain that "defies communication through language," in the words of Jean Améry, who experienced Nazi torture.[8]

Teuta shut down completely as she was reunited with her family and the other captives. "I lost consciousness. I was so terrified, so upset, that I let my body go, I didn't know anything anymore." Qëndresa returned home after two weeks of detention and violence and could not answer her anxious relatives' questioning. "I was almost crazy, I was so embarrassed that I didn't want to look my father in the eyes, or my mother, and didn't know anything anymore. I didn't know whether it was day or night, nothing at all. I only knew that my life was over, but life continued. I no longer remember how long I was unconscious. I only knew that my mother was feeding me. I couldn't even drink some water with my own hands, I was completely distraught, I felt paralyzed. I know that my mother cleaned me up and changed my clothes. I fell asleep and no longer knew where I was until the next morning. And for one week I was lost. Everything roared all week. I remembered the noise, the noise of those big knives when they came closer to me, of the automatic weapons, of all the beatings, I mean, everything roared, and I cried all the time, I remained locked in my room, unable to go out."

The feeling of helplessness that Qëndresa experienced when she was in the hands of her captors, facing not only sexual torture but a life-threatening situation, stayed with her for a long time.

Often women kept silent because there was simply no need to talk. Their families had heard their screams when they were taken away and saw them distraught and bedraggled when they returned. They knew. And there were more pressing needs. After the war ended, the task of rebuilding and the overwhelming grief of mourning the dead muted all other concerns. Going back home turned into a shock. Which home? As Ganimete tells it, there was not much of their former life left. And her case was not unique. Valbona returned to her village poorer than ever, having lost all she had during the displacement of her family across the hills of central Kosovo. She found only destruction: "It was all reduced to rubbish, they had flattened the house across the meadow to its foundations. At first [Serbs] had pretty much kept the roof because they were stationed in the house and took their rest there, later they flattened it."

Edona's house had been burned at the beginning of the war, and so were Liridona's, Shpresa's, Teuta's, and Fitore's, the latter by her Serbian neighbors. The charred remains of their home—in Albanian, *shpi*, home but also family—looked to them like an accurate representation of their destroyed lives.

In June 1999, after the Kumanovo Agreement that ended the NATO war against Serbia, Serbian security forces withdrew from Kosovo, leaving behind a scarred wasteland. In the vacuum of security created by the inability of the NATO mission, KFOR, to establish order, reprisal attacks against Serbs, their properties, and their religious sites accounted for human losses and a notable destruction of Orthodox churches.[9] However, the scale of the devastation deliberately planned and organized by the Serbian security forces remained unparalleled. A United Nations survey conducted in the summer of 1999 revealed that 64 percent of housing stock assessed had suffered severe damage and an additional 20 percent showed light to moderate damage.[10]

In the Drenica region, destruction was much greater than the national figures. Mosques were similarly affected. The entire old center of Gjakova, with the Ottoman architecture of the wooden shops in the Old Bazaar and the beautiful sixteenth-century Hadum mosque, had turned into piles of charred debris. The same destruction had been delivered to the center of Peja, a lively regional market on the northwestern border with Montenegro, where 80 percent of the houses were heavily damaged.[11] The southern part of the once prosperous mining and industrial city of Mitrovica had been leveled, leaving intact only the Serb neighborhoods across the river Ibar. In Prizren—the old Ottoman town with its Sinan Pasha mosque, also the center of the Catholic Diocese and home to a stately Serbian Orthodox Seminary adjacent to the fourteenth-century church of Bogodorica of Ljeviska—most of the historic sites were spared destruction.[12] The exception was the League of Prizren Complex, a compound of Ottoman-style houses where the first Albanian insurrection for autonomy from Istanbul was organized in the nineteenth century: Serbian troops razed it to the ground on the last day of the war.

Of the major towns, only the center of Gjilan and Pristina had kept their housing stocks standing, though shops had been gutted and apartments pillaged like everywhere else; among the most precious spoils, the VHS players, at the time cutting-edge technology and very common in Albanian households. There was not one urban river, whether the Lumbardh in Prizren, the Bistrica in Peja, or the Ibar in Mitrovica, that was not strewn with kitchen appliances, old clothes, and other spoils of war. Hundreds, if not thousands, of crows, large birds fattened even more by ready available waste, blackened the sky of every city as they rose from their perches to move to their next resting place.

In the rural areas, the devastation had been complete. Through June and July 1999, the UN World Food Programme (WFP) flew its helicopter over Kosovo daily to bring food and supplies to the most remote areas. It was impossible to reach them by truck, as Serbian troops had mined most roads. The view from the sky was a string of half-burned villages, one after another, some of them still smoldering. On June 26, a WFP crew spotted a cluster of burned houses perched on top of a high hill, none of which had a roof.[13] As they landed, they were welcomed by a group of people who said they had not seen a friendly face since the beginning of the war. For the previous two weeks, the villagers had been eating only boiled wheat, as the carcasses of their livestock lay in the fields. The UN crew took note of the situation for a country-wide assessment of war damage: in that village, Serbian security forces had completely or severely burned 80 percent of a total of 109 houses, and partially burned the remaining 20 percent; they had killed 40 percent of the livestock. Of the 870 inhabitants, only 630 were left there, almost two weeks after the ceasefire.[14] That was Shpresa's village.

Teuta and her family left the refugee camp and returned to Kosovo in one truck, "but the road had been destroyed by the war, and because there were no people around and the truck could not take us to the house, it stopped precisely near the place where the incident happened. When it left us there, my two legs buckled under me. As we lie down to sleep, oh my! I could not tell anyone, it was precisely the place where it happened. I was very upset, I didn't want to live, I could not pull myself together. We had returned to Kosovo, and we began our lives from the beginning. The house was burned, nothing was left. The night we came back, we had only one or two mattresses to lie down on."

After more perilous wandering in the mountains, Liridona and her mother went back home, where only a month earlier she had been tortured by Serbian security forces, and from which they had escaped after the murder of her father and her sister. "They told us that they had been buried, though not there, but when we returned, we found their dead bodies. My sister was where I left her, my father also, and because his body was older, he had putrefied more slowly, she was more...I pulled my mother to one side, so she wouldn't see them. The neighbors came over and buried them. My sister had not done anything to anybody, she was a child. My mother died a year after that, she died of heartbreak. As for me, I told you what happened to me and all, but the murder of my sister killed me more than what they did to me. Animals don't do that."

Valbona's grief for the rape and murder of her sister ran deep. When she realized that the eight women, among them her sister, would never come back to the barn that Serbian security forces had turned into a rape camp, she feared the worst but did not know what had happened to them. So she waited, thinking her sister might be back one day because, without the evidence of a dead body, she always had a reason to hope. On July 2, 1999, French NATO troops came to the village of Kozhiça, a village of 572 inhabitants where twenty civilians had been killed and only three of the seventy-seven houses had been left untouched, to dig up three wells that had been suspiciously filled with rocks, pieces of wood, and brush.[15] Under the debris, they found the remains of the eight women. It did hurt very much that they had been left without burial for a long time, "Our hearts became stones."

The exhumation was carried out in the presence of experts from the International Criminal Tribunal for Former Yugoslavia (ICTY). "Only my husband was present when they pulled out his own mother. My uncles on my father's side were there, but not us. The foreigners, whoever they were, I don't know, called every day, they said that they would pull them out, they were looking for them. Now, my husband knew when they did it, but he didn't tell us. About the three sisters killed in the same place as their mother, he said, 'There was only a bag.' They all fit in just one bag, nobody could tell which body was which. They buried them somewhere, in a bag. About my sister, my brother said, 'She lay there as if she was dead, her right arm like this, and the two hands like that, but the right arm didn't seem dead.' My mother-in-law was also there."

The wakes for the two women were held simultaneously, each at their own family's house, and Valbona's first duty, as a married woman, was to sit with the women of her husband's family and host visitors. "Women didn't have rights back then, maybe it's better now. I was very upset. I went to my father's to see my sister for just one hour, not even an hour. I went with a woman from the *fis*, and then I left. I did not stay long enough with my sister, only half an hour. At my husband's, the house was chockablock with women, because my mother-in-law had five daughters and lots of sisters, while my mother was left to receive everyone alone. I said to myself, 'Why don't they let me stay for the whole day by my sister's side?' 'Come on, we have the wake over there!' It was like that back then. Now, I would spend a whole day at my sister's wake, which they didn't let me do. I went back to attend my mother-in-law's wake. I was always very well-behaved. I stayed with my mother only a little."

Fitore stayed closer to her mother: "My mother is like all the other mothers of Kosovo. She went through a lot because eleven people in her family were killed. And even today I don't know how to tell her anything about myself because we all suffered from great trauma. So many bad things happened!"

Ardita felt the pain of a mother: "When I returned home, I found the house burnt, we didn't know where to go or what to do. We were left with some clothes, and some livestock, upset, crying: my daughters were upset, my sons were killed, my husband killed, and I was the head of the family. My life was a catastrophe, but I could not kill myself. I never found my second son, he is still missing. My older son was killed with my in-laws' son and all the other men in a big massacre. When they found their clothes they put them in a warehouse, they came to the municipality and called us, 'Come to identify the clothes of your husband and children.' I found my husband's keys and also my son's, I found their things there. And I found the things of my in-laws' son but found absolutely nothing of my other son. We took those things home, and someone said, 'No, these are not his keys.' So I went back and asked, 'Are these keys for a car or a tractor?' He said, 'They are for a tractor.' When he said that, I left. I went a second time, and I recognized my son's sweater, it was a piece of a torn sweater, and I recognized the keys to their car and said, 'Here, this is his sweater. I made it, I washed it, I did it all.' We took those things, and we went home to cry with my other children."

After the war, families were a world of sorrow. Blerta lost seventeen relatives on her father's side of the family. "My uncle's son was killed at the crossing of Morina. The others were killed in Meja.... We were there. I was with my young daughter, my son, a toddler, and a newborn daughter, three children, and with my mother's sister, my cousin's wife, and my sister's sister-in-law, and after that we went from Meja to Beleg, where what happened happened to everyone." Afërdita lost three cousins in the war, fifteen, twenty, and thirty-four years old, "the young generation in the family, all gone." "My sister died after the war, but she was always troubled after she was raped in Drenica. They had taken her husband to the police station and for three–four days she didn't know where her husband was, whether he was alive or dead. He was an only child and so she went after him to the police station and there she was raped. Everyone said, 'Why did you go into the wolf's mouth?' She thought, 'I am going with my children and will save my husband.'"

The Dead Can't Talk

Having survived the war would have been a reason to rejoice. Yet, being alive after sexual violence was quickly downgraded as worse than death. "It would have been better if you were dead," was the refrain that many survivors heard from their families as they were turned from victims into wrongdoers who had victimized those close to them. This death wish implicitly doubts the innocence of the victims, as in the rape myth that evaluates the criminality of a sexual assault by the degree of violence suffered by the victim. The evidence of lack of consent can only be found in a martyred body or a lifeless corpse. Death is a defense of individual and collective honor in the folktale *Bunari i Çikave* (The girls' well), both a story and the name of a place celebrating a group of girls who jump into a well to their death to avoid being "dishonored."[16] It's not that the survivors did not have similar thoughts, Fatime, among all the others. "I said it one million times, 'Why am I not dead? Oh God, why haven't they killed me there? I am not dead, I am not, but you see, I feel cold inside, it's cold because it always comes back and it hurts here, in my head." However, when the same death wish felt so strongly by almost all survivors was expressed by others, especially the people closest to them, it sounded different.

Both Merita and her husband could have been killed or could have gone missing when Serbian troops raided their home. Instead, after he was beaten and she was gang-raped in his presence, they were still alive, though incapable of moving from the pain and the shock. Merita's husband could only cry, "Today is a black day for me. There is nothing that will give me my life back." When later they reunited with the rest of the family as refugees in Macedonia, after a perilous escape from Kosovo, he was still reeling from his lost honor. "'What are you coming to see? Are you coming to give me condolences or what?' he said to my father, who had come to visit." Merita received the first medical help in the camp and was still in extreme distress:

"The doctor wanted to take me to Skopje. He said, 'Indeed, we must keep her lying down for two weeks.' But my husband did not let me go. Another doctor came, and they gave me four infusions. I felt it was so little, just a crumb of help, to calm me down! My husband cried, 'It would have been better to be dead, better to be dead than what happened to me.'"

In the refugee camp of Çegran, in Macedonia, Nazlie Bala met a thirteen-year-old, a survivor of gang rape, who had not left her tent or uttered a word for almost two months.[17] "Her mother noticed that I was taking statements for the OSCE, but she was pressured by her father-in-law and did not dare seek help, because for the oldest man in the family what happened to that teenage girl brought shame to the family. Every night, he asked his son and his daughter-in-law to kill the girl, because what had happened was a shame for the family." Eventually, the woman found the courage to speak out, and her daughter was invited to join the safe space that women's rights activists had created. There, the girl who had been shocked into silence regained her voice and began to sing along with the other women the songs she had known from childhood.

Selvi Izeti, an experienced psychologist at the Kosova Rehabilitation Centre for Torture Victims (KRCT), has treated a survivor who was deeply burdened by her parents' death wish for her.[18] The woman was raped together with her sister, but she was the only one to survive. Her father never spoke to her again, except on the day on which he buried his other daughter. "I would have liked to bury you as well," he said. Her own mother's comment was, "What a torment is having to face you now!"

I Want to Be Heard

After the initial shock, when they finally found sympathetic listeners, whether among their family or foreign journalists, or ICTY investigators, survivors of rape relished the opportunity to share their stories. It took some time for Vlora and her family to be able to rebuild some sort of normalcy after the vicissitudes of the war, including the fact that they had lost their home. When they finally returned to their town, they met the neighbors whom they had not seen for months. "They all talked about the war, you know, how we had gone through it and so on. I didn't know it was wrong to talk and I told everyone there, 'This happened to me during the war.' I began to talk. When my mother heard me, she said, 'Never again do

I want to hear what you are saying now!' you know, to those neighbors, 'Never again open that conversation with anybody.'" Dutifully, Vlora never raised the issue again or ever answered questions about her experience of the war.

Ganimete was chastised by her mother for talking to journalists, and she understood that her family did not want her to confide in anyone. However, she needed medical attention for her health problems, which were becoming chronic. She went to see a doctor, who immediately directed her to a psychologist who could better treat the "hurt in my heart." It was the year 2000, and the memory of what had happened to her was still fresh, giving her an anger that was becoming an unbearable weight to bear. "It seemed to me that I was talking not to a doctor, but to a prosecutor to whom I wanted to tell everything because I wanted to denounce those people. And I felt sort of weak and talked very slowly. The doctor listened to me for about two hours, no, four hours. I said to him, 'Don't write that I am ill, listen to me, that God's willing I feel better now as I talk because I always had to keep it close to my chest.'"

The chief prosecutor at the ICTY, Carla Del Ponte, sent a team of investigators to interview witnesses and survivors, and visited sites alleged to have been used for rapes and murders of young women during the conflict.[19] Investigators from The Hague came to interview Teuta when she was still in the refugee camp. Informed of her case by her sister, they thought that they could use her testimony to build the prosecution of Slobodan Milošević and other Serbian leaders for war crimes and crimes against humanity. She remembers that there was no hesitation in her voice when she agreed to testify. "In 2002 people from the Tribunal came again for me, sometime in February. In February 2002 I testified against Milošević. I was very happy to tell the court what they had done to me. It was difficult for me to speak in front of him, I felt pain in my body. I don't know how to describe it, I felt it, but I could not wait to talk. And I testified."

The trust built with sympathetic investigators could be easily broken. In the case of Fatime, it was a court translator who intervened, in lieu of her family, perhaps for the same reasons: "I only said that part when they took me and raped me and nothing else. I did not have the courage to talk anymore because as I began, he began to go like this, 'Don't talk!' I don't know why he did not let me tell my story... any time I began to talk, he interrupted me, and I did not dare speak. People forget that I was very young at the time because if it was today, I would talk, and I would know what to do."

Investigators from The Hague met with Merita six times, hoping that they could persuade her to testify. "I hid it from my husband, I hid it because he did not want me to talk, not at all. 'Go ahead! Pick up a walkie-talkie and tell everybody if you wish!' he said, 'let everybody know what happened to us.' But I gave a statement about everything they did. They thanked me. 'You,' they said, 'must go with us to America. There we will change your life. You must go, so you will get better, you will change what is not good in this horrible life.' But I didn't go."

Among close relations, the cost of disclosure might be very high, but it is often unavoidable. Shpresa waited to be alone with her husband to tell him. "I said to myself, 'Let him say what he wants.' You know, there had been moments when my husband had screamed at me, but this wasn't something to scream over, this was war. When we finally came together in a refugee camp in Albania, after weeks of separation, he asked, 'How did it go? How did you get out of Kosovo?' and everything else because he knew nothing, we had had no contact with my husband for a long time. 'Yes, I will tell you something that maybe....' He said, 'That's war. I didn't even know whether I would see you and the children again.' I told him, 'They came in'—he had heard this already from his own nephew—'four men took us.' Perhaps I didn't want to tell all, perhaps my husband didn't want me to tell him everything, but he saw the marks on my legs. I still have scars today, although at that point I was beginning to heal, two and a half months had passed. And I said, 'Yes, I will tell you everything.' My husband cried so much that I couldn't talk anymore, I had to stop, I talked and paused, talked and paused."

Fitore decided that her boyfriend should know, even though the gossip in her social circle was that he would no longer marry her once he knew, or that he would marry her only to honor her late brother, whom he loved dearly as his best friend. "He kept me. He never said anything, he never reminded me of what I told him, and I credit him for never reminding me."

At first, Fatime said nothing. However, she felt so bad for so long and became so withdrawn from her husband that he became suspicious. "I postponed telling him, yes, I postponed it one million times, because I wanted and did not want to tell him. But I overdid it, and he said, 'I don't trust you anymore, you cheated on me with someone else, you are nothing for me anymore. Let's split!' I cried and swore to him, but did not persuade him, I could not. So I said, 'OK, I will tell you. This, this, and this happened to me. Your father knows. They shot at us, but he was spared and saw everything, and protested. Can't you see? He always defended me. But this happened. It was a war. Did you like being wounded? You did not, but you are wounded. Do you see that there are different destinies? You over there, and I somewhere else. I was left alone with a child and found myself in a situation with no way out, where a person only wants to say, 'Take what you want, but spare my life.' You must believe that I am clean. Serbs raped me, I did not want that, they took me by force. I am standing in front of you clean. Do as you please, if we split I will find a place, and people with whom I can stay. I am who I am.' He said, 'Oh no, I understood.'"

How happy was Edona's husband when he saw she had survived the war! She too felt relieved, "but I had a problem, how to tell my husband. The neighbor came to visit and said, 'It's wonderful that you survived.' I froze." For the next few days, when visitors talked over the events of the war, Edona quickly turned the conversation to them and never said a word about her story. Then one day she felt she could no longer hold her secret and sat down with her husband. "'I want to tell you something.' 'Come on, you have nothing to tell me.' 'I want to talk, I decided. It's better.' 'You have nothing to tell me. It was a war. They could have cut your legs, they could have cut your hands, they could have killed the boy. You were in their hands, you and I, and he and everybody. And never talk to me about this business. Never. I am proud of you.' Blessed that day when he told me those words! It seemed to me that I was born a second time and that I had no more wounds in my body."

The day Ajshe went back home, she saw her husband move from distress and shock to happiness. "When he saw us it was as if the entire world were his. He hugged us and said, 'Oh God, I got my life back seeing you once again. Oh my son, what happened to you?' because the child was a little black and blue where they had beaten him. And the child, 'They did not beat me, but once or twice I saw....' I burst into wailing. My husband said, 'Is it possible to leave us alone for three–four hours?' This is what he said. I cried. I said, 'I am dead, they killed me, leave me, I am who I am. I went to give help to your people, without foreseeing that they could do this to me. I am not what I was before this was done to me, but what happened happened, and this is who I am now.' And he took his head into his hands and went into the room, he said, 'Come on woman, it will be OK.'"

It was not OK. It got much worse within a month. Ajshe could not take the name-calling: "Eating bread three, four times a day is too much, and so is hearing bad words four times a day...words, words, words. Sometimes he came to apologize, 'Woman, forgive me because I know that you didn't do it for pleasure, but I cannot accept it.' But how much money were his apologies worth?" They have been separated ever since.

How did Kimete make the decision to tell her husband? "Some twenty-thirty families knew what happened, they were there. I said, 'Better I tell him that he hears it from someone else.' I began to talk. Except that I expected he would take it better. He just argued, argued the whole time. One day he got up and left the house. I did not hear from him for seven years. I heard he emigrated. His parents were dead, thus he never came back. I tried to establish contact with him, and he said, 'Don't contact me.' I thought about going to the TV program *Missing People* and telling them, 'I have no contact with him.' I raised my children alone, they are good but withdrawn. We did not deserve this life. I told you my daughters have an education, and they all have an apartment and a salary of their own. I told them, 'Don't trust people.'"

Knowing and Not Knowing

Who knows and who does not know? Who has been told and who has not? What do they know? There are no simple answers to those questions. As Vlora put it, "My family, the people closest to me, all the uncles, and so on, knew everything, and I know that also the neighbors knew, but they never knew."

If there was one person in which Blerta could confide, it would have been her sister-in-law. They knew each other as girls, had grown up together, and had become young wives at the same time. Blerta had been so happy when she married her brother. Family ties kept them even closer. "She said, 'Blerta, there is something wrong with you. I know about the war and so on.' I said, 'They raped me, yes, but I don't want the children to know, my husband, to know.'" Blerta did not fear her sister-in-law's judgment and found in her a good listener and a friend. What she had not considered was the possibility that her friend would in turn confide in someone else, tell her own husband, for example. Once Blerta's brother and mother knew, the secret so closely held was in the open within the family. Has her husband also heard? "I don't know. Maybe yes, but he never talks about it. I cannot really tell yes or no. He knows that there is a women's organization working with survivors, but he doesn't ask me where I go when I go there or what I do."

What happened to Blerta in the war remains the elephant in the room. She doesn't want it to become a topic of conversation in the *rrethi* because she cannot suffer people's reaction, their unrelenting gossip, the shame that they make her feel, and that will be transmitted to her children. "I would like to talk but don't have the courage. Not that I don't have the courage, maybe I do have the courage, but I wonder, what will happen after? I want my children to walk in the streets with their heads up." Is she afraid that casting her eyes down as a defense from stigma is a behavior that she will pass to the children along with the story of her violation?[20] That's perhaps why she prefers to balance "knowing and not knowing" at home, and when she leaves the house to meet with counselors, she tells her children that she talks to professionals about "something bad" that happened to her during the war.

Teuta got married in 2009. "Until then, I couldn't accept anybody in my life, I felt the need to be by myself. My husband asked me only at the beginning. I told him, 'This and this happened,' and he was much more upset about what happened to me than I was. We never talked about it again, and he never reminds me, never offends me. Only now, when he hears something, he tells me, 'Don't get upset because you don't have anything to be upset about.' Oh my! Do I have his support!" Teuta's family knows. Her own father was in the basement, hiding with the other older men when she was taken away. When she returned in the morning, "as I said before, I lost consciousness and never, whether they understood it or not, did they ask me about it." Had they asked, she would not have been able or willing to answer. Her body, however, spoke for her. When she went to the bathroom to clean up, she wanted to do it alone and tried to keep even her mother out, but her mother got in to help. "I couldn't see my back, nobody can see their back, but when my mother saw it, she saw horror. I had many marks all over my body. I had wounds because they took me to a burnt house. The debris on the floor cut me, but I did not feel it because I was dead, my body was dead." Teuta has always been quick in shutting down her mother's reminiscence of the war. "Let it go, mom, it's all in the past," she says when she sees her too upset.

"A mother is very dear," says Shpresa, "a mother feels even more pain than her children for what happens to them, and I don't plan to ever talk to my mother about the incident." Shpresa too was kidnapped in front of everyone, and everyone knows. "My oldest sister-in-law told me, 'What happened to you happened to everyone.'" Yet, Shpresa has refused to discuss the matter and has tried to hide all evidence of the incident. In the beginning, when she was still in the camps, her legs were in terrible pain from cuts and burns, but she tried to bury that pain and hid the wounds. Afraid of the revealing intimacy of the washroom, she refused her sister-in-law's invitation to go in together, as all other women did. She went in alone and cleaned up as fast as she could so as not to show her body.

Adelina's mother was a victim as well, and a courageous one who tried to resist the assault and defend her daughters. Adelina knows this because she heard her mom screaming as she grabbed a weapon from her torturer, "Do what you want with me, but leave them." All her sisters suffered the same violence, but none of them has since talked about it. None of her sisters even acknowledge the incident, and since they were separated, though they could hear each other's screams, nobody can claim to have been a witness to the other's ordeal. Her mother never went over the events of that day. She never talked, never acknowledged it. She moved away from home to join a son who lives abroad, never to return to Kosovo.

Everyone in Qëndresa's own family knows, but she talks only to her sister about it and finds great support from her. As for the rest, "We all lived together, but after what happened to me, you didn't hear one word about it because we are not very open, we don't talk." Her brother, a child during the war, still suffers from the beating he got when he jumped to help her. "However, he has no desire to talk about this, absolutely, never. Both of my brothers don't even want to mention it. If someone mentions the war, they leave the room because they want nothing to do with it. But I know that they know. As they say, 'the heart knows.'" Still protective of her little brother, Vlora remains silent because of him: "I don't like that he feels bad because it happened when I went out to get some milk for him, I don't like that he feels guilty. As far as knowing, he knows everything but he never touches this topic and neither do I."

Psychologist Selvi Izeti, who treats scores of survivors, sees a pattern in this behavior: "There is an internal agreement, an agreement not to speak, not verbalize, sort of, I know that this happened, you know that this happened, but we don't talk about it. I often understood, for example, that the men pretend not to know, but they know."[21] The consequences of knowing could be serious. Lumnije, who was an adolescent during the war, did not want anyone to know, or her chances to marry and have children would have evaporated. What did the fiancé of Fitore's younger sister know? "Nothing happened to her, and we have a medical certificate to prove it. But the fiancé said, 'I am no longer marrying you.' We had to return the money he had paid for her through the matchmaker, and we didn't have that kind of money." Liridona sent her mother to speak to her fiancé just before they got married. "Maybe she told him more or less everything, but he never spoke with me and never asked me, never in my life."

Qëndresa summoned all her courage to tell her story to the man she met a few years after the war when they began talking seriously about getting married. She knew it was a risky gamble for her. At first, he struggled with the idea, but in fact, "he accepted everything. He said, 'You didn't want that to happen, it was the war, it could have happened to me too, it could have happened to my sister, you did not look for it.'" With her husband's family, she had to be very cautious, since they knew nothing, but they found out because "someone said something," and relationships with them became cold. She felt lucky because her husband chose her over his parents. And so felt Vlora at first, when thanks to the mediation of an aunt she met a young man and married him: "I had his words in my mind, 'Your past will never bother me, and I will never mention it.' That did it." The troubles started immediately after her husband told his mother. He expected that she would understand. Vlora does not live near her husband's family, also because she knows that she would occupy a lower position than her sisters-in-law in the internal order of the household. She never visits her mother-in-law and never receives her visits. When her husband returns home from seeing his mother, she sees him upset and begins to argue with him. Yet, they kept the family together.

In psychologist Izeti's experience, only the minority of survivors are open within the family about what happened to them, because talking uncovers the pretense of not knowing. Those who are open with their families pay for it with ostracism, if not further violence. She mentioned the case of a woman who had been married for just five or six months and was pregnant when she was raped.[22] She was not with her family at the time, but with other relatives and neighbors. When she told her husband, he said, "Let's keep it between us." Shortly after, someone who was also present when she was raped told the mother-in-law. Without taking into consideration that the couple had decided to stay in the marriage, her husband's family insisted on taking her back to her mother, pregnant as she was, and then they went to pick up her baby daughter, who was never seen again. The woman's anguish for the loss of her daughter is still evident. Such stories are cautionary tales for any survivor; they may risk losing their children or their families. In

Fitore's words: "I don't want my husband's family to know because I have children and I wouldn't know where and how to raise them on my own."

Talk and the Creation of Stigma

In 2002, when Teuta confronted Milošević and other Serbian officials indicted at The Hague, she did so as a protected witness. Yet the tribunal did not succeed in keeping her identity hidden, and she has since relocated to a third country. "My experience was very bad with those who are farther from me in the village, not with my family, which supported me. I no longer wanted to live in that place, I asked for help to move because I didn't have a life there. My family also agreed with my decision because they said that there was no life for me in the village. How does the saying go? 'Freedom or death.' And when I came to this new country, I asked to go to a place where there were no Albanians. When I came here, they took me to a mountain, and I said, 'I don't want to meet any Albanians.' Only after five, or six years, I began little by little to meet Albanians again, but no, at the beginning I didn't want to meet them, I didn't want to see any of them, I didn't want to know any of them. I socialized much more with non-Albanians, people from here rather than from that place because they didn't know what had happened to me."

The notoriety acquired by Teuta through the media reports of the Milošević trial uncovered the secret that surrounded her war experience, and although she was able to testify in court, she was silenced by local society. The most powerful authority that imposes silence on survivors of sexual violence is not a single person, it is the ordered universe in which they live, which punishes exposure. The parting words of Valbona's mother on the occasion of her marriage were, "Don't talk!" That teaching has an enduring life for women, who have little or no power in the family, let alone the broader society.

As a human rights defender, Nazlie Bala was investigating an ethnic murder in a rural community when she learned the same lesson.[23] Begrudgingly allowed in the *oda*, the men's room, she was joined by the grandmother of the family, who was called to keep her company. When Nazlie asked her to say something, the grandma replied: "What do I have to say? When I was little, they told me, 'Be silent, you are too young to speak.' When I grew up a little and reached puberty, they said, 'Be silent, because it's shameful if you talk.' When I got married, they told me, 'You, as a woman in the *fis*, cannot talk.' When I got older, they told me, 'Be silent, because you don't know anything, you're stupid.'"

Women who know their place do not talk. To remind them of the order reigning in the world where they live, there is the *rrethi*, the social circle of family and neighbors, with their endless gossip that spreads all news, whether good or bad, very fast. Adding superstition to this dynamic produces further marginalization. Counseling survivors, Selvi Izeti learned from several of them that even during the mass expulsion of Albanians in the spring of 1999, though they had barely escaped death, they were shunned, whereas those who had been wounded in different circumstances were immediately helped.[24] Nobody let rape survivors even get on a tractor, as if they had some infectious disease. The thinking, a mix of superstition and fear of sullen honor, was, "You will bring us bad luck because we know what happened to you and it might happen to us because it happened to you."

After the war, relentless gossip set in. Merita could not stand the flippant and accusatory comments about survivors. "Someone said, 'She did it for pleasure.' Maybe someone does it for pleasure, pardon my expression, but with another Albanian. *Shki*, what should I call them? Serbs, the occupiers, came to our house. They came to take us from our place and our home, to take our life, to kill us, to rape us, to beat us, to do all that. This is a crime, how come they don't know that this happens during the war?" Teuta regrets mostly the lack of support from her local community. "A person in this situation does not need offense added to the trauma. They don't say it directly, but when two people get together, they go, 'This happened to her,' 'Did you hear this?' 'They did this to her.' And on top of that, the neighbors come to your home and say, 'I heard this, I heard that about you.' We, survivors, are very interesting to people, but we are not supported by people. For example, they all knew what happened, they all saw me, and they still offended me."

Qëndresa finds that "the *rrethi* is perfidious. I wanted so much to talk to someone outside the family, but if I went out alone, in the village, in our village, they would say, 'Oh look! The wife of such and such is going out. Where is she going? What is she doing?' My family has been supportive, but they kept me hidden at home. But you cannot keep the story hidden, it was war, it happened everywhere." She was left asking herself again and again, "Where can I go to talk with another woman as much as I like? And where do I go to hear someone telling me of a case that maybe is worse than mine?"

The neighbors' malicious surveillance made life difficult for Afërdita. "They would say, 'Eiii! This merry widow is going out to have fun somewhere!' But I went out anyway. I wasn't interested in having fun or not having fun. But because they gossiped, I got dressed up and made up, put on pants, and went out and didn't give it five cents. If someone wanted to follow me, where would I go to hide?"

Kosovo is a very small country. It is made up of even smaller communities. There is no place that is far enough from home. The new social environment that Ganimete found in her husband's town was no better than the one back home. "I was judged. They never wanted to be with me, they wanted to be with others, they very often treated me like a crazy person, even my family, my husband's closest *rrethi*. Whenever I said something, they said, 'Leave her alone, she suffered a lot during the war.' The moment I asked for something that was my right, the moment I said anything, or went to a social gathering, if somebody said something and I said, 'No, it's not like this, but like that,' because I wanted to participate in the conversation as an equal, they said, 'Leave her alone, maybe she says that because she suffered during the war.' I did not want to let them say that about me, I did not want to be always linked to that war, and I did not want to be connected with that past. I wanted to be told, 'Yes, good, you are right if that's what you think.' Anytime people in my husband's *rrethi* used a word I didn't know because I am from another village and we have a different dialect... for example, if they said, '*Hoshxhollden*' whatever, '*Hoshbollden*' [Turkish for welcome], they would say, 'She doesn't know that word because she suffered a lot during the war.' I knew that somebody respected me for what I suffered, but nobody in my village used the word '*Hoshxhollden*'—'*Hoshbollde*,' do you understand? Everybody connected me to the war, and the worst is that I felt very bad. On an everyday basis, I always felt very bad."

Over time, Vlora became more withdrawn and less likely to leave the bedroom to greet guests. She did not talk at gatherings and reacted sharply when someone asked her a question. "Somehow, when I had something to say, they treated me like an idiot, and I know that when they talked about me, about my case, I got lost somehow, I didn't know what to do, how to behave, or what to say. My paternal aunt came to visit, and I remember I was wearing a big, long sweater since we didn't have many clothes because everything had been burned. I sat down on the couch like everyone else, but before sitting down, I remember that I had pulled my sweater, and adjusted it. My aunt, who knew about me, approached me and took me to another room. 'My girl, it didn't happen, right? Are you pregnant? Go to the doctor for a check-up.' 'Aunt, I did go already.' 'But with this sweater here, didn't something else happen?' 'No, aunt, I went to the doctor.' Then there were my friends, my cousins, who came to visit and said, 'We are getting married, we are creating a family.' And the way they looked at me! They looked in such a way that it touched me at my weakest point. I always said, 'Why, God, are people like that? Why do they have a bad spirit?' For example, come New Year's Eve or Bajram...when Bajram comes, the whole house says, 'Happy Bajram!' I felt like crying, and the whole house cried for me. And at that moment, I faced a very difficult situation because, for example, when they wished 'Happy Bajram!' to the others, to my sisters, they all hugged each other. With me, it was always different. And in this case, I always felt terrible because they all looked at me differently. Why do they look at me differently? They treat me differently."

The lack of support from other women killed Ganimete's spirit. "If I said, 'This happened to me in the war,' I would be put down. Women always told me, 'Let it go, don't tell anyone.' You know, people did not want to deal with this issue. The worst is that it made me feel guilty. The fact is, I am not guilty, but the fact is also that the *rrethi a*nd people made me feel guilty, ashamed, and at no time did I want to feel ashamed."

Vlora experienced the same. "Women are always sticking their noses into someone else's business. I saw women whispering, and I knew they were talking about me. I felt psychologically ill. You see people talking about you. They say, 'Do you know what happened?' What to do? You keep to yourself, you know? I was growing up confined at home and ill, and they began to say I was ill. Why am I not as active as the others? Why don't I go out like that one? Why don't I dress like this one? Why don't I take care of myself like that one? All the others were in some way higher or better than me. I was the lowest. The words they said went to my head; they whisper into my head all the time, and they make me anxious."

"Acceptance" might be a vague term, but the lack of it denotes a key aspect of the situation in which a stigmatized individual finds herself. When those who surround a survivor fail to pay the respect that she anticipates must be due to her as a person with a specific role in society, she feels rejected and echoes this denial, by thinking that some of her qualities justify it.[25] Vlora saw her younger sister get married, but nobody wanted her. "When my sister came to visit, she instilled some sort of hatred in me. They made me feel bad, like a retarded person, like I didn't want to be married, I was sick.... They said things such as, 'She got married, she has a daughter, we are happy with her, she has shoes, clothes, she is happy....' My father said many things that made me feel bad psychologically and spiritually. I never expected that from my father, nor from my sister.... And my mother too said things like, 'Shush,' or 'Go wear this,' 'Wear what you had before,' 'Don't hurt me,' 'Don't make me feel bad.'... They put me in the position of being jealous. But no, I am glad that my sister is married and she has a daughter and all, but they put me in that position to hurt me."

Ganimete anticipated pressure and criticism from family and community by hiding from public view. "I didn't want to go anywhere, and I didn't want to know anybody, I absolutely didn't want to. This place is judgmental, and I didn't want anybody to know me as a person, where I lived, where I was from, or what happened. Whenever someone talked about what happened to them during the war, I always left. When the topic of rape during the war comes up, a victim always thinks that everyone knows everything about her, do you understand? And at that time, I thought that after the war, who knows, my name circulated everywhere."

The fear of being identified and labeled was overwhelming from day one, as in the experience of Teuta in the refugee camps immediately after the war: "I took some tablets and lay down all the time. I didn't want to get out, and I didn't want to see anybody. I didn't want to meet anybody because I said to myself, 'Everybody knows what happened to me,' as if they knew as if they saw everything." It was a combination of withdrawal and imposed seclusion that kept Qëndresa from resuming the life she had before the war. When the school called her father asking for her, she told him to tell them that she had left the village. "I said, 'They don't know I am here.' I did not go out once, never, never, and no friend or anybody else came to see me, nobody. I always stayed inside the house. How could I go out when someone could see me and know what I had survived?"

For Blerta, even accompanying her child on a simple school field trip was daunting. There was no chance she would go, "I am so afraid. For a very long time, I didn't go anywhere, absolutely anywhere. I didn't have the courage. I couldn't hang out where there were many people. I only wanted to stay home alone, not see anyone." Fatime fears that her withdrawal made her a bad mother. "I didn't raise my children as I should have. I never took them to the park just five minutes from my home. I couldn't; I didn't have the strength to leave the house." Her husband had to force her to attend a surprise party because he could not even coax her into joining him in town for coffee, a simple pleasure she no longer enjoys. At the party, she felt lost. "I stayed in a corner the whole time. Not because they moved away from me, it was I who didn't feel well. I always found some reason not to go to the center of town, not to see anyone or be seen by anyone who knew me, who knew all that happened to me, and I stayed home, you know, alone." Vlora had the same reaction during a party at her home. "I couldn't wait to go to my room and be alone there. I felt calm only there and relaxed because I was away from people. It felt good that I was far from their words."

The war devastated families and communities to such an extent that mourning the dead and celebrating the living occupied and continues to occupy the lives of survivors in ritualized collective remembrances. Sexual violence survivors could never go along with this custom. For a long time, Edona avoided paying her condolences to relatives or acquaintances. "I couldn't cross the threshold because I thought, if I go through that door, the women will say, 'This happened to you,' and even though they didn't, all the same, I thought that they would say it. And I did not go anywhere. I stayed home." Ardita avoided going anywhere at all. "I never dared go out. I didn't even go to a women's meeting because someone would gossip. I always stayed home. I only went to the doctor for checkups because I was sick and nowhere else. I have many illnesses, including high sugar levels and high blood pressure. I am the head of the family, and I am sick."

The Strongest Link: An Oral History of Wartime Rape Survivors in Kosovo. Anna Di Lellio and Garentina Kraja, Oxford University Press. © Oxford University Press 2025. DOI: 10.1093/9780197699324.003.0008

8

Justice

At 9:00 a.m. on Saturday, March 11, 2006, the two guards on duty at the United Nations Detention Unit in the Scheveningen Penitentiary Facility at The Hague unlocked the cells of E1 wing.[1] On weekends, the detainees slept in before their exercise. "Good Morning!" called a guard opening the cell of Slobodan Milošević, the most famous defendant in the trials conducted by the International Criminal Tribunal for Former Yugoslavia (ICTY). There was no answer from the president of Serbia, who never exercised, but was scheduled to take medications for his hypertension every morning. The guards decided to let him sleep a bit longer. Only when they got back to the cell block at 10 a.m., they realized that something was wrong. They called him again, shook his foot, tried to detect a pulse, but got no response. Milošević was dead. His widow, Mirjana Marković, living in Moscow, was quick to comment on CNN, "The Hague tribunal has killed my husband," a conclusion shared by family and political allies.[2] Forensic investigation confirmed instead that Milošević had died of natural causes, from a heart attack. An autopsy found no poison or any other chemical substance in his body that might have contributed to the death.

The first head of state to be tried by international justice had been indicted on May 24, 1999, in the midst of the Kosovo war, for war crimes and crimes against humanity in Kosovo, Bosnia Herzegovina, and Croatia. His trial had lasted a little more than fifty-six months since his first appearance in court on July 3, 2001, and it ended without a verdict. It was not what the chief prosecutor Carla Del Ponte had hoped for, as she made clear in her opening statement to the trial: "The history of the disintegration of the former Yugoslavia and the fratricidal conflicts of another age which it brought about is a complex process which must be written by many people. This Tribunal will write only one chapter, the most bloody one, the most heartbreaking one as well; the chapter of individual responsibility of the perpetrators of serious violation of international humanitarian law."[3]

Among the 124 witnesses for the prosecution were five Albanian women called to testify against the defendant, as the charge of sexual assault, prominent in the Bosnia-Herzegovina indictment, was added to the Kosovo indictment in October 2001, mostly owing to pressure from human rights organizations.[4] "Sexual assault" in this context was intended as a form of persecution; it included rape as well as all other attacks to the fundamental human right of physical integrity, such as torture and any cruel, inhuman, or degrading treatment of a sexual nature. The death of Milošević closed his case, but not the case against his co-defendants, a "Who's Who" of Serbian politics. Among them, the president of Serbia, Milan Milutinović; the deputy prime minister of the Federal Republic of Yugoslavia and head of the Kosovo Joint Command of Army and Police, Nikola Šainović; and the chief of the Yugoslav Army General Staff, General Dragoljub Ojdanić.[5] The minister of internal affairs of Serbia, Vlajko Stojilikovič, was also part of the indictment, but he was never transferred to the ICTY; he shot himself on the steps of the National Assembly of Serbia on April 11, 2002, on the day the Law on Cooperation with the Hague Tribunal was passed, allowing his extradition to The Hague.[6]

A few months before Milošević's death, more defendants were added to the original group, all on the same charges: the commander of the Third Army, General Nebojša Pavković; the commander of the Yugoslav Army Pristina Corps, Vladimir Lazarević; the head of the Serbian Ministry of Internal Affairs for Kosovo, Sreten Lukić; and the Assistant Minister of the Ministry of Internal Affairs of Serbia and Chief of the Ministry's Public Security Department, Vlastimir Djordjević.[7] None of them had been accused of having "physically perpetrated any of the crimes charged, personally," but of having "planned, instigated, ordered, committed or otherwise aided and abetted in a deliberate and widespread or systematic campaign of terror and violence directed at Kosovo Albanian civilians living in Kosovo in the FRY."[8]

The verdict for the six remaining defendants, after Milošević's death and Stojilikovič's suicide, finally arrived in 2009. As Chief Judge Lord Ian Bonomy, a former judge of Scotland's Supreme Court, read the judgment, those once powerful men sat in the very back of the court, behind three rows of defense lawyers, expressionless. With the exception of Milutinović, who was acquitted on all counts, all the defendants were found guilty either of participating in, or aiding and abetting a joint criminal enterprise to change the ethnic balance of Kosovo that targeted the Albanian population.[9]

In 2011, Vlastimir Djordjević received a similar judgment.[10] The Court stopped short of concluding that "sexual assault" had been a tool of the campaign of ethnic cleansing planned and executed by the defendants. The judges did find that the survivors who testified had been credible, and that the sexual assaults described by them had happened, but they could not establish without reasonable doubt that the defendants knew of or could foresee the commission of such crimes. With one exception, General Pavković, all were acquitted of the charge.

Years earlier, Dragoljub Kunarac, Radomir Kovac, and Zoran Vuković, all members of a Bosnian Serb military unit in Foča, had been found guilty of rape, which they personally used as an instrument of terror and arbitrarily applied in detention centers.[11] Journalist Slavenka Drakulić, an observer at the trial, wrote about the unbearable pain of the many women who testified against the defendants, a pain she could hear and feel despite the screen that hid the witnesses from the public.[12] It must have been a harrowing experience, but Bosnian witnesses faced their torturers and saw them sentenced to long prison terms.

It was different for witnesses from Kosovo. They thought they would be vindicated by speaking out against the instigators, the organizers, and the commanders of their torturers. They felt protected by the power of the court. They could not have known how ill-prepared that court was, despite the experience garnered in the trials against Bosnian perpetrators, to prosecute sexual assault as a crime of war and a crime against humanity.

Though public knowledge of widespread rape during the Kosovo War had been ensured by several media reports as early as April 1999 and by the investigations of human rights groups in the summer of 1999, sexual assault was arguably a concern of relative urgency for the office of the prosecutors at The Hague. They collected very little information on this particular crime before the first Kosovo-related indictment against Milošević and his co-defendants, and when they finally added sexual assault to the other charges, they failed to gather more evidence. By their own account, the prosecutors blame their lack of success only partially on the unwillingness of survivors to testify. Facing an overwhelming number of crimes, and under pressure for time, they exercised discretion on what to prioritize and what evidence to collect. Sexual violence was never a priority.[13]

At The Hague, sexual violence was prosecuted as a war crime and also a crime against humanity. In Bosnia, mass detention sites where women were systematically raped, the so-called rape camps, had sadly created the opportunity for the testimonies of so many witnesses that it had been impossible to disregard the crime of sexual violence as part of a strategy of ethnic cleansing. In Kosovo, prosecutors could count only on the evidence of discrete cases. Neither the prosecutors nor the judges understood how to handle traumatized witnesses who contradicted themselves, who mixed up dates, who could not remember some details of their experience, and who were exposed to the aggressive, often offensive cross-examination by the defense—in the case of Milošević, conducted by the defendant himself, an arrogant man who showed only contempt for the court and the witnesses.

At times, even the sharp chief prosecutor Sir Geoffrey Nice found himself incapable of shielding a witness of sexual violence from the aggressiveness of the defendant. When the truthfulness of protected witness K31, a teenager who was held for days in Prishtina hospital and used as a sex slave, was challenged by Milošević, the prosecutor raised the issue of "whether a man who has no apparent sympathy for victims should be allowed to cross-examine witnesses like this." Judge May upheld the right of the defendant to cross-examine witnesses, and Nice apologized for his objection, by citing his own inexperience about "the associated problems of this type of witness."[14]

Facing Milošević

On April 8, 2002, Teuta had her first day in court at the ICTY. Her identity protected by a number, she stood in front of prosecutor Cristina Romano, Chief Judge Robert May, and Slobodan Milošević for most of the morning's closed session, which lasted more than four hours. During her testimony, she had to search her memory to avoid even the smallest contradiction with her initial statement during the preparatory stage of the trial, or with her own words during the same session. She had to describe in excruciating detail what had happened to her on the night of March 29, 1999. The most difficult part was answering Milošević's leading questions during cross-examination without being too distracted by her own emotions. "When I saw Milošević, it seemed to me that each of my legs weighed two hundred kilos. I didn't even know how I felt, I just said to myself, 'Why did this man do that?'"

Her deposition was consistent and straightforward. There were no KLA fighters in her village, just the usual unarmed and un-mobilized civilians, although she had heard of a base three villages distant. Even her brothers had not sought out the KLA until they were expelled from their home and found protection with the guerrillas located in mountains nearby. When a mix of Serbian forces arrived, both police and army (easily distinguishable from their uniforms, blue for the former and greenish-brown for the latter), they took up stations on the second story of a house and began to snipe downward. The usual sequence of terrorizing ensued.

First they beat up a refugee from another village, quite badly, because he had dared to ask to speak with the commander, an Albanian-speaking policeman previously known to him. Then they systematically robbed the civilians, both men and women, of valuables and documents, and began to force-march them first to a field, then into a basement, then back to the field for more beatings, then back to the houses. Five men never made that return. To those who cried from sheer terror, the soldiers said, "You shouldn't cry. You should have thought [about it] earlier, because now you're at war with the state. But NATO will come and help you."[15]

Men and women were then separated, with the men taken to the second story of a house, and women to a cowshed, where Teuta was picked out, along with others, and pushed into another house and gang-raped. Early on the morning of March 30, the soldiers ordered the villagers to leave. But where to go? "You are going to Albania and you will live there as if in America," was the answer.[16] In a final act, before they set off toward Albania, Serbian forces held back forty men from the group. Those men have not been found since.

Milošević contested Teuta's testimony by reframing the events of March 1999, according to his line of defense, and presenting the war as one of national defense against terrorists. Why would soldiers shoot if they did not have an enemy? Didn't she say the KLA were nearby? Wouldn't protection from the shooting be the most plausible reason for pushing villagers into a basement? Milošević tried alternately to insinuate that his army was fighting terrorist-separatists and that the armed men who had attacked her village might have been not Serbs but Albanians, KLA fighters. He found it unbelievable that police officers could command soldiers and even more unbelievable that Serbs spoke Albanian. He disputed her memory of the forty men who were separated from the rest after soldiers had burned homes and raped women, and who had been missing ever since: Were they really forty? Fewer? More? What were their names? Why did the others leave for Albania, lining up with hundreds of other displaced people, if no police or army escorted them? He even suggested that one of the many displacements to which Teuta and the others were subjected was indeed inspired by noble intentions. Milošević asked her: "Wasn't the case that they wanted to protect you from the danger, to get you away from the danger of that shooting that was taking place in front of you, or not?" And Teuta answered: "There was no danger whatsoever. The danger was coming from them."[17]

Teuta did not buckle under pressure. She carefully listened to an interpreter who had to repeat Milošević's wording, as some of the questions were at times so leading or absurd as to be incomprehensible. Once she lost it, "I snapped at him because he tried to make me look like a liar." She calmly went over the events of those three days, from March 28 to 30, 1999, once again. No, surely police and soldiers "were not protecting me, and there was no fighting. They were shooting downwards, but there was no fighting in the meantime. It was only them, shooting downwards into the village. And I said—I did not say the KLA was in a nearby village. I said it was stationed three villages away from my village."[18] And no, she and the villagers did not want to go to Albania. Though nobody was escorting them, all the roads were crowded with threatening police and army and dotted with checkpoints that served as interrogation points for all the displaced. There was no way they could stay in Kosovo.

Teuta tried to halt the needlessly detailed cross-examination, which was focused on discrediting her by exposing minor inconsistencies in the testimony: "I will not answer this question. I came here just for what regards my case, what happened to me."[19] She had gone to The Hague to pursue justice for what she and other women endured on the night of March 29, 1999, when they were taken to different houses and gang-raped by soldiers as a policeman stood guard at the door, controlling the rapists' shifts. Milošević's line of questioning of her story of collective violence against her and the other women in the village took off on a very hostile and offensive path. First, he sowed doubts: "I'm sorry to hear what happened to you, if it happened to you, but my question is: What proof do you have that this did happen to you?" to which she answered: "I did not come here to lie. That happened. I'm not here to lie. That is true." He insisted: "Yes, but this is a very serious crime which in any proceedings needs to be corroborated with evidence. Do you have any evidence in addition to your statement?" Judge May had to intervene: "Well, that will be...that will be it for the Prosecution. Whether corroboration is required is a matter of law. It's not required in this Tribunal for such an allegation."[20]

Undeterred in his strategy of discrediting the witness, Milošević continued to prod her, attributing her lack of initiative to the cultural backwardness of Albanian society: Why had she not immediately reported the rape suffered at the hand of the soldiers? And why had she not asked for their names? When Teuta acknowledged that there were many rape victims in Kosovo two years after the war, and admitted that survivors had remained silent, Milošević tried to make it appear as if NATO troops were responsible for the sexual violence, deflecting the blame from his own troops: "Do you know whether heads of state or government whose troops are stationed in Kosovo are being held responsible for that?"[21] It was not the first time that Milošević attempted to turn accusations against Serbian troops to other actors. In the cross-examination of another protected witness, K15, also a victim of rape, he said he felt sorry for her but was sure that the perpetrators were common criminals who would be arrested by the Serbian army and police, and pointed at the situation in postwar Kosovo as catastrophic: "When Serbs ran it, there was no rape. But rape is a speciality of Albanian criminal that they used in 1987 and 1988."[22]

Testifying at The Hague was a mixed experience for Teuta, but certainly harrowing. "It felt good to look for justice in front of the one who committed the crime, but for me it was also difficult to talk, I don't know why. It was very difficult because I was not prepared. I didn't meet anyone beforehand, I wasn't prepared to be stronger and even though they said I was strong, I was psychologically exhausted." She did go back to The Hague twice more, in 2007 and in 2009. "In 2007 it seems to me, if I am not mistaken, it seems to me that the defendant was a minister or something like that, and I testified against him, while in the other case it was six commanders and officers because what I described had a lot to do with them. But it was a good feeling to face them." The "them" she faced remain nameless for her, and perhaps rightly so.

Though their identities and ranks were key to the trial, Teuta remained focused on telling her story to a court judging a group of perpetrators she never knew or encountered. "The first time was the most difficult, maybe because it was the first time and keep in mind that Milošević was the leader. For them I only felt…angrier. It was easier, but it was never easy. The third time, I felt very bad, somewhat liberated but also somehow upset. It seems to me that I hurt because it was too much. I was liberated a little, but again it all came back with the tapes that said everything. What made it difficult was that I could forget them, but it all came back again, so I could not forget them, leave them behind and move on with my life. The prosecutors kept coming, and the last time they begged me a lot. Once, they called me on the phone, 'Please, you are key for us. Come on, because if you don't come this time we will go down.' I said, 'Good, I understand that, but I want to move on, I don't want to suffer all my life.' Because anytime I went there I had to tell the whole story again and everything came back. And it is not easy to appear in front of an international court."

Not all witnesses, in fact, went back after their first appearance.

If Teuta was not prepared for the difficult task of testifying, neither was the court prepared to assist her and the other women. In hindsight, prosecutors regret their lack of expertise, which could not be compensated by the sympathy and solidarity shown to the witnesses. Focused on criminal responsibility, they did not make more use of expert testimony to provide context, and when they tried to do just that in the *Milutinović et al.* case, they were rebuffed by both the defense and the judges.[23] Ingeborg Joachim, a German doctor with medica mondiale and plenty of experience with survivors in Gjakova, was ready to explain both the cultural and social contexts in which the survivors had to make their testimonies and their subjective, psychological conditions. The court rejected her testimony, since there was no need, argued the judge, for an explanation of the depth of a woman's trauma or the social circumstances in which publicly testifying about sexual violence would be nearly impossible. Medica mondiale would not be credible, said Judge Ian Bonomy, since "the objective of medica mondiale is to support these women, to give them help. It would be contrary to the ethos of the organisation [sic], I think, to challenge the accusation of rape." And how credible would be the doctor's report, given that "the objective of the person compiling the report is to encourage complaints of rape?"[24]

Valbona's first appearance at the tribunal was in the late morning of July 16, 2002. Like Teuta, she was identified by a number and questioned in the closed-door session in which she faced Milošević. "Oh my! I didn't know whether to feel freer or more constrained, I didn't know how to manage the situation. Today, when I think about how scared I was! I didn't dare look at him from fear. Believe me, I didn't dare look because I was still afraid of *Shki*. I told myself, 'Say everything, face everything.' But that one no, I never wanted to see him, because I didn't like to look at him, not in photos, not anywhere. The terror stayed and I cannot shake it. It was bad, I am telling you. I didn't eat nor drink, when they gave me some food I turned it back. I didn't even go for a walk, I stayed inside, terrified."

The court—the judge, the prosecutor, and the defendant—was well prepared for her testimony, since she had laid out the fundamental narrative of the events of late March 1999 in a statement of November 22 of the same year. One day earlier, she had gone through that statement with the prosecutors once again, making some edits here and there.[25] That written statement would have had the same legitimacy of an oral statement because of the particular vulnerability of the witness, according to the court's rule of procedure 92bis, a novelty in international justice. Yet she did not shy away from taking the witness stand. She had been shown the forensic pictures of the eight bodies recovered in the well, and had identified her sister and her mother-in-law.[26] She was as ready as she could be. "I faced Milošević. Twice. I could manage the situation when Milošević said that it wasn't like I said. But the trauma! I spoke without knowing that I was speaking. I said horrible words. They said twice or three times, 'Look, tell us if anything is the matter. We can take a break and walk out.' But like we Albanians often do, I got hold of myself and managed."

The prosecutor read her statement in the monotone of a detached official. It was indeed an official document, eloquent in its simplicity, and forever entrusted to history as a public transcript of the Milošević trial; only names and localities have been redacted from it. Early one morning at the end of March, or beginning of April, she could not remember exactly the date but it was just after the start of NATO bombing, Yugoslav army soldiers surrounded her village. For safety reasons, she and some other women and children, a total of twenty-two people, hid in a house on a hill further up. The men, including her father and brother, fled to the mountains to escape the soldiers. The following morning, soldiers arrived at the house where the women and children were sheltering, searched them, robbed them of everything, including their IDs, then marched them to another village. However, before arriving at their destination, they were intercepted by an army truck carrying other troops and ordered to go back. The women and children were held at a house where they were searched and robbed again by a Serbian-speaking woman named Mirdita, who assisted the soldiers.

After three days, they were told to walk to the mosque: one soldier said it was to protect them from NATO bombing, and Mirdita said, "They're asking for a group of you there." When they reached the village, the soldiers held the women and children in a cowshed and handed them over to other soldiers with tiger badges on their arms. The women were taken out in small groups to be "checked," each forced to strip naked and improperly touched by the soldiers in their private parts. She was threatened of rape as well as death. Back in the cowshed, she saw the soldiers remove five younger women, her sister among them, and three older women from the group and then heard three shots from outside. None of the women returned. Only after the war they were all found dead in a well near the shed where they had been held.[27]

In the cross-examination, Milošević ridiculed Valbona because she said that in order to escape the fighting she and her family had left their home just to find shelter in a house up the hill, "You just moved into the neighborhood?" Except that this is precisely what everyone did, in villages or in cities, as we heard in countless narrations: they cautiously moved from one place to another, trying to outwit the soldiers and the police, as the hills and the streets crawled with armed men who barked orders and kept the night lit with the flashing of their guns, shooting in order to terrorize when not to kill.

Valbona could not remember how long after the bombing started she left her house, nor could she tell with precision where her cousin's house was in relation to hers. "A few meters further up, above our house. About one kilometer."[28] Was it twenty-two or sixteen the number of desperate women and children whom the soldiers shuffled back and forth for almost a week on the hills of Kosovo? Valbona and a second witness, Xhevahire Rrahmani, could not agree on the exact number. Milošević argued that imprecision and contradictions invalidated their testimonies.

As was customary, Milošević framed the events as part of a legitimate counterinsurgency, painting the men who fled to the mountains as fighters who had engaged in fire with his soldiers. "Did you move from your own house to the house next door because you thought that the police knew that your husband was a member of the KLA and would come to your house to look for him?"[29] But whatever role Valbona's husband had in the war, he was not wearing the uniform and he was not armed. Milošević again tried to confuse the narration, placing the KLA at the scene of the crime and even stating that Mirdita, the Albanian woman who collaborated with his army, must have been with the KLA.

To transfer the responsibility of the crime to someone other than his men, Milošević used Valbona's distinction between the soldiers and the "criminals" who assaulted her. He painted a picture of the soldiers as honorable, exploiting the witness's testimony on the confounding behavior of his army, which robbed and tortured its unlawful captives but also fed them and played with the babies. Why would they do such horrible things to her and the other women if instead they were only sheltering them? He asked her: "Did you go to hide in the mosque when they told you to hide in the mosque? Did you think that they wished you well, that they wished to protect you because they assumed that NATO would not bomb a mosque?" Valbona responded: "No, I don't think they wished us well. We only thought that something worse awaited us. And that's what happened."[30]

The corroborating evidence that Milošević had sought in every case of sexual violence brought against him was present in this case. Forensic pathologists had confirmed that the eight women thrown into the well had been raped first. Besides, Valbona had been a credible witness from the beginning. After the discovery of the bodies, journalists had come every day to her village, asking for interviews; they had talked to her mother, to the neighbors, but her statements sounded the most accurate and caught the attention of the prosecutors at The Hague. "I talked so much that now I don't remember in detail what I said, I gave so many statements! Can you believe that I forgot some things? Sometimes I remember, why did I forget? But sometimes I couldn't talk, I saw that I was shaking. The Tribunal called me, but I was pregnant with my daughter, I was close to the delivery. They waited two months for me to deliver my baby and then they waited until she was four months old, because I said, 'I don't want the baby to be in the balloon' [colloquial for airplane]. But I was ready to give it all, all."

By that time, the prosecutor's team had improved how they dealt with sexual violence witnesses: they and the court-assigned psychologists helped her in giving her testimony, but so did medications. Nothing helped any more when she went back to the hotel after the testimony and to her husband and daughter. "I argued with my husband. He asked what happened to me, and who? what? I had such stress in my head, I wanted to cry, and I didn't know what to say. You know, they killed my life and I just wanted to cry. My daughter cried too, because I wasn't picking her up, I didn't feel that she was mine. I suddenly felt, how to put it, paralyzed, cold, I no longer had any feeling. I know that my husband too is a survivor, and I don't know why I felt that way."

It took years, and many hours of counseling, for Valbona to understand the trauma she suffered from what she saw during the war and what she survived. She went back to testify at The Hague four years later in the trial of Milutinović, but this time her transcripts were sealed. "They came to Kosovo, those people from The Hague, and visited me. When they came, do you know how I felt? Like with the people who are with the association working with survivors. I felt with them as with my family, I felt well, I felt warmth for them. I will never forget Judge May. When I faced Milošević, when he attacked me, Mr. May, with his white hair, interrupted him. He supported me as best as he could. I went through a lot, and they knew. Mr. May said, about me, 'Let her stay,' grant me asylum, you know? I thought about it and thought and thought...and oh God! They called me to the reception, 'Come downstairs, we need to talk.' 'Didn't I already go to give my testimony? Must I go again?' They said, 'No, they sent us here to offer you to stay in Holland.' I remember as if it was today the conditions they offered me; they were very good, money and all, but I didn't stay. My father-in-law had only one son. There was no telephone at that time in the village where I lived but he found a phone and called us, 'Where are you?' He called his son, he didn't let me stay, 'She must come back here.' Those who were with the Court, asked, 'Why not? Tell us the reason. Why did you say yes, then no? We didn't offer this to everybody, because you were pregnant at the time and went through a lot.' My children now say, 'Don't tell us we could have gone...do you know how much better off we would be?'"

Eyewitnesses

Teuta and Valbona were not the only victims who spoke at the ICTY about sexual assault. Three women, all identified only by a number, testified they had been sexually assaulted in Pristina. Just one week after the start of the NATO bombing, three masked men in green camouflage uniforms barged into K62's apartment in the center of town, robbed and assaulted her—a crime repeated in many other private homes.[31] K14 was only a teenager in late May 1999 when a group of policemen wearing blue and green camouflage uniforms with blue ribbons on their right arms kidnapped her from her apartment, took her to the Bozhur Hotel, raped her, and took her back home only when she agreed she would return with her sister; a friend told her that she too had been kidnapped, taken to a private house, and raped.[32] Another teenager, K31, was taken by Serbian soldiers to the hospital of Prishtina with her wounded brother in May 1999: she was assaulted during the trip from her village and once in the hospital she was taken to the basement with other women, and she was gang-raped.[33] The three witnesses also testified that, like tens of thousands of other Prishtina residents, they were later expelled from their homes under threat of violence, whether directly or indirectly, by a combination of army soldiers, paramilitaries, and armed Serb civilians—in other words, a panoply of different forces that needed expert coordination to act so effectively.

Milošević's defense was consistent. K31 could just describe, but not explain, what happened after her father was killed, her brother wounded, and Serbian soldiers approached her group: "They gave first aid to my brother. A soldier gave him first aid. And at the same time, a group of soldiers murdered my sister and several other people, four or five other people. And we were surprised that my brother was given first aid, where at the same time they were murdering other people."[34] Soldiers put her and her wounded brother in a vehicle to take them to the hospital and from that moment began to harass her. The absurdity of such behavior was great fodder for Milošević's aggressive questioning, which attacked the veracity of the witness, provoking her reaction: "You're making me nervous, you're trying to make me guilty of something, and I don't accept what you're insinuating."[35] She added, "And if it wasn't the truth that I was telling you, I wouldn't have bothered to come here to tell you anything but the truth."[36]

The prosecutor Geoffrey Nice stepped in: "This is an aggressive cross-examination without a positive case against a woman who is extremely vulnerable according to all the learning. I've raised before whether a man who has no apparent sympathy for victims should be allowed to cross-examine witnesses like this, and I must repeat our concern. We know imperfectly, others know better, the damage that is done and is sometimes intended to be done to witnesses in this position by this form of cross-examination. It is distasteful and, in my respectful submission, should be carefully monitored."[37] Judge May upheld the right of the accused to cross-examine, but shared the prosecutor's concern as he warned Milošević that "many witnesses have been through very traumatic experiences, and that should be reflected in the way that they're treated in this court."[38]

In the judgment, the court leaned back on the more conventional view that sexual assault had been an opportunistic crime, the type that always happens in wars. The judges said that he could not conclude that the violence had been part of a planned campaign, because "while the victims in each of these incidents were Kosovo Albanians and the perpetrators were members of the Serbian forces, considering the limited number of incidents relied on to support this underlying act of persecutions...the ethnicity of the two victims alone is not a sufficient basis to establish that the perpetrators acted with discriminatory intent."[39]

Thus, the Serbian leaders could not be held accountable for the behavior of "rogue elements" among the plurality of forces deployed in Kosovo. General Pavković was convicted on charges of sexual assault as a crime against humanity for the events in Beleg and Qirez—the first also the site of a large massacre of civilians, and the second corroborated by forensic evidence—but not for incidents brought up in court by other witnesses from Prishtina.[40] In judging Djordjević, the court concluded that the witnesses had been sexually assaulted but their number was still too small to draw the conclusion that rape had been used to persecute Albanians. It took the Judgment on Appeal in 2014 to convict Lukić and Šainović, extending to Pavković as well the responsibility of all the other incidents of sexual assaults brought by the prosecution.[41] The same year, Djordjević's appeal also reversed the judgment in the first instance and concluded that the Chamber had made an "error of law" in not including sexual assault in the crimes that had the intent of terrorizing Albanians.[42]

They Should Have Known

At The Hague, the men formerly at the head of the political and military institutions of Serbia alternately played the role of not only patriots and humanitarians, but also powerless bureaucrats. Milutinović said he protected the constitution and worked for peace, but he was acquitted mostly on the grounds that he was a powerless figurehead, a puppet of Milošević. Šainović, Milošević's coordinator of the activities of the army and police in Kosovo, claimed he had neither authority nor control over those forces, that he was simply one of the many persons who were sent to Kosovo to find a solution to the crisis, and that he could not have known of any crimes, let alone sexual crimes, committed by Serbian troops, because nobody reported to him. General Ojdanić argued that all his actions were legitimate responses to the threats posed by both the KLA and NATO, that he operated only within the chain of command of the army, with a very marginal role, if any, in the Supreme Defense Council. The ambitious General Pavković, known for having pushed early on for an all-out war in Kosovo and for micromanaging all operations, always maintained that he was a leading figure in protecting his country from terrorism, but he couldn't have any knowledge of crimes because he was "six levels removed from the actual fighting on the ground, and that information was corrupted and often incomplete by the time it reached him."[43]

All Milošević's co-conspirators shared a twisted version of reality, according to which they were defenders of their country and their fellow Serbs from terrorists, going as far as arming Serb civilians and disarming Albanian civilians. According to their presentation of the war, Serbian army and police checkpoints along the main roads were not instruments of control and violence, but instead provided services to refugees fleeing KLA and NATO violence. They all denied that the army could be involved in crimes such as the widespread and systematic burning, looting, killing, destruction of cultural property and sexual violence. Maybe rogue groups that escaped detection?

The court concluded otherwise. The prosecution proved that despite the many different groups that made up the Serbian armed presence in Kosovo in the years 1998 and 1999, their command structure was clear and well-functioning.[44] The army, under the leadership of its top brass and the supreme commander, FRY President Slobodan Milošević, in coordination and cooperation with the Ministry of Interior (MUP) groups, ran all operations, with oversight over all armed groups.[45] That included from 1,400 to 2,500 volunteers, recruited from paramilitary groups, inmates, and reservists who had already distinguished themselves as war criminals in Bosnia, according to the army's own reports, and who in Kosovo, like in Bosnia, were no rogue elements: they reported to the army.[46]

We learn about these Serbian volunteers and other "irregulars" in their own words, as they testified at the ICTY, talked to American public radio journalists immediately after the war, or were interviewed on camera in two revealing documentaries, *The Unidentified* and *The Scorpions*—the latter composed almost exclusively from the videos proudly filmed by one of them with his brand new camcorder.[47] In the film that shows paramilitaries in action or in repose, they are well equipped and uniformed, on a par with regular soldiers or police, and working alongside them.

The defendants maintained that soldiers had received the order to behave honorably and follow the Geneva Convention regarding civilians, and that when they knew of crimes, they had them properly investigated and punished. They were aware of the work of the ICTY since its establishment in 1993 and of the numerous guilty sentences handed down to Bosnian Serb leaders, and that international prosecutors had intensified their investigation of war crimes in Kosovo immediately after the January 15, 1999, massacre of civilians in Reçak. Thus, they had left a paper trail that included several orders to protect civilians during NATO raids, even to distribute aid, and to punish any violation of the law. The Serbian military has, after all, a fully functional military justice system.

The evidence, however, shows that crimes were reported only episodically, and when they were reported, they were not investigated, whether because of a deliberate policy, negligence on the part of the commanders, or obstruction of justice by the army itself.[48] In fact, evidence points to a practice of general denial of the legal order. In one telling example, General Pavković reportedly lost his patience when asked about the authorization to requisition civilian vehicles: he just ordered that cars be taken and distributed among army and police during the war, and kept as booty after.[49] There are records of a high-level meeting held on May 17, 1999, including the top leadership and Slobodan Milošević, convened in the same week Milošević was served the ICTY indictment for war crimes and crimes against humanity in Bosnia and Kosovo. The meeting discussed mass killing and rapes and punishment for the perpetrators. Yet, ICTY prosecutors found no indication of a follow-up. Rade Marković, head of Serbia's state security, said during that meeting that all volunteers, the same people who had been signaled as the perpetrators of those crimes, were "a necessary evil."[50]

After going through a range of testimonies and reports by the army and Defense Ministry, prosecutors never found evidence of a conviction of any army soldier for any serious crime, despite thousands of criminal reports and indictments.[51] The court learned that of the many prosecutions by the Yugoslav army, including the very few on war crimes, none were for crimes committed against Albanians or civilians. The overwhelming majority of crimes involved evasion of military service, desertion, refusal to implement orders, and robberies. Not only was there no significant action on war crimes, but evidence was suppressed.[52] Lakic Dorović, the prosecutor of the Military District Court of Prishtina, testified that 1,400 criminal reports had disappeared from his office.[53] These actions effectively decriminalized what everyone knew was a crime, even though *de jure* the appearance of legality was maintained. Not only the armed forces on the ground "knew that they could act with near impunity,"[54] they knew that criminal behavior would be seen positively.

An army soldier testified that he participated in the killing of fifteen Albanian civilians, as ordered, because "if you followed these orders you were a hero."[55] Regular soldiers are less frequently mentioned as perpetrators of sexual violence, although they were often present when crimes were committed, were the enablers of crimes, and sometimes joined in. Typically, the army would surround and shell an area, then the police and paramilitaries would move in, call people out of their homes, separate the men from the women, rob everybody, and beat up and/or kill the men. Rapes happened in those circumstances, as we heard from several survivors. The army was in charge of emptying out the capital Pristina, calling people out of their homes and channeling them to the rail or bus station. Fatime, who told us her story, was one of those women who were pulled out of the crowd and raped.

Most of the evidence identifies police and paramilitaries as perpetrators. Their behavior was known before the trials. Two members of the paramilitaries active on the western mountains of Kosovo told American Public Radio in 1999 that "the main interest [of their group] was in robbing people and raping women," "they killed everybody except for women they might want to rape first," and "they had license to kill and rape."[56] Yet, when volunteers recruited into paramilitary formations were indicted for rape, the cases were quickly transferred to a municipal court and there is no evidence of a sentence.[57] What they received was, instead, a license to do whatever they felt like. After the March 29, 1999, massacre of fourteen civilians in Podujevo, the army sent the Scorpions away but called them back within two weeks.[58] The commander of the army's 125th Motorized Brigade, Dragan Zivanović, in charge of a unit which was nicknamed the Jackals, congratulated its leader Nebojša Minić, aka. Mrtvi (The Dead) for his April 1, 1999, massacre of forty-eight civilians in Lubeniq, a "cleaning" operation, as he called it, and sent the same unit to Qyshk and Zahac, where two other massacres were committed on May 14 for a total of forty-six civilian casualties.[59] Zivanović described a distinct group known as "Brazil" as the best-trained police anti-terrorist unit, knowing that Brazil was the code sign for Milorad Ulemek Luković (aka Legija). A former associate of the paramilitary group formed at the time of the war in Bosnia and Croatia, Arkan's Tigers, Legija was the operational commander of the Special Operation Units (JSO), who wore green camouflage uniforms and often sported black facemasks, the same type of masks that survivors remember.[60]

Paramilitaries in Kosovo were close-knit networks of families or criminal groups, loyal to brutal commanders who showed them by example how to fight. It was the brother of the Scorpions commander Boca who opened fire without warning on civilians in Podujevo, killing fourteen. He then bragged about it. Bragging about atrocities, says the anonymous fighter K. in the documentary *The Scorpions*, was the way to recruit fresh members to the group. Mrtvi, the charismatic leader of the Jackals, fired the first shot, point blank, to kill an old villager in Lubeniq who had pleaded with him; the others followed his example.[61] Ajshe told us how, kidnapped in the street and taken twice to the police station on the same day, she was raped twice, even as some police hesitated to assault her, after one superior moved first and gave them permission. Liridona was not killed when a commander ordered a soldier to "man up" and shoot her only because that soldier refused to pull the trigger, but she was subsequently raped.

Orders to expel Albanians were never written, only oral. Sometimes the order was well-defined. Two members of the regular army testified that a commanding officer said that "not a single Albanian was to remain in Kosovo and their identification papers were to be torn, so as to prevent them from coming back."[62] Testifying as protected witness K90, a Serbian soldier said that they were told to "relocate" Albanian villagers near Gjakova, and "clear" more than a dozen villages.[63] Other witnesses recounted how they were told to "mop up" and "clear" a village, but that was a partial and vague order, which never indicated what "mopping" precisely meant. Paramilitaries were given lists of people, usually Albanian community leaders, "to take dead or alive," but without further instruction.[64] The handling of civilians was left to the discretion of military units. This is the context in which several testimonies of survivors recount the occurrence of mass rapes of which they were victims. And so the ICTY, on appeal, concluded that sexual violence, as part of a repertoire of violence that strategically targeted Albanians for ethnic cleansing during the years 1998 and 1999, was known to Serbian leaders, even though there was no written order for it and no more than five women had come forward to testify against them.

Trials at Home

The crime of sexual violence in Kosovo had not been a priority at the ICTY, nor was it for the UN Mission in Kosovo (UNMIK), which took over the administration of police and justice immediately after the war. Cases were handed to UNMIK by Sevdije Ahmeti, the director of the Center for the Protection of Women and Children, or by other individuals, including victims such as Vasfije Krasniqi-Goodman, whose story is now widely known. On April 14, 1999, a local Serb, a policeman, showed up at Vasfije's house and forced her to follow him to his station on the pretext that she had to give an account of the whereabouts of the men in her family. Instead, he assaulted her at gunpoint, claiming that his revenge was for an unrelated KLA attack. Then he handed her over to another Serb. She reported the incident the next day to the KLA and later to UNMIK. She knew her first assailant and provided investigators with his photo. The photo was lost, as most evidence did go missing, and no case was ever prosecuted. Krasniqi-Goodman continued to lobby for justice and presented her case to the European Union Rule of Law Mission (EULEX), UNMIK's successor in handling war crimes in Kosovo. But in October 2014, she saw her two assailants walk free after the Supreme Court of Kosovo acquitted them on procedural grounds. Her case has been analyzed by rule of law monitors and human rights groups as an example of how the judicial system fails survivors by not knowing or not applying international standards.[65] It is only due to her determination and vocal protest that the case has since been reopened.[66]

The Krasniqi-Goodman case was only one of two cases of sexual violence that had gone to trial in Kosovo since 2009, when EULEX received nine files related to this crime from UNMIK and later added four cases of its own.[67] One was Vasfije's. Long gone from Kosovo and living in the United States with her husband and two children, she had the courage to speak up publicly about her experience and seek justice.

Merita's husband did not allow her to testify at The Hague when prosecutors asked for her help, but circumstances have changed. "My happiness is that EULEX recently summoned me, because my husband knows one of the persons who attacked us. He was a policeman from Kosovo, from Vranjevc. I didn't know that man, because they all had masks, but to spite my husband he showed himself to him, he took off his mask when he left the room. And he had a house a bit uphill from us. They say that he and a certain Dragan committed massacres and rapes. Seven people were killed in Kolovica, and he killed them. It was difficult that day, because there was an offensive. I know about two young girls, I know about those women. It happened in the house nearby. There were close to twenty women there, yes. To tell you the truth, what makes my soul heal, because I don't feel good about taking up weapons and going to war against them, what would make me happy is that if I die, I know that I died with honor, but that idiot is in jail. It would make me happy to be face to face with that idiot in the tribunal and to denounce that shameless criminal. And I don't know what I would say at that moment or what I would feel. But I know that I desire with all my soul and all my life to denounce them. For a woman it's very difficult to raise the head from deep water and fall in the fire, so to speak, to have a rather normal life and have it completely destroyed. You are standing on your feet, everything goes well and then.... My heart is burned, it's in bits and pieces."

Despite her pessimism, Ganimete never stops fighting: "I have zero hope in justice, very honestly, I don't, we don't have hope in international or domestic justice. Some time ago we met with this prosecutor, I am serious, who complained, 'You don't have many witnesses, you don't have witnesses.' I said, 'We have twenty-five witnesses.' She said, 'They aren't enough.' Do twenty-five seem few to you? I'd say, start with this. We are in peacetime now, but in the event of a murder, shouldn't I tell you—you are a prosecutor—that there was a crime? And would you answer, 'I need one hundred cases to put together a dossier'? We are more and more disillusioned."

The Strongest Link: An Oral History of Wartime Rape Survivors in Kosovo. Anna Di Lellio and Garentina Kraja, Oxford University Press. © Oxford University Press 2025. DOI: 10.1093/9780197699324.003.0009

9

What Remains

The trauma is written on Afërdita's body, literally: "I have these two scars on my face that don't show much now, because many years have passed. Oh my! At the time you could see them a lot. But I know that they are here and here on my face, and they have begun to give me wrinkles. When I went out, I kept my head down. I said to myself, 'All those who see me will know what happened to me.' My daughter has tried all sorts of things to cover those scars, but I told her, 'Not this, daughter, this is not what is going to improve my face.'"

Though they may not be as visible as scars, illness and pain haunt Fatime: "I still have problems, I feel sick in my stomach, I have my stomach all tied up in knots, because those scoundrels put sharp objects in, they wounded me with sharp objects."

Merita, too, still suffers from the torture: "Though I have begun to improve a little, I still have pain in my body because they hit me in the back. I never knew what they hit me with." The violence left a trail of other health issues. "Ah! I forgot that I had an abortion! I had to kill a three-month-old baby. It was right after we came back from the war. I was pregnant and went to the doctor because I was all swollen and he said, 'You don't want to have a child with this infection.' I did all my tests, and it came out that I had a sexual infection. The doctor asked, 'Did anything happen in the war?' 'Yes, this and this happened.' Seven months passed and we monitored the situation. They told me at first that they had given me AIDS. I didn't know what to do. When I took the test a second time, the doctor said, 'No, your situation has improved, don't be too worried.' No fewer than six people raped me. Who knows what they did to me!"

She was a victim, yet was tormented by guilt. "My heart felt that although I wasn't terminally ill, because I didn't have cancer, you know, which is incurable everywhere but is a disease from God, I had a disease which was curable, but came from something immoral. I don't know how to explain it, but that knowledge killed me more than terminal illness. Four years later, I went to talk to the doctor because I wanted to have a child. I wanted to have ten children, because I like children so much! I thought that since I no longer had the infection, I could be pregnant again. Well, the infection was always there, but I used all the means I knew to get rid of it. The doctor finally said yes, and I gave birth. The infection began to clear, but later came back. I have problems again with that infection and those problems remind me of everything."

While Merita was raped, her husband was beaten to a pulp. He has his own trauma, and she must shoulder that too. "My husband began to abuse me. He would come up to me and say, 'The Serbs raped you.' Is there anything worse? I have not eaten, drunk, or slept without being beaten, without crying and without being upset because of him. I asked him many times, 'Do you know what you did to me?' because he forgot. 'I didn't do anything, what did I do?' I know that he is sick. He had such headaches, not to be found on heaven or earth. My family said, 'Take the child and leave.' I said, 'What happened to me wasn't his fault and in that moment, he spoke up for me. I will never leave.'"

Life at home became so unbearable that even her mother-in-law encouraged her to leave. "She said, "Go back to your mother, because here it's bad for you." Then my husband got sicker. Now, the children too saw he had lost his mind. Once I woke up and he was having a seizure, he lost consciousness, and then he threw up. The doctor said, 'No, this is not the flu,' and with his uncle I took him to the emergency room. The doctor was surprised that he was still alive after the beating he received in the war. 'Had you brought him to me ten years ago, when it happened, I could have treated him. I am just wondering how he could have survived, and how you could still be alive.' When they opened his head, they found his brain full of liquid, full of pus, and they drained it. Since he had surgery, he talks and listens a bit better, and he is calmer. Now I am OK, it's not that bad."

The Skin of Memory

The violence suffered by survivors has also left no "tellable story" inside,[1] but the story is there. In her Auschwitz memoir, Charlotte Delbo wrote that, however silenced, the story of violence remains under the "skin of memory," a skin so tough and thick that it does not allow the filtering out of anything underneath, yet it cracks unexpectedly to release its content when one least expects it, as "the will has no power on dream."[2] What remains unsaid bursts out in nightmares, sudden flashbacks, somatic reactions, gush of tears, and an overwhelming sense of guilt. None of that should surprise. Now we know that trauma produces physiological alterations in the body and the brain, and that those effects last through life; as noted in van der Volk's bestseller, "the body keeps the score."[3]

For Shpresa, the impulse of crying comes suddenly when she is home alone. "Yesterday my third daughter found me. 'Mom, what's up?' 'Nothing, I am not crying about anything in particular, I must be nervous.' I am nervous about myself. Because when I am by myself, an ill feeling comes back. When I remember, my body does not feel well."

Years after the war, Qëndresa realized that questions about herself and her surrounding world crowd her solitude: "Even now, when I am alone, I become quieter and just think about the incident. Everything that happened, I am telling you, is in front of me. Sometimes, when I am by myself, I say, 'Why did it happen to me?' Sometimes I say, again, when I am alone, 'But this is war, what didn't happen!?' They killed my relatives, they beat up my relatives, they did everything possible, those *Shki*. Sometimes I can take some distance from it, you know, and say, 'Get a grip on yourself!' and I calm myself down."

Controlling her emotions is possible for Qëndresa when she puts her experience into context, when she becomes aware of her past as a collective past. But involuntary memories intrude in even the most hidden parts of the self. Her husband told her, "You know, when we got married you cried during your sleep, you cried so much, you seemed frightened." Even when she sleeps, she is very scared. And so is Shkurta: "I can never go to sleep because everything comes back to me. Three people I lost, no less. It's a lot to lose three people, but it would have been better if they killed everyone. Once they kill you, you are dead, but instead I stayed alive and always with bad thoughts. Something gets into me and says, 'Uhhh, they are coming in!'"

Liridona's surroundings, not just her mind, are filled with traumatic memories: "When memory comes back at night, I am afraid. Two nights ago I woke up two–three times because dreams brought it all back. Because I have no means, I still live in the house where I was raped. At home, I am afraid." Fear seizes Merita, despite the strength and the willpower she has. She is, as the saying goes, "a person with a head stronger than a rock," but like Liridona, she feels that she has no safe haven. "When I came back after the war, I didn't even want to see my house, where it all happened, but the family said, 'Come on, we must live here. You should go to a doctor.' But I wasn't insane. I would have rather killed myself than live there. But they built a new house in the same place and that killed me, because I cannot sleep in that house."

The survivors' memory of the fear they felt during the attack stays buried inside, ready to be revived and to rise to the surface with traumatic flashbacks at the first reminder. Shkurta is afraid of any army uniform: "My legs shake like leaves when I see NATO soldiers. I shake, and they have done nothing to me. Good God! When I think of it, my heart drops, and if I see them, I am afraid."

Ganimete, a woman who seems indomitable, fears political protests that might turn violent: "Any time I see a demonstration against the Parliament, any time I see the Parliament in flames, I feel stressed.[4] I cannot hear police or ambulance sirens. I don't want to see sparks or someone starting a fire, because any time something like that happens, my trauma is reactivated. I want to see good debates on our TV, my desire is to have calm around me, I want to see calm, I want to see better institutions, working hard for the good of society. I don't want to see shooting in our institutions, I don't want to see our buildings in flames. On that day when we had a provocation from Serbia, when we heard that a train left Belgrade to come here, I called other survivors at about noon and said, 'Let's go together to the Center!' We had no guts to stay home alone. We are always stressed, everything is difficult, going on living is difficult."

As unpleasant as they are, traumatic memories could be evoked, says Ajshe, even on pleasant occasions: "Weddings, *kanagjegj*, and banquets are over for me. I didn't go to my brother's wedding, nor my sister's, I didn't go to any wedding or banquet. I didn't celebrate my son's birthday nor anyone else's, because when I hear music, I must hide somewhere else. Music could play here right now, and I would feel blocked, and tak! I would suddenly begin to cry, and as I begin to cry someone always comes to me and asks, 'What do you cry about and what for?' I am telling you, I'd rather stay home. Once, after work, I went to a restaurant on the way to the seacoast, on a field trip organized by a colleague. But when I saw the crowd of people in tank tops and shorts, I froze. I said, 'Why did you take me here?' He didn't know that I had sores, that I scratched my sores a little and they were bleeding. I saw the shorts and the tank tops covered in blood, ripped, and began to cry. I went to the beach four or five times just to please my husband. Did I volunteer or was I forced? There is that word in Serbo-Croatian that you never heard because you are too young, '*dobrovoljno*,' working voluntarily, which really means you are forced to work.[5] I went to the seacoast by force, and no, I did not enjoy it, I remained fully dressed. But I went and sat down, like those ducks. I went in the water fully dressed two–three times, and a woman made some comments, but I didn't want to make a scene and thought nothing bad."

There is no single pattern; traumatic memories remain paradoxically both surprising and predictable. Vlora: "Even today it can happen that I may be hanging out with someone and if some memories come suddenly to mind, my body shakes, and somehow I feel paralyzed and cannot talk anymore, I feel so bad! Now, all that makes me psychologically ill, ill in my head. I have been very upset for a long time when spring comes, because it was spring when it happened to me, when I experienced that evil, and I always remembered the incident." Afërdita also dreads the spring: "Every year since 2000, when March comes, I feel sick and have to go to the hospital, because it happened in March."

As memories of the violence continue to be omnipresent, they destroy many other memories, anchoring a survivor's past to the traumatic experience that upended their lives. Fatime has now problems with forgetfulness. "I grew up in Pristina, I came here when I was three years old, but sometimes I don't know where I am. Maybe it's because I spend so much time alone, by myself. I hide at home, and I forget." She is not alone in feeling forgetful.

Ajshe: "Now I am forgetting everything. Someone once asked me, 'Where does your daughter-in-law work?' I said, 'Somewhere.' 'What is her name?' I didn't know. I paused, and paused, then said, 'I am sorry, I had a nervous breakdown, sorry.' I went home and told my husband and he said, 'Why didn't you give a whatever name, so you don't make people think that you have become crazy? You must know the name of a young bride to finish the story and not give people material to point the finger at you.' I don't know, maybe I am forgetful from that trauma because it's not normal that I forget. I opened the refrigerator three times because I forgot what I was looking for. When those memories come back, I forget everything; what happens is that I get defensive and forget."

Valbona is of two minds about the memories that come unexpectedly to haunt her. Some are unbearable: "When the memory of the war was fresher, it unfolded in front of me, and I cried so much that I didn't know how to manage. Life continued, and I could not find closure. I cried until I wanted to explode, I got so tired. And after two–three days, I was like garbage from all that crying." But then there are the equally vivid memories of the dead, especially her young sister, and those are healing: "When I held my sister's things, everything came back. I always see my sister in dreams. I see her in a stream of flowers, of water. And I always see my mother-in-law. My husband says, '*Ku ku*, I never see my mom,' while I always see them, and in the dreams, I am with them. But when I wake up in the morning I am upset I don't know for how many days, because they are not real. When I wake up, I don't see them anymore. They say, 'Give it up.' But I don't want to because I am happy to be with them. They told me that I was still young, and I should give a sister to my daughter, but she doesn't know, like I do, what a sister is. To know a sister and enjoy her presence, and then lose her, that is very hard."

Blerta visits the cemetery more than her living relatives. "I often go to see my brother's grave. Any time I yearn for him, I go."

A Life No Longer Worth Living

In her philosophical reflection as a survivor of sexual violence, the ethicist Susan Brison touches upon the apparently contradictory stance of a trauma victim between life and death, best defined by Samuel Beckett's line, "I can't go on, I'll go on."[6] It is truly an existential question for Merita: "To kill myself or not to kill myself? This was the problem." As one "gets a grip on herself," as Qëndresa puts it, and goes on living, the thought of suicide remains always present.

Ajshe: "After the war I went back to work, but everything came back to me every day after 5 p.m. I would go to the window and say, 'Oh God, why didn't you take me when you took my mother?' People go to work every day, they contribute to society, and though I am in the position of contributing, I cannot. I don't enjoy my work. I took Apaurin, ten milligrams, twenty milligrams, then I got used to it, and now it no longer helps. Do you know what they say about Dino Hasanaj, who wouldn't have been able to stab himself?[7] Even though everyone says he couldn't do that, I say that he could. Why? I drank one liter of bleach, that's why. I drank one glass, then a second…I wanted to give up, and I drank again and again till I finished it. I took advantage of a moment when nobody was home because someone would have stopped me. Since that day my stomach hurts, I vomited blood, but I didn't die. I am left with nothing."

After the failure of her first suicide attempt, Ajshe tried again. "I always thought that I would use a rope to kill myself, and after three–four days someone would find me, but it would be worse. I calculated that I would drink bleach and I would be gone, like that! But it was bad. Another time I stole the revolver of a friend who works with the police. I excused myself from work, finding a pretext. I left a letter, apologizing to all my family. I felt bad mostly for my son, who would grow up an orphan because of me. Allah wanted my husband to find the letter, just five minutes before I was committing suicide. He came closer to me and said, 'Are you normal? This happened to many, you are not the only one, it happened to this friend and that other friend, there are many that we don't even hear about. Come on, I will do my best, I will try, and will find a job at all costs. And now you have your young daughter-in-law in the house and don't need to do the housework.' But I did all the work of a young bride, it felt good. I worked very hard so I wouldn't think. And whenever I saw a dead body, I said, 'Why can't I be in her place?' But God knows his works, he decides, not me."

Feeling broken, survivors despair at the possibility of rebuilding their whole old self and world, and that makes life unworthy of living. Valbona was able to return to her routine with great difficulty: "In the morning I couldn't get up, even though work was waiting for me—the fields, the cows, the guests. I had many guests, during the day I had two or three. If nobody came, I would say, 'What happened?' And I always felt so tired! Now it's a bit better, but for a long time I didn't have any life in me. I only knew I could no longer go on living. Very often I tried to commit suicide. And very often my husband stopped me, he stopped me at the last minute."

Holocaust survivor Jean Améry wrote, "whoever was tortured, stays tortured."[8] It is that condition that brought him, and like him many others, to commit suicide years after surviving Nazi concentration camps. Sexual violence is torture and similarly refashions people in its own image, destroying their past and all that gave meaning to it. This is clearly what happened to Vlora: "When those bad memories fill my head, I feel very bad, become nervous and worried, my life seems like a catastrophe, because in those moments you also lose the good things that you experienced, you don't know how to go on living, you don't feel happy anymore."

Because survivors believe they lack a meaningful past, they cannot look to the life ahead. Edona found that she has lost the will to live because she has lost the capacity of seeing herself in the future: "What more would life bring me? Why live anymore? Even today I thought about how to kill myself, how to finish it. Once I said, 'How can I disappear from this life?' and went to my room. My husband came after me and said, 'What's going on? Are you crazy? Look at how many men they killed! Did those men want to be killed? Which man wanted to drop his weapons and say, kill me? They overpowered them and killed them. And you, you didn't want to. You didn't say yes, they did what they wanted to do. What could you have done?'"

Those words help, but only in the moment. "Anytime I am left alone because everyone goes to work, I think about what happened to me, and all the memories come back. One friend who was with me that night is dead now, we are not sure how she died, I can only tell you what I heard. They say that she killed herself by electrocution. She was always so nervous that she began to smoke. She was thirty years old. The day she died, she went to visit my mother and said, 'I wash clothes all day.' And my mother, 'It's so good that you are so healthy and strong and help your mother with her housework.' She said, 'I am not good, I have flashbacks and think, Why does the morning come for me? And why the night? Why did they kill our neighbors and not me?' She left my mother's place in the evening to return home, where they were getting ready for dinner. The beans were already on the table when they heard that cry of hers, 'Iuuuuuu!' It was so loud it got to the ears of God. She took my soul. I am telling you, I think of her often because I tried to kill myself one hundred times. I tried one hundred times to drink bleach, even though I have children. They are all grown up and their father can take a better wife who can raise them better, because I failed as a mother."

Edona, like the others, understood from a very early age the meaning of "good wife" and "good mother." She felt she was one, but the war happened, and she lost her sense of self as a wife and mother. Objectified and tortured, she already experienced what Cathy Winkler, an anthropologist and a rape survivor, calls a "social death," a feeling of hopelessness at being able to reassert oneself in the context of the family.[9] This remains subjectively important, even when the family plays a key supporting role. Edona's husband, for example: "He never leaves home anymore because he watches over me. Never. He said, 'Until I trust that you wouldn't do anything stupid when I leave, I will not go to work. We will not have anything to eat, but I won't leave.' Once I went somewhere in the yard and there he was, just behind me. I said, 'I didn't know that someone would be so close to me, especially you. I didn't expect anything from you.' I never expected all that from my husband, even though he was educated and understanding, he was always a good man. Always. He supported me and gave me an opening in life."

If the impossibility of a meaningful future looms tragically over the present, children provide the needed comfort. When Vlora feels dejected, as if she never had any happiness in her life, she knows that indeed there is some happiness for her in the present, and that is because of her son. "He gives me the will to live. Sometimes my life is like a dream. Hop! I close my eyes and then I open them, and say, 'Oh God, is this my life? Is this my son?' I don't know what my life looks like. It's like I lived in a dream." If Merita has nine lives, as her mother often tells her, she knows that she has used almost all of them, but she is left with the one that belongs to her child. "Where is greater happiness than seeing your child and creating a family?," asks Fitore, who after the war felt all her good memories disappear. "How did I feel after the war? To tell you the truth, I feel dead. I am done for all purposes. I have regrets about everything. My only happy memory is when my first child was born. That time I saw my husband happier than any other time in my life."

Children do not just give hope or restore the place a woman has in the family and the community. They literally rescue their mothers from sure death. Merita: "It was a few days after they told me that I had AIDS that I tried to kill myself. I stuck my head in the oven, being in the oven would have been better than what had become of my life. I said to myself, 'I did not heal, I am not completely healed, my soul is not healed, and what is the meaning of my life now? Let them put me in a grave.' My daughter found me, she screamed, 'Mommy, mommy!' My daughter is an angel. She knows everything, what happened to me, the beating of my husband, and she supports me. She told me just now, 'Mom, it's wonderful that you are alive. It is so important for me that I can call you mother and that I can see you. You gave me life and you are the light of my eyes.' And this is everything for me."

Afërdita was saved by her daughter as well. "Once I was very upset and drank one liter of bleach. My daughter called an old woman, a friend, for help. I kept thinking, 'Who the hell is she calling? She is not going to stop me,' because the anger about that time came back. I stayed in the hospital, in the neuropsychiatric ward, for maybe three weeks."

Shared Trauma

Individuals suffer trauma in solitude, but that trauma is also experienced, in different ways, by the whole family. Qëndresa: "My parents don't feel well since then, since they saw me after the incident. And they are young, they are still in their fifties. My father has hypertension, he had three heart attacks. My mother says, 'I was never well, when I think of you, I am never happy.'" Serbian soldiers and paramilitary targeted several members of the same nuclear family, as in the case of Adelina and Shkurta, or members of the larger group of relatives. Afërdita's brother was raped in prison: "I said to him, 'Oh brother, you never went through what we did!' 'Eh sister, you don't know what rape for a man is.' He told me the horror he experienced."

Psychologist Selvi Izeti told us of the case of a mother and her son, one of the most touching in her work with survivors:[10] "When the rape happened, her eleven-year-old son was present. She also had two other children in another room, but the eldest was there with her. Later, she felt that her son felt hatred for her. I asked her, 'How does he express his hatred toward you?' 'He doesn't say a word to me, never. He never speaks to me and never comes close to me. With me he is always very formal.' This story struck me, and I insisted on meeting with the son, now an adult. And when he came to my office, I said, 'What do you think of the fact that your mother thinks you hate her?' He began to cry. 'I don't hate my mother,' he said, 'I hate myself because I couldn't help her when she most needed my help.' They were both burdened by the weight of suffering from something of which none of them was guilty."

Ajshe's son saw what happened to his mother. "He kept it inside, but he suffered emotionally. We have been silent, very quiet. Whenever he looked at me, growing up, his eyes filled with tears." Afërdita's daughter, a toddler at that time, told her mother that she remembers everything: "They pushed me away from you, they grabbed your hair and I felt bad for the hair. I didn't know what they were doing though I knew that those people did evil things to you. Today I understand everything." The soldiers made Fatime's little girl watch everything. "On July 2nd, after we returned, there was a celebration, and they all fired their weapons in the air so much that my daughter was terrified. Nobody could approach her. She was so afraid! Until I gave birth to my boy, I kept her with me all night, because she couldn't sleep from fear and when she did, she cried and wailed all night, she shook as if she was electrocuted. Neither did I sleep at all, I could not calm down my child."

When their mothers were attacked, some children were like extras in a horror movie. Merita's oldest son was a baby in the crib when it happened, and he has never lived with his mother since. "He was raised by my mother-in-law. I told her, 'I am not interested in my son.' She washed him, wiped him with what she had, and gave him food while I could only give him food when I was OK: everything he ate, she gave him. She loves him more than I do. And I am happy that she loves him. I wouldn't know how to return the favor; I don't know how to reward her. Now he never talks to me, not even for a minute. But I never regretted having left him."

In Valbona's family, sadness can seize anybody at any time. "From where do I begin? I feel very sad that my child was in the war. I feel very sad that he drank water from the well, that I filled bottles with the water from the well where my sister and my mother-in-law had been left dead. I feel very sad that my second child was in diapers in the months immediately after the war, and I didn't have where to put him. When he began to walk, he crawled out and in the mud. Once my big brother, who lived with me because my place was nearer his job, didn't wake up to go to work. I called him, 'Wake up brother! Wake up that you will be late.' With tears in his eyes, he said, 'I had a dream last night. I saw our sister. She asked for help, she wailed, I got up and grabbed her and cried.' We know that until she died, she went through a lot.... My father and my mother helped me and the psychologist who treated me said they were good, so they didn't seek treatment. But my mother goes to the doctor for her eyes. There are nights when she cannot open her eyes from the pain, *ku ku*, she complains about those eyes. Some women told her, 'You cry too much. You cry a lot, day after day.' She spares me from seeing her cry, but the other women see it."

Standing by her father at her sister's wake, Valbona saw his tears. "He cried, 'Ah, look at her!' My sister was healthier and better looking than me. 'Had I had a boy, I would have let him go to get married instead of her. I anticipated her to get married and leave, and that would have been fine, but not that the war would take her away.' My father changed a lot after the war. He had to break the habit of driving his tractor to the mountain with my sister. She tended the cows that he kept and still keep in the village, she took all the manure, and brushed the cows. She was as hardworking as a man. You know, the only place I like to visit when I go out is the house of my sister's best friend. Those two went into the well together. They killed this woman's only brother as well, and the television people come often to interview their mother. But I go just to have some conversation, to warm up my spirit somehow. I like to stay at her place very much, we are very sad together, we share feelings."

Teuta missed the proximity of her family when she relocated abroad after her testimony at The Hague: "I moved to a state that I didn't know, I didn't know the language. It was a catastrophe in the beginning. The state welcomed us, four protected witnesses, offered us everything, they also helped with psychologists, but it is very difficult to meet with a psychologist, a doctor, someone like that, when you don't know the language. It is not the same if you express your own feelings when there is someone translating your words. But a person reconciles with anything. So, we began a new life. A person will never forget the past, but she can keep it a little behind. I could integrate very little, because when I came to this new country, I asked to go to a place where there were no Albanians. When much later I began to meet them, they were from this country rather than from our place, and they didn't know what happened to me."

Although she feels ambivalent about Kosovo, Teuta feels ambivalent about it. "Things might have changed in Kosovo in comparison with when I lived there. But I cannot really tell you my opinion because I don't stay much when I visit. I stay a maximum of one month and I don't have much time. You see, my children have other obligations. Sometimes I feel very cold inside because I was born there, I grew up there, I could not put distance between me and Kosovo. It's just that they did very little for us in Kosovo. I have the duty to live here, but I always have Kosovo in my mind. I always think about returning. Look, I am telling you, I will never reconcile with this life here. I always knew that I had no place here. Even though I have a life, I have documents in place, I am a citizen of this state, it does not attract me. I always think of returning."

Building a Network

When the director of the Kosova Centre for Rehabilitation of Torture Victims (KRCT) Feride Rushiti met Teuta for the first time, she realized that the young woman was afraid of talking to her.[11] "I saw that she was unable to breathe, she was fidgety. It was in December and it was cold. She wore a shawl over a shirt and when she began to talk, she also began to push the shawl back, revealing large red spots on her neck. Suddenly, she cried. I cried. You can't be indifferent when a person is showing those kinds of emotion. She enters a well of emotions and takes you down there with her."

A leading advocate of sexual violence survivors, Rushiti has never lost the empathy that first drew her to working for them. Looking backward, she reckons that while she was engaged as a health worker from the start of the war, caring primarily for survivors was not a foregone conclusion. She left her home in Gjilan on the snowy day of the massacre of civilians at Reçak, January 15, 1999, a young woman still dreaming to finish her studies at the University of Tirana to become a gastroenterologist. Just one day earlier, the police had come searching for her as someone whose name was linked to the KLA. She was not a fighter, but had treated anyone who needed help, including fighters. With other young Kosovars, she had reported to the Kosovo liaison office in Tirana. Her expertise was first used to sort out foreign donations of medicines whose prescription was unknown to relief workers. She did not need money, and was glad to volunteer at the hospital, where she had been helping with the care of the refugees already for a year. It did not take long for the doctors to realize that she was underutilized, and she quickly became a psychosocial coordinator in charge of a mobile team serving different refugee camps across Albania.

In the spring of 1999, she was hired by UNICEF to work with children in the northern Albania camps of Kukës, the home of the tens of thousands of refugees flowing daily through the border with Kosovo. Kukës is a small, isolated village in the middle of the mountains, at the time reachable from Tirana by a ten-hour car drive on a narrow and tortuous road. For UN personnel, it was just a quick fifteen minutes by helicopter, and in fifteen minutes they moved from a bustling city to total chaos. The high plateau of Kukës, with its unpaved streets strewn with garbage and a mosque as its only distinguishing building, was packed with refugees, mostly women, children, and old people. During the first weeks, there was not enough shelter for everyone as UN agencies and other relief organizations scrambled to find tents and food. When Rushiti arrived in Kukës at the end of March, flown in with other UN personnel by an Apache, she was so distraught that for three days she could not leave her bed. Her boss thought she might need counseling herself and offered to let her go back home. She decided to stay. If she was ready to fight for her people, she might as well put up with sharing a room with four other colleagues and hundreds of lice.

In Kukës, Rushiti learned skills other than medicine, dealing with scores of children roaming the camp and playing in the mud of spring and the dust of the following summer. She focused on a big group of them camping inside the big mosque on the square, using "the gifts of my childhood," as she likes to say, which proved more effective than the impromptu training in psychosocial care that she had received. That meant that she made children sing the repertoire of Albanian songs that she knew, keeping them busy and content as their mothers fetched food. When UNICEF director Carol Bellamy made a visit to Kukës, she was directed to the mosque to check the excellent job done by the local team. She rewarded them with two helicopters full of toys for children who had lost everything.

At Bar Amerika, a tavern of sorts where journalists and aid workers congregated after hours, Rushiti also found a small role as intermediary and interpreter between refugees and the foreign media. One day, they asked her to go to the camp run by Italians. The journalists wanted to interview a woman whom they knew had been raped; she had lost all connections with her family and had only a child with her. Rushiti remembers everything about that meeting, even the sunlight shining over the refugee camp, on Kukës plateau: "'Hello, how are you?' I said when I met the woman, but she did not reply, she stood completely frozen, no emotions. I am an emotional person and had no clue of what it meant to be frozen like that, it was at the very beginning of my career. 'How are you feeling?' 'Fine.' The journalists, who were American, were trying to get into the room. I said that we had to close the door, that if we didn't create a safe environment, I couldn't continue the interview with the woman. She kept repeating, in a mumble, 'Fine, I am fine, I lost my child on the way….' You could barely understand what she said. Suddenly, she said, 'They killed my husband.' Nobody was thinking of asking after her husband. Husbands were not around back then; all the women were alone in the camps. Talking to her was like trying to put together the pieces of a puzzle. I started to cry. Behind the door, the journalists began to push to enter. And then she too began to cry and to speak in voices that sounded different from her own, I don't quite know how to explain."

Only after some meetings, she began to tell the whole story, how she had been attacked and her husband killed, and how she had to leave her wounded child behind.

Rushiti could speak the language of the survivors she met, but most importantly she knew their world. She felt she could have been one of them. For the previous decade, she had faced serious risks for her safety. In 1989, her second cousin Afrim Rushiti, a well-known boxer, had been shot dead in the streets of Gjilan during a demonstration against Milošević. His crime was trying to stop the police from beating a woman who sold street food in the hospital courtyard where demonstrators had been trapped; he managed at first to escape and hide down a pothole, but a Serbian nurse with a view of the courtyard revealed his position to the police. By association with him, the entire extended family was targeted for surveillance, even Rushiti, a young and successful student back then. With higher education shut down for Albanians in Kosovo after 1990, she enrolled in the University of Tirana.

She often took the dangerous, illegal trek across the border in the company of smugglers, and knows she was lucky that nothing happened to her. It was more dangerous at home, because she was doing something illegal from the point of view of the Serbian government. It was 1992 or 1993, she cannot remember precisely. One early morning, the police came for her. She still does not know who had informed the police that she was home for the holidays. "My father told the police that I wasn't there, that I was on holiday. They returned after a few days and it did look like I had been on holiday because I had a tan after a few days spent at the beach in Albania. They invited me to follow them for an 'informational interview.' Although it was summer, I got dressed for winter, I wore a big sweater, just to not look provocative. Imagine that! People did not openly talk about it, but women were raped at the police station, and I am not referring to wartime. I know a woman who was raped by a medical doctor before the war at the hospital, while on detention."

Growing up, Rushiti had heard her grandmother's stories from the Second World War, how she covered herself and even smeared her face with ashes as a form of defense from possible assaults, whether by Bulgarian or Serbian soldiers. Those memories seemed forgotten, but decades later she noticed that Grandma could not watch a war movie on TV without reliving the threats and the fear of her youth. Remembering her grandmother's stories was enough to make Feride not only wary of Serbian police and soldiers, but also conscious of her vulnerability as a woman.

Immediately after the war, Rushiti set up the KRTC to treat war traumas, but survivors of sexual violence, today a major focus of the organization's activities, were slow in seeking help. Sometimes the reason was just ignorance. Teuta, among others, did not know that she could find help in Prishtina: "Nobody helped, there was no psychologist at that time in Kosovo. Maybe there was one, but I did not meet her, I didn't know, I didn't have anyone to contact. And I went through it all on my own, I mean, you helped yourself. I had to because I saw I was going crazy. My soul was not dead." The problem was that it was also very hard for the professionals to offer help. In the immediate aftermath of the war, Rushiti found it impossible to penetrate the rural communities where sexual violence had been more widespread. "There was not just silence, it was a taboo to speak about sexual violence. It was impossible for survivors, but also for us, we were threatened."

At the Center, Selvi Izeti worked at first mostly with individuals and families who had lost loved ones. Those were clients who could not wait to talk, who would find solace in telling their stories. It was much different for survivors of sexual violence. They had not talked to anyone since the war, and when they began to visit the center, they spoke solely of their dead or their missing. They had multiple traumas. Only when they understood that they could trust the therapist did they open up about their own personal experience of violence. But that change took months, if not years. What never changed was the demand for absolute anonymity. For a long time, even the work of organizations such as KRTC could not be made public. As late as 2006, when the law providing compensation for veterans and civilian victims of the war was first debated, Rushiti unsuccessfully proposed that survivors be included, perhaps not as such, but as civilians suffering from psychological problems. "Don't even go there," was the answer of the minister of welfare, whom she found sympathetic, yet not ready to take on the cause of survivors. Had he agreed, she would have found another sort of opposition to publicity, this time among the very same women who had become KRTC's clients.

There have been and there continue to be so many obstacles for women to independently contact psychotherapists that the relationship was inverted. The therapists and the advocates looked for them. In the immediate aftermath of the war, Veprore (Lola) Shehu was so moved by the few cases of sexual violence she stumbled upon while working as a researcher of war crimes with the International Crisis Group (ICG) that she joined Medica Kosova, a spinoff from the feminist organization medica mondiale, based in Germany but active in several conflict zones.[12] Together with a professional staff trained by German and Bosnian psychologists, she managed to circumvent the problem of silence by relying both on medical expertise and on the very traditionalist culture that feminists saw as a possible obstacle. It took some field research in the rural areas, where the war had been most brutal.

Medica Kosova went to the village leaders, usually the oldest men or even clergy, whether an imam or a priest, and learned from them which were the families where there had been casualties, and "women had experienced terrible things when militaries and paramilitaries entered their houses."[13] Under the pretext of offering condolences, Shehu visited those families, a possibility allowed by the tradition that opens ritual mourning wakes to anyone. That was also the opportunity to offer trauma and medical counseling to the women as a service to heal their war trauma in general. An all-women medical team traveling in a mobile clinic followed up this first approach, identified survivors, and later referred them to psychologists.

A word-of-mouth campaign brought so many more survivors to Medica Kosova that a second organization, Medica Gjakova, was set up to satisfy the growing demand for services. After a stint with the Norwegian Refugee Council immediately after the war, Mirlinda Sada had been working with a local NGO focused on women when medica mondiale recruited her in 2013 to head the office in Gjakova.[14] Though she had no specific skills to treat trauma, Sada had a firsthand experience of the war and its impact on people. For the entire duration of the war, she had been in this city, where civilians were targeted with more brutality than in any other urban center. NATO intervention brought happiness at first, she recalls, "but then the terror began and it lasted three months. We tried to leave twice for Albania, but my grandmother wasn't able to walk, and we could not abandon her."

In a span of three months, more than one thousand civilians were killed in Gjakova, most of them men, and hundreds are still missing. Hundreds of women were raped. Sada recalled, "What had happened in Bosnia was always on our mind, we knew it could happen here in Kosovo, but we worried about our men. If they went out, they would be killed, so we sacrificed for them. I did, for my father and my younger brother. Fortunately, nothing happened to me, but I had several encounters with police and soldiers at checkpoints. It was easier if you knew Serbian, and I did. It was terrifying of course, but when they stopped me, they would say, 'It's good that Albanian women speak Serbian in Gjakova.'"

To expand its reach, Medica Gjakova strategically used information regarding war operations to identify the specific areas where sexual violence had been most widespread. At the beginning, it was easier to enlist gynecological services that could direct the psychologists toward survivors. With time, the psychologists themselves began to scout villages ravished by the war, asking the mayor, or the imam, whether they could identify survivors. Making contact with women so wounded takes a painstaking effort that includes persuading local community leaders to break the conspiracy of silence enveloping the crime of sexual violence. The rest is much easier, as Medica Gjakova's staff combines an innate empathy with the professional skills acquired through formal training. For Blerta, for instance, meeting psychologist Shpresa Frrokaj opened up for the first time the possibility of talking about what hurt, "and I felt seventy percent happier, coming to Medica was like going who knows where... I had felt like an orphan before, I didn't have friends, never met anyone."

In Drenas, a small town in Drenica, one of the other areas hit hardest by the war, Kadire Tahiraj began her work with survivors one day in 2004, after she approached a traumatized woman at the hospital and heard her testimony.[15] Tahiraj immediately understood the plight of that stranger. In the following month, six more women came to her to talk about their wartime experience, and they kept coming. The Drenas Center for the Promotion of Women's Rights, the small organization she founded in 2008, is now a prominent center engaged in improving the living conditions of almost two hundred marginalized women in the surrounding areas.

The sympathetic mayor of Drenas, KLA co-founder Ramiz Lladrovci, turned over to Tahiraj the old municipal building at the center of town. It is a sizable space that can accommodate all the activities the center organizes for women from all walks of life, but it has no central heating or running water. Yet, the director, as everyone calls Kadire, welcomes visitors or clients with the grace of the lady of a manor and manages it as efficiently as one can under the circumstances. The center has trained women to make all sorts of handicrafts that are sold at the center, in one shop in downtown Prishtina, and in a corner dedicated to their crafts inside Kosovo's Assembly. By mid-2022, the center had screened and helped about three hundred clients with the application for survivors' pensions.

On a busy day in May 2022, the director received Fatmire and Luljeta, who had just shown up for consultation on private matters.[16] Then she drove half an hour to an isolated house on the nearby hills to check on Drita, who lives in poverty with her brother's family. After some more driving, she finally reached a small town to see Arbana and her husband, a former guerrilla fighter mutilated in the war, one of the few openly supportive spouses of survivors; he does not agree with the other men and their conviction that if the women did not leave or did not defend themselves from their rapists it meant that they "liked it." He said, "If I could not defend her, and I was armed, how could she have defended herself?"

At the center, the director comforted Fatmire, whose son, now the head of a household of fifteen, criticized her for receiving a pension that he considered an exchange of money for sex. Devalued as a survivor in her own house, Fatmire was demoted to second place after her daughter-in-law, who insultingly reminded her during the pandemic that she obtained aid from the center only because she was raped. Fatmire dreamed of living alone and being able to speak up about her experience. "I would like to scream it to the world." Her friend Luljeta, much younger than Fatmire, found the courage to leave a home where she was abused, but she was alone with an epileptic son who was traumatized by the violence he witnessed at home. She too did not feel accepted anywhere. Even as the silence surrounding wartime sexual violence has now been broken, talking about it brought new criticism, as in the common complaint: "Why do you always talk about rape?"

Dealing with a population of clients who have many pressing needs is exhausting, but the director seems to possess an endless reservoir of empathy and pragmatism: she never studied psychology, but she is quick in detecting signs of depression, and her knowledge of state policies and administrative procedures has become refined with practice. Her skills showed during the visit to Drita. It was a very sad house of women up in the hills, where Drita's mother still mourns her two boys, eighteen and fifteen, murdered by Serbian forces, and Drita cares for her son but mostly works thanklessly in the house. The director whispered something to Drita while the young sister-in-law, who was not supposed to know what happened in the war, left the room with the baby. When the sister-in-law returned, the director turned to her and advised her about her rights for a social pension: with four small children and an unemployed husband, she met all the criteria required by law. Later, noticing that the women sat in a dark house, the windows and door hidden behind laundry hanging on a clothesline, the director pointed to the beautiful nature all around and reproached them in a friendly way, "Why don't you hang your laundry in the garden, sweep the terrace, and sit outside to enjoy the sun?"

Women seeking counseling do so because they fully trust the service providers' staff to keep their commitment to confidentiality. At the start, some women continue to talk around rape as something that happened to a third person, but do not reveal their individual experience, even in closed group discussions. Adelina: "We didn't even ask the question among ourselves, like for example, 'Were you raped?' You know? No, no, no." At the KRTC, Selvi Izeti knows well that most of her clients come to her office under some pretext, because they do not want their families to know. They find hundreds of excuses to visit her office, and they often bring their children, but they are always afraid of being found out. It is troublesome for the psychologist to know that the women she treats find additional stress in the very action of coming to her. She understands that "they are not yet free." Most survivors travel long distances to visit counselors working in regions other than their own to avoid being seen entering their premises. And thus in Prishtina, Selvi Izeti sees clients from Drenica, and Fehmije Luzha at Medica Gjakova counsels women from Prishtina, while Kadire Tahiraj in Drenica advises those from Dukagjin. Traveling costs money and time, but it allows privacy and preserves confidentiality.

It is still very common that as the KRTC or Medica Gjakova are made aware of a case, a professional therapist visits the woman and tries first to establish a relationship of trust with her in her own home. It can also happen that a member of the family encourages a woman to seek counseling. Shpresa's husband heard about the KRTC on TV, took down the phone number, and told her about it. Since 2013, a few husbands have begun to accompany their wives to their psychotherapy sessions. It is rarer that women approach this type of service on their own. Fatime did, but she is a rarity: "I went on the internet and searched, searched, wrote all sort of stupid things until I found the Center and I wasn't sure it was the right place until I heard, 'This is it, you have come to a good, safe place.'"

Medications provided some help; they were a quick answer to an overwhelming pain, and a promising one, given the prospect of an elusive healing. Vlora: "I began to take tranquilizers in May, I could because I wasn't pregnant anymore. I feel better with pills. Now, when there are arguments with my husband, even the pills I take don't make me feel calmer because I am always nervous.... Because I don't feel like the others but sicker." Edona:

"I never stopped taking tranquilizers. I told the psychologist, 'The stomach, I am up all night because of stomach pain.'...Then a woman suggested that I drink milk, and that helps me a lot. I leave a bottle in the fridge and drink a cold glass at night and I cut down the pills. Now I only take pills when I get too upset."

Afërdita: "I am spending a lot of time without sleeping but I fought back against pills, because taking sleeping pills for seventeen years is too much. I took one, two, three pills. Whenever I was seized by crises, 'vup!' and I was knocked out. Not five milligrams or ten milligrams, but fifteen, I was down for three-four days and then I woke up." Talking to a psychologist, finding acceptance, has at least reduced medicalization by breaking the isolation. For Fatime, it is clear how that happened: "Now I have friends, I have very good friends who have the same problem, the same happened to them."

Organizations working with survivors provide a safe space where survivors can talk more freely, whether to a professional therapist or to other survivors. Like Fatime, Lumnije found great comfort in realizing she was not the only one to have gone through the harrowing experience of sexual violence, trauma, and stigma: "Now I have friends here, good friends." For Shpresa, it was just important to talk to sympathetic ears: "As I talked, as I said everything that happened to me, somehow it seemed as if I was relieved of a lot of pain. I couldn't talk to my mother, because a mother is very dear, she feels even more everything her children feel, and I cannot talk to her, nor I plan to ever do that, not to my mother, not to my daughters, not to anyone."

There is no longer a taboo in Kosovo about wartime sexual violence, which thanks to advocates is freely addressed in the public sphere. Art exhibitions, plays, and awareness campaigns devoted to survivors have increased since 2015. Survivors had their own champion in Parliament when Vasfije Krasniqi-Goodman was elected in 2021, though she retired two years later for health reasons. As a "professional" representative of survivors in many venues, from the domestic Assembly to the U.S. Congress and the global platform of the Nobel Prize–winning Mukwege Foundation, Krasniqi-Goodman has to live with the contradiction of being like all the others though she is set apart from them, and that is a heavy burden.[17] Her courage in speaking up has hardly been contagious. For all other survivors, silence remains the preferred option, and they live in a world divided in two parts, as Goffman would put it: the larger group to which they tell nothing, and the small group on which they can rely for confidentiality and to which they talk.[18]

Talking Is a Duty and a Right

In 2012, Nazlie Bala and former KLA fighter Aida Derguti met with Igo Rogova of the Kosova Women's Network, and the two women agreed that survivors had been trapped for too long between the desire to talk about what happened to them and the compulsion to stay silent, whether this silence was externally imposed or self-imposed. For International Women's Day, on March 8, they staged a sit-in in the center of Prishtina under the banner, "We don't want flowers. We want justice for women who suffered sexual violence during the war."[19] Never before had such a closely kept public secret been disclosed so publicly. Advocates felt they had an opening with a new generation of women leaders, such as the minister of European integration, Vlora Çitaku, and the president of the Republic, Atifete Jahjaga, who were galvanized into action after meeting survivors privately and hearing their stories. For their part, survivors were happy to talk to and be recognized by powerful women. Within the family, they became the object of envy. The custom was for men to meet with public officials if any meeting was necessary. When the women returned home from their afternoon chats over coffee with the president of the Republic, they inevitably gained a higher standing in their *rrethi*.

Seeing an opening in the institutions, advocates laid out specific demands. They raised the issue of including wartime rape survivors as a separate category in the law on veterans and civilian victims of the war and won that battle against strong political opposition.[20] Members of the Assembly made the specious argument that too much time had passed since the war and there was no evidence for the alleged crimes of sexual violence. The War Veterans Association wanted to include survivors of sexual violence in the broad category of civilian victims.

In the veterans' narrative of the war, there is no room for victimization—or for women, for that matter. The heroes are only manly warriors. Celebrations and commemorations are first of all for the fallen in battle, the "active victims," and only two known early memorials have been dedicated to women, both located in the western village of Burim (formerly Istog): two statues in the semblance of Luljeta Shala Bujupi (Suliotja) and Mervete Maksutaj, who were about twenty years old when they joined the KLA and were killed in 1998. More recently, two other women fighters have been recognized. In 2017, a statue of Hyrë Emini-Mira was erected in Ferizaj, and in 2018 a statue of Xhevë Krasniqi Ladrovci was placed in the main square of

Drenas.[21] This is a remarkably small number of memorials and monuments devoted to women, since at least thirty-two women appear in the available list of the *dëshmorët* (war martyrs) compiled by the *Shoqata e Veteranëve të Luftës të Ushtrisë Çlirimtare të Kosovës* (Association of War Veterans of the KLA).[22] If thirty-two women died, many more should be the survivors of the war, but with a few exceptions, veteran women are not known or celebrated as men are.

The war that was fought over the bodies of women left no heroine behind, says Ganimete: "All types of people who have been in the war are proud. There is pride in saying, 'I am the wife of a martyr.' There is pride in saying, 'I am a civilian victim.' There is pride in saying, 'I am the wife of a veteran.' But a raped woman doesn't feel pride. There is no pride in saying, 'I was raped.' There is no pride because there is no pride for the family either, or the husband or the children or a daughter because nobody will say, 'My mother was raped.' This has killed all our lives; this has taken away from us the hope for life....Had I been without an arm, without a leg, I would have been happier. I would have been much happier if I were blind. I would not have to see anything, nor feel anything. Had I been blind, I would have gone out and someone would have given me a hand, because I am blind. Someone would have helped me. But my wound is inside and burns my heart every day."

Women survivors of sexual violence are not classified as veterans, but they feel they should have been. Shkurta says: "I went to war, my body went to war, and there was never a moment when I didn't fight. And all my life I had to keep silent. Soldiers fought. We didn't fight in the same way, but we fought more than they did. We were face to face with Serbs. We all had to face them. Men left. They went far away. We all stayed with the Serbs. They seized us, took us where they wanted and did what they wanted with us and you couldn't even say a word. Nothing. I very much want to be recognized, not exaggeratedly, but I don't have any photos of myself showing that I fought."

As in every guerrilla war, many women were involved in logistics as mothers, sisters, and wives of the KLA fighters—real, not just metaphorical, fighters. Ajshe was caught as she was bringing clothes to her KLA relatives. The Serbian counterinsurgency deployed disproportionate violence, and the conflict quickly morphed into a campaign of ethnic cleansing, a total war against all Albanian civilians. In this context, it is not unreasonable to consider almost everybody a veteran. Uniquely recognized by her husband as partaking in a collective trauma, Edona draws much support from it: "I have a brother and a friend in my husband. He says, 'You too fought in the war. This was your war. It wasn't you who went to them. You made me proud, and your thoughts and your suffering must be known. The day has come.' I said, 'Which day has come? Ishallah, we should never even mention it.' But the day came. Those who wanted to talk did it, and it went well. Ishallah, those who suffered and were hit felt happy, even though nobody carries the dishonor we do and we will always suffer from it until we die."

In Prishtina, women's activists had realized early on in the war that women would be extremely vulnerable to sexual assault. That did not deter them from risking exposure. On the contrary, to avoid being caught they used improvised strategies that foregrounded their femininity, playing on gender stereotypes and ethnic prejudice. The conventional wisdom was that Albanian women were more modest in their appearance than Serbian women, and less assertive when talking to men, whether because of their cultural context or because their relationship with the police and army was objectively hostile. Hence, looking more like a Serbian woman would be a rational line of defense. For Nazlie Bala, who since childhood had preferred sports and music to grooming, it meant that she had to conduct her investigations of human rights violations around the country wearing a dress and using an exaggerated quantity of makeup.[23] Shpresa Mulliqi, a journalist interested in covering the front line, thought she would be safer traveling disguised as a Serbian woman and exploiting the stereotype that sees blond women like her as more feminine and less threatening. She hid her camera and recorder under a stash of women's magazines in Serbian, beaming an ingratiating smile any time she was stopped at a checkpoint, and she was never searched.[24]

In Peja, activists like Lumka Krasniqi drove a car full of medical supplies and food across the war zone, together with another woman from the Council for Emergencies, a support group created by local youth. "My father was very worried. He said, 'I don't care if they kill you or do something, I care if they do to you what they usually do.'"[25] The two women were determined not to fall victim to anyone. They always kept a bomb in their car, hidden under a towel by the gear. Once the police stopped them and pulled Lumka out of the car for an interrogation. Her friend Angjelina, who stayed inside, quickly told her, "Don't worry about it because if something happens, I will take action." Fortunately for them, nothing ever happened.

This awareness of women's vulnerability, perhaps surprisingly, was not universally shared at first. Izeti was a young woman in the southeastern town of Ferizaj, where the war was fought less violently, and she never thought it could happen there, certainly not to her, though soldiers and paramilitaries swarmed her neighborhood. She heard no warning from her mother or grandmother, though the latter had experienced war.[26] When the men took to the mountains and left their families behind, at first it seemed to Valbona that there was nothing wrong with it. "Up in the mountains it would have been riskier because men fought with men…we did not know that women also fought. What would they do to womenfolk? Maybe a kick here or there but that's nothing, perhaps some shouting too. My father-in-law said, 'If something happens to our women, may God blind your eyes. This is war.' He foretold the violence and said it to the younger men. Look, I did not hear this myself, I heard it from the men. We did not know. They told us, 'Let's go women, go here, go there….' We womenfolk just shuffled along with our bags. And we did not dare say no, or make noise, because they were expecting the worst, and saying that we needed help was out of the question, we did not dare throw a tantrum."

Ganimete thinks that deep cultural reasons meant that women, though vulnerable, would be spared the worst: "Our mentality, the Albanian tradition of the *kanun*, is that women are not killed even in blood feuds. I heard stories from my mother, such as the story of someone who killed another man and was involved in a blood feud. He was not given permission by the offended party to leave his house, so when he went out, he would take his wife with him. The one who was coming to kill him in revenge would say, 'No, because he is with his children'—back then, they called women children, you know? 'He is with his wife,' and he was not killed. And we thought that like in the *kanun*, which prevailed in Kosovo, they would not hurt the children and would not hurt the women."

In fact, in the oral tradition there is an explicit permission for men and women to walk hand in hand when a man is targeted for revenge killing, trumping the customary modesty that does not allow public forms of intimacy between adults.[27] So strong were those beliefs that they defied the growing evidence of sexual violence crimes emerging from the Bosnian war, and of women's vulnerability at home. How was it possible that Ganimete never heard of the horror stories of rape camps that were making headlines in news all over the world in the mid-1990s? Still, she recalls that nobody in rural Kosovo had an inkling of the mass rapes in Bosnia. They were too isolated.

Poverty also ran deep. When visiting the village of Obri e Epërme in Drenica to chronicle life in rural Kosovo, *Koha Ditore*'s journalists, all urban youth, were stunned when they saw a woman burst out of a closet where she hid, apparently too ashamed to witness how strangers would react to seeing their impoverished abode: a mud house, a wooden stove, and earth for floor.[28] Ganimete: "We heard of the killed, the wounded, but no media ever mentioned rapes. We barely had electricity, we used to watch Albanian news, but from the moment Serbs came in, we had to break the antenna and were left only with their TV because if they found you watching the TV from Albania they would kill you."

Would warnings have made a difference? Ganimete thinks they would have, and for this reason the survivors have a duty to talk. "My most burning desire is that all young people, that everybody in Kosovo will be aware of this crime. Maybe they will transmit the knowledge of how rape happens in war, Ishallah, to their children and their grandchildren, so nobody has to ever go through this. Thank you very much for this opportunity to tell you my story, maybe in one hundred years it will fall in someone's hands. In time, it will be known how someone survives the war and there will be greater awareness of what can happen and of the worst things that can happen. Maybe rape is the gravest crime against humanity that remains silent all your life."

Would knowledge change behavior? Ganimete is certain it would. "I went to school, I was an excellent student in primary school and also in high school and at no moment in my life has anyone told us about this history, told us that rape occurs in war. I never heard about it. Have you? If someone had told us about it and our husbands were made aware of it, and our families were made aware of it, first and foremost they would have protected their wives, they would have shielded their twelve-year-old daughters from rape, they would have protected them and wouldn't have fled for their lives into the mountains and wouldn't have left the women behind. And now they wouldn't judge their wives or refuse them support. You know what? When the men went to the mountains, the women would have gone as well."

The Strongest Link: An Oral History of Wartime Rape Survivors in Kosovo. Anna Di Lellio and Garentina Kraja, Oxford University Press. © Oxford University Press 2025. DOI: 10.1093/9780197699324.003.0010

10
The Strength Inside

We were writing this book when Russia began the invasion of Ukraine, and we heard the first reports of rape almost immediately. So did people in Kosovo, and they were gripped by feelings of fear and anxiety. Across the country, survivors of sexual violence were plunged into a state of renewed alarm, even though the war was never an immediate or real threat for them. Reports of rapes during Hamas's attack in Israel on October 7, 2023, produced a similar reaction. The Kosovo War ended more than twenty years ago, but it left a mark on individual psyches, a trauma that, unlike the historical event that caused it, has no time limit. Still, it can be reactivated as a "real" experience by any trigger such as a not-too-distant war.[1] When the narrators in this book told us of the fear reawakened by crimes committed in current conflicts, they revealed that their trauma is not just a problem of the emotional sphere, and that they experience a collective trauma in which the threshold between the social and the psychological is subtle. Having this awareness in mind is crucial for trauma experts to formulate effective therapeutic strategies across generations.[2] For us, it was the necessary frame to compose our own narrative plot.

We thus began from the historical context that created a transgenerational legacy of traumatizing events for Albanians in Kosovo. We broadly traced the crucial influence of state formation on ethnic relations between Serbs and Albanians from the beginning of the twentieth century to the establishment of Socialist Yugoslavia after the Second World War. The state, always ruled by Serbs or Yugoslavs, has been an organ of repression and violence against Albanians, applying collective punishment to movements for national independence. It does not follow that the plot of this book is solely political, though politics is always present.

Unlike most recent histories of Kosovo based on testimonies, including those focused on women, we are not presenting narrations of agency and heroism. Our narrators are not known figures of protest and resistance. Their stories are important to recover ordinary lives, and more precisely, the ordinariness permitted in a context of repression. They tell how daily life was shaped by tradition and describe the struggle to keep families together against the odds, especially as the growing state violence increasingly intruded in the domestic sphere. As young girls, our narrators experienced the alteration of time's expected flow when increasing insecurity added new obstacles to education. They learned how murderous was the security apparatus that damaged their male kin both physically and psychologically.

War broke out in March 1998, and everything experienced before that seemed a premonition of the total devastation that followed: the looting, the body searches, the forced marches, the use of civilians as human shields, the destruction of religious sites, homes, and livestock, the killings, and the rapes. The pain was and is individual, but the persecution and trauma were and are collective. The rapes were often perpetrated by gangs of soldiers, police, and paramilitaries, in plain view and with total impunity, sometimes in public to force families, husbands, and children to witness the event. Sexual violence was intended to humiliate and was accompanied by beating, cutting, burning, and branding the victims. The victims always asked for human compassion and tried to resist. It was all in vain, because empathy is a sentiment alive only among humans, and Albanians no longer were human for their torturers after years of pounding state propaganda. The women were reduced to washing machines and breeding factories, the men to either sexual animals or feminine versions of themselves—that is, objects of derision for other men, as in Edona's memory of those forced to dance naked before being deported and disappeared.[3]

Broken Selves

For women survivors of sexual violence, the story of the aftermath of that violence is a punishing story of stigmatization that led to secrecy and isolation. The question arises: How was it possible for mass victimization and traumatization to become an individual burden? Trauma studies provide some answers. Because a healthy society always maintains the conservative notion that there is justice in this world and that people generally get what they deserve, it considers victims a liability, and shuns them. In the Albanian society of Kosovo, emerging horribly scarred from the war, victims of sexual violence found even less acceptance than they would have in a healthier society because they embodied what everyone wanted to forget.[4] This rejection is political as much as social.

Politically, only by denying the widespread and systematic sexual violence against their women were Albanians able to hide their own humiliation and victimization behind a conventional history of heroism. This dynamic, far from being unique, can be observed in several historical examples across the world. Until the mid-1990s, postwar Italy utterly denied the estimated 12,000 rapes by French colonial troops after the victorious campaign for Monte Cassino in late spring 1944. Recognizing those crimes would have meant criticizing Italy's new allies in NATO, and would have been incompatible with a public discourse extolling the masculine warrior figure of the antifascist partisans.[5] Germany acknowledged the mass rapes by the Soviet army in 1945 only sixty years later because recognition would have been an admission of men's impotence and dishonor in the context of an already inglorious defeat.[6] In China, the state silenced the horrific stories of rape by the Japanese army in Nanking, because competition for recognition between the People's Republic of China and the Republic of China suppressed any claim to memory, let alone justice.[7] Cultural and institutional restrictions silenced memories of widespread sexual violence under the Khmer Rouge, a denial readily embraced by the Extraordinary Chambers in the Courts of Cambodia (ECCC), known as the Khmer Rouge tribunal.[8]

The social dynamic of rejection is as effective as politics in silencing and isolating survivors. We felt the narrators' disorientation from the very immediate aftermath of the rapes, when it was made very clear to them that they had become a barely tolerable burden for even their closest family, even their female relatives. It is the women's judgment that hurts the most. A successful Kosovo film, the 2021 Sundance Film Festival winner *Hive*, suggests a possible reading of the power dynamic among women.[9] The film is the real-life story of a war widow, Fahrije Hoti, who lives in Krusha e Madhe, a village where almost all the men have been killed, but the few remaining are still in command.[10] Cornered into poverty and despair, she must struggle against the opposition of the whole *rrethi* to her driving a car and starting a small business, and the other widows are no less hostile than the other villagers before they join her. In a few scenes, Fahrije tends a beehive, at the beginning struggling under the attack of the bees, later much calmer and in control. The director, Blerta Basholli, explained those scenes: "Bees sting people who are restless or upset. They can sense it. The women in the story are like bees, they sting Fahrije but stop when they feel and recognize her inner resolve."[11] Ganimete told us that the sting of women's rejection was what hurt her the most.

The narrators in this book are strong women, but even for the strongest it took extraordinary effort and time to absorb the rejection of her closest circle, a rejection which was psychologically devastating, a "vicarious" traumatization perhaps worse than the primary.[12] They knew, without hesitation, what had gone wrong. They felt a widening gap between what they had been and ought to be and what they had become after defilement, and felt that shame.[13] As girls, they had learned and internalized the role and position of a woman in the family and society by observing their mothers and other adults perform their roles. We know that by listening to their memories of childhood, which sometimes are infused with nostalgia for a prelapsarian past—a feeling which is consonant with the mass culture trope of "poor but happy"—but most importantly reveal a very early training in the rules of the dominant social and moral order.

That is where the girls learned that not fitting in has a price: the ostracism of the *rrethi*, the social circle which has enormous power on an individual as a monitor and judge of their behavior. They learned that the *rrethi* has a collective dimension but is also layered, with the men, the elder, the stronger, and the richer on top, and that they may find little support among other women, who are at the bottom. In remembering how, as children, they dutifully performed their assigned role without ever questioning it, our narrators expressed great pride. There is pride in their memories of being "good girls," working in the fields, tending the animals, helping build the house, and making their bridal trousseau. These memories make the sadder recollections of poverty, fear, and insecurity fade, and the narrators yearn for a past life that promised to stay unbroken, a life in which they would be certain of their position in the world. *Grua*, meaning "woman" in Albanian, is the same word as "wife." To be a woman, one must be a wife, and a good one.

After what happened to them in the war, they could no longer feel pride, just shame about their "spoiled identity."[14] Yet, their war stories are all about exceptional performances of "unspoiled" roles of wife, daughter-in-law, mother, daughter, and sister. Hunted by Serbian security forces who were scouring the countryside and the cities, the men left. They went to fight or into hiding, because they were the first target for assassination. Women were charged with the task of keeping together the elderly and the children. They were the ones carrying babies, food, and bundles of clothes when displaced across the countryside, keeping the toddlers quiet when in hiding, and doing all the things a woman does for the family in peacetime, such as making sure everyone is clean and fed—except that there was no peace.

At the end of an interview with Shemsi Syla, then a high-ranking KLA fighter and currently the deputy minister of defense, his wife, Tevide, when asked how she experienced the war, let out in a matter-of-fact way, "While he was up in the mountains playing war with his friends, I was here, answering the door when Serbian soldiers knocked, standing between them and the children and his parents."[15] Women were at the front line even when they did not fight. They were the ones who were often selected, or volunteered, to come out of safety and brave the streets, on the reasonable assumption that they ran fewer risks of being killed than men, like Fatime who was sent to look for food by her relatives, Ajshe who was carrying winter clothes to KLA fighters, or Vlora who went to fetch milk for her baby brother. None thought of recusing herself from any difficult task or dangerous mission; their main concern was to protect their fathers, sons, husbands, or brothers.

As girls they had always obeyed, even when at puberty they were withdrawn from the community of children they loved, and realized the time had come to take their mothers' path of hard work and submission to a new, alien family. They accepted the fact that marriage was not an individual choice, that their role was to produce children, preferably boys rather than girls, in exchange for protection and respect. As insecurity increased in the 1980s and 1990s, families did not believe they could protect their daughters, and they shifted that responsibility to a husband who could. Once they entered into a new family, girls knew that their power depended on the power of their men. In fact, they felt they had no choice other than accepting all of that. The broader context helps explain such conformity. Albanian rural society was always alienated from the state in Kosovo, especially in Drenica, where many of our narrators are from and where the war lasted longer and was more destructive.

It was not much different elsewhere. Families were a world apart, where rebellion against adults who were often under attack from the police was not an option. In all of the interviews, the narrators lowered their heads and their voices came down to a whisper when talking about being taken out of school to be given in marriage with a man they did not know. Some cried, remembering that first shocking loss of agency. Gone were all dreams of becoming a doctor or a teacher, somebody other than a wife and mother; still, they accepted their fate without failing. In their own words, "What could I do?"

Gender Games

We added other narrators, women who broke with their assigned role either on their own, or with their fathers' permission and support. Having challenged their community, those rebel girls and women were sanctioned with demotion or exclusion from the family. In the end, they completed their studies. Several did not marry. They did not conform to the dominant gender roles and could take a step back, intuitively understanding that gender is performative. Cross-dressing or manipulating gender stereotypes, especially their ethnic variants, was for them one means of expressing agency and most of all protecting their vulnerability in a complex range of circumstances. It was a form of resistance.[16]

Dressing like a boy gave a sense of security to girls during the long treks to school. It allowed young women militants to run across town at night undisturbed, and thus freed them from being confined in the domestic sphere. During the war, it was women's presumed harmlessness that activists used to trick security forces when carrying hidden weapons, medicine, cameras, or recorders. What worked in their case, however, was not the performance of an archetypal woman, but rather of a stereotypical "Serbian woman," showing all the right signifiers: fluency in Serbian, fearlessness of the police, fairer complexion and hair, and an urban look that accentuated modern traits such as Western clothing and makeup. We heard those stories from women who felt happy and proud of their courage and cunning.

Our narrators were socialized to the local standards that consider women untouchable in the public sphere. They tried to exploit this notion of femininity but failed. Neither Qëndresa, who was fourteen years old, nor her grandmother, who dressed her up as an older woman and sent her out with a child, thought that Serbian forces would not honor the sacredness of the mother figure. Thinking along the same lines, Fatime and Ajshe ventured out of their homes, thinking that with children by their side they would be spared the violence. When Vlora volunteered to walk out of a refuge to fetch milk for her baby brothers, her family did not stop her because they all thought that nobody would touch a thirteen-year-old girl. In fact, none of these devices worked. In the retelling, those stories of courage and abnegation to the family are not a source of pride. They cannot be told outside a safe space where sympathetic listeners can be found, because there is no redemptive quality in the violation the women suffered on account of their daring. Those stories do not belong in the repertory of stories of self-sacrifice for the nation that is an exclusive reserve of male fighters. There is no victim's story that is read as sacrifice in postwar Kosovo; on the contrary, the distinction between stories of civilians' victimization and stories of heroism is sharp.[17]

The Eloquence of Silence

What remains is the option of silence, though silence is a much more complex phenomenon than just complete absence of speech, or an imposed ban of communication. To guide us through a closer reading of what we heard about silence, we used a road map suggested by an anthropologist of the ancient world, Luigi Spina.[18] We started with the recognition that silence can be equivalent to talk or thought, that silence can be eloquent,[19] and that for every silence one needs to provide its context, indicate its actors, genesis, and outcomes.[20] We thus composed a narration of the many silences we found in the interviews, drawing from them insights that could broaden our understanding of gender and power in war and peacetime.

Our narrators told us about being physically unable to speak in the immediate aftermath of rape. They regained the capacity to talk about their experience only later, interacting with friendly and sympathetic people.[21] However, that was not always true, and often survivors chose silence to protect themselves from the fear of not being believed. Rape myths are still so prevalent, in Kosovo as elsewhere, that victims continue to be suspected of consenting to their attackers. Ajshe gave us photos of her bruised and cut body taken immediately after the war, as if providing forensic evidence of torture was necessary to be believed. We understood why the dead are always more credible than survivors. Raped, killed, and then dumped into a well, Valbona's sister and five other women bore silent witness of their violation, and their martyred corpses gave their families and the international court impeccable testimony.

Sometimes, the families of the narrators wished that they were dead, making a not too subtle exhortation to go away, disappear from sight, or at least stay forever silent, as only a dead person can be. Some narrators tried to commit suicide, and we know of their attempts only because they failed. We still ignore how many others found a way out from their pain in death. The death-wishers deserve attention because of who they are and because of their intentions and goals. As family, they are intimate with survivors, yet less inclined to accept them. They impose silence because they are afraid of being associated with "discreditable" women, capable of "passing" but who could become "discredited" if publicly identified.[22] They did not always need to order silence as much as allude to the undesirable difference of survivors with a thoughtless comment, or a gesture, adding to the shame and anxiety of those who already feel defective. They became a moralizing collective eye that triggered shame.[23] In Bangladesh, the word *khota* (a scornful remark that reminds one of an unpleasant event) denotes the judgment that the local community imparts on all women raped during the Partition of 1971, even those who were made into icons of the war of independence as national heroines.[24] Place, time, language, and customs may differ, but the story is the same.

Self-imposed silence is a rational reaction to stigmatizers' pressure. The alternative would be leaving home. Teuta fled her stigmatizers and built an entirely new life abroad. For years now, she has been free of gossiping relatives, neighbors, and villagers in her daily life, but she has struggled to bridge her two biographies, at first avoiding Albanians in her host country for fear of bumping into someone who knew, and always maintaining a love-hate relationship with her birthplace.[25] Key changes have happened in Kosovo since 2015, breaking the public secret surrounding wartime sexual violence and achieving public and even institutional acknowledgment. The topic is no longer taboo on television. However, it remains taboo at home, in the neighborhood, and in the village.

As we thought about the silence of survivors, it occurred to us that the greatest and hardest silence to break is that of the perpetrators. Dori Laub and other scholars have explained how the key event in trauma is the perpetrators' destruction of empathy as a human feeling, both in their own internal world and in the victims', eliminating any possibility of speech, let alone dialogue.[26] As expected, no individual perpetrator has acknowledged his crimes in Kosovo, nor in Serbia. When we try to imagine what they might say if they spoke, we think about what history tells us, that even when they testify, perpetrators give up very little in terms of information about their criminal actions. They follow a script that mostly tries to minimize and rationalize their behavior.[27]

Milošević was not a direct perpetrator, but he was tried as responsible for sexual violence in Kosovo, among other war crimes and crimes against humanity. When he faced witnesses, he behaved precisely as other perpetrators who are forced to confront their actions. He portrayed himself and his country as victims of terrorism and claimed to have performed his duty as defender of the nation, maintaining that the Yugoslav army had fought terrorists and protected civilians from them. None of that was true, of course, as is evident from court records and from the testimonies we gathered. The direct perpetrators were men wearing different uniforms, belonging to different armed formations, army, police, and paramilitaries, but all moving at the same time and in a coordinated way across Kosovo. They were almost always drunk or drugged, often in a rage, erratic in their behavior, a few times ambivalent, but always cruel and omnipotent. They were, as a comprehensive report of war crimes by Human Rights Watch wrote, "under orders."

A Language of Rights and Justice

All our narrators shared a thirst for justice, accompanied by the realization that they may never get it. Justice is more like a guiding principle than a reality. The narrators often use the terms "we" and "category" when talking about themselves, and especially in the context of their long-deserved acknowledgment and reparations. Since the war pension allocated to survivors has grouped them in a separate category from the other civilian victims, it has also provided them with a language of rights and justice. In the context of the pension, a story of victimization is much easier to tell than a story of shame.[28] On the contrary: it helps more individuals seek reparations, which are understood as financial and moral recognition.

There have been many changes in the field of justice for sexual violence survivors, not only in Kosovo but in the world. Since the first convictions for sexual violence as a war crime, a crime against humanity, and genocide, at the ICTY and at the International Criminal Court for Rwanda (ICTR), international law has established a solid jurisprudence in the matter.[29] Prosecutors are now supported by new actors in their pursuit of evidence. In the ethnic cleansing campaign begun in 2017 against the Rohingya by the Myanmar state, reports of widespread and systematic sexual violence were gathered early on, contributing to the 2019 decision of the International Criminal Court (ICC) prosecutor to open an investigation into the crisis.[30] Since February 2022, a network of international and domestic prosecutors, human rights organizations, and investigative journalists has wasted no time in collecting evidence and testimonies on thousands of war crimes and crimes against humanity perpetrated by Russian forces in Ukraine, with a focus on sexual violence.[31] In 2024, a similar dynamic has led the ICC prosecutor to investigate rape as a war crime and crime against humanity in the context of the Hamas-Israeli conflict and charged Hamas leaders with this crime in his call for their arrest warrant.[32] It is good progress, but not enough to give justice to hundreds of thousands of victims across the world, as narrow political considerations continue to trump their needs, demands, and rights.

This is particularly true in Kosovo, where the conflict that caused so much violence has not been resolved as yet. The international community and the domestic society have acknowledged survivors, but their recognition appears to be thin. At the international level, acknowledgment is limited to the human rights world and is far from being fully adopted by governments and international organizations, which always yield to realist concerns. Two examples illustrate the issue. Serbia has been successful in its demand, backed by Russia, to exclude Kosovo from the annual UN report on conflict-related sexual violence to the secretary general until 2021.

In November 2022, the British host of the London World Conference on the Prevention of Conflict-Related Sexual Violence invited Ivica Dačić, Serbian deputy prime minister and foreign minister who was Milošević's right arm during the war, to sit with survivors of Serbian crimes from Bosnia, Croatia, and Kosovo.[33] Dačić was not there to issue an apology, but to deliver a de-contextualized, generic speech on the evil of sexual violence that sounded like a cynical string of platitudes.[34] The Kosovo foreign minister and a host of regional human rights organizations protested.[35] However, the damage was done. For Ganimete, the presence at the summit of a leader of the Serbian state, one of the instigators of sexual violence, was a "double confrontation"; the support expected from the international conference turned into additional anxiety.[36] In Kosovo, acknowledgment stops at public discourse. It is not enough to defeat or even alleviate the stigma that degrades, humiliates, and isolates survivors at home.

Women's Networks: The Strongest Link

The lives of the narrators of this book share a common plotline. It is not a linear one, but it has a beginning and a middle. The end is not that clear. The middle is an interruption of the plot, which destroyed what made sense before the war, but also any vision for the future. Dreams were replaced by suicidal thoughts and a feeling that it is impossible to go on living. There is no end to this book, not just because the narrators go on living, but because they live in an endless present. The path of recovery depends on what goes on around them at any given time.

We interviewed narrators who were introduced to us by service providers and advocates, so we heard a selected group of individuals. It is clear, however, that it was possible for them to talk to us freely and safely because of the "everyday work of repair," in Veena Das's words, which they have begun with the professionals, who helped them reconnect with people.[37] For now, they have reconnected just with other survivors as a first step to break their isolation, and the hope is that they will be able to talk more freely also with their families and communities. Funds and support to the organizations that are devoted to help survivors have come from transnational organizations, but it was the women of Kosovo who picked up the pieces of their broken selves to create a support network. It should never be forgotten that the traumatic experience of the Kosovo War was a moment of collective change, which devastated the society like the individual bodies of survivors.[38] Through interviews and observations, we learned that counselors feel a moral commitment to survivors, which is precisely what trauma experts require to promote recovery.[39] It is not just their professional training that taught them how to show moral solidarity to their clients, or how to love them. They knew instinctively from their own experience.

Holocaust survivor Primo Levi once wrote that "every human being possesses a reserve of strength whose extent is unknown to him, be it large, small, or nonexistent, and only through extreme adversity we can evaluate it."[40] The women we got to know while working on this book showed that they possessed a great reserve of force that kept recharging during very trying times because they were not alone. When they felt they had reached the bottom, they found, as mothers, a reason to live in their children, whose greater freedom they cherish, whose care they always feel could be more and better, and whose "normality" they protect. Other women, empathetic counselors and committed advocates, established with them the human bonds of trust that had been broken by the traumatic experience of sexual violence and the subsequent stigmatization. Thanks to them, it was possible for us to be included among what Goffman calls the "wise" people, those who are privy to conditions of the stigmatized and accept them.[41]

Qëndresa put it clearly: "I want to decide with whom I talk, and I talk with those whom I consider worthy. Now for example, you met me to do something...it is still difficult for me to talk to you but I have decided to tell you what happened in my life." We sought access to survivors because we wanted to give them a speaking position, insofar as their voices have been sidelined or repressed, especially in front of an international audience. In exchange, they showed us that they are the strongest link.

The Strongest Link: An Oral History of Wartime Rape Survivors in Kosovo. Anna Di Lellio and Garentina Kraja, Oxford University Press. © Oxford University Press 2025. DOI: 10.1093/9780197699324.003.0011

Appendix

List of Interviews

This appendix is organized in three sections. The first list contains the life story interviews conducted by the authors with the narrators who are the protagonists of this oral history. The second includes all the structured interviews conducted by the authors with key figures in women's rights organizations, as well as other protagonists of Kosovo social and political life. The third is a list of those life story interviews conducted by researchers of the Kosovo Oral History Initiative, which were used to illustrate events and provide context.

The Narrators

The order of this list reflects the numbers we used to codify the interviewees, who remain anonymous as per their request. The names we attribute to each have been selected by the authors; they are the names that were more frequently given in the generation to which the woman belonged, based on information retrieved from the Kosovo Agency of Statistics' records. The full identity of the narrators is known only to the organizations that facilitated their selection and on whose premises the interviews were conducted: the Kosova Rehabilitation Center for Torture Victims in Prishtina, Medica Gjakova in Gjakova, and the Center for the Promotion of Women's Rights in Drenas. Only with one survivor we spoke remotely because she no longer lives in Kosovo. One did not agree to being recorded, and notes from the interview are on file with the rest of the transcripts. All the recorded interviews are archived in a hard drive at the Kosovo Oral History Initiative and will remain unpublished.

1. Ganimete, interviewed by Garentina Kraja, October 17, 2017, and Anna Di Lellio and Garentina Kraja, January 12, 2018
2. Fatime, interviewed by Garentina Kraja, October 18, 2017
3. Qëndresa, interviewed by Garentina Kraja, October 24, 2017
4. Vlora, interviewed by Garentina Kraja, October 26, 2017
5. Ajshe, interviewed by Garentina Kraja, October 31, 2017
6. Afërdita, interviewed by Garentina Kraja, November 2, 2017
7. Liridona, interviewed by Garentina Kraja, November 7, 2017
8. Edona, interviewed by Garentina Kraja, November 8, 2017
9. Merita, interviewed by Garentina Kraja, November 9, 2017
10. Shpresa, interviewed by Garentina Kraja, November 9, 2017
11. Fitore, interviewed by Anna Di Lellio and Garentina Kraja, January 11, 2018

12. Blerta, interviewed by Anna Di Lellio and Garentina Kraja, January 11, 2018
13. Adelina, interviewed by Anna Di Lellio and Garentina Kraja, January 12, 2018
14. Teuta, interviewed by Garentina Kraja via end-to-end encryption app Viber, January 13, 2018
15. Valbona, interviewed by Garentina Kraja, January 14, 2018
16. Kimete, interviewed by Garentina Kraja, January 15, 2018
17. Shkurta, interviewed by Kadire Tahiraj, August 17, 2015
18. Lumnije, interviewed by Kadire Tahiraj, August 18, 2015
19. Ardita, interviewed by Kadire Tahiraj, September 14, 2015
20. Drita, interviewed by Kadire Tahiraj, September 19, 2015

Structured Interviews by the Authors

Ahmeti, Sevdije (co-founder and former director of the Center for the Protection of Women and Children). Interview via skype by Anna Di Lellio, December 27, 2014.

Bala, Nazlie (human rights activist and politician). Interview via skype by Anna Di Lellio, December 22, 2014.

Basholli, Blerta (film director). In-person interview by Anna Di Lellio. New York, November 6, 2021.

Haradinaj, Ramush (KLA commander and former prime minister of Kosovo). In-person interview by Garentina Kraja, Prishtina, January 4, 2010.

Izeti, Selvi (psychologist). In-person interview by the authors. Prishtina, January 14, 2018.

Jashari, Iliriana and Selvete (members of the Jashari family, killed in March 1998). In-person interview by Garentina Kraja, Prekaz, February 1998.

Musa, Pranvera (financial officer). In-person interview by Anna Di Lellio, New York, October 20, 2019.

Qena, Nebi (journalist). In-person interview by Garentina Kraja, Jerusalem, February 12, 2023.

Rogova, Igballe (Igo) (executive director of Kosova Women's Network). Interview via phone by Anna Di Lellio, December 26, 2014.

Rushiti, Feride (director of the Kosovo Rehabilitation Centre for Torture Victims). In-person interview by Anna Di Lellio, Prishtina, January 14, 2018.

Sada, Mirlinda (Linda) (director of Medica Gjakova). In-person interview by the authors, Gjakova, January 12, 2018.

Selimi, Rexhep (former KLA commander). In-person interview by Anna Di Lellio, Prishtina, November 16, 2004.

Shehu, Veprore (Lola) (director of Medica Kosova). Interview via email by Anna Di Lellio, December 3, 2014.

Syla, Tevide (wife of KLA commander Shemsi Syla). In-person interview by Anna Di Lellio, Prishtina, September 14, 2005.

Tahiraj, Kadire (director of the Center for the Promotion of Women's Rights). In-person interview by Anna Di Lellio, Drenas, May 30, 2022.

Tahiraj, Shukrije (teacher and LDK city councilor in Skënderaj). In-person interview by Anna Di Lellio, Skënderaj, August 25, 2002.

Kosovo Oral History Initiative Interviews

These interviews are available to the public on the Kosovo Oral History Initiative website, https://oralhistorykosovo.org.

Bala, Nazlie (human rights activist and politician). Interview by Zana Rudi. Kosovo Oral History Initiative, Prishtina, June 21 and July 3, 2012. Video, 135 minutes. https://oralhistorykosovo.org/nazlie-bala/.

Berisha Lushaj, Zyrafete (high school teacher). Interview by Anita Susuri. Kosovo Oral History Initiative, Prishtina, November 17, 2021. Video, 75 minutes. https://oralhistorykosovo.org/zyrafete-berisha-lushaj/.

Brovina, Flora (poet, pediatrician, former political prisoner, and women's rights activist). Interview by Aurela Kadriu. Kosovo Oral History Initiative, Prishtina, June 27–28 and August 12, 2018. Video, 532 minutes. https://oralhistorykosovo.org/flora-brovina/.

Dida, Nadire (teacher). Interview by Donjeta Berisha. Kosovo Oral History Initiative, Prishtina, July 10 and October 8, 2014. Video, 11:43 minutes. https://oralhistorykosovo.org/nadire-dida/.

Dobruna, Vjosa (pediatrician and women's rights activist). Interview by Mimoza Paçuku. Kosovo Oral History Initiative, Prishtina, July 3 and 11, 2013. Video, 267 minutes. https://oralhistorykosovo.org/vjosa-dobruna/.

Gashi, Shukrije (director of the Center for Conflict Management—Partners Kosova and former political prisoner). Interview by Jeta Rexha and Kaltrina Krasniqi. Kosovo Oral History, Prishtina, February 14, and March 21, 2015. Video, 388 minutes. https://oralhistorykosovo.org/shukrije-gashi/.

Gjergji, Dom (Father) Lush (Catholic Bishop Vicar of the Kosovo Diocese). Interview by Erëmirë Krasniqi. Kosovo Oral History Initiative, Prishtina, May 18 and 25, 2015. Video, 132 minutes. https://oralhistorykosovo.org/dom-lush-gjergji/.

Gjurgjeala, Jehona (director of the NGO TOKA). Interview by Aurela Kadriu. Kosovo Oral History Initiative, Prishtina, May 18, 2017. Video, 57 minutes. https://oralhistorykosovo.org/jehona-gjurgjeala/.

Haradinaj Demiri, Hatmone (high school teacher, former political prisoner). Interview by Anita Susuri. Kosovo Oral History Initiative, Prishtina, March 11, 2022. Video, 94 minutes. https://oralhistorykosovo.org/hatmone-haradinaj-demiri/.

Hoti, Shaqir (musician). Interview by Jeta Rexha and Kaltrina Krasniqi. Kosovo Oral History Initiative, Prishtina, April 22, 2015. Video, 122 minutes. https://oralhistorykosovo.org/shaqir-hoti-2/.

Hyseni, Hydajet (journalist, former political prisoner, politician). Interview by Jeta Rexha. Kosovo Oral History Initiative, Prishtina, June 7, 2015. Video, 147 minutes. https://oralhistorykosovo.org/hydajet-hyseni/.

Krasniqi, Lumturije (Lumka) (accountant, former logistics officer of the KLA). Interview by Anna Di Lellio. Kosovo Oral History Initiative, New York, March 12, 2017. Video, 143 minutes. https://oralhistorykosovo.org/lumturije-lumka-krasniqi/.

Kraja, Mehmet (writer and co-founder of the LDK). Interview by Jeta Rexha and Kaltrina Krasniqi. Kosovo Oral History Initiative, Prishtina, November 4, 2014. Video, 130 minutes. https://oralhistorykosovo.org/mehmet-kraja/.

Lokaj, Xhejrane (midwife and women's rights activist). Interview by Dafina Beqiri. Kosovo Oral History Initiative, Peja, September 5, 2013. Video, 154 minutes.
https://oralhistorykosovo.org/xhejrane-lokaj/.
Maçastena, Naime Sherifi (human rights and women's rights activist, former political prisoner). Interview by Anita Susuri. Kosovo Oral History Initiative, Prishtina, March 4, 2022. Video, 84 minutes.
https://oralhistorykosovo.org/naime-macastena-sherifi/.
Muharremi, Beti (director of the NGO Dera e Hapur). Interview by Jeta Rexha and Kaltrina Krasniqi. Kosovo Oral History Initiative, Prishtina, February 7, 2015. Video, 54 minutes.
https://oralhistorykosovo.org/beti-muharremi/.
Prekpalaj, Marta (school principal and women's rights activist). Interview by Anita Prapashtica and Nicole Farnsworth. Kosovo Oral History Initiative, Prizren, June 5, 2013. Video, 105 minutes.
https://oralhistorykosovo.org/marta-prekpalaj/.
Rogova, Safete (actress and women's rights activist). Interview by Mimoza Paçuku. Kosovo Oral History Initiative, Prishtina, June 3, 2012. Video, 79 minutes. https://oralhistorykosovo.org/safete-rogova/.
Shala, Hava (social worker, former political prisoner, and leader of the blood feud reconciliation mass movement). Interview by Erëmirë Krasniqi. Kosovo Oral History Initiative, Prishtina, August 13 and October 14, 2016. Video, 170 minutes.
https://oralhistorykosovo.org/hava-shala/.
Surlić, Stefan (political scientist). Interview by Marjana Toma. Kosovo Oral History Initiative, Belgrade, June 19, 2017. Video, 110 minutes.
https://oralhistorykosovo.org/stefan-surlic/.
Syla, Ola (human rights activist). Interview by Jeta Rexha. Kosovo Oral History Initiative. Prishtina, November 23, 2014. Video, 106 minutes.
https://oralhistorykosovo.org/ola-syla/.
Tahiri, Edita (political scientist, co-founder of the LDK, former chief negotiator with Serbia). Interview by Aurela Kadriu. Kosovo Oral History Initiative, Prishtina, May 4, 2018. Video, 153 minutes.
https://oralhistorykosovo.org/edita-tahiri/.

Notes

Introduction

1. Patricia Laurence, "Women's Silence as a Ritual of Truth: A Study of Literary Expression in Austen, Brontë, and Woolf," in *Listening to Silences: New Essays in Feminist Criticism*, ed. Elaine Hedges and Fishkin Fisher (Oxford: Oxford University Press, 1994), 156–157.
2. Silvia Amati, "Ambiguity as a Defense in Extreme Trauma," in *Bearing Witness: Psychoanalytic Work with People Traumatised by Torture and State Violence*, ed. Andres Gautier and Anna Sabatini Scalmati (London: Taylor & Francis Group, 2010), 44. We are aware of the limits of expressing our indignation and denunciation of the crime of sexual violence through writing, limits explored by the French sociologist Luc Boltanski in *Distant Suffering. Morality, Media and Politics* (Cambridge: Cambridge University Press, 1999).
3. Anonymous diplomat, in-person communication with Anna Di Lellio, New York, April 26, 2018.
4. Dori Laub and Nanette C. Auerhahn, "Knowing and Not Knowing Massive Psychic Trauma: Forms of Traumatic Memory," *International Journal of Psycho-Analysis* 74 (1993): 288; Philip M. Bromberg, "The Nearness of You: Navigating Selfhood, Otherness and Uncertainty," in *Knowing, Not-Knowing, and Sort-of-Knowing: Psychoanalysis and the Experience of Uncertainty*, ed. Jean Petrucelli (London: Karnac, 2010), 36.
5. Kreshnik Gashi and Xhorxhina Bami, "Kosovo's Special Prosecutor: 'Wartime Rape Victims Must Speak Out,'" BIRN, July 8, 2021, https://balkaninsight.com/2021/07/08/kosovo-special-prosecutor-wartime-rape-victims-must-speak-out/.
6. Anna Di Lellio, "Authors of Their Own Transitional Justice: Survivors of Wartime Sexual Violence," in *Kosovo and the Pursuit of Justice after Large Scale Conflict*, ed. Aidan Hehir, Robert Muharremi, and Furtuna Sheremeti (London: Routledge, 2021), 92–110.
7. Integra and forumZFD, *I Want to Be Heard* (Prishtinë: Integra and forumZFD, 2017); Medica Gjakova and Salie Gajtani-Osmankaq, *I Am Anemone* (Gjakovë: Medica Gjakova, 2017); forumZFD and KRCT, *Beyond Pain, Towards Courage: Stories about the Trauma of Wartime Sexual Violence* (Prishtinë: forumZFD and Kosova Rehabilitation Centre for Torture Victims, 2021).
8. Arber Kadriu and Die Morina, "Pioneering Kosovo Rape Victim Relives Battle for Justice," BIRN, October 18, 2018, https://balkaninsight.com/2018/10/18/pioneering-kosovo-rape-victim-relives-battle-for-justice-10-18-2018/.
9. Xhorxhina Bami, "Kosovo War Rape Survivor Seeks Attacker's Prosecution," BIRN, October 14, 2019, https://balkaninsight.com/2019/10/14/kosovo-war-rape-survivor-seeks-attackers-prosecution/.
10. Kadire Tahiraj (director of the Center for the Promotion of Women's Rights), personal communication with the authors, Drenas, January 12, 2018.
11. Jonathan Steele (foreign correspondent for *The Guardian*), in-person interview with Anna Di Lellio, London, October 22, 2005; Babak Bahadori, *The CNN Effect in Action: How the News Media Pushed the West Towards War in Kosovo* (Basingstoke, UK: Palgrave Macmillan, 2007); Philip Hammond and Edward S. Herman, eds., *Degraded Capability: The Media and the Kosovo Crisis* (London: Pluto Press, 2000).
12. Among many others, for different perspectives see Independent International Commission on Kosovo, *The Kosovo Report: Conflict, International Response, Lessons Learned* (New York: Oxford University Press, 2000) and Danilo Zolo, *Invoking Humanity. War, Law, and Global Order* (London: Bloomsbury, 2002).
13. Human Rights Watch, *Rape as a Weapon of "Ethnic Cleansing"* (New York: Human Rights Watch, 2000), https://www.hrw.org/legacy/reports/2000/fry/index.htm#TopOfPage; OSCE and ODIHR, *Kosovo/Kosova: As Seen, As Told, Part I: October 1998–June 1999* (Warsaw:

OSCE, 1999), https://www.osce.org/files/f/documents/d/d/17772.pdf; Dominique Serrano Fitamant, *Assessment Report on Sexual Violence in Kosovo* (New York: United Nations Population Fund, 1999), https://reliefweb.int/report/serbia/assessment-report-sexual-violence-kosovo; Rachel Wareham, *No Safe Place: As Assessment of Violence Against Women in Kosovo* (New York: United Nations Population Fund for Women, 2000), https://iknowpolitics.org/sites/default/files/nosafeplace_kosovo.pdf.

14. Anna Di Lellio and Stephanie Schwandner-Sievers, "The Legendary Commander: The Construction of an Albanian Master-Narrative in Post-War Kosovo," *Nations & Nationalism* 12, no. 3 (2006): 513–529.
15. Amnesty International, *"Wounds That Burn Our Souls": Compensation for Kosovo's Wartime Rape Survivors, but Still No Justice* (New York: Amnesty International, 2017), https://www.amnesty.org/en/documents/eur70/7558/2017/en/.
16. ICTY, "Haradinaj and Balaj Acquitted of All Charges. Brahimaj Guilty of Cruel Treatment and Torture in Jablanica Compound," press release (April 3, 2008), https://www.icty.org/en/press/haradinaj-and-balaj-acquitted-all-chargesbrahimaj-guilty-cruel-treatment-and-torture-jablanica.
17. Xhorxhina Bami, "Kosovo Finds Serb Ex-Policeman Guilty of Wartime Rape After Retrial," BIRN, November 11, 2022, https://balkaninsight.com/2022/11/11/kosovo-finds-serb-ex-policeman-guilty-of-wartime-rape-after-retrial.
18. Office of the Special Representative of the Secretary General on Sexual Violence in Conflict, *In Their Own Words: Voices of Survivors of Conflict-Related Sexual Violence and Service-Providers*, October 29, 2021, https://www.un.org/sexualviolenceinconflict/in-their-own-words-voices-of-survivors-of-conflict-related-sexual-violence-and-service-providers/.
19. Anna Di Lellio, "Seeking Justice for Wartime Sexual Violence in Kosovo: Voices and Silence of Women," *Eastern European Politics and Societies and Cultures* 30 (2016): 621–643; and Anna Di Lellio and Garentina Kraja, "Sexual Violence in the Kosovo Conflict: A Lesson for Myanmar and Other Ethnic Cleansing Campaigns," *International Politics* 58 (2021): 148–167.
20. The authors, with the clinical psychologist Rachel Cohen, were the consultants who designed the study. The sample of survivors in the study was composed of 200 survivors, including nine men, thirty-seven Roma women, and one Serbian woman. The research is published in a medica mondiale and Medica Gjakova's report, *Am I Guilty for What Happened to Me? A Study of the Long-Term Consequences of War Rape in Kosovo* (Cologne and Prishtina: medica mondiale and Medica Gjakova, 2024).
21. Olivera Simić, *Silent Victims of Wartime Sexual Violence* (London: Taylor & Francis, 2018).
22. Dafina Halili, "I Never Imagined This Could be Done Also to Men," Kosovo 2.0, October 27, 2022, https://kosovotwopointzero.com/en/i-never-imagined-this-could-be-done-also-to-men/.
23. Nancy Dowd, *The Man Question* (New York: New York University Press, 2010), 17.
24. Caroline Blyth, *The Narrative of Rape in Genesis 34: Interpreting Dinah's Silence* (Oxford: Oxford University Press, 2010), 18.
25. Feride Rushiti (director of the Kosovo Rehabilitation Centre for Torture Victims), in-person interview by Anna Di Lellio, Prishtina, January 14, 2018.
26. Ronald J. Grele, "Movement Without Aim: Methodological and Theoretical Problems in Oral History," in *Envelopes of Sound: The Art of Oral History*, 2nd ed., rev. and enl. (Westport, CT: Praeger Pub, 1991); Alessandro Portelli, *The Death of Luigi Trastulli and Other Stories: Form and Meaning in Oral History* (Albany: State University of New York Press, 1991); and Luisa Passerini, *Fascism in Popular Memory: The Cultural Experience of the Turin Working Class* (Cambridge: Cambridge University Press, 1987).
27. Georg Simmel, "The Stranger," in *On Individuality and Social Forms: Selected Writings*, edited and with an Introduction by Donald N. Levine (Chicago: Chicago University Press, 1971 [1908]).
28. Susan Brison, *Aftermath: Violence and the Remaking of a Self* (Princeton, NJ: Princeton University Press, 2002), 90–91 and 96–97.
29. Nayanika Mookherjee, *The Spectral Wound: Sexual Violence, Public Memories, and the Bangladesh War of 1971* (Durham, NC: Duke University Press, 2015), 251–263.
30. Sarah K. Loose and Amy Starecheski, "Oral History for Building Social Movement: Then and Now," in *Beyond Women's Words: Feminism and the Practice of Oral History in the Twenty First Century*, ed. Katrina Srigley, Stacey Zembrzycki, and Franca Iacovetta (London: Taylor & Francis Group, 2018).

31. Yasmin Saikia, *Women, War and the Making of Bangladesh: Remembering 1971* (Durham, NC: Duke University Press, 2011), 90; Veena Das and Arthur Kleinman, "Introduction" to *Remaking the World: Violence, Social Suffering and Recovery*, ed. Veena Das, Arthur Kleinman, Margaret M. Lock, Mamphela Ramphele, and Pamela Reynolds (Berkeley and Los Angeles: University of California Press, 2001), 19.
32. Marianne Hirsch, "Ce Qui Touche à la Mémoire," *Esprit* 438 (October 2017): 60.
33. Anna Di Lellio, Feride Rushiti, and Kadire Tahiraj, "Art Activism Against the Stigma of Sexual Violence: The Case of Kosovo," *Violence Against Women* 25, no. 13 (2019): 1546–1557.
34. For a short discussion of the campaign for blood feuds reconciliation, see Howard Clark, *Civil Resistance in Kosovo* (London: Pluto, 2000), 60–64.
35. Dom Lush Gjergji, "Në vjetorin e pajtimit të gjaqeve," interview, *RTV 21*, June 2015, video, 19:18, https://www.youtube.com/watch?v=H9hDD471bq0.
36. Di Lellio and Kraja, "Sexual Violence in the Kosovo Conflict."
37. Anna Sheftel, "Talking and Not Talking About Violence: Challenges in Interviewing Survivors of Atrocity as Whole People," *Oral History Review* 54, no. 2 (2018): 280.
38. Mary Marshall Clark, "Resisting Attrition in Stories of Trauma," *Narrative* 13, no. 3 (2005): 296.
39. Portelli, *The Death of Luigi Trastulli*, 256.
40. Alessandro Portelli, *The Order Has Been Carried Out: History, Memory and Meaning of a Nazi Massacre in Rome* (New York: Palgrave Studies in Oral History, [1999] 2007).
41. Seada Vranić, *Breaking the Wall of Silence: Voices from Raped Bosnia* (Zagreb: Antibarbarus, 1996); Selma Leydesdorff, *Surviving the Bosnian Genocide: The Women of Srebrenica Speak* (Indianapolis: Indiana University Press, 2011); Inger Skjelsbæk, "Victims and Survivors: Narrated Social Identities of Women Who Experienced Rape During the War in Bosnia-Herzegovina," *Feminism and Pshychology* 16 (2006): 373–403.
42. Wendy Bracewell, "Rape in Kosovo: Masculinity and Serbian Nationalism," *Nations and Nationalism* 6 (2000): 563–590; Katherine Verdery, "From Parent-State to Family Patriarchs: Gender and Nation in Contemporary Eastern Europe," *East European Politics and Societies* 8, no. 2 (1994): 225–255; and Dubravka Žarkov, *The Body of War: Media, Ethnicity and Gender in the Break-Up of Yugoslavia* (Durham, NC: Duke University Press, 2007).
43. Di Lellio and Kraja, "Sexual Violence in the Kosovo Conflict," 154–155 and 161–163; Anna Di Lellio, "Gender and Sexual Violence in Genocide," in *Handbook of Genocide Studies*, ed. David Simon and Leora Kahn (Cheltenham, UK, and Northampton, MA: Edward Elgar, 2023), 214–218.
44. Nuto Revelli, *L'anello piú forte. La donna: Storie di vita contadina* (Torino: Einaudi, 1985).
45. Bruce G. Link and Jo Phelan, "Stigma Power," *Social Science & Medicine* 103 (2014): 24–32.
46. Judith Herman, *Trauma and Recovery* (New York: Basic, 1992).
47. Dori Laub, "An Event Without a Witness: Truth, Testimony and Survival," in *Testimony: Crisis of Witnessing in Literature, Psychoanalysis and History*, ed. Shoshana Felman and Dori Laub (London: Taylor & Francis, 1991), 85. See also Elisabeth Porter, "Gendered Narratives: Stories and Silences in Transitional Justice," *Human Rights Review* 17 (2016): 36.

Chapter 1

1. Viktor Meier, *Yugoslavia: A History of Its Demise* (London: Routledge, 1999), 79–89; Anna Di Lellio, *La Jugoslavia crollò in miniera. Kosovo 1989: Lo sciopero di Trepça e la lotta per l'autonomia* (Milano: Prospero Editore, 2024), 197–217.
2. Sevdije Ahmeti (cofounder and former director of the Center for the Protection of Women and Children), interview via Skype by Anna Di Lellio, December 27, 2014; Sevdije Ahmeti, *Journal d'une femme du Kosovo: La guerre avant la guerre* (Paris: Karthala 2003), 27; Nicole Farnsworth, ed., *History Is Herstory Too: The History of Women in Civil Society in Kosovo 1980–2004* (Prishtina: Qendra Kosovare për Studime Gjinore 2008), 59–72.
3. Ahmeti, interview.
4. Robert D. Kaplan, *Balkan Ghosts* (New York: St. Martin's Press 1993); Jasna Dragović-Soso, "Why Did Yugoslavia Disintegrate?," in *State Collapse in South-Eastern Europe*, ed. Lenard J. Cohen and Jasna Dragović-Soso (West Lafayette, IN: Purdue University Press, 2008).
5. Kosovo was a *vilayet*, a large Ottoman administrative unit introduced in 1864 that included part of modern Macedonia, Albania, and Serbia. The annexation included an area comprising Prishtina, Prizren, and Mitrovica; Peja, Gjakova, and Deçan were ceded to Montenegro.

6. Ivo Banac, *The National Question in Yugoslavia: Origins, History, Politics* (Ithaca, NY: Cornell University Press, 1988), 291–306.
7. Noel Malcolm, *Kosovo: A Short History* (New York: New York University Press, 1998), 253–254. A campaign of killing and destruction of Albanian villages in Kosovo and Macedonia was reported by, among others, Leon Trotsky, correspondent for the Ukrainian newspaper *Kjevskia Mysl*, and by the international commission of inquiry set up by the Carnegie Endowment.
8. Nathalie Clayer, *Aux origines du nationalisme albanais: La naissance d'une nation majoritairement musulmane en Europe* (Paris: Karthala, 2007), 524–531. Anti-Slavism emerged first in northern Albania among the Franciscan clergy, influenced by Austro-Hungarian interests.
9. Malcolm, *Kosovo*, 28–40.
10. Wayne S. Vucinich and Thomas Allan Emmert, *Kosovo: Legacy of a Medieval Battle* (Minneapolis: University of Minnesota, 1991); Malcolm, *Kosovo*, 58–80.
11. Ivan Čolović, *Smrt na Kosovu Polju* [Death on the field of Kosovo] (Beograd: Biblioteka XX Vek, 2017). The oral tradition of the Battle of Kosovo is shared by different nations besides Serbs, feeding a myth of exclusionary identities used at different times by power groups since the fourteenth century.
12. However, Albanians have their own narrative of the Battle of Kosovo. In their epic songs, which are less known than the Serbian, Albanians are represented as both loyal subjects of the sultan and rebels to his authority; the murderer of the sultan is also Albanian, Millosh Kopiliq. See Anna Di Lellio, *The Battle of Kosovo 1389: An Albanian Epic* (London: IB Taurus, 2009).
13. Larry Wolff, *Inventing Eastern Europe: The Map of Civilization on the Mind of the Enlightenment* (Redwood, CA: Stanford University Press, 1994).
14. Jovan Cvijić, *La Peninsule Balkanique: Geographie humaine* (Paris: Libraire Armand Colin, 1918), 285; Vladan Georgevitch (Djordjević), *Les Albanais et le grandes puissances* (Paris: Calmann-Lévy, 1913), 8. Vladan Djordjević was a noted Serbian diplomat who indulged in racialist observations, such as the measurement of Albanians' skulls: a "thin and small type, which has something typical of the gypsies and the phoenicians."
15. Sonja Biserko, "Serbian Nationalism and the Remaking of the Yugoslav Federation," in *Yugoslavia Implosion: The Fatal Attraction of Serbian Nationalism*, ed. Sonja Biserko (Oslo: Norwegian Helsinki Committee, 2012), 33–124.
16. Mehmet Konitza, "The Albanian Question," *The Adriatic Review* I, no. 4 (1918): 145–164.
17. Noel Malcolm, "Is the Complaint About the Serb State's Deportation Policy of Albanians Between the Two World Wars Based on Myth?," in *The Case for Kosova: Passage to Independence*, ed. Anna Di Lellio (London: Anthem Press, 2006); Vladan Jovanović, "Land Reform and Serbian Colonization," *East Central Europe* 42, no. 1 (2015): 87–103.
18. Grigorije Božović, "Kačaki," *Policija* 7, no. 13–14 (1920): 559, quoted in Banac, *The National Question*, 303.
19. Jozo Tomasevich, "Italian-Albanian Rule in Kosovo and Western Macedonia," in *War and Revolution in Yugoslavia, 1941–1945: Occupation and Collaboration* (Stanford, CA: Stanford University Press, 2001); Ali Hadri, *Lëvizja nacionalçlirimtare në Kosovë 1941–1945* (Prishtinë: Bashkësia e Institucioneve Shkencore të KSA të Kosovës, 1971); Muhamet Shatri, *Kosova në luftën e dytë botërore 1941–1945* (Prishtinë: Botimet Toena, 1997).
20. Carlo Umiltà, *Jugoslavia e Albania: Memorie di un diplomatico* (Milano: Garzanti, 1947); Luca Micheletta, *La resa dei conti, Il Kosovo, L'Italia e la dissoluzione della Jugoslavia (1939–1941)* (Rome: Nuova Cultura, 2008); Davide Rodogno, *Il nuovo ordine mediterraneo: Le politiche di occupazione dell'Italia fascista in Europa 1940–1943* (Milano: Bollati Boringhieri Editore, 2003).
21. The Italian king's envoy Francesco Jacomoni proposed to expel twelve thousand Montenegrin settlers, as cited in Rodogno, *Il nuovo ordine mediterraneo*, p. 356, and in Francesco Jacomoni di San Savino, *La politica dell'Italia in Albania nelle testimonianze del Luogotenente del Re Francesco Jacomoni di San Savino* (Bologna: Cappelli, 1956), 316.
22. We thank historian Vladan Jovanović for pointing to Vladimir Dedijer and Anton Miletić, *Proterivanje Srba sa ognjišta 1941–1944* (Beograd: Prosveta, 1989), for testimonies of colonists expelled from Kosovo.
23. Anna Di Lellio et al., *Fostering a Critical Account of History in Kosovo: Engaging with History Teachers' Narratives of the Second World War* (Prishtina and Belgrade: Oral History Kosovo and CFCCS, 2017), 48–50.

24. Emily Greble, "Conflict in Post-War Yugoslavia: The Search for a Narrative," The National World War II Museum, September 21, 2021, https://www.nationalww2museum.org/war/articles/conflict-post-war-yugoslavia; Mrika Limani, *Perspectives on Ideology and Violence in the Second World War in Kosova* (Prishtinë: Instituti i Historisë "Ali Hadri," 2021).
25. Bette Denich, "Dismembering Yugoslavia: Nationalist Ideologies and the Symbolic Revival of Genocide," *American Ethnology* 21, no. 2 (1994); Anna Di Lellio, "The Narrative of Genocide as Cosmopolitan Memory and its Impact on Humanitarian Intervention," paper, Interdisciplinary Workshop on Collective Memory and Collective Knowledge in a Global Age, London School of Economics, June 17–18, 2007.
26. Anna Di Lellio and Dardan Luta, *The Long Winter of 1945: Tivari* (Toronto: University of Toronto Press, 2023). The massacre at Tivari of scores of Albanian recruits by Serbian and Montenegrin partisans at the end of the Second World War is an episode that continues to nurture feelings of resentment. Communist partisan leader Fadil Hoxha talks about the violent suppression of an Albanian insurrection of Drenica in his memoir, *Fadil Hoxha në veten e parë, Me shënime dhe parathënie të Veton Surroi* (Prishtinë: Koha, 2010), 233–255.
27. Serbian nationalists have consistently labeled Albanians *ballist* from the armed groups who fought not only for the liberation of Albania from foreign occupation but also against the Communist partisans during the Second World War. In the 1980s, the theme of Albanian rebellion in 1945 was used by the wartime head of the Communist Intelligence Service, Spasoje Djaković, to attack the credibility of the Kosovo leadership that emerged from the partisan war in *Sukobi na Kosovu* (Beograd: Narodna Knjiga, 1984).
28. Ivo Banac, *With Stalin Against Tito: Cominformist Splits in Yugoslav Communism* (Ithaca, NY: Cornell University Press, 1988), 29.
29. Elidor Mëhilli, *From Stalin to Mao: Albania and the Socialist World* (Ithaca, NY: Cornell University Press, 2017), 43–44.
30. Arbnora Dushi, "Intergenerational Memory on the Border History," *Ethnologica Balcanica* 21 (2018): 291–308.
31. Roger Brubaker, *Nationalism Reframed: Nationhood and National Question in the New Europe* (Cambridge: Cambridge University Press, 1996). Brubaker places ethnic conflicts in the framework of competing nationalisms at the center of a "triadic nexus" of nationalizing states, national minorities and external national homelands.
32. Banac, *With Stalin*, 243–254.
33. Shkëlzen Maliqi, *Shembja e Jugosllavisë, Kosova dhe rrëfime të tjera: Dialog me Baton Haxhiun* (Tiranë: Universiteti Evropian i Tiranës, 2011), 69–70. Once Ranković retired, a regional Commission was set up to investigate his actions in Kosovo. Shkelzen Maliqi learned from his father Mehmet, the regional minister of the interior, that about seventy Albanians had been murdered extrajudicially by Ranković's police, perhaps an underestimation of human losses during that time.
34. Malcolm, *Kosovo*, 323.
35. Malcolm, *Kosovo*, 326.
36. Bogdan Denitch, "Notes on the Relevance of Yugoslav Self-Management," *Politics and Society* 3, no. 4 (1973): 479.
37. Besnik Pula, "The Emergence of the Kosovo 'Parallel State,' 1988–1992," *Nationalities Papers* 32, no. 4 (2004): 797–826.
38. Atdhe Hetemi, *Student Movements for the Republic of Kosovo 1968, 1981 and 1997* (London: Springer International, 2020), 9.
39. Malcolm, *Kosovo*, 329–330.
40. Stephanie Schwandner-Sievers, "The Bequest of *Ilegalja*: Contested Memories and Moralities in Contemporary Kosovo," *Nationalities Papers* 41, no. 6 (2013): 953–970.
41. Sabrina P. Ramet, *The Three Yugoslavias: State-Building and Legitimation 1918–2005* (Bloomington, IN: Indiana University Press, 2006), 227–261. The 1971 events in Croatia were "reformist" and not "separatist," as the regime called them. On the events following the death of Tito, see Sabrina P. Ramet, *Balkan Babel: The Disintegration of Yugoslavia from the Death of Tito to the Fall of Milosevic* (London: Routledge, 2002), 3–25, and Meier, *Yugoslavia*, 1–32.
42. Julie A. Mertus, *Kosovo: How Myths and Truths Started a War* (Oakland: University of California Press, 1999), 17–86; Mehmet Kraja, *Vite të humbura* (Prishtinë: Rozafa, [1995], 2003), 129–162; Branka Magaš, *The Destruction of Yugoslavia: Tracking the Break-Up, 1980–1992* (London: Verso, 1993), 6–48.

43. Short for *Uprava Državne Bezbednosti*, or Administration of State Security, that is, the secret police.
44. Amnesty International, *Yugoslavia: Prisoners of Conscience*, AI INDEX: EUR 48/031/81, 1981, https://www.amnesty.org/en/wp-content/uploads/2021/06/eur480311981en.pdf; Sabile Keçmezi-Basha, *Të burgosurit politikë shqiptarë në Kosovë 1945–1990* (Shkup: Logos A, 2009), 88–98; and *Organizata dhe grupet ilegale në Kosovë 1981–1989 (sipas aktgjykimeve të gjykatave ish-jugosllave)* (Prishtinë: Instituti i Historisë, 2003), 27–87; Ethem Çeku, *Shekulli i ilegales: Proceset gjyqësore kundër ilegales në Kosovë. Dokumente* (Prishtinë: Brezi '81, 2004), 498–744.
45. Malcolm, *Kosovo*, 336.
46. Rozita Dimova, "From Past Necessities to Contemporary Friction: Migration, Class and Ethnicity in Macedonia," Max Planck Institute for Social Anthropology Working Papers, 94, 2007, 6.
47. Nebojša Vladisavljević, *Serbia's Antibureaucratic Revolution: Milošević, the Fall of Communism and Nationalist Mobilization* (New York: Palgrave MacMillan, 2008), 253; Goran Musić, *Making and Breaking the Yugoslav Working Class: The Story of Two Self-Managed Factories* (Budapest: Central European University Press, 2021), 217–226.
48. Aziz Abrashi and Burhan Kavaja, *Epopeja e minatorëve: Marshet e tubimet protestuese dhe grevat minatorëve të "Trepçes" në vitet 1988–1990* (Prishtinë: Koha, 1996); Di Lellio, *La Jugoslavia*.
49. Shkëlzen Maliqi, *Nyja e Kosovës: As Vllasi as Millosheviqi* (Ljubljana: Knjižna zbirka KRT, [1989] 1998), 264, and "The Albanian Intifada," in Magaš, *The Destruction of Yugoslavia*, 180–186.
50. Mehmet Kraja, *Vite të humbura* (Prishtinë: Rozafa [1995] 2003), 175–178.
51. Human Rights Watch/Helsinki, *Open Wounds: Human Rights Abuses in Kosovo* (New York: Human Rights Watch, 1993), https://www.hrw.org/sites/default/files/reports/Kosovo943.pdf; Marc Weller, *The Crisis in Kosovo, 1989–1999: From the Dissolution of Yugoslavia to Rambouillet and the Outbreak of Hostilities* (Cambridge: Cambridge University Press, 1999).
52. Clark, *Civil Resistance*, 224.
53. Malcolm, *Kosovo*, 346–347.
54. Shkëlzen Maliqi, *Kosova: Separate Worlds: Reflections and Analyses* (Prishtinë: Dukagjini Publishing House, 1998), 261, and Besnik Pula, "The Emergence."
55. Malcolm, *Kosovo*, 347.
56. Denisa Kostovicova, *Kosovo: The Politics of Identity and Space* (New York: Routledge, 2005), 314.
57. Renaud de la Brosse, *Political Propaganda and the Plan to Create a "State for all Serbs": Consequences of Using Media for Ultra-Nationalist Ends* (The Hague: International Criminal Tribunal for Yugoslavia, IT-02-54-T, 2003), http://balkanwitness.glypx.com/de_la_brosse_pt1.pdf; Bracewell, "Rape in Kosovo"; Muhamedin Kullashi, *Humanisme et Haine: Les intellectuels et le nationalisme en ex-Yougoslavie* (Paris: L'Harmattan, 1998); Žarkov, *The Body of War*.
58. Mertus, *Kosovo*, 95–121; Dubravka Ugrešić, *The Culture of Lies: Antipolitical Essays* (Philadelphia: Penn State University Press, 1998), 288; Mark Thompson, *A Paper House: The Ending of Yugoslavia* (New York: Pantheon, 1992), 129; Nick Miller, *The Nonconformists: Culture, Politics, and Nationalism in a Serbian Intellectual Circle, 1944–1991* (Budapest: Central European University, 2008), 260–267.
59. Malcolm, *Kosovo*, 340. For a collection of petitions promoted by the Serbian Orthodox Church demanding the revocation of Kosovo's autonomy and claiming genocide of Serbs, see Archimandrite Anastasije Jevtich, *Dossier Kosovo* (Lausanne: L'Age d' Homme, 1991).
60. Kosta Mihailović and Vasilije Krestić, *Memorandum of the Serbian Academy of Sciences and Arts: Answers to Criticisms* (Belgrade: SANU, 1995), 129.
61. Croatian commentator and politician Slaven Letica, as quoted in Lynda E. Boose, "Crossing the River Drina: Bosnian Rape Camps, Turkish Impalement, and Serb Cultural Memory," *Signs: Journal of Women in Culture and Society* 28, no. 1 (2002): 86.
62. Ugrešić, *The Culture of Lies*, 71.
63. The quote from Djordje Vuković is in *Theoria* no. 3–4 (1987): 56, as cited in English translation by Biserko, *Yugoslavia Implosion*, 211.
64. Malcolm, *Kosovo*, 339.

65. Žarkov, *The Body of War*, 40–41.
66. Bracewell, "Rape in Kosovo," 582.
67. Žarkov, *The Body of War*, 21–42.
68. Hoxha, *Fadil Hoxha*, 424–430.
69. Žarkov, *The Body of War*, 37.
70. Bahtije Abrashi (educator), interview by Anita Susuri, Kosovo Oral History Initiative, Prishtina, February 14, 2022, video, 122 minutes, https://oralhistorykosovo.org/bahtije-abrashi/.
71. Nazlije Bala (political activist), interview by Zana Rudi, Kosovo Oral History Initiative, Prishtina, June 21 and July 3, 2012, video, 135 minutes, https://oralhistorykosovo.org/nazlie-bala/.
72. Vjosa Dobruna (pediatrician and human rights activist), interview by Mimoza Paçuku, Kosovo Oral History Initiative, Prishtina, July 3 and 11, 2013, video, 135 minutes, https://oralhistorykosovo.org/vjosa-dobruna/.
73. Raffaella Lamberti, in-person communication, Bologna, January 20, 2015.
74. Julie Mertus, "Gender in Service of Nation: Female Citizenship in Kosovar Society," *Social Politics: International Studies in Gender, State & Society* 3, Issue 2–3 (Summer 1996): 261–277.
75. David L. Phillips, *Liberating Kosovo. Coercive Diplomacy and U.S. Intervention* (Cambridge, MA: MIT Press, 2012), 61.
76. Tim Judah, *Kosovo. War and Revenge* (New Haven, CT: Yale University Press, 2000); James Pettifer, *The Kosova Liberation Army. Underground War to Balkan Insurgency, 1948–2001* (New York: Columbia University Press, 2012); Henry H. Perritt, *Kosovo Liberation Army: The Inside Story of an Insurgency* (Champaign, IL: University of Illinois Press, 2008).
77. Information Counseling and Referral Service, *Socio-Economic and Demographic Profiles: Socio-Economic and Demographic Profiles of Former KLA Combatants Registered by IOM*, Vol. I (Prishtina: International Organization for Migration, 2000). Of the 25,723 self-declared KLA members, only 2 percent said they joined before 1998; more than half joined in 1998.
78. Di Lellio, "Gender and Sexual Violence in Genocide," 219.
79. Patrick Ball, Ewa Tabeau, and Philip Verwimp. *The Bosnian Book of the Dead: Assessment of the Database* (Brighton: Households in Conflict Network/University of Sussex, 2007), https://hrdag.org/wp-content/uploads/2013/02/rdn5.pdf.
80. Independent International Commission on Kosovo, *Kosovo Report: Conflict, International Response and the Lessons Learned* (Oxford: Oxford University Press, 2000), 67. For the reception of the war in different national contexts, see Mary Buckley and Sally N. Cummings, eds., *Kosovo: Perceptions of War and Its Aftermath* (London and New York: Continuum, 2001).
81. Ivo Daalder and Michael E. O'Hanlon, *Winning Ugly: NATO's War to Save Kosovo* (Washington, DC: Brookings Institution Press, 2000), 120–124.
82. Katarina Ristić and Elisa Satjukow, "The 1999 NATO Intervention from a Comparative Perspective: An Introduction," *Comparative Southeast European Studies* 70, no. 2 (2022): 193.
83. Humanitarian Law Center, *Kosovo Memory Book 1998–2000* (Belgrade: Humanitarian Law Center, 2011), 478. See the online edition of the database: http://www.kosovskaknjigapamcenja.org/?page_id=660&lang=de
84. Kathleen Kuehnast, Chantal de Jonge Oudraat, and Helga Hernes, eds., *Women and War: Power and Protection in the 21st Century* (Washington, DC: United States Institute of Peace 2011), 72.
85. Human Rights Watch, *Rape as a Weapon of "Ethnic Cleansing"*; OSCE and ODIHR, *Kosovo/Kosova: As Seen, As Told*; Serrano Fitamant, *Assessment Report on Sexual Violence*; Vincent Iacopino, Martina W Frank, Heidi M Bauer, Allen S Keller, Sheri L Fink, Doug Ford, Daniel J. Pallin, and Ronald Waldman, "A Population-Based Assessment of Human Rights Violations Against Albanian Ethnic Refugees from Kosovo," *American Journal of Public Health* 91, no. 12 (2001): 2013–2018.
86. Raghild Nordås and Dara Kay Cohen, "Conflict-Related Sexual Violence," *Annual Review of Political Science* 24 (2021): 193–211.
87. Di Lellio and Kraja, "Sexual Violence in the Kosovo Conflict," p. 158.
88. Laurel Baig, Michelle Jarvis, Elena Martin-Salgado, and Giulia Pinzauti, " Contextualizing Sexual Violence. Selection of Crimes," in *Prosecuting Conflict-Related Sexual Violence at the ICTY*, ed. Serge Baron Brammertz and Michelle Jarvis (Oxford: Oxford University Press, 2016), pp. 172–219.

89. International Criminal Court, "*Elements of Crime*," Document No. ICC-PIDS-LT-03-002/11 (2011), https://www.icc-cpi.int/sites/default/files/Publications/Elements-of-Crimes.pdf.
90. *Prosecutor v. Šainović et al.*, ICTY- IT-05-87-A, Appeal Judgment (January 23, 2014), paras. 580 and 1604, https://www.icty.org/x/cases/milutinovic/acjug/en/140123.pdf; *Prosecutor v. Djordjević*, ICTY-IT-05-87/1-A, Appeal Judgment (January 27, 2014), para. 929, https://ucr.irmct.org/LegalRef/CMSDocStore/Public/English/Judgement/NotIndexable/IT-05-87%231-A/JUD265R0000406863.pdf.
91. *Djordjević*, para. 887.
92. *Djordjević*, para. 877.
93. Sophie Richardot, "'You Know What to Do with Them': The Formulation of Orders and Engagement in War Crime," *Aggression and Violent Behavior* 19 (2014): 85.
94. Bracewell, "Rape in Kosovo," 572.
95. Verdery, "From Parent-State to Family Patriarchs," 228.
96. Claude Cahn and Tatjana Peric, *Roma and the Kosovo Conflict* (Brussels: European Roma Rights Center, 1999), https://www.errc.org/cikk.php?cikk=798.
97. Amnesty International, *Wounds That Burn*, 19.
98. Tatiana Peric and Martin Demirovski, "Unwanted: the Exodus of Kosovo Roma (1998–2000)," *Cambridge Review of International Affairs* 13, no. 2 (Spring 2000): 83–96.
99. Human Rights Watch, *Under Orders*, 459–460, and *Federal Republic of Yugoslavia: Abuses Against Serbs and Roma in the New Kosovo* (New York: Human Rights Watch, 1999), https://www.hrw.org/reports/1999/kosov2/; OSCE, *As Seen, as Told, Part II*; Cahn and Peric, "Roma and the Kosovo Conflict."
100. *Prosecutor v. Haradinaj et al.*, ICTY- IT-04-84 and IT-04-84bis, Case Information Sheet, https://www.icty.org/x/cases/haradinaj/cis/en/cis_haradinaj_al_en.pdf.
101. "Coming out of the cave," as stated by survivor no. 16 in the survey conducted by Medica Gjakova on February–April 2022, in Gjakova, for the study by medica mondiale and Medica Gjakova, *Am I Guilty for What Happened to Me?*.

Chapter 2

1. Margaret Mead, "Introduction: Philip E. Mosely's Contribution to the Comparative Study of the Family," in *Communal Families in the Balkans: The Zadruga. Essays by Philip E. Mosely and Essays in His Honor*, ed. Robert F. Byrnes (Notre Dame: University of Notre Dame Press, 1976), xxv. On the origin of the joint family in the Balkans and its defensive, economic, and social functions in a pastoral society see Karl Kaser, "The Balkan Joint Family Household: Seeking its Origins," *Continuity and Change* 9, no.1 (1994): 45–68.
2. Borba-Politika, *Косово/Kosova* (Beograd: Kultura, 1973), 257.
3. Borba-Politika, *Косово/Kosova*, 277; Anton Çetta, *Prozë popullore nga Drenica* (Prishtinë: Rilindja, 1972), 12.
4. Carlton Coon, "The Mountain of Giants: A Racial and Cultural Study of the North Albanian Mountain Ghegs," *Papers of the Peabody Museum* 23, no. 3 (1950): 3–105, and Juliet Reineck, "The Past as Refuge: Gender, Migration and Ideology Among the Kosova Albanians" (PhD diss., University of California, Berkeley, 1991).
5. Reineck, "The Past as Refuge," 41.
6. Albert Doja, *Naître et grandir chez les Albanais. La construction culturelle de la personne* (Paris: L'Harmattan, 2000), 195.
7. E. A. Hammel and Djordje Šoć, "The Lineage Cycle in Southern and Eastern Yugoslavia," *American Anthropologist* 75, no. 3 (1973): 802–814.
8. Clayer, *Aux origines*, 26–27.
9. Doja, *Naître et grandir*, 26.
10. Margaret Hasluck, *The Unwritten Law in Albania*, ed. J. H. Hutton (London: Cambridge University Press, 1954), 51–72; Berit Backer, *Behind Stone Walls: Changing Household Organisation Among the Albanians of Kosovo* (London: Center for Albanian Studies, 2015), 235–251; and Reineck, "The Past as Refuge," 59–60.
11. Hava Shala (social worker, former political prisoner, and leader of the blood feud reconciliation mass movement), interview by Erëmirë Krasniqi, Kosovo Oral History Initiative, Prishtina, August 13 and October 14, 2016, video, 170 minutes, https://oralhistorykosovo.org/hava-shala/.
12. Dom Lush Gjergji (Catholic bishop vicar of the Kosovo Diocese), interview by Lura Limani, Kosovo Oral History Initiative, Prishtina, May 19 and 25, 2015, video, 132 minutes,

https://oralhistorykosovo.org/dom-lush-gjergji/. In postwar Kosovo, the long distance from school and the risks involved in traveling alone for young children was still a major reason for girls to drop out of school, see Farnsworth, ed., *History Is Herstory Too*, p. 245, ft.18. In 2003, only 17 percent of the rural women had completed education beyond primary school. Although the gender gap in education is currently closing fast in the cities, the countryside remains a different world for girls, who still now feel threatened and unsafe, see Nicole Farnsworth, ed., *1325 Facts and Fables: A Collection of Stories about the Implementation of the United Nations Security Council Resolution 1325 on Women, Peace and Security in Kosovo*, 2nd ed. (Prishtinë: Kosova Women's Network, 2002), 211–213, https://womensnetwork.org/wp-content/uploads/2022/10/1325-Facts-and-Fables.pdf.
13. Hasluck, *The Unwritten Law*, 14.
14. This is also the title of one of the best books on the subject, edited by the Jesuit father and Albanologist Giuseppe (Zef) Valentini, *La legge delle montagne albanesi nelle relazioni della missione volante 1880–1932* (Firenze: Olschki Ed, 1969).
15. Shtjefen Gjeçovi, *Kanuni i Lekë Dukagjinit: The Code of Lekë Dukagjini* (New York: Gjonlekaj, 1989). An ethnographer and Franciscan father, Gjeçovi began to publish this compilation of the orally transmitted laws, in 1913 in the Franciscan order's periodical *Hylli i Dritës* (Morning Star), founded and edited by Father Gjergj Fishta, as Albanians were struggling to ensure their national independence. Gjeçov perhaps intended to align the traditional culture with the precepts of the Church, but he principally used the *kanun* to "imagine" a political and legal space based on a defined Albanian national culture, rooted in language and preceding Islam and Ottoman culture as argued in Eleanor Pritchard, "Nested Comparisons: Nation-Building Through Comparative Thinking about Albanian Law," *International Journal of Law in Context* 12, no. 4 (2016): 469–483.
16. Reineck, "The Past as Refuge," 40.
17. Backer, *Behind Stone Walls*, 130 and 137. Backer's informant equated the unwritten law to what is specific to Albanian culture.
18. From our interviews with the narrators.
19. Pierre Bourdieu, *Outline of a Theory of Practice* (Cambridge: Cambridge University Press, 1977), 17.
20. Hasluck, *The Unwritten Law*, 25.
21. Reineck, "The Past as Refuge," 72, 169–172, 174–176.
22. Reineck, "The Past as Refuge," 60–91.
23. Xhejrane Lokaj (midwife and women's rights activist), interview by Dafina Beqiri, Kosovo Oral History Initiative, Peja, September 5, 2013, video, 154 minutes, https://oralhistorykosovo.org/xhejrane-lokaj/.
24. Kostovicova, *Kosovo: The Politics of Identity and Space* (London: Routledge, 2005), 41.
25. Hivzi Islami, *Fshati i Kosovës. Kontribut për studimin sociolologjiko-demografik të evolucionit rural* (Prishtinë: Rilindja, 1985), 160–161. In 1981, 78 percent of the age group over 65 were illiterate, 33 percent of those between 35 and 64. The cover of Ann Christine Eek, *Albanian Village Life: Isniq-Kosovo 1976* (Sweden: Tira Book, 2021), a beautiful book of photos taken during Berit Backer's fieldwork during the summer of 1976, shows a small group of rural girls on the road to high school looking both confident and quizzical about their newly acquired freedom.
26. Farnsworth, ed., *History Is Herstory Too*, 21–23; Backer, *Behind Stone Walls*, 93; and Kostovicova, *Kosovo*, 40–41.
27. Dobruna, interview, Kosovo Oral History Initiative.
28. Marta Prekpalaj (school principal and women's rights activist), interview by Anita Prapashtica and Nicole Fransworth, Kosovo Oral History Initiative, Prizren, June 5, 2013, video, 105 minutes, https://oralhistorykosovo.org/marta-prekpalaj/.

Chapter 3

1. Reineck, "The Past as a Refuge," 67–68.
2. Hasluck, *The Unwritten Law*, 25.
3. Backer, *Behind Stone Walls*, 255.
4. Reineck, "The Past as Refuge," 52.
5. Ernesto Cozzi, "Le vendette del sangue nelle montagne dell'Alta Albania," *Anthropos* 5, no. 3 (1910): 660.

NOTES TO PAGES 58-74

6. Backer, *Behind Stone Walls*, 265.
7. Backer, *Behind Stone Walls*, 103-128; Reineck, "The Past as Refuge," 55-57.
8. Reineck, "The Past as Refuge," 97.
9. Reineck, "The Past as Refuge," 99-100.
10. Reineck, "The Past as Refuge," 100-101.
11. *Mahalla*: Arabic word = neighborhood. In this context, a neighborhood or section of a village respecting exogamy and solidarity in case of blood feuds.
12. Christopher Bohem, *Blood Revenge: The Anthropology of Feuding in Montenegro and Other Tribal Societies* (Lawrence: Kansas University Press, 1984).
13. Mary Motes, "Bloody Albanians!," in *Kosovo: Prelude to War 1966-1999* (Homestead, FL: Redland Press, 1998), 191-197; Isabel Ströhle, "Speaking of Vendetta in the Century of the Atom: The Anti-Feuding Campaign in Late Socialist Kosovo," in *Violence After Stalin: Institutions, Practices, and Everyday Life in the Soviet Bloc 1953-1989*, ed. J. Claas Behrends, Pavel Kolár, and Thomas Lindenberger (Stuttgart and Hannover, Germany: Ibidem Press, 2024).
14. The mass movement of blood feud reconciliation of 1990-1991 is still waiting to be analyzed. The web archive of Kosovo Oral History Initiative, with dozens of interviews with participants and various secondary sources, is a trove of information for those who are interested in knowing more. For a broad reference to the events of 1990, see Clark, *Civil Resistance*, 60-64.
15. Gjergj Fishta, "A janë t'zott shqyptarët me u majtë shtet n'vedi? [Are Albanians capable of being an independent state?]," *Hylli i Dritës* Vjeti I, no. 2 (1913): 36-42.
16. In the culturally comparable context of North Africa, anthropologist Lila Abu-Lughod revealed a similar dynamic in *Veiled Sentiments: Honor and Poetry in a Bedouin Society* (Berkeley and Los Angeles: University of California Press, 1986), 253.
17. *Amanet*: Turkish loanword = ancestor's will or pledge which is expected to be fulfilled.
18. Bala, interview, Kosovo Oral History Initiative.
19. Branislav Nusić was a famous Serbian playwright and writer, and Ivan Ribar was a Yugoslav Communist leader and partisan commander. Gjergj Fishta was an Albanian Franciscan writer, essayist, and leader of the movement for national independence, and Sami Frashëri a prominent Albanian writer and essayist based in Istanbul and leader of the National Renaissance movement in Albania.
20. *Kismet*: Turkish loanword = fate.
21. Ola Syla (human rights activist), interview by Jeta Rexha, Kosovo Oral History Initiative, Prishtina, November 23, 2014, video, 106 minutes, https://oralhistorykosovo.org/ola-syla/.
22. Yugoslav Communist leader Fadil Hoxha describes the giddy atmosphere of the destruction of the Ottoman heritage of the city in his memoir, *Fadil Hoxha në veten e parë*, p. 306. See also Valbona Shujaku, *Prishtina: Poetic Memories* (Prishtinë: Republic, 2011) and Besnik Pula, "Dissecting Prishtina," *Kosovo 2.0*, June 3, 2013, http://kosovotwopointzero.com/en/dissecting-prishtina/.
23. Nadire Dida (teacher), interview by Donjeta Berisha, Kosovo Oral History Initiative, Prishtina, July 10 and October 8, 2014, video, 11: 43 minutes, https://oralhistorykosovo.org/nadire-dida/.
24. Safete Rogova (actress and women's rights activist), interview by Mimoza Paçuku, Kosovo Oral History Initiative, Prishtina, June 3, 2012, video, 79 minutes, https://oralhistorykosovo.org/safete-rogova/.
25. The description of life in Prishtina during the 1970s is drawn from Migjen Kelmendi, *To Change the World: A History of the Traces* (Prishtina: Java Multimedia Production, 2001).
26. Bala, interview, Kosovo Oral History Initiative.
27. Ahmeti, *Journal*, 29.
28. Ahmeti, interview.

Chapter 4

1. Farnsworth, ed., *History Is Herstory Too*, 25-27. Conventional accounts of the protest do not mention women at all: Magaš, *The Destruction*, 16, and Clark, *Civil Resistance*, 42.
2. Mertus, *Kosovo*, 17-55. Mertus interviewed more than fifty individuals in Kosovo, both Serbs and Albanians, on how they remembered the events, 56-74.
3. Mertus, *Kosovo*, 31.
4. Kraja, *Vite të humbura*, 149-157.

5. *Malësore* = mountain girl, girls from the mountainous area of Malësia, in Montenegro.
6. Shaqir Hoti (musician), interview by Jeta Rexha and Kaltrina Krasniqi, Kosovo Oral History Initiative, Prishtina, April 22, 2015, video, 122 minutes, https://oralhistorykosovo.org/shaqir-hoti-2/.
7. Mehmet Kraja (writer and cofounder of the LDK), interview by Jeta Rexha and Kaltrina Krasniqi, Kosovo Oral History Initiative, Prishtina, November 4, 2014, video, 130 minutes, https://oralhistorykosovo.org/mehmet-kraja/.
8. Amnesty International, *Yugoslavia: Prisoners of Conscience*.
9. Ahmeti, *Journal*, 25.
10. Sabile Keçmezi Basha, *Qëndresa shekullore e familjes—Tahir Meha* (Prishtinë: Instituti i Historisë, 2015).
11. Hatmone Haradinaj Demiri (high school teacher, former political prisoner), interview by Anita Susuri. Kosovo Oral History Initiative, Prishtina, March 11, 2022, video, 94 minutes, https://oralhistorykosovo.org/hatmone-haradinaj-demiri/.
12. Naime Maçastena Sherifi (women's rights activist, former political prisoner), interview by Anita Susuri, Kosovo Oral History Initiative, Prishtina, March 4, 2022, video, 84 minutes, https://oralhistorykosovo.org/naime-macastena-sherifi/.
13. *Kuku* is an onomatopoeic Albania idiom that expresses disbelief, distress, or wonder, depending on the context.
14. Judah, *Kosovo: War and Revenge*, 124–125.
15. Bujar Dugolli, *The Turning Point of 1 October: The Student Movement in Kosovo 1997–1998* (Prishtinë: University of Prishtina, 2020).
16. Comunità di Sant' Egidio, "Kosovo Statement" (Prishtina and Belgrade: Comunità di Sant'Egidio, September 1, 1996), https://archive.santegidio.org/archivio/pace/kosovo_19960109_EN.htm; Clark, *Civil Resistance*, 161.
17. Dugolli, *The Turning Point*, 270.
18. Amnesty International, *Yugoslavia.: Prisoners of Conscience*; Eraldin Fazliu, "Kosovo's Political Prisoners," Kosovo 2.0., April 26, 2016, https://kosovotwopointzero.com/en/kosovos-political-prisoners/.
19. Kushtrim Krasniqi, "My Grandfather Metush Krasniqi," n.d., https://oralhistorykosovo.org/my-grandfather-metush-krasniqi/.
20. Hydajet Hyseni (journalist, former political prisoner, politician), interview by Jeta Rexha, Kosovo Oral History Initiative, Prishtina, June 7, 2015, video, 147 minutes, https://oralhistorykosovo.org/hydajet-hyseni/.
21. Enver Dugolli, *Unbroken: Surviving Milosevic's Prisons* (London: The Center for Albanian Studies, 2021).
22. Enver Dugolli, personal communication via Facebook messenger with Anna Di Lellio, January 21, 2023.
23. Dugolli, *Unbroken*; Amnesty International, *Federal Republic of Yugoslavia: Ethnic Albanians. Victims of Torture and Ill Treatment by Police in Kosovo Province*, AI INDEX: EUR 48/18/92 (June 1992), https://www.amnesty.org/en/wp-content/uploads/2021/06/eur480181992en.pdf.
24. Shala, interview, Kosovo Oral History Initiative.
25. Zyrafete Berisha Lushaj (high school teacher), interview by Anita Susuri, Kosovo Oral History Initiative, Prishtina, November 17, 2021, video, 75 minutes, https://oralhistorykosovo.org/zyrafete-berisha-lushaj/.
26. Bajram Kelmendi was a prominent lawyer and human rights activist. On the same day that the NATO bombing began, on March 24, 1999, Serbian police took him and his two sons from their home. Their bodies were found the next day. He had begun to work on an indictment of Milošević at the ICTY.
27. Human Rights Watch, *Yugoslavia: Human Rights Abuses in Kosovo 1990–1992* (New York: Human Rights Watch, 1992), https://www.hrw.org/legacy/reports/1992/yugoslavia/#P800_140238.
28. Gjergji, interview, Kosovo Oral History Initiative.
29. Mertus, *Kosovo*, 135–164.
30. Mertus, *Kosovo*, 147.
31. Arbnora Dushi, personal communication via email with Anna Di Lellio, January 20, 2023.
32. Judah, *Kosovo*, 113–114.
33. Gjergji, interview, Kosovo Oral History Initiative.

34. *Bac* = uncle, respectful term used to address older men.
35. Dobruna, interview, Kosovo Oral History Initiative.
36. Jehona Gjurgjeala (director of the NGO TOKA), interview by Aurela Kadriu, Kosovo Oral History Initiative, Prishtina, May 18, 2017, video, 57 minutes, https://oralhistorykosovo.org/jehona-gjurgjeala/.
37. Stefan Surlić (political scientist), interview by Marjana Toma, Kosovo Oral History Initiative, Belgrade, June 19, 2017, video, 110 minutes, https://oralhistorykosovo.org/stefan-surlic/.
38. Mertus, *Kosovo*, 187–204.
39. Malcolm, *Kosovo*, 345.
40. Mertus, *Kosovo*, 197.
41. Di Lellio et al., *Fostering*, 43.
42. Shukrije Tahiraj (teacher and Skënderaj city councilor for LDK), interview with Anna Di Lellio, August 25, 2002, notes.
43. Mehmet Gradica was a *ballist* and a collaborator of the occupying Axis during the Second World War. He was killed in Drenica as he fought against Yugoslav Communist partisans in 1945.
44. Rexhep Selimi (cofounder and commander of the KLA), in-person interview with Anna Di Lellio, Prishtina, November 16, 2004.
45. Elizabeth Rubin, "Editor in Exile," *New Yorker*, May 17, 1999, pp. 46–53.
46. "Fjala e Ushtarëve të UÇK-së në Varrimin e Mësuesit Halit Geci në Llaushë," *Zëri i Kosovës*, no. 45 (1997): 11–12; Fisnik Abrashi and Ylber Bajraktari, "UÇK: Dalja nga ilegaliteti?" *Koha Ditore*, December 1, 1997, 1–2.
47. Selimi, interview. Selimi was the masked man who read the war declaration.
48. Steele, interview.
49. Garentina Kraja and Nebi Qena, "Na s'kem ku shkojmë, në vendin tonin jem," *Koha Ditore*, February 14, 1998.

Chapter 5

1. Borba-Politika, *Kocobo/Kosova*, 957.
2. General Wesley Clark, Testimony in *Prosecutor vs. Milošević*, ICTY- IT-02-54, Transcripts (December 15, 2003), 30396, https://ucr.irmct.org/Search/PreviewPage/?link=http%253A//icr.icty.org/LegalRef/CMSDocStore/Public/English/Transcript/NotIndexable/IT-02-54/TRS1154R0000087703.doc. Similar statements can be found in Duško Doder and Laura Branson, *Milošević: Portrait of a Tyrant* (Los Angeles: Free Press, 1999), 241–242; Louis Sell, *Slobodan Milošević and the Destruction of Yugoslavia* (Durham, NC: Duke University Press, 2002), 281; and Lenard J. Cohen, *Serpent in the Bosom: The Rise and Fall of Slobodan Milosevic* (Boulder, CO: Westview Press, 2001), 236–237.
3. Human Rights Watch, *Humanitarian Law Violations in Kosovo* (New York: Human Rights Watch, October 1998), https://www.hrw.org/legacy/reports98/kosovo/.
4. Amnesty International, *Federal Republic of Yugoslavia, A Human Rights Crisis in Kosovo Province, Drenica, February–April 1998: Unlawful Killings, Extrajudicial Executions and Armed Opposition Abuses* (AI INDEX: EUR 70/033/1998, June 30, 1998), https://www.amnesty.org/en/documents/eur70/033/1998/en/. In 1997, Adem Jashari had been convicted in absentia for a number of attacks on Serbian police.
5. Human Rights Watch, *Humanitarian Law Violations*; KMLDNJ, *Buletini*, Viti VIII, no. 6, (Janar–Mars 1998): 15–16; Bardh Hamzaj and Faik Hoti, *Jasharët* (*Histori e rrëfyer nga Rifat, Besarta, Bashkim, Murat dhe Lulzim Jashari*) (Prishtinë: Zëri, 2003), 95; Besarta Jashari, "War in Europe: Three Albanian Victims of Serbian Ethnic Cleansing and Atrocities," interview, FRONTLINE, *PBS*, 2000, transcripts, https://www.pbs.org/wgbh/pages/frontline/shows/kosovo/interviews/victims.html; Marie Colvin, "Kosovo's Silent Houses of the Dead," *The Sunday Times*, March 15, 1998.
6. Dejan Anastasijević, "Bloody Game," *Vreme*, January 13, 1998; Humanitarian Law Center, *Spotlight on Kosovo: Human Rights in Times of Armed Conflict*, Report No. 26 (Beograd: Humanitarian Law Center, May 1998), 7. The news also disappeared from all archived official records of violence in Kosovo on that same date collected by the Federal Ministry of Foreign Affairs of the Federal Republic of Yugoslavia, *Terrorist Acts of Albanian Terrorist Groups in Kosovo and Metohija: Documents and Evidence, 1 January 1998–10 June 1999*, III Part One (Belgrade: Službeni glasnik, 2000), 344.

NOTES TO PAGES 96–112   243

7. Besa Ilazi and Agim Zogaj, "Dihet se si na zë nata, por nuk dihet se si dhe a do të na çelë sabahi!," *Zëri*, January 31, 1998, p. 10.
8. Iiriana and Selvete Jashari, interview by Garentina Kraja, Prekaz, February 1998.
9. Reportage notes from the visit to Jashari compound of the *Koha Ditore* crew (Garentina Kraja, Nebi Qena, and Visar Kryeziu), Prekaz, February 1998. Garentina Kraja and Nebi Qena, "Na s'kem ku shkojmë, në vendin tonin jem," *Koha Ditore*, February 14, 1998.
10. Dukagjin Gorani and Baton Haxhiu, "Prekazi, edhe një herë në zjarr," *Koha Ditore*, January 23, 1998; Baton Haxhiu, *Lufta Ndryshe* (Prishtinë: Kumti, 2008).
11. Philip Smucker, "Serbia: Kosovo Crackdown Over. West Mulls Action Today," *Newsday*, March 9, 1998, p. A15.
12. Federal Republic of Yugoslavia, *Terrorist Acts of Albanian Terrorist Group*, 346.
13. Anastasijević, "Dead Man's Dance," *Vreme*, March 14, 1998. https://serbiandigest.libraries.rutgers.edu/336/dance-dead
14. Nebojša Pavković, "War in Europe. Commander Nebojsa Pavkovic," interview, FRONTLINE, PBS, 2000, https://www.pbs.org/wgbh/pages/frontline/shows/kosovo/interviews/pavkovic.html.
15. Anastasijević, "Final Score," *Vreme*, March 21, 1998; Miloš Vasić, "How Serbs and Albanians Perceive Each Other and Themselves. If They Were Really Like That," *Vreme*, March 14, 1998. https://serbiandigest.libraries.rutgers.edu/336/if-only-it-were-really-so
16. Nebi Qena (*Koha Ditore* journalist and witness to the burial on March 11, 1998), interview by Garentina Kraja, Jerusalem, February 12, 2023. *Šiptar* is used instead of *albanski* as a derogatory term for Albanian, a distortion of the term *shqiptar*, which means Albanian.
17. Di Lellio and Schwandner-Sievers, "The Legendary Commander."
18. Fron Nazi, "Balkan Diaspora: The Albanian-American Community," in *Contending Voices on Balkan Interventions*, ed. William Joseph Buckley (Grand Rapids, MI: William B. Eerdmans, 2000), 149–152; Stacy Sullivan, *Be Not Afraid, for You Have Sons in America: How Albanians in the US Fought for Their People in Kosovo* (New York: St. Martin's Press, 2004), 166; and Paul Hockenos, *Homeland Calling: Exile Patriotism and the Balkan Wars* (Ithaca, NY: Cornell University Press, 2004), 246.
19. Garentina Kraja, "Recruitment Practices of Europe's Last Guerrilla: Ethnic Mobilization, Violence and Networks in the Recruitment Strategy of the Kosovo Liberation Army" (BA/MA thesis, Yale University, 2011), 48.
20. ICTY, "The Prosecutor's Statement Regarding the Tribunal's Jurisdiction over Kosovo," The Hague, March 10, 1998, https://www.icty.org/en/press/prosecutors-statement-regarding-tribunals-jurisdiction-over-kosovo.
21. Human Rights Watch, *A Week of Terror in Drenica* (New York: Human Rights Watch, October 1998), https://www.hrw.org/legacy/reports/1999/kosovo/. In the village of Abri të Epërme, twenty-one people of the Delija family were killed, including an eighteen-month-old infant.
22. Robert Elsie, *Historical Dictionary of Kosovo* (Lanham, MD: The Scarecrow Press, 2011), 85.
23. Elsie, *Historical Dictionary*, 185.
24. Ramush Haradinaj (KLA commander and former prime minister of Kosovo), in-person interview by Garentina Kraja, Prishtina, January 4, 2010.
25. Bardh Hamzaj, *A Narrative About War and Freedom (Dialog with the Commander Ramush Haradinaj)* (Prishtinë: Zëri, 2000), 54.
26. *Hasret* is a Turkish word that means "longing," but in Albanian it means "the only son."
27. Radio Kosova e Lirë, "Mervete Salih Maksutaj (10.4.1978–4.12.1998)," n.d. https://www.radio-kosovaelire.com/mervete-salih-maksutaj-10-4-1978-4-12-1998/.
28. UNHCR, *IDP/Shelter Survey Kosovo: Joint Assessment in 20 Municipalities* (Geneva: UNHCR, 1998).
29. Humanitarian Law Center, *Kosovo Memory Book Database. Presentation and Expert Evaluation* (Prishtina, February 4, 2015), http://www.kosovomemorybook.org/wp-content/uploads/2015/02/Expert_Evaluation_of_Kosovo_Memory_Book_Database_Prishtina_04_02_2015.pdf.
30. The Independent International Commission on Kosovo, *The Kosovo Report*, 89.
31. Derogatory for Serb: *Shki* is the plural form, *Shka* the singular.
32. Derogatory expression for Roma.
33. Human Rights Watch, *Under Orders*, 145–146. Though the laws of war prohibit it, there is evidence that Serbian forces deliberately contaminated water wells by disposing of chemicals, dead animals, and even human corpses in the wells.

34. Ger Duijzings, *Religion and the Politics of Identity in Kosovo* (New York: Columbia University Press, 2001), 81. In Kosovo, the day of Saint George has a sincretic appeal for different faiths. An important religious holiday for many Orthodox Eastern European Countries, it falls on April 23 by the Julian calendar and May 6 by the Gregorian calendar.
35. Human Rights Watch, *Under Orders*, 149–150.

Chapter 6

1. Nebi Qena, "Jeta e mirë atje n'Prishtinë, a? Si n'Zvicër?" *Koha Ditore*, June 16, 1998.
2. Farnsworth, ed., *History Is Herstory Too*, 139.
3. Flora Brovina (poet, pediatrician, former political prisoner, and women's rights activist), interview by Aurela Kadriu, Kosovo Oral History Initiative, June 27–28 and August 12, 2018, video, 532 minutes, https://oralhistorykosovo.org/flora-brovina/.
4. The reference is to the massacre in Likoshan and Qirez, mentioned in Chapter 5, "War," section "Counterinsurgency."
5. Edita Tahiri (political scientist, cofounder of the LDK, former chief negotiator with Serbia), interview by Aurela Kadriu, Kosovo Oral History Initiative, Prishtina, May 4, 2018, video, 153 minutes, https://oralhistorykosovo.org/edita-tahiri/.
6. Wesley Clark, *Waging Modern War: Bosnia, Kosovo, and the Future of Combat* (New York: Public Affairs, 2002), 133.
7. Operation Storm (August 1995) was a major military operation by Croatian and Bosnian troops, supported by U.S. military advisers, against the self-styled Republic of Serbian Krajina. It resulted in the expulsion of thousands of Serbs from the reconquered areas of Croatia and Bosnia.
8. Dobruna, interview, Kosovo Oral History Initiative.
9. Lumturije (Lumka) Krasniqi (accountant, former KLA logistics officer), interview by Anna Di Lellio, Kosovo Oral History Initiative, New York, March 12, 2017, video, 143 minutes, https://oralhistorykosovo.org/lumturije-lumka-krasniqi/.
10. Beti Muharremi (director of the NGO *Dora e Hapur*), interview by Jeta Rexha and Kaltrina Krasniqi, Kosovo Oral History Initiative, Prishtina, February 7, 2015, video, 54 minutes, https://oralhistorykosovo.org/beti-muharremi/.
11. Dobruna, interview, Kosovo Oral History Initiative.
12. Nataša Kandić is a leading human rights activist in Belgrade, founder of the Humanitarian Law Center.
13. Ola Syla (human rights activist), interview by Jeta Rexha, Kosovo Oral History Initiative, Prishtina, November 23, 2014, video, 106 minutes, https://oralhistorykosovo.org/ola-syla/.
14. Pranvera Musa (financial officer), in-person interview with Anna Di Lellio, New York, October 20, 2019, notes.
15. Safete Rogova, interview, Kosovo Oral History Initiative.
16. Chris Bird and Nicholas Watt, "Kosovan Leader's Death Condemned," *The Guardian*, May 9, 1999, https://www.theguardian.com/world/1999/may/10/balkans7.
17. Human Rights Watch, *Under Orders*, 147–148.
18. Translated as the Feast of Sacrifice, it is one of the major Islamic holidays, commemorating Abraham's (Ibrahim) willingness to sacrifice his son in obedience to God's order.
19. Di Lellio and Kraja, "Sexual Violence in the Kosovo Conflict," 156–157; Human Rights Watch, *Under Orders*, 399–406. The school of Studime was a rape camp and Studime was the site of a massacre of more than one hundred men on May 2 and 3, 1999.
20. Reports of the massacre are confirmed by the war casualties database of the Kosovo Memory Book, which is searchable by name, date of birth, place of birth, ethnicity, status (civilian or combatant), locality and date of killing, http://www.kosovskaknjigapamcenja.org/?page_id=48&lang=de
21. Human Rights Watch, *Under Orders*, 150–151.

Chapter 7

1. Reuters, "Kosovo Rape Testimony Shown in Britain," April 13, 1999, https://reliefweb.int/report/serbia/london-kosovo-rape-testimony-shown-britain. Articles on rape began to appear in April, obtaining a wide audience through BBC interviews with survivors and information pointing to rape camps similar to Bosnia; those shocking stories were strongly denied by the Serbian government. To mention the major source in the English language: John Daniszewski,

"Death of Belanica," *Los Angeles Times,* April 25, 1999, https://www.latimes.com/archives/la-xpm-1999-apr-25-ss-31093-story.html; Bruce Johnston, "Refugee Girls Stripped, Gang Raped by Militia," *The Independent,* April 12, 1999, https://www.independent.ie/world-news/refugee-girls-stripped-gang-raped-by-militia-26152948.html; Vernon Loeb and R. Jeffrey Smith, "Evidence Mounts of Atrocities by Yugoslav Forces," *Washington Post,* April 10, 1999, A16, https://www.washingtonpost.com/wp-srv/inatl/longterm/balkans/stories/atrocities041099.htm; David Rohde, "An Albanian Tells How Serbs Chose Her, 'the Most Beautiful' for Rape," *New York Times,* May 1, 1999, A8, https://www.nytimes.com/1999/05/01/world/crisis-balkans-crimes-albanian-tells-serbs-chose-her-most-beautiful-for-rape.html; Carol J. Williams, "In Kosovo, Rape Seen as Awful as Death," *Los Angeles Times,* May 27, 1999, A1, https://www.latimes.com/archives/la-xpm-1999-may-27-mn-41524-story.html. Journalists kept reporting on the issue throughout the year: Peter Finn, "Signs of Rape Scar Kosovo: Families' Shame Could Hinder Investigation," *Washington Post,* June 2, 1999, https://www.washingtonpost.com/wp-srv/inatl/longterm/balkans/stories/rape062799.htm; Elisabeth Bumiller, "Deny Rape or Be Hated: Kosovo Victims' Choice," *New York Times,* June 22, 1999, A1, https://www.nytimes.com/1999/06/22/world/crisis-in-the-balkans-crimes-deny-rape-or-be-hated-kosovo-victims-choice.html; Christine Toomey, "Speak No Evil, See No Evil," *Sunday Times Magazine,* November 18, 1999, 32–42, https://www.christinetoomey.com/pdfs/Speak_No_Evil.pdf.
2. Paul Fussell, *The Great War and Modern Memory* (New York: Oxford University Press, 1975), 51.
3. Roberta Culberston, "Embodied Memory, Transcendence, and Telling: Recounting Trauma, Re-Establishing the Self," *New Literary History* 26, no. 1 (1995): 169–195.
4. Pat Barker, *The Silence of the Girls* (Doubleday, 2018).
5. Goffman, *Stigma*, 42.
6. Elaine Scarry, *The Body in Pain* (New York and Oxford: Oxford University Press, 1985), 49.
7. As quoted in Scarry, *The Body in Pain*, 4.
8. On the notion of speechless terror, see Jean Améry, *At the Mind's Limits: Contemplation by a Survivor on Auschwitz and Its Realities* (Bloomington and Indianapolis: Indiana University Press, 1980): 158–182; and Bessel A. van der Kolk and Onno van der Hart, "The Intrusive Past: The Flexibility of Memory and The Engraving of Trauma," in *Trauma: Explorations in Memory*, ed. Cathy Caruth (Baltimore, MD, and London: Johns Hopkins University Press, 1995): 158–182.
9. Andrew Herscher and András Riedlmayer, "Monument Crime: The Destruction of Historical Architecture in Kosovo," *Grey Room Autumn* 1 (2000): 108–122; Andrew Herscher, *Violence Taking Place: The Architecture of the Kosovo Conflict* (Stanford, CA: Stanford University Press, 2010).
10. UNHCR, *Kosovo Rapid Village Assessment: First Cut,* July 7, 1999. file:///Users/annadilellio/Downloads/2CD5068A624F58B5C12567AE002F0399-KosovoVillageAssmt.pdf
11. Sabri Bajgora, *Destruction of Islamic Heritage in the Kosovo War, 1998–1999* (Prishtina: Interfaith Kosovo, Ministry of Foreign Affairs of the Republic of Kosovo, 2014).
12. The Orthodox Seminary was targeted for destruction in March 2004, when Albanians rioted after a period of escalating ethnic hostilities, as perspectives of a quicker resolution of Kosovo status dwindled. A complete review and discussion of these riots is in UN Security Council, *Report on the Situation in Kosovo,* S/2004/932, 2004 (also known as the Eide Report after the principal author, Norwegian Diplomat Kai Eide), https://www.securitycouncilreport.org/atf/cf/%7B65BFCF9B-6D27-4E9C-8CD3-CF6E4FF96FF9%7D/kos%20S2004%20932.pdf.
13. During the months of June and July 1999, Anna Di Lellio traveled widely across Kosovo as press officer of the UN World Food Programme. Di Lellio's observations were recorded in a diary, from which the description of the village is drawn.
14. Data collected by the WFP team through a questionnaire, on file with Di Lellio.
15. Ahmeti, *Journal,* 239.
16. The girls' well is located between Strellcë and Deçan, in Dukagjin, but folklore scholar Anton Çetta collected the folktale in Drenica, see *Nga Folklori Ynë,* 314.
17. Nazlie Bala (human rights activist), interview via phone by Anna Di Lellio, December 22, 2014.
18. In-person interview by the authors, Prishtina, January 14, 2018.
19. Human Rights Watch, *Kosovo: Rape as a Weapon,* 38.
20. Goffman, *Stigma,* 17.

21. Izeti, interview.
22. Izeti, interview.
23. Bala, interview, Kosovo Oral History Initiative.
24. Izeti, interview.
25. Goffman, *Stigma*, 7.

Chapter 8

1. ICTY, *Report to the President: Death of Slobodan Milošević* (The Parker Report), 2006, http://www.icty.org/x/cases/slobodan_milosevic/custom2/en/parkerreport.pdf.
2. "The Death of Milosevic Called Justice Denied," *New York Times*, March 3, 2006, https://www.nytimes.com/2006/03/12/world/europe/death-of-milosevic-called-justice-denied.html.
3. *Prosecutor v. Milošević et al.*, ICTY-IT-99-37-PT, Prosecution Opening Statement (February 12, 2002), 10, https://www.icty.org/x/cases/slobodan_milosevic/trans/en/020212IT.htm.
4. *Prosecutor v. Milošević et al.*, ICTY-IT-99-37-PT, "Kosovo"—Second Amended Indictment (October 16, 2001), para. 67-68, https://www.icty.org/x/cases/slobodan_milosevic/ind/en/mil-2ai011029e.htm. The five women were protected witnesses and appeared anonymously, identified by a code: K14, raped at the hotel Bozhur with her sister; K62, raped at home in front of her husband, who also testified as K63; K31, sexually assaulted for days at the Pristina hospital; K20 and K24, who have been interviewed for this book. Another protected witness, K15, who had been called to testify about mass killing, said during her testimony that she and another young girl had been taken from a convoy of refugees and raped by Serbian soldiers.
5. Milutinović, Šainović, and Ojdanić were indicted with Milošević on May 22, 1999, see *Prosecutor v. Milutinović et al.*, ICTY-IT- 99-37, Indictment (May 23, 1999), https://ucr.irmct.org/scasedocs/case/IT-02-54#eng.
6. BBC, "Top Serb Suspect Dies," April 14, 2002, http://news.bbc.co.uk/2/hi/europe/1928491.stm.
7. *Prosecutor v. Milutinović et al.* and *Prosecutor v. Pavković et al.*, ICTY, IT-99-37-PT and IT-03-70-PT, Decision on Prosecution Motion for Joinder (July 8, 2005), https://www.icty.org/x/cases/pavkovic/tdec/en/050708.htm.
8. *Prosecutor v. Milošević et al.*,"Kosovo"—Second Amended Indictment, para. 53.
9. The video of the sentencing is available on YouTube (https://www.youtube.com/watch?v=_6xcplUyZ10). ICTY, "Five Senior Serb Officials Convicted of Kosovo Crimes, One Acquitted," Press Release, The Hague (February 26, 2009), https://www.icty.org/en/press/five-senior-serb-officials-convicted-kosovo-crimes-one-acquitted; *Prosecutor v. Milutinović et al.*, ICTY-IT-05-87, Trial Judgment (February 26, 2009), 4 volumes, https://www.icty.org/x/cases/milutinovic/tjug/en/jud090226-e1of4.pdf.
10. *Prosecutor v. Djordjević*, ICTY, IT-05-87/1-T, Judgment (February 23, 2011), para 1796, https://www.icty.org/x/cases/djordjevic/tjug/en/110223_djordjevic_judgt_en.pdf.
11. *Prosecutor v. Kunarac et al.*, ICTY-IT-96-23-T & IT-96-23/1-T, Judgment (February 22, 2001), https://www.icty.org/x/cases/kunarac/tjug/en/kun-tj010222e.pdf.
12. Slavenka Drakulić, *They Would Never Hurt a Fly: War Criminals on Trials in The Hague* (New York: Penguin, 2004), 6-48.
13. Michelle Jarvis and Kate Vigneswaran, "Challenges to Successful Outcomes in Sexual Violence Cases," in *Prosecuting Conflict-Related Sexual Violence at the ICTY*, ed. Serge Brammertz and Michelle Jarvis (Oxford: Oxford University Press, 2016), 54.
14. *Prosecutor v. Milošević*, ICTY-IT-99-37-PT, Public Redacted Version of Previous Closed Session Transcript of Witness Testimony by Order of the Trial Chamber (July 16, 2002), 8143, on file with authors.
15. *Prosecutor v. Milošević et al.*, Transcripts (April 8, 2002), 2522.
16. *Milošević et al.*, Transcripts, 2533.
17. *Milošević et al.*, Transcripts, 2554.
18. *Milošević et al.*,Transcripts, 2553.
19. *Milošević et al.*, Transcripts, 2554.
20. *Milošević et al.*, Transcripts, 2537.
21. *Milošević et al.*, Transcripts, 2552.
22. *Milošević et al.*, Public Redacted Version of Previous Closed Session Transcript of Witness Testimony by Order of the Trial Chamber (March 1, 2002), 1384-1385, on file with authors.
23. Prya Gopalan, Daniela Kravetz, and Aditya Menon, "Proving Crimes of Sexual Violence," in *Prosecuting Conflict-Related Sexual Violence at the ICTY*, ed. Serge Baron Brammertz and Michelle Jarvis (Oxford: Oxford University Press, 2016), 111.

NOTES TO PAGES 176–186   247

24. *Prosecutor v. Šainović et al.*, ICTY-IT-05-87, Pre-Trial Conference (July 7, 2006), 292, https://www.icty.org/x/cases/pavkovic/trans/en/060707ED.htm.
25. Transcripts (July 16, 2002), 8167, 2–13.
26. Transcripts, 8167, 14–15, reference to Exhibits 269 and 269A.
27. *Milošević et al.*, Transcripts (July 16, 2002), 8167–8169, https://ucr.irmct.org/scasedocs/case/IT-02-54#transcripts.
28. *Milošević et al.*, Transcripts, 8171.
29. *Milošević et al.*, Transcripts, 8174.
30. *Milošević et al.*, Transcripts, 8174.
31. The testimony of K62 was held in closed session when the actual incident of sexual violence occurred, see *Milošević et al.*, Transcripts (August 24, 2006), 2267. Her husband, protected witness K63, testified about finding his wife in distress and receiving her first account of the incident, see Transcripts (August 23, 2006), 2232, https://ucr.irmct.org/scasedocs/case/IT-05-87#transcripts.
32. *Milošević et al.*, Public Redacted Version of Previous Closed Session Transcript of Witness Testimony by Order of the Trial Chamber (March 1, 2002), 1405–1436, on file with authors.
33. *Milošević et al.*, Transcripts (July 16, 2002), 8128–8164.
34. *Milošević et al.*, Transcripts, 8156.
35. *Milošević et al.*, Transcripts, 8156.
36. *Milošević et al.*, Transcripts, 8162.
37. *Milošević et al.*, Transcripts, 8142–8143.
38. *Milošević et al.*, Transcripts, 8145.
39. *Djordjević*, Trial Judgment (2011), para. 1796.
40. *Milutinović et al.*, Trial Judgment, Vol. II, paras. 785 and 1245.
41. *Šainović et al.*, Appeal Judgment, para. 573–600 and 1603–1604.
42. *Djordjević*, Appeal Judgment, para. 929.
43. *Milutinović et al.*, Trial Judgment, III, para. 714.
44. Human Rights Watch, *Under Orders*, 61–98; *Milutinović at al.*, Judgment, I, para. 413–789. We drew closely from Di Lellio and Kraja, "Sexual Violence in the Kosovo Conflict," 160–161, to discuss the organized impunity of the Serbian security forces in Kosovo.
45. *Milutinović et al.*, Judgment, I, para. 1023, 1024, and 1039.
46. *Milutinović et al.*, Judgment, I, para. 645 and 650.
47. "Excerpts from interviews with Militia Members," conducted by Montgomery Michael and Stephen Smith of America Radio Works in September 1999, https://americanradioworks.publicradio.org/features/kosovo/more1.htm; *The Scorpions—A Home Movie*, directed by Lazar Stojanović (Belgrade: Humanitarian Law Center, 2007); and *The Unidentified*, directed by Marija Ristić (Balkan Investigative Reporting Network, 2015).
48. *Milutinović et al.*, Prosecution Public Redacted Final Trial Brief and Corrigendum (July 29, 2008), para. 272–275, https://www.icty.org/x/cases/milutinovic/pros/en/080728.pdf.
49. *Milutinović et al.*, Judgment, I, para. 563–564.
50. *Milutinović et al.*, Judgment, III, para. 351.
51. *Milutinović et al.*, Judgment, I, para. 544 and 546.
52. *Milutinović et al.*, Judgment, I, para. 544.
53. *Milutinović et al.*, Judgment, I, para. 550.
54. *Djordjević*, Appeal, para. 922.
55. *Milutinović et al.*, Judgment, I, para. 537.
56. "Excerpts from Interviews."
57. *Milutinović et al.*, Judgment, I, para. 543.
58. *Djordjević*, Appeal, para. 923.
59. A description of how those crimes were planned and executed is in the documentary *The Unidentified*, which contains interviews with the perpetrators. Fred Abrahams and Eric Stover, in *A Village Destroyed, May 14, 1999: War Crimes in Kosovo* (Berkeley and Los Angeles: University of California Press, 2002), chronicle the killing in Qyshk based on testimonies and photographic evidence left in the village by the perpetrators.
60. *Djordjević*, Appeal, para. 678–714.
61. As told by a witness in *The Unidentified*.
62. *Milutinović et al.*, Judgment, III, para. 34.
63. *Milutinović et al.*, Judgment, III, para. 43, 44, and 696.
64. "Excerpts from Interviews."

65. Amnesty International, *Wounds That Burn*, 21.
66. Arber Kadriu and Die Morina, "Pioneering Kosovo Rape Victim Relives Battle for Justice," BIRN (October 18, 2018), https://balkaninsight.com/2018/10/18/pioneering-kosovo-rape-victim-relives-battle-for-justice-10-18-2018/.
67. Amnesty International, *Wounds That Burn*, 20.

Chapter 9

1. Laub, "From Speechlessness to Narrative," 257.
2. Charlotte Delbo, *Days and Memory* (Marlboro, VT: Marlboro Press, 1985).
3. Bessel A. van der Bolk, *The Body Keeps the Score: Brain, Mind, and Body in the Healing of Trauma* (New York: Penguin Books, 2014).
4. The reference is to attacks against the Kosovo Assembly, both inside and outside, by members of the same Assembly in October 2015; see Radio Free Europe/Radio Liberty, "Western Leaders Warn Tear Gas Attacks Hurting Kosovo, October 24, 2015, https://www.refworld.org/docid/56813c9d15.html.
5. The reference is to the Yugoslav Youth Labor Actions, volunteer squads of young people who lent their labor to build the country after the devastation of the Second World War, and whose organization had some elements of coercion; see Carol S. Lilly, "Problems of Persuasion: Communist Agitation and Propaganda in Post-War Yugoslavia, 1944–1948," *Slavic Review* 53, no. 2 (1994): 395–413.
6. Susan Brison, *Aftermath: Violence and the Remaking of a Self* (Princeton, NJ: Princeton University Press, 2002), 106.
7. Dino Hasanaj, the head of Kosovo Privatization Agency, died from several stab wounds in June 2012. An international investigative team concluded that the cause of his death was suicide. However, the fact that he was a businessman, a high-profile public figure nearing retirement, and that he appeared to have stubbed himself multiple times, encouraged rumors of murder and cover-up; see Fatos Bytyci, "Kosovo Privatization Head Took Own Life: Autopsy," Reuters, June 18, 2012, https://www.reuters.com/article/us-kosovo-official-suicide-idUSBRE85H1G620120618.
8. Améry, *At the Mind's Limits*, 34.
9. Cathy Winkler, "Rape as Social Murder," *Anthropology Today* 7, no. 3 (1991): 14.
10. Izeti, interview.
11. Rushiti, interview.
12. Veprore Shehu (director of Medica Kosova), interview via email by Anna Di Lellio, December 3, 2014.
13. Shehu, interview.
14. Linda Sada (director of Medica Gjakova), in-person interview by the authors, Gjakova, January 12, 2018.
15. Kadire Tahiraj (director of Center for the Protection of Women and Girls, Drenas), interview via skype by Anna Di Lellio, January 2015.
16. This and the following paragraphs are based on fieldwork and an interview with Kadire Tahiraj by Anna Di Lellio, May 30, 2022.
17. Goffman, *Stigma*, 108.
18. Goffman, *Stigma*, 95.
19. The development of a women's network advocating for justice is described in Di Lellio, "Seeking Justice," and "Authors of Their Own Transitional Justice."
20. Edona Peci, "Kosovo Wartime Rape Controversy Sparks Protest," BIRN, March 29, 2013, https://balkaninsight.com/2013/03/29/war-rape-issue-sparks-public-reactions/.
21. Eurisa Rukovci, "Women in Bronze," *Dealing with the Past*, July 19, 2019, https://dwp-balkan.org/women-in-bronze/. About the two women to whom the statues are dedicated, Radio Kosova e Lirë maintains an online archive with short biographies of all the fallen KLA. Luljetë Jahir Shala: https://www.radiokosovaelire.com/luljete-jahir-shala-2-10-1977-14-12-1998/; Myrvete Maksutaj: https://www.radiokosovaelire.com/mervete-salih-maksutaj-10-4-1978-4-12-1998/.
22. Ahmet Qeriqi (director of Radio Kosova e Lirë and member of the editorial board of a multi-volume collection of KLA biographies, *Fenikset e Lirisë*), email message to Anna Di Lellio, October 3, 2020.
23. Bala, interview.
24. Shpresa Mulliqi, Facebook message to Anna Di Lellio, January 24, 2023.
25. Krasniqi, interview.

26. Izeti, interview.
27. Anton Çetta, "Gjakmarrja në traditën tone popullore gojore," *Gjurmime Albanologjke Folklor dhe Ethnologje* X (1980): 215–217.
28. As witnessed by *Koha Ditore* reporters Garentina Kraja, Nebi Qena, and Visar Kryeziu in November, 1997.

Chapter 10

1. For the connection between history and trauma, see leading experts on trauma: Cathy Caruth, *Unclaimed Experience: Trauma, Narrative, and History* (Baltimore, MD, and London: Johns Hopkins University, 1996), 24; and Clara Mucci, *Trauma e perdono: Una prospettiva psicoanalitica intergenerazionale* (Milano: Raffaello Cortina, 2014), 49.
2. Mucci, *Trauma e perdono*, 50–51 and 189–235; Dori Laub, "On Holocaust Testimony and Its Reception Within Its Own Frame, as a Process in Its Own Right," *History and Memory* 21, no. 1 (2009): 135.
3. In Michael Kimmel, "Masculinity as Homophobia: Fear, Shame, and Silence in the Construction of Gender Identity," in *Theorizing Masculinities*, ed. Harry Brod and Michael Kaufman (Thousand Oaks, London, New Delhi: Sage Publications, 1994), 133, there is a reference to a survey, in which "women and men were asked what they were most afraid of. Women responded that they were most afraid of being raped and murdered. Men responded that they were most afraid of being laughed at."
4. van der Kolk and McFarlane, "The Black Hole of Trauma," in *Traumatic Stress: The Effects of Overwhelming Experience on Mind, Body, and Society*, ed. Bessel van der Kolk, Alexander McFarlane, and Lars Weisaeth (New York City: Guilford Press, 1996), 28–29.
5. Tommaso Baris, "Le corps expéditionnaire français en Italie. Violences des 'libérateurs' durant l'été 1944," *Vingtième Siècle: Revue d'Histoire* 93 (janv–mars 2007): 60.
6. Hans Magnus Enzensberger, "Afterword by the German Editor," in Anonyma, *A Woman in Berlin* (London: Virago Press, 2004), 310.
7. Iris Chang, *The Rape of Nanking: The Forgotten Holocaust of World War II* (New York: Basic Books, 1997), 11.
8. Teresa De Langis, "Speaking Private Memory to Public Power: Oral History and Breaking the Silence on Sexual and Gender-Based Violence During the Khmer Rouge Genocide," in *Beyond Women's Words: Feminisms and the Practices of Oral History in the Twenty-First Century*, ed. Katrina Srigley, Stacey Zembrzycki, and Franca Iacovetta (London: Taylor & Francis Group, 2018), 158.
9. *Hive*, directed by Blerta Basholli (2021; New York: Zeitgeist Film, 2022).
10. Human Rights Watch, *Under Orders*, 364–365.
11. Blerta Basholli (film director), in-person interview by Anna Di Lellio, New York, November 6, 2021.
12. On second traumatization based on non-acceptance by a third party after a traumatic event, see Mucci, *Trauma e perdono*, 63.
13. Goffman, *Stigma*, 7.
14. Goffman, *Stigma*, 5.
15. Tevide Syla, in-person interview by Anna Di Lellio, Prishtina, September 14, 2005.
16. James Scott, "Voice Under Domination: The Arts of Political Disguise," in *Domination and the Art of Resistance: Hidden Transcripts* (New Haven, CT: Yale University Press, 1990), 162. On the South African case, see Fiona Ross, *Bearing Witness: Women and the Truth and Reconciliation Commission in South Africa* (London: Pluto Press, 2002), 154–157.
17. Autobiographies of heroes are much better known than memoirs of refugees and civilian victims; see Anna Di Lellio and Mevlyde Salihu, "Albanian Personal Narratives of the Kosovo War," *Культура/Culture* 5 (2014): 105–124.
18. A philologist and Greek scholar, Luigi Spina is one of the founders of L'Accademia del Silenzio, at the Libera Università di Lingue e Comunicazione (IULM) in Milan, Italy.
19. Luigi Spina, "Shhhh, la sfida etimologica e onomatopeica," in *Il paradosso del silenzio. Percorsi alternativi nel caos contemporaneo*, ed. Nicoletta Polla-Mattiot (Padova: Il Poligrafo, 2009), 63–69.
20. Luigi Spina, "Imporre il silenzio," in *Antichi silenzi*, ed. Giorgio Ieranò e Luigi Spina (Milano; Udine: Mimesis. Accademia del Silenzio, 2015), 11.

21. Veena Das, "Language and Body: Transactions in the Construction of Pain," *Daedalus* 125, no. 1 (1996): 67–92.
22. Goffman, *Stigma*, 42.
23. Agnes Heller, "Five Approaches to the Phenomenon of Shame," *Social Research* 70, no. 4 (2003): 1019.
24. Mookerjee, *The Spectral Wound*, 27. Chapter 3 of this book focuses on how the scorn of villagers brings back to the present the memory of rape, all the while keeping it a public secret.
25. Goffman's "double living," *Stigma*, 78–79.
26. Dori Laub, "Traumatic Shutdown of Narrative and Symbolization: A Death Instinct Derivative?" *Contemporary Psychoanalysis* 41, no. 2 (2005): 329–330.
27. Leigh A. Payne, "Unsettling Accounts: Perpetrators' Confessions in the Aftermath of State Violence and Armed Conflict," in The *Routledge International Handbook of Perpetrator Studies*, ed. Susan C. Knittel and Zachary J. Goldberg (London and New York: Routledge, 2019), 131–133.
28. Sidonie Smith, "Narrating the Right to Sexual Well-Being and the Global Management of Misery: Maria Rosa Henson's Comfort Woman and Charlene Smiths' Proud of Me," *Literature and Medicine* 24, no. 2 (2005): 159.
29. Alexandra Adams, "The Legacy of the International Criminal Tribunals for the Former Yugoslavia and Rwanda and Their Contribution to the Crime of Rape," *European Journal of International Law* 29, no. 3 (2018).
30. ICC, *Decision Pursuant to Article 15 of the Rome Statute on the Authorisation of an Investigation into the Situation in the People's Republic of Bangladesh/Republic of the Union of Myanmar*, ICC-01/19-27, November 14, 2019, https://www.icc-cpi.int/sites/default/files/CourtRecords/CR2019_06955.PDF.
31. Lauren Wolfe, "Ukraine's True Detectives: the Investigators Closing in on Russian War Criminals, *The Guardian*, October 20, 2022, https://www.theguardian.com/world/2022/oct/20/ukraine-true-detectives-investigators-closing-in-on-russian-war-crimes.
32. ICC, *Statement of ICC Prosecutor Karim A.A. Khan KC: Applications for Arrest Warrants in the Situation in the State of Palestine*, May 20, 2024. The call for arrest warrants also includes Israeli leaders, but they are charged with other crimes than rape. https://www.icc-cpi.int/news/statement-icc-prosecutor-karim-aa-khan-kc-applications-arrest-warrants-situation-state.
33. Alexandra Rogers, "British Ministers Under Fire After Serb deputy PM Ivica Dacic, Former Ally of Milosevic, Spoke at Prevention of Sexual Violence in Conflict Conference in London" *Argumentum*, December 1, 2022, https://www.argumentum.al/en/british-ministers-under-fire-after-serb-deputy-pm-ivica-dacic-former-ally-of-milosevic-spoke-at-prevention-of-sexual-violence-in-conflict-conference-in-london/.
34. J. Diković, "Dačić na Konferenciji o prevenciji seksualnog nasilja: Važno je detekovati govor mržnje, ekstremističke ideologije i znake napetosti" *Danas*, November 28, 2022, https://www.danas.rs/svet/dacic-na-konferenciji-o-prevenciji-seksualnog-nasilja-vazno-je-detekovati-govor-mrznje-ekstremisticke-ideologije-i-znake-napetosti/.
35. Kosovo Foreign Minister Donika Gërvalla Speaking About Victims of Sexual Violence @ London Conference, https://www.youtube.com/watch?v=ToVQmqavNfc; Autonomni Ženski Centar Beograd, "Saopštenje za javnost: Ratni huškači nemaju pravo da govore o seksualnom nasilju u ratu [Press Release: Warmongers have no right to talk about sexual violence in war]," published in English on the Facebook page of Medica Gjakova, November 28, 2022, (https://www.facebook.com/100064492130347/posts/522542579905475/). The same sentiments of indignation were expressed on twitter by prominent regional activists: https://twitter.com/atifetejahjaga/status/1597569536441491456?s=46&t=KEqMQMAGacDldM8apIJQog&fbclid=IwAR3DuaVTZHj5ZnrxxF27qoTxZxN0MkNytZ8otF8J4oi2e0EqoECnnfXe6hc; https://twitter.com/SandraOrlovic/status/1597190433058103296.
36. Personal communication via messenger, February 3, 2023.
37. Das, *Life and Words*, 62.
38. Erikson, "Notes on Trauma and Community," *American Imago* 48, no. 4 (1991): 460.
39. Mucci, *Trauma e Perdono*, 200.
40. Primo Levi, *The Drowned and the Saved* (New York: Vintage International, 1989), 60.
41. Goffman, *Stigma*, 28.

Bibliography

Abrahams, Fred, and Eric Stover. *A Village Destroyed, May 14, 1999: War Crimes in Kosovo*. Berkeley and Los Angeles: University of California Press, 2002.

Abrashi, Aziz, and Burhan Kavaja. *Epopeja e Minatorëve: Marshet e tubimet protestuese dhe grevat minatorëve të "Trepçes" në vitet 1988–1990*. Prishtinë: Koha, 1996.

Abrashi, Fisnik, and Ylber Bajraktari. "UÇK: Dalja nga ilegaliteti?" *Koha Ditore*, A1. December 1, 1997.

Abu-Lughod, Lila. *Veiled Sentiments: Honor and Poetry in a Bedouin Society*. Berkeley and Los Angeles: University of California Press, 1986.

Adams, Alexandra. "The Legacy of the International Criminal Tribunals for the Former Yugoslavia and Rwanda and Their Contribution to the Crime of Rape." *European Journal of International Law* 29, no. 3 (2018): 749–769.

Ahmeti, Sevdije. *Journal d'une femme du Kosovo, février 1998–mars 1999: La guerre avant la guerre*. Paris: Karthala, 2003.

Amati Sas, Silvia. "Ambiguity as a Defense in Extreme Trauma." In *Bearing Witness: Psychoanalytic Work with People Traumatised by Torture and State Violence*, edited by Andres Gautier and Anna Sabatini Scalmati, 32–45. London: Taylor & Francis Group, 2010.

Améry, Jean. *At the Mind's Limits: Contemplation by a Survivor on Auschwitz and Its Realities*. Bloomington and Indianapolis: Indiana University Press, 1980.

Amnesty International. *Federal Republic of Yugoslavia: Ethnic Albanians. Victims of Torture and Ill-Treatment by Police in Kosovo Province*. AI INDEX: EUR 48/18/92 (June 1992). https://www.amnesty.org/en/wp-content/uploads/2021/06/eur480181992en.pdf.

Amnesty International. *A Human Rights Crisis in Kosovo Province: Drenica. February–April 1998: Unlawful Killings, Extrajudicial Executions and Armed Opposition Abuses*. AI INDEX: EUR 70/033/1998 (June 30, 1998). https://www.amnesty.org/en/documents/eur70/033/1998/en/.

Amnesty International. *Kosovo: Incidents of Multiple Rape*. AI INDEX: EUR 70/76/1999 (May 26, 1999). https://www.amnesty.org/download/Documents/148000/eur700761999en.pdf.

Amnesty International. *"Wounds That Burn Our Souls": Compensation for Kosovo's Wartime Rape Survivors, but Still No Justice*. New York: Amnesty International, 2017. https://www.amnesty.org/en/documents/eur70/7558/2017/en/.

Amnesty International. *Yugoslavia: Prisoners of Conscience*. AI INDEX: EUR 48/031/1981 (1981). https://www.amnesty.org/en/wp-content/uploads/2021/06/eur480311981en.pdf.

Anastasijević, Dejan. "Bloody Game." *Vreme*, January 31, 1998.

Anastasijević, Dejan. "Dead Man's Dance." *Vreme*, March 14, 1998. https://serbiandigest.libraries.rutgers.edu/336/dance-dead.

Anastasijević, Dejan. "Final Score." *Vreme*, March 21, 1998. https://serbiandigest.libraries.rutgers.edu/337/final-settlement.

Autonomni Ženski Center Beograd. *Saopštenje za javnost: Ratni huškači nemaju pravo da govore o seksualnom nasilju u ratu*, November 29, 2022. https://womenngo.org.rs/vesti/1943-ratni-huskaci-nemaju-pravo-da-govore-o-seksualnom-nasilju-u-ratu?fbclid=IwAR35qQqdMTxfFGFrMnxNRUbDTiEEMZ0oibq7wDvcoxnjhnzEFjF90oHaC1k.

Backer, Berit. *Behind Stone Walls: Changing Household Organisation Among the Albanians of Kosovo*. London: Center for Albanian Studies, 2015.

Bahadori, Babak. *The CNN Effect in Action: How the News Media Pushed the West Towards War in Kosovo.* Basingstoke, UK: Palgrave Macmillan, 2007.

Baig, Laurel, Michelle Jarvis, Elena Martin-Salgado, and Giulia Pinzauti. "Contextualizing Sexual Violence: Selection of Crimes." In *Prosecuting Conflict-Related Sexual Violence at the ICTY*, edited by Serge Baron Brammertz and Michelle Jarvis, 172–219. Oxford: Oxford University Press, 2016.

Bajgora, Sabri. *Destruction of Islamic Heritage in the Kosovo War, 1998–1999.* Prishtina: Interfaith Kosovo, Ministry of Foreign Affairs of the Republic of Kosovo, 2014.

Ball, Patric, Ewa Tabeau, and Philip Verwimp. *The Bosnian Book of the Dead: Assessment of the Database.* Households in Conflict Network, University of Sussex, 2007. https://hrdag.org/wp-content/uploads/2013/02/rdn5.pdf.

Bami, Xhorxhina. "Kosovo Finds Serb Ex-Policeman Guilty of Wartime Rape After Retrial." *BIRN*, November 11, 2022. https://balkaninsight.com/2022/11/11/kosovo-finds-serb-ex-policeman-guilty-of-wartime-rape-after-retrial/.

Bami, Xhorxhina. "Kosovo War Rape Survivor Seeks Attacker's Prosecution." *BIRN*, October 14, 2019. https://balkaninsight.com/2019/10/14/kosovo-war-rape-survivor-seeks-attackers-prosecution/.

Banac, Ivo. "Is It True That Tito's Yugoslav Policies Favored Albanians in Kosova?" In *The Case for Kosova: Passage to Independence*, edited by Anna Di Lellio, 63–67. London: Anthem Press, 2006.

Banac, Ivo. *The National Question in Yugoslavia: Origins, History, Politics.* Ithaca, NY: Cornell University Press, 1984.

Banac, Ivo. *With Stalin Against Tito: Cominformist Splits in Yugoslav Communism.* Ithaca, NY: Cornell University Press, 1988.

Baris, Tommaso. "Le corps expéditionnaire français en Italie: Violences des 'libérateurs' durant l'été 1944." *Vingtième Siècle: Revue d'Histoire* 93 (janv–mars 2007): 47–61.

Barker, Pat. *The Silence of the Girls.* New York: Doubleday, 2018.

Basholli, Blerta, dir. *Hive.* 2021. New York: Zeitgeist Film, 2022.

BBC. "Top Serb Suspect Dies," April 14, 2002. http://news.bbc.co.uk/2/hi/europe/1928491.stm.

Bird, Chris, and Nicholas Watt. "Kosovan Leader's Death Condemned." *The Guardian*, May 9, 1999. https://www.theguardian.com/world/1999/may/10/balkans7.

Biserko, Sonja. "Serbian Nationalism and the Remaking of the Yugoslav Federation." In *Yugoslavia Implosion: The Fatal Attraction of Serbian Nationalism*, 33–124. Oslo: The Norwegian Helsinki Committee, 2012. https://www.nhc.no/content/uploads/2018/07/YugoslaviasImplosion_book.pdf.

Blyth, Caroline. *The Narrative of Rape in Genesis 34: Interpreting Dinah's Silence.* Oxford: Oxford University Press, 2010.

Boehm, Christopher. *Blood Revenge: The Anthropology of Feuding in Montenegro and Other Tribal Societies.* Lawrence: Kansas University Press, 1984.

Boltanski, Luc. *Distant Suffering: Morality, Media, and Politics.* Cambridge: Cambridge University Press, 1999.

Boose, Lynda E. "Crossing the River Drina: Bosnian Rape Camps, Turkish Impalement, and Serb Cultural Memory." *Signs: Journal of Women in Culture and Society* 28, no. 1 (2002): 71–96.

Bourdieu, Pierre. *Outline of a Theory of Practice.* Cambridge: Cambridge University Press, 1977.

Božović, Grigorije. "Kaçaki." *Policija* 7, no. 13–14 (1920).

Bracewell, Wendy. "Rape in Kosovo: Masculinity and Serbian Nationalism." *Nations and Nationalism* 6 (2000): 563–590.

Brison, Susan. *Aftermath: Violence and the Remaking of a Self.* Princeton, NJ: Princeton University Press, 2002.

Bromberg, Philip M. "The Nearness of You: Navigating Selfhood, Otherness and Uncertainty." In *Knowing, Not-Knowing, and Sort-of-Knowing: Psychoanalysis and the Experience of Uncertainty*, edited by Jean Petrucelli, 23–44. London: Karnac, 2010.

Brubaker, Rogers. *Nationalism Reframed: Nationhood and the National Question in the New Europe*. Cambridge: Cambridge University Press, 1996.
Buckley, Mary, and Sally N. Cummings, eds. *Kosovo: Perceptions of War and Its Aftermath*. London and New York: Continuum, 2001.
Bumiller, Elizabeth. "Deny Rape or Be Hated: Kosovo Victims' Choice." *New York Times*, June 22, 1999, A1. https://www.nytimes.com/1999/06/22/world/crisis-in-the-balkans-crimes-deny-rape-or-be-hated-kosovo-victims-choice.html.
Bytyci, Fatos. "Kosovo Privatization Head Took Own Life: Autopsy." *Reuters*, June 18, 2012. https://www.reuters.com/article/us-kosovo-official-suicide-idUSBRE85H1G620120618.
Cahn, Claude, and Tatjana Peric, *Roma and the Kosovo Conflict*. Brussels: European Roma Rights Center, 1999. http://www.errc.org/cikk.php?cikk=798.
Caruth, Cathy. *Unclaimed Experience: Trauma, Narrative, and History*. Baltimore, MD, and London: Johns Hopkins University Press, 1996.
Çeku, Ethem. *Shekulli i Ilegales: Proceset gjuqësore kundër ilegales në Kosovë. Dokumente*. Prishtinë: Brezi' 81, 2004.
Çetta, Anton. "Gjakmarrja në traditën tone popullore gojore." *Gjurmime Albanologjke Folklor dhe Ethnologje* X (1980): 207–228.
Çetta, Anton. *Nga folklori ynë*. I. Prishtinë: Instituti Albanologjik, 2020.
Çetta, Anton. *Prozë popullore nga Drenica*. I. Prishtinë: Rilindja, 1972.
Chang, Iris. *The Rape of Nanking: The Forgotten Holocaust of World War II*. New York: Basic Books, 1997.
Clark, Howard. *Civil Resistance in Kosovo*. London: Pluto, 2000.
Clark, Mary Marshall. "Resisting Attrition in Stories of Trauma." *Narrative* 13, no. 3 (2005): 294–298.
Clark, Wesley. *Waging Modern War: Bosnia, Kosovo, and the Future of Combat*. New York: Public Affairs, 2002.
Clark, Wesley. Testimony in *Prosecutor v. Milošević*, Case IT-02-54 (ICTY Transcripts, December 15, 2003). https://ucr.irmct.org/Search/PreviewPage/?link=http%253A//icr.icty.org/LegalRef/CMSDocStore/Public/English/Transcript/NotIndexable/IT-02-54/TRS1154R0000087703.doc.
Clayer, Nathalie. *Aux origines du nationalisme albanais: La naissance d'une nation majoritairement musulmane en Europe*. Paris: Karthala, 2007.
Cohen, Lenard J. *Serpent in the Bosom: The Rise and Fall of Slobodan Milosevic*. Boulder, CO: Westview Press, 2001.
Ćolović, Ivan. *Smrt na Kosovu polju*. Beograd: Biblioteka XX vek, 2017.
Colvin, Marie. "Kosovo's Silent Houses of the Dead." *The Sunday Times*, March 15, 1998. https://advance-lexis-com.proxy.library.nyu.edu/api/document?collection=news&id=urn:contentItem:3S9H-5FC0-008G-H33P-00000-00&context=1519360.
Comunità di Sant'Egidio. "Kosovo. Statement." September 1, 1996. https://archive.santegidio.org/archivio/pace/kosovo_19960109_EN.htm.
Coon, Carlton. "The Mountain of Giants: A Racial and Cultural Study of the North Albanian Mountain Ghegs." *Papers of the Peabody Museum* 23, no. 3 (1950): 3–105.
Cozzi, Ernesto. "Le vendette del sangue nelle montagne dell'Alta Albania." *Anthropos* 5, no. 3 (1910): 654–687.
Culbertson, Roberta. "Embodied Memory, Transcendence, and Telling: Recounting Trauma, Re-Establishing the Self." *New Literary History* 26, no. 1 (1995): 169–195.
Cvijić, Jovan. *La Péninsule balkanique: Géographie humaine*. Paris: Librairie Armand Colin, 1918.
Daalder, Ivo H., and Michael E. O'Hanlon. *Winning Ugly: NATO's War to Save Kosovo*. Washington, DC: Brookings Institution Press, 2000.
Daniszewski, John. "Death of Belanica." *Los Angeles Times*, April 25, 1999. https://www.latimes.com/archives/la-xpm-1999-apr-25-ss-31093-story.html.
Das, Veena and Arthur Kleinman. "Introduction" to *Remaking the World: Violence, Social Suffering and Recovery*, edited by Veena Das, Arthur Kleinman, Margaret M. Lock,

Mamphela Ramphele, and Pamela Reynolds, 1–22. Berkeley and Los Angeles: University of California Press, 2001.

Das, Veena. "Language and Body: Transactions in the Construction of Pain." *Daedalus* 125, no. 1 (1996): 67–92.

Das, Veena. *Life and Words: Violence and the Descent into the Ordinary*. Berkeley and Los Angeles: University of California Press, 2006.

Dedijer, Vladimir, and Anton Miletić. *Proterivanje Srba sa ognjišta 1941–1944*. Beograd: Prosveta, 1989.

de la Brosse, Bernard. *Political Propaganda and the Plan to Create a "A State for All Serbs": Consequences for Using the Media for Ultra Nationalist Ends*. The Hague: International Criminal Court for Yugoslavia, 2003. http://balkanwitness.glypx.com/de_la_brosse_pt1.pdf.

de Langis, Teresa. "Speaking Private Memory to Public Power: Oral History and Breaking the Silence on Sexual and Gender-Based Violence During the Khmer Rouge Genocide." In *Beyond Women's Words: Feminisms and the Practices of Oral History in the Twenty-First Century*, edited by Katrina Srigley, Stacey Zembrzycki, and Franca Iacovetta, 155–169. London: Taylor & Francis Group, 2018.

Delbo, Charlotte. *Days and Memory*. Marlboro, VT: Marlboro Press, 1985.

Denich, Bette. "Dismembering Yugoslavia: Nationalist Ideologies and the Symbolic Revival of Genocide." *American Ethnologist* 21, no. 2 (1994): 367–390.

Denitch, Bogdan. "Notes on the Relevance of Yugoslav Self-Management." *Politics & Society* 3, no. 4 (1973): 473–489.

Diković, J. "Dačić na Konferenciji o prevenciji seksualnog nasilja: Važno je detekovati govor mržnje, ekstremističke ideologije i znake napetosti." *Danas*, November 28, 2022. https://www.danas.rs/svet/dacic-na-konferenciji-o-prevenciji-seksualnog-nasilja-vazno-je-detekovati-govor-mrznje-ekstremisticke-ideologije-i-znake-napetosti/.

Di Lellio, Anna. *The Battle of Kosovo 1389: An Albanian Epic*. London: I. B. Tauris, 2009.

Di Lellio, Anna. "Authors of Their Own Transitional Justice: Survivors of Wartime Sexual Violence." In *Kosovo and the Pursuit of Justice After Large Scale Conflict*, edited by Aidan Hehir, Robert Muharremi, and Furtuna Sheremeti, 92–110. London: Routledge, 2021.

Di Lellio, Anna. "Gender and Sexual Violence in Genocide." In *Handbook of Genocide Studies*, edited by David Şimon and Leora Kahn, 214–225. Cheltenham, UK, and Northampton, MA: Edward Elgar, 2023.

Di Lellio, Anna. *La Jugoslavia crollò in miniera: Kosovo 1989: lo sciopero di Trepça e la lotta per l'autonomia*. Milano: Prospero Editore, 2024.

Di Lellio, Anna. "Seeking Justice for Wartime Sexual Violence in Kosovo: Voices and Silence of Women." *Eastern European Politics and Societies and Cultures* 30 (2016): 621–643.

Di Lellio, Anna, Abit Hoxha, Orli Fridman, and Srđan Hercigonja. *Fostering a Critical Account of History in Kosovo: Engaging with History Teachers' Narratives of the Second World War*. Prishtina and Belgrade: Oral History Kosovo and CFCCS, 2017.

Di Lellio, Anna, and Garentina Kraja. "Sexual Violence in the Kosovo Conflict: A Lesson for Myanmar and Other Ethnic Cleansing Campaigns." *International Politics* 58 (2021): 148–167.

Di Lellio, Anna, and Dardan Luta. *The Long Winter of 1945: Tivari*. Toronto: Toronto University Press, 2023.

Di Lellio, Anna, Feride Rushiti, and Kadire Tahiraj. "Art Activism Against the Stigma of Sexual Violence: The Case of Kosovo." *Violence Against Women* 25, no. 13 (2019): 1543–1557.

Di Lellio, Anna, and Mevlyde Salihu. "Albanian Personal Narratives of the Kosovo War." *Култура/Culture* 5 (2014): 115–124.

Di Lellio, Anna, and Stephanie Schwandner-Sievers. "The Legendary Commander: The Construction of an Albanian Master-Narrative in Post-War Kosovo." *Nations & Nationalism* 12, no. 3 (2006): 513–529.

Dimova, Rozita. "From Past Necessities to Contemporary Friction: Migration, Class and Ethnicity in Macedonia." Max Planck Institute for Social Anthropology Working Papers, 94, 2007.

Djaković, Spasoje. *Sukobi na Kosovu*, Beograd: Narodna Knjiga, 1987.
Doder, Duško, and Laura Branson. *Milosevic: Portrait of a Tyrant*. Los Angeles: Free Press, 1999.
Doja, Albert. *Naître et grandir chez les Albanais: La construction culturelle de la personne*. Paris: L'Harmattan, 2000.
Dowd, Nancy. *The Man Question*. New York: New York University Press, 2010.
Dragović-Soso, Jasna. *Saviours of the Nation: Serbia's Intellectual Opposition and the Revival of Nationalism*. Montreal: McGill-Queen's Press, 2002.
Dragović-Soso, Jasna. "Why Did Yugoslavia Disintegrate?" In *State Collapse in South-Eastern Europe: New Perspectives on Yugoslavia's Disintegration*, edited by Lenard J. Cohen and Jasna Dragović-Soso, 1–39. West Lafayette, IN: Purdue University Press, 2008.
Drakulić, Slavenka. *They Would Never Hurt a Fly: War Criminals on Trial in The Hague*. New York: Penguin, 2004.
Dugolli, Bujar. *The Turning Point of 1 October: The Student Movement in Kosovo 1997–1998*. Prishtinë: University of Prishtina, 2020.
Dugolli, Enver. *Unbroken: Surviving Milosevic's Prisons*. London: The Center for Albanian Studies, 2021.
Duijzings, Ger. 2001. *Religion and the Politics of Identity in Kosovo*. New York: Columbia University Press, 2001.
Dushi, Arbnora. "Intergenerational Memory of the Border History." *Ethnologia Balkanica* 21 (2018): 291–308.
Eek, Ann Christine. *Albanian Village Life: Isniq-Kosovo 1976*. Sweden: Tira Books, 2021.
Elsie, Robert. *Historical Dictionary of Kosovo*. Lanham, MD: Scarecrow Press, 2011.
Enzensberger, Hans Magnus. "Afterword by the German Editor." In Anonyma, *A Woman in Berlin*, 309–311. London: Virago, 2004.
Erikson, Kai. "Notes on Trauma and Community." *American Imago* 48, no. 4 (1991): 455–472.
"Excerpts from Interviews with Militia Members Conducted by Montgomery Michael and Stephen Smith of America Radio Works in September 1999." https://americanradioworks.publicradio.org/features/kosovo/more1.htm.
Farnsworth, Nicole. *1325 Facts and Fables: A Collection of Stories About the Implementation of the United Nations Security Council Resolution 1325 on Women, Peace and Security in Kosovo*. 2nd edition. Prishtinë: Kosova Women's Network, 2002. https://womensnetwork.org/wp-content/uploads/2022/10/1325-Facts-and-Fables.pdf.
Farnsworth, Nicole, ed. *History Is Herstory Too: The History of Women in Civil Society in Kosovo, 1980–2004*. Prishtinë: Kosova Gender Studies Center, 2008.
Fazliu, Eraldin. "Kosovo's Political Prisoners." *Kosovo 2.0*. April 26, 2016. https://kosovotwopointzero.com/en/kosovos-political-prisoners/.
Federal Republic of Yugoslavia, Federal Ministry of Foreign Affairs. *Terrorist Acts of Albanian Terrorist Groups in Kosovo and Metohija: Documents and Evidence, 1 January 1998–10 June 1999*, III, Part One. Belgrade: Službeni glasnik, 2000.
Finn, Peter. "Signs of Rape Scar Kosovo: Families' Shame Could Hinder Investigation." *Washington Post*, June 2, 1999. A1. https://www.washingtonpost.com/wp-srv/inatl/longterm/balkans/stories/rape062799.htm.
Fishta, Gjergj. "A janë t'zott shqyptareët me u majtë shtet n'vedi?" *Hylli i Dritës* Vjeti I, no. 2 (1913): 36–42.
"Fjala e Ushtarëve të UÇK-së në Varrimin e Mësuesit Halit Geci në Llaushë." *Zëri i Kosovës*, no. 45 (1997): 11–12.
ForumZFD and Kosova Rehabilitation Centre for Torture Victims. *Beyond Pain, Towards Courage: Stories About the Trauma of Wartime Sexual Violence*. Prishtinë: forumZFD and Kosova Rehabilitation Centre for Torture Victims, 2021.
Fussell, Paul. *The Great War and Modern Memory*. New York: Oxford University Press, 1975.
Gashi, Kreshnik, and Xhorxhina Bami. 2021. "Kosovo's Special Prosecutor: 'Wartime Rape Victims Must Speak Out.'" *BIRN*, July 8. https://balkaninsight.com/2021/07/08/kosovo-special-prosecutor-wartime-rape-victims-must-speak-out/.

Georgevitch (Djordjević), Vladan. *Les Albanais et les grandes puissances*. Paris: Calmann-Lévy, 1913.
Gjeçovi, Shtjefen. *Kanuni i Leke Dukagjinit: The Code of Leke Dukagjini*. New York: Gjonlekaj, 1989.
Gjiergji, Dom Lush. "Në vjetorin e pajtimit të gjaqeve." Interview. RTV June 21, 2015. Video, 19:18. https://www.youtube.com/watch?v=H9hDD471bq0.
Goffman, Ervin. *Stigma: Notes on the Management of Spoiled Identity*. New York, London, and Toronto: Simon and Schuster, 1963.
Gopalan, Prya, Daniela Kravetz, and Aditya Menon. "Proving Crimes of Sexual Violence." In *Prosecuting Conflict-Related Sexual Violence at the ICTY*, edited by Serge Baron Brammertz and Michelle Jarvis, 111–171. Oxford: Oxford University Press, 2016.
Gorani, Dukagjin, and Baton Haxhiu. "Prekazi, edhe një herë në zjarr." *Koha Ditore*, January 23, 1998.
Greble, Emily. "Conflict in Post-War Yugoslavia: The Search for a Narrative," The National WWII Museum, New Orleans, September 21, 2021. https://www.nationalww2museum.org/war/articles/conflict-post-war-yugoslavia.
Grele, Ronald J. "Movement Without Aim: Methodological and Theoretical Problems in Oral History." In *Envelopes of Sound: The Art of Oral History*, 126–143. 2nd edition, revised and enlarged. Westport, CT: Praeger Pub, 1991.
Hadri, Ali. *Lëvizja nacionalçlirimtare në Kosovë, 1941–1945*. Prishtinë: Bashkësia e Institucioneve Shkencore të KSA të Kosovës Rilindja, 1971.
Halili, Dafina. "I Never Imagined This Could Be Done Also to Men," Kosovo 2.0, October 27, 2022. https://kosovotwopointzero.com/en/i-never-imagined-this-could-be-done-also-to-men/.
Hammel, E. A., and Djordje, Šoć. "The Lineage Cycle in Southern and Eastern Yugoslavia." *American Anthropologist* 75, no. 3 (1973): 802–814.
Hammond, Philip, and Edward S. Herman, eds. *Degraded Capability: The Media and the Kosovo Crisis*. London: Pluto Press, 2000.
Hamzaj, Bardh. *A Narrative About War and Freedom (Dialog with the Commander Ramush Haradinaj)*. Prishtinë: Zëri, 2000.
Hamzaj, Bardh, and Faik Hoti. *Jasharë (Histori e rrrëfyer nga Rifat, Besarta, Bashkim, Murat dhe Lulzim Jashari)*. Prishtinë: Zëri, 2003.
Hasluck, Margaret. *The Unwritten Law in Albania*. Edited by J. H. Hutton. London: Cambridge University Press, 1954.
Haxhiu, Baton. *Lufta Ndryshë*. Prishtinë: Kumti, 2008.
Heller, Agnes. "Five Approaches to the Phenomenon of Shame." *Social Research* 70, no. 4 (2003): 1015–1030.
Herman, Judith Lewis. *Trauma and Recovery*. New York: Basic, 1992.
Herscher, Andrew. *Violence Taking Place: The Architecture of the Kosovo Conflict*. Stanford, CA: Stanford University Press, 2010.
Herscher, Andrew, and András Riedlmayer. "Monument Crime: The Destruction of Historical Architecture in Kosovo." *Grey Room* 1 (Autumn 2000): 108–122.
Hetemi, Atdhe. *Student Movements for the Republic of Kosovo, 1968, 1981, and 1997*. London: Springer International, 2020.
Hirsch, Marianne. "Ce qui touche à la mémoire." *Esprit* 438 (October 2017): 42–61.
Hockenos, Paul. *Homeland Calling: Exile Patriotism and the Balkan Wars*. Ithaca, NY: Cornell University Press, 2004.
Hoxha, Fadil. *Fadil Hoxha në veten e parë: Me shënime dhe parathënie të Veton Surroi*. Prishtinë: Koha, 2010.
Humanitarian Law Center. *Kosovo Memory Book Database: Presentation and Expert Evaluation*. Prishtina, February 4, 2015. http://www.kosovomemorybook.org/wp-content/uploads/2015/02/Expert_Evaluation_of_Kosovo_Memory_Book_Database_Prishtina_04_02_2015.pdf.

Humanitarian Law Center. *Kosovo Memory Book 1998–2000*. Beograd: Humanitarian Law Center, n.d. http://www.kosovskaknjigapamcenja.org/?page_id=660&lang=de.
Humanitarian Law Center. *Spotlight on: Kosovo, Human Rights in Times of Armed Conflict*, Report No. 26, May. Beograd: Humanitarian Law Center, 1998.
Human Rights Watch. *Federal Republic of Yugoslavia: Abuses Against Serbs and Roma in the New Kosovo*. August. New York: Human Rights Watch, 1999. https://www.hrw.org/reports/1999/kosov2/.
Human Rights Watch. *Humanitarian Law Violations in Kosovo*. New York: Human Rights Watch, October 1998. https://www.hrw.org/legacy/reports98/kosovo/.
Human Rights Watch. *Kosovo: Rape as a Weapon of "Ethnic Cleansing."* New York: Human Rights Watch, 2000. https://www.hrw.org/legacy/reports/2000/fry/index.htm#TopOfPage.
Human Rights Watch. *Open Wounds. Human Rights Abuses in Kosovo*. New York: Human Rights Watch, 1993. https://www.hrw.org/sites/default/files/reports/Kosovo943.pdf.
Human Rights Watch. *Under Orders*. New York: Human Rights Watch, 2001. https://www.hrw.org/reports/2001/kosovo/?gad_source=1&gclid=CjwKCAjw1920BhA3EiwAJT3lS-WoqlCf7oKSCT28l4VY4iUIJEUpe8fMLjtTJvggSiR4zCOb6ZAv-ARoCmhIQAvD_BwE.
Human Rights Watch. *A Week of Terror in Drenica*. New York: Human Rights Watch, October 1998. https://www.hrw.org/legacy/reports/1999/kosovo/.
Human Rights Watch. *Yugoslavia: Human Rights Abuses in Kosovo 1990–1992*. New York: Human Rights Watch, 1992. https://www.hrw.org/legacy/reports/1992/yugoslavia/#P800_140238.
Iacopino, Vincent, Martina W Frank, Heidi M Bauer, Allen S Keller, Sheri L Fink, Doug Ford, Daniel J. Pallin, and Ronald Waldman. "A Population-Based Assessment of Human Rights Violations against Albanian Ethnic Refugees from Kosovo." *American Journal of Public Health* 91, no. 12 (2001): 2013–2018.
I Begged Them to Kill Me: Crimes Against the Women of Bosnia-Herzegovina. Sarajevo: Center for Documentation and Investigation of the Association of Former Prison Camp Inmates of Bosnia-Herzegovina, 2000.
Ilazi, Besa, and Agim Zogaj. "Dihet se si na zë nata, por nuk dihet se si dhe a do të na çelë sabahi!" *Zëri*, January 31, 1998, p. 10.
Independent International Commission on Kosovo. *The Kosovo Report: Conflict. International Response. Lessons Learned*. New York: Oxford University Press, 2000. https://www.law.umich.edu/facultyhome/drwcasebook/Documents/Documents/The%20Kosovo%20Report%20and%20Update.pdf.
Information Counseling and Referral Service (ICRS). *Socio-Economic and Demographic Profiles of Former KLA Combatants Registered by IOM*, Vol. I, January 21, 2000. Pristina: IOM Kosovo.
Integra and forumZFD. *I Want to Be Heard*. Prishtinë: Integra and forumZFD, 2017.
Islami, Hivzi. *Fshati i Kosovës: Kontribut për studimin sociolologjiko-demografik të evolucionit rural*. Prishtinë: Rilindja, 1985.
Jacomoni, Francesco. *La politica dell'Italia in Albania nelle testimonianze del Luogotenente del Re Francesco Jacomoni di San Savino*. Bologna: Cappelli, 1956.
Jarvis, Michelle, and Kate Vigneswaran. "Challenges to Successful Outcomes in Sexual Violence Cases." In *Prosecuting Conflict-Related Sexual Violence at the ICTY*, edited by Serge Brammertz and Michelle Jarvis, 33–72. Oxford: Oxford University Press, 2016.
Jashiri, Besarta. "War in Kosovo: Three Albanians Victims of Serbian Ethnic Cleansing and Atrocities." Interview. FRONTLINE, *PBS*, 2000. Transcript. https://www.pbs.org/wgbh/pages/frontline/shows/kosovo/interviews/victims.html.
Jevtich, Anastasije. *Dossier Kosovo*. Lausanne: L'Age d' Homme, 1991.
Johnston, Bruce. "Refugee Girls Stripped, Gang Raped by Militia." *The Independent*, April 12, 1999.https://www.independent.ie/world-news/refugee-girls-stripped-gang-raped-by-militia-26152948.html.

Jovanović, Vladan. "Land Reform and Serbian Colonization." *East Central Europe* 42, no. 1 (2015): 87–103.
Judah, Tim. *Kosovo: War and Revenge*. New Haven, CT: Yale University Press, 2000.
Kadriu, Arber, and Die Morina. "Pioneering Kosovo Rape Victim Relives Battle for Justice." *BIRN*, October 18, 2018. https://balkaninsight.com/2018/10/18/pioneering-kosovo-rape-victim-relives-battle-for-justice-10-18-2018/.
Kaplan, Robert. *Balkan Ghosts: A Journey Through History*. New York: Picador, 1993.
Kaser, Karl. "The Balkan Joint Family Household: Seeking Its Origins." *Continuity and Change* 9, no. 1 (1994): 45–68.
Keçmezi-Basha, Sabile. *Organizata dhe grupet ilegale në Kosovë 1981–1989 (sipas aktgjykimeve të gjykatave ish-jugosllave)*. Prishtinë: Instituti i Historisë, 2003.
Keçmezi-Basha, Sabile. *Qëndresa shekullore e familjes—Tahir Meha*. Prishtinë: Instituti i Historisë, 2015.
Keçmezi-Basha, Sabile. *Të burgosurit politikë shqiptarë në Kosovë 1945–1990*. Shkup, Prishtinë, Tiranë: Logos-A, 2009. Kelmendi, Migjen. *To Change the World: A History of the Traces*. Prishtina: Java Multimedia Production, 2001.
Kimmel, Michael. "Masculinity as Homophobia: Fear, Shame, and Silence in the Construction of Gender Identity." In *Theorizing Masculinities*, edited by Harry Brod and Michael Kaufman, 119–141. Thousand Oaks, London, and New Delhi: Sage Publications, 1994.
KMLDNJ. *Buletini*, Viti VIII, no. 6 (Janar-Mars 1998).
Косово/Kosova. Beograd: Borba, 1973.
Konitza, Mehmet. "The Albanian Question." *The Adriatic Review* 1, no. 4 (1918): 145–164.
Kostovicova, Denisa. *Kosovo: The Politics of Identity and Space*. London: Routledge, 2005.
Kraja, Garentina. "Recruitment Practices of Europe's Last Guerrilla: Ethnic Mobilization, Violence and Networks in the Recruitment Strategy of the Kosovo Liberation Army." Bachelor of arts and master of arts thesis, Yale University, 2011.
Kraja, Garentina, and Nebi Qena. "Na s'kem ku shkojmë, në vendin tonin jem." *Koha Ditore*, February 14, 1998.
Kraja, Mehmet. *Vite të humbura*. Prishtinë: Rozafa, [1995] 2003.
Krasniqi, Gëzim. "'Quadratic Nexus' and the Process of Democratization and State-Building in Albania and Kosovo: A Comparison." *Nationalities Papers* 41, no. 3 (2013): 395–411.
Krasniqi, Gëzim. "Revisiting Nationalism in Yugoslavia: An Inside-Out View of the Nationalist Movement in Kosovo." In *Debating the End of Yugoslavia*, edited by Florian Bieber, A. Galijaš, and Roy Archer, 225–240. London: Routledge, 2016.
Krasniqi, Kushtrim. *My Grandfather Metush Krasniqi*. n.d. https://oralhistorykosovo.org/my-grandfather-metush-krasniqi/.
Kuehnast, Kathleen, Chantal de Jonge Oudraat, and Helga Hernes, eds. *Women and War: Power and Protection in the 21st Century* Washington, DC: United States Institute of Peace, 2011.
Kullashi, Mehmedin. *Humanisme et haine: Les intellectuels et le nationalisme en ex-Yugoslavie*. Paris: L'Harmattan, 1998.
Laub, Dori. "Bearing Witness as the Vicissitudes of Listening." In *Testimony, Crisis of Witnessing in Literature, Psychoanalysis, and History*, edited by Dori Laub and Shohana Felman, 57–74. New York and London: Routledge, 1992.
Laub, Dori. "An Event Without a Witness: Truth, Testimony and Survival." In *Testimony: Crisis of Witnessing in Literature, Psychoanalysis and History*, edited by Shoshana Felman and Dori Laub, 75–92. London: Taylor and Francis, 1991.
Laub, Dori. "From Speechlessness to Narrative: The Cases of Holocaust Historians and of Psychiatrically Hospitalized Survivors." *Literature and Medicine* 24, no. 2 (2005): 253–265.
Laub, Dori. "On Holocaust Testimony and Its Reception Within Its Own Frame, as a Process in Its Own Right." *History and Memory* 21, no. 1 (2009): 127–150.
Laub, Dori. "Traumatic Shutdown of Narrative and Symbolization. A Death Instinct Derivative?" *Contemporary Psychoanalysis* 41, no. 2 (2005): 307–326.

Laub, Dori, and Nanette C. Auerhahn. "Knowing and Not Knowing Massive Psychic Trauma: Forms of Traumatic Memory." *International Journal of Psycho-Analysis* 74 (1993): 287–302.

Laurence, Patricia. "Women's Silence as a Ritual of Truth: A Study of Literary Expression in Austen, Brontë, and Woolf." In *Listening to Silences: New Essays in Feminist Criticism*, edited by Elaine Hedges and Fishkin Fisher, 156–167. Oxford: Oxford University Press. 1994.

Levi, Primo. *The Drowned and the Saved*. New York: Vintage International, 1989.

Leydesdorff, Selma. *Surviving the Bosnian Genocide: The Women of Srebrenica Speak*. Indianapolis: Indiana University Press, 2011.

Lilly, Carol S. "Problems of Persuasion: Communist Agitation and Propaganda in Post-War Yugoslavia, 1944–1948." *Slavic Review* 53, no. 2 (1994): 395–413.

Limani, Mrika. *Perspectives on Ideology and Violence in the Second World War in Kosova*. Prishtinë: Instituti I Historisë "Ali Hadri," 2021.

Link, Bruce G., and Jo Phelan. "Stigma Power." *Social Science & Medicine* 103 (2014): 24–32.

Loeb, Vernon, and R. Jeffrey Smith. "Evidence Mounts of Atrocities by Yugoslav Forces." *Washington Post*, April 10, 1999, A16. https://www.washingtonpost.com/wp-srv/inatl/longterm/balkans/stories/atrocities041099.htm.

Loose, Sarah K., with Amy Starecheski. "Oral History for Building Social Movement: Then and Now." In *Beyond Women's Words: Feminism and the Practice of Oral History in the Twenty-First Century*, edited by Katrina Srigley, Stacey Zembrzycki, and Franca Iacovetta, 236–243. London: Taylor & Francis Group, 2018.

Magaš, Branka. *The Destruction of Yugoslavia: Tracking the Break-Up 1980–1992*. London: Verso, 1993.

Malcolm, Noel. "Is the Complaint About the Serb State's Deportation Policy of Albanians Between the Two World Wars Based on Myth?" In *The Case for Kosova: Passage to Independence*, edited by Anna Di Lellio, 59–61. London: Anthem Press, 2006.

Malcolm, Noel. *Kosovo: A Short History*. New York and London: Macmillan, 1998.

Maliqi, Shkelzen. "The Albanian Intifada." In Branka Magaš, *The Destruction of Yugoslavia: Tracking the Break-Up 1980–1992*, 179–186. London: Verso, 1993.

Maliqi, Shkelzen. *Kosova: Separate Worlds. Reflections and Analyses*. Pristina: Dukagjin, 1998.

Maliqi, Shkelzen. *Nyja e Kosovës, as Vllasi as Millosheviqi*. Ljubljana: Knjižna zbirka KRT, [1989a] 1998.

Maliqi, Shkelzen. *Shembja e Jugosllavisë, Kosova dhe rrëfime të tjera: Dialog me Baton Haxhiun*. Tiranë: UET Press, 2011.

Mead, Margaret. "Introduction: Philip E. Mosely's Contribution to the Comparative Study of the Family." In Communal Families in the Balkans: The Zadruga.Essays by Philip E. Mosely and Essays in His Honor, edited by Robert F. Byrnes, xvii–xxvii. Notre Dame, IN: University of Notre Dame Press, 1976.

Medica Gjakova and Salie Gajtani-Osmankaq. *I Am Anemone*. Gjakova: Medica Gjakova, 2017.

medica mondiale and Medica Gjakova. *Am I Guilty for What Happened to Me? A Study of the Long-Term Consequences of War Rape in Kosovo*. Cologne and Prishtina: medica mondiale and Medica Gjakova, 2024.

Mehilli, Elidor. *From Stalin to Mao: Albania and the Socialist World*. Ithaca, NY: Cornell University Press, 2017.

Meier, Victor. *Yugoslavia: A History of Its Demise*. London: Routledge, 1999.

Mertus, Julie. "Gender in Service of Nation: Female Citizenship in Kosovar Society." *Social Politics: International Studies in Gender, State & Society* 3, no. 2-3 (Summer 1996): 261–277.

Mertus, Julie. *Kosovo: How Myths and Truths Started a War*. Berkeley: California University Press, 1999.

Micheletta, Luca. *La resa dei conti: Il Kosovo, l'Italia e la dissoluzione della Jugoslavia (1939–1941)*. Roma: Edizioni Nuova Cultura, 2008.

Mihailović, Kosta, and Krestić Vasilije. *Memorandum of the Serbian Academy of Sciences and Arts. Answers to Criticisms*. Belgrade: SANU, 1995.

Miller, Nick. *The Nonconformists: Culture, Politics, and Nationalism in a Serbian Intellectual Circle, 1944–1991*. Budapest: Central European University Press, 2007.

Mookherjee, Nayanika. *The Spectral Wound: Sexual Violence, Public Memories, and the Bangladesh War of 1971*. Durham, NC: Duke University Press, 2015.

Motes, Mary. "Bloody Albanians!" In *Kosova, Kosovo: Prelude to War 1966–1999*, 191–197. Homestead, FL: Redland Press, 1998.

Mucci, Clara. *Trauma e perdono: Una prospettiva psicoanalitica intergenerazionale*. Milano: Raffaello Cortina, 2014.

Murtezi Shala, Ramize. *Unë e përdhunuara...Bazuar në ngjarje të vërtetë*. Prishtinë: Faik Konica, 2018.

Musić, Goran. *Making and Breaking the Yugoslav Working Class: The Story of Two Self-Managed Factories*. Budapest: Central European University Press, 2021.

Nazi, Fron. "Balkan Diaspora: The Albanian-American Community." In *Contending Voices on Balkan Interventions*, edited by William Joseph Buckley, 149–152. Grand Rapids, MI: William B. Eerdmans, 2000.

Nordås, Raghild, and Dara Kay Cohen. "Conflict Related Sexual Violence." *Annual Review of Political Science* 24 (2021): 193–211.

Office of the Special Office of the Special Representative of the Secretary General on Sexual Violence in Conflict. *In Their Own Words: Voices of Survivors of Conflict-Related Sexual Violence and Service-Providers*, October 29, 2021. https://www.un.org/sexualviolencein-conflict/in-their-own-words-voices-of-survivors-of-conflict-related-sexual-violence-and-service-providers/.

OSCE and ODIHR. *Kosovo/Kosova: As Seen, As Told. Part I October 1998–June 1999 and Part II, June to October 1999*. Organization for Security and Cooperation in Europe. Warsaw: OSCE, 1999. https://www.osce.org/files/f/documents/d/d/17772.pdf.

Passerini, Luisa. *Fascism in Popular Memory: The Cultural Experience of the Turin Working Class*. Cambridge: Cambridge University Press, 1987.

Payne, Leigh A. "Unsettling Accounts. Perpetrators' Confessions in the Aftermath of State Violence and Armed Conflict." In *The Routledge International Handbook of Perpetrator Studies*, edited by Susan C. Knittel and Zachary J. Goldberg, 130–141. London: Routledge, 2019.

Pavković, Nebojša. Interview, "War in Europe," FRONTLINE, *PBS*, n.d. https://www.pbs.org/wgbh/pages/frontline/shows/kosovo/interviews/pavkovic.html.

Peci, Edona. "Kosovo Wartime Rape Controversy Sparks Protest." *BIRN*, March 29, 2013. https://balkaninsight.com/2013/03/29/war-rape-issue-sparks-public-reactions/.

Perič, Tatiana, and Martin Demirovski. "Unwanted: The Exodus of Kosovo Roma (1998–2000)." *Cambridge Review of International Affairs* 13, no. 2 (2000): 83–96.

Perritt, Henry H., Jr. *Kosovo Liberation Army: The Inside Story of an Insurgency*. Champaign, IL: University of Illinois Press, 2008.

Pettifer, James. *The Kosova Liberation Army: Underground War to Balkan Insurgency, 1948–2001*. New York: Columbia University Press, 2012.

Phillips, David L. *Liberating Kosovo: Coercive Diplomacy and U.S. Intervention*. Cambridge, MA: MIT Press, 2012.

Portelli, Alessandro. *The Death of Luigi Trastulli and Other Stories: Form and Meaning in Oral History*. Albany: State University of New York Press, 1991.

Portelli, Alessandro. *The Order Has Been Carried Out: History, Memory, and Meaning of a Nazi Massacre in Rome*. London: Palgrave Studies in Oral History, [1999] 2007.

Portelli, Alessandro. "What Makes Oral History Different." In *The Oral History Reader*, edited by R. Perks and A. Thomson, 63–74. London: Routledge, 1998.

Porter, Elisabeth. "Gendered Narratives: Stories and Silences in Transitional Justice." *Human Rights Review* 17, no. 1 (2016): 35–50.

Pritchard, Eleanor. "Nested Comparisons: Nation-Building Through Comparative Thinking About Albanian Law." *International Journal of Law in Context* 12, no. 4 (2016): 469–483.

Pula, Besnik. "Dissecting Prishtina." *Kosovo 2.0.* June 3, 2013. http://kosovotwopointzero.com/en/dissecting-prishtina/.

Pula, Besnik. "The Emergence of the Kosovo 'Parallel State,' 1988–1992." *Nationalities Papers* 32, no. 4 (2004): 797–826.

Qena, Nebi. "Jeta e mirë atje n'Prishtinë, a? Si n'Zvicër?" *Koha Ditore*, June 16, 1998.

Radio Free Europe/Radio Liberty. "Western Leaders Warn Tear Gas Attacks Hurting Kosovo." October 24, 2015. https://www.refworld.org/docid/56813c9d15.html.

Radio Kosova e Lirë. "Luljetë Jahir Shala (2.10.1977–14.12.1998)." n.d. https://www.radiokosovaelire.com/luljete-jahir-shala-2-10-1977-14-12-1998/.

Radio Kosova e Lirë. "Mervete Salih Maksutaj (10.4.1978–4.12.1998)." n.d. https://www.radiokosovaelire.com/mervete-salih-maksutaj-10-4-1978-4-12-1998/.

Ramet, Sabrina Petra. *Balkan Babel: The Disintegration of Yugoslavia from the Death of Tito to the Fall of Milosevic*. London: Taylor & Francis Group, 2002.

Ramet, Sabrina Petra. *The Three Yugoslavias: State Building and Legitimation, 1918–2005*. Washington, DC: Woodrow Wilson Center Press; Bloomington: Indiana University Press, 2006.

Reineck, Janet. "The Past as Refuge: Gender, Migration and Ideology Among the Kosova Albanians." PhD dissertation, University of California, Berkeley, 1991.

Reuters. "Kosovo Rape Testimony Shown in Britain." April 13, 1999. https://reliefweb.int/report/serbia/london-kosovo-rape-testimony-shown-britain.

Revelli, Nuto. *L'anello più forte. La donna: Storie di vita contadina*. Torino: Einaudi, 1985.

Richardot, Sophie. "'You Know What to Do with Them:' The Formulation of Orders and Engagement in War Crime." *Aggression and Violent Behavior* 19 (2014): 83–90.

Ristić, Katarina, and Elisa Satjukow. "The 1999 NATO Intervention from a Comparative Perspective: An Introduction." *Comparative Southeast European Studies* 70, no. 2 (2022): 189–201.

Ristić, Marija, dir. *The Unidentified*. 2015. Belgrade: Balkan Investigative Reporting Network.

Rodogno, Davide. *Il nuovo ordine mediterraneo. Le politiche di occupazione dell'Italia fascista in Europa (1940–1943)*. Milano: Bollati Boringhieri, 2003.

Rogers, Alexandra. "British Ministers Under Fire After Serb Deputy PM Ivica Dacic, Former Ally of Milosevic, Spoke at Prevention of Sexual Violence in Conflict Conference in London." *Argumentum*, December 1, 2022. https://www.argumentum.al/en/british-ministers-under-fire-after-serb-deputy-pm-ivica-dacic-former-ally-of-milosevic-spoke-at-prevention-of-sexual-violence-in-conflict-conference-in-london/.

Rohde, David. "An Albanian Tells How Serbs Chose Her, 'the Most Beautiful' for Rape." *New York Times*, May 1, 1999, A8. https://www.nytimes.com/1999/05/01/world/crisis-balkans-crimes-albanian-tells-serbs-chose-her-most-beautiful-for-rape.html.

Ross, Fiona. *Bearing Witness: Women and the Truth and Reconciliation Commission in South Africa*. London: Pluto Press, 2002.

Rubin, Elizabeth. "Editor in Exile." *The New Yorker*, May 17, 1999, 46–53.

Rukovci, Eurisa. "Women in Bronze." *Dealing with the Past*, July 19, 2019. https://dwp-balkan.org/women-in-bronze/.

Saikia, Yasmin. *Women, War and the Making of Bangladesh: Remembering 1971*. Durham, NC: Duke University Press, 2011.

Scarry, Elaine. *The Body in Pain*. New York and Oxford: Oxford University Press, 1985.

Schwandner-Sievers, Stephanie. "The Bequest of *Ilegalja*: Contested Memories and Moralities in Contemporary Kosovo." *Nationalities Papers: The Journal of Nationalism and Ethnicity* 41, no. 6 (2013): 953–970.

Scott, James. "Voice Under Domination: The Arts of Political Disguise." In *Domination and the Art of Resistance: Hidden Transcripts*, 136–182. New Haven, CT: Yale University Press, 1990.

Sell, Louis. *Slobodan Milosevic and the Destruction of Yugoslavia*. Durham, NC: Duke University Press, 2002.
Serrano Fitamant, Dominique. *Assessment Report on Sexual Violence in Kosovo*. United Nations Population Fund, 1999. https://reliefweb.int/report/serbia/assessment-report-sexual-violence-kosovo.
Shatri, Mehmet. *Kosova në luftën e dytë botërore, 1941–1945*. Prishtinë: Botimet Toena, 1997.
Sheftel, Anna. "Talking and Not Talking About Violence: Challenges in Interviewing Survivors of Atrocity as Whole People." *Oral History Review* 54, no. 2 (2018): 278–293.
Shujaku, Valbona. *Prishtina Poetic Memories*. Prishtinë: Republic, 2011.
Simić, Olivera. *Silent Victims of Wartime Sexual Violence*. London: Taylor & Francis, 2018.
Simmel. Georg. "The Stranger." In *On Individuality and Social Forms: Selected Writings*, edited and with an Introduction by Donald N. Levine, 143–149. Chicago: Chicago University Press, [1908] 1971.
Skjelsbæk, Inger. "Victims and Survivors: Narrated Social Identities of Women Who Experienced Rape During the War in Bosnia-Herzegovina." *Feminism and Psychology* 16 (2006): 373–403.
Smith, Sidonie. "Narrating the Right to Sexual Well-Being and the Global Management of Misery: Maria Rosa Henson's Comfort Woman and Charlene Smiths' Proud of Me." *Literature and Medicine* 24, no. 2 (2005): 153–180.
Smucker, Philip. "Serbia: Kosovo Crackdown Over: West Mulls Action Today." *Newsday*, March 9, 1998.
Sorguc, Albina. "Srebrenica Anniversary: The Rape Victims' Testimonies=." *BIRN*, July 11, 2014. A15. https://balkaninsight.com/2014/07/11/srebrenica-anniversary-the-rape-victims-testimonies/.
Spina, Luigi. "Imporre il silenzio." In *Antichi Silenzi*, edited by Giorgio Ieranòe Luigi Spina, 9–29. Milano; Udine: Mimesis. Accademia del Silenzio, 2015.
Spina, Luigi. "Shhhh, la sfida etimologica e onomatopeica." In *Il paradosso del silenzio: Percorsi alternativi nel caos contemporaneo*, edited by Nicoletta Polla-Mattiot, 63–69. Padova: Il Poligrafo, 2009.
Stojanović, Lazar, dir. *The Scorpions—A Home Movie*. 2007. Belgrade: Humanitarian Law Center.
Ströhle, Isabel. "Speaking of Vendetta in the Century of the Atom: The Anti-Feuding Campaign in Late Socialist Kosovo." In *Violence After Stalin: Institutions, Practices, and Everyday Life in the Soviet Bloc 1953–1989*, edited by J. Claas Behrends, Pavel Kolár, and Thomas Lindenberger. Stuttgart and Hannover, Germany: Ibidem Press, 2024.
Sullivan, Stacy. *Be Not Afraid, for You Have Sons in America: How Albanians in the US Fought for Their People in Kosovo*. New York: St. Martin's Press, 2004.
"The Death of Milosevic Called Justice Denied." *New York Times*, March 3, 2006. https://www.nytimes.com/2006/03/12/world/europe/death-of-milosevic-called-justice-denied.html.
Thompson, Mark. *A Paper House: The Ending of Yugoslavia*. Vintage, 1992.
Tomasevich, Jozo. "Italian-Albanian Rule in Kosovo and Western Macedonia." In *War and Revolution in Yugoslavia, 1941–1945: Occupation and Collaboration*, 148–156. Stanford, CA: Stanford University Press, 2001.
Toomey, Christine. "Speak No Evil, See No Evil." *Sunday Times Magazine*, November 18, 1999, 32–42. https://www.christinetoomey.com/pdfs/Speak_No_Evil.pdf.
Ugrešić, Dubravka. *The Culture of Lies: Antipolitical Essays*. University Park, PA: Pennsylvania State University Press, 1998.
Umiltà, Carlo. *Jugoslavia e Albania: Memorie di un Diplomatico*. Milano: Garzanti, 1947.
UN Security Council. 2004. *Report on the Situation in Kosovo*, S/2004/932. https://www.securitycouncilreport.org/atf/cf/%7B65BFCF9B-6D27-4E9C-8CD3-CF6E4FF96FF9%7D/kos%20S2004%20932.pdf.

UNHCR. *IDP/Shelter Survey Kosovo: Joint Assessment in 20 Municipalities.* November 12, 1998.
UNHCR. *Kosovo Rapid Village Assessment: First Cut*, July 7, 1999. https://reliefweb.int/report/serbia/kosovo-rapid-village-assessment-first-cut-7-jul-1999
Vacsić, Miloš. "How Serbs and Albanians Perceive Each Other and Themselves. If They Were Really Like That." *Vreme*, March 14, 1998. https://serbiandigest.libraries.rutgers.edu/336/if-only-it-were-really-so
Valentini, Giuseppe, ed. *La legge delle montagne albanesi nelle relazioni della missione volante 1880–1932.* Firenze: Olschki Ed, 1969.
van der Kolk, Bessel A. *The Body Keeps the Score: Brain, Mind, and Body in the Healing of Trauma.* New York: Penguin Books, 2014.
van der Kolk, Bessel A., and Alexander Mc Farlane. "The Black Hole of Trauma." In *Traumatic Stress: The Effects of Overwhelming Experience on Mind, Body, and Society*, edited by Bessel van der Kolk, Alexander McFarlane, and Lars Weisaeth, 3–23. New York City: Guilford Press, 1996.
van der Kolk, Bessel A., and Onno van der Hart. "The Intrusive Past: The Flexibility of Memory and the Engraving of Trauma." In *Trauma: Explorations in Memory*, edited by Cathy Caruth, 158–182. Baltimore, MD, and London: Johns Hopkins University Press, 1995.
Verdery, Katherine. "From Parent-State to Family Patriarchs: Gender and Nation in Contemporary Eastern Europe." *East European Politics and Societies* 8, no. 2 (1994): 225–255.
Villapadierna, Ramiro. "Drenica, Después de la Matanza," *ABC*, March 15, 1998.
Vladisavljević, Nebošja. *Serbia's Antibureaucratic Revolution.* New York: Palgrave Macmillan, 2008.
Vranić, Seada. *Breaking the Wall of Silence: Voices from Rapes Bosnia.* Zagreb: Antibarbarus, 1996.
Vucinich, Wayne S., and Thomas A. Emmert, eds. *Kosovo: Legacy of a Medieval Battle.* Minneapolis, MN: University of Minnesota Press, 1991.
Wareham, Rachel. *No Safe Place: An Assessment of Violence Against Women in Kosovo.* United Nations Development Fund for Women, 2000. https://iknowpolitics.org/sites/default/files/nosafeplace_kosovo.pdf.
Weller, Marc. *The Crisis in Kosovo, 1989–1999: From the Dissolution of Yugoslavia to Rambouillet and the Outbreak of Hostilities.* Cambridge: Cambridge University Press, 1999.
Williams, Carol J. "In Kosovo, Rape Seen as Awful as Death." *Los Angeles Times*, May 27, 1999, A1. https://www.latimes.com/archives/la-xpm-1999-may-27-mn-41524-story.html.
Winkler, Cathy. "Rape as Social Murder." *Anthropology Today* 7, no. 3 (1991): 12–14.
Wolfe, Lauren. "Ukraine's True Detectives: The Investigators Closing in on Russian War Criminals." *The Guardian*, October 20, 2022. https://www.theguardian.com/world/2022/oct/20/ukraine-true-detectives-investigators-closing-in-on-russian-war-crimes.
Wolff, Larry. *Inventing Eastern Europe: The Map of Civilization on the Mind of the Enlightenment.* Stanford, CA: Stanford University Press, 1994.
Žarkov, Dubravka. *The Body of War: Media, Ethnicity and Gender in the Break-Up of Yugoslavia.* Durham, NC: Duke University Press, 2007.
Zolo, Danilo. *Invoking Humanity: War, Law, and Global Order.* London: Bloomsbury, 2002.

THE OXFORD ORAL HISTORY SERIES

Erin Jessee (University of Glasgow)
Nicholas Ng-A-Fook (University of Ottawa)
Annie Valk (CUNY Graduate Center)
Series Editors

Donald A. Ritchie (Historian Emeritus, US Senate)
Senior Advisor

Dreaming the New Woman: An Oral History of Missionary Schoolgirls in Republican China
Jennifer Bond

Sound Writing: Voices, Authors, and Readers of Oral History
Shelley Trower

Oral History and the Environment
Edited by Stephen M. Sloan and Mark Cave

Rethinking Oral History and Tradition: An Indigenous Perspective
Nepia Mahuika

Sisterhood and After: An Oral History of the UK Women's Liberation Movement, 1968–present
Margaretta Jolly

Narrating South Asian Partition: Oral History, Literature, Cinema
Anindya Raychaudhuri

Voices of Guinness: An Oral History of the Park Royal Brewery
Tim Strangleman

Fly Until You Die: An Oral History of Hmong Pilots in the Vietnam War
Chia Youyee Vang

Edward M. Kennedy: An Oral History
Barbara A. Perry

The Land Speaks: New Voices at the Intersection of Oral and Environmental History
Edited by Debbie Lee and Kathryn Newfont

The Voice of the Past: Oral History, Fourth Edition
Paul Thompson with Joanna Bornat

When Sonia Met Boris: An Oral History of Jewish Life Under Stalin
Anna Shternshis

Inside the Clinton White House: An Oral History
Russell L. Riley

Escape to Miami: An Oral History of the Cuban Rafter Crisis
Elizabeth Campisi

Velvet Revolutions: An Oral History of Czech Society
Miroslav Vaněk and Pavel Mücke

Pioneers and Partisans: An Oral History of Nazi Genocide in Belorussia
Anika Walke

Doing Oral History, Third Edition
Donald A. Ritchie

A Guide to Oral History and the Law, Second Edition
John A. Neuenschwander

Chinese Comfort Women: Testimonies from Imperial Japan's Sex Slaves
Peipei Qiu, with Su Zhiliang and Chen Lifei

Listening on the Edge: Oral History in the Aftermath of Crisis
Edited by Mark Cave and Stephen M. Sloan

Dedicated to God: An Oral History of Cloistered Nuns
Abbie Reese

Lady Bird Johnson: An Oral History
Michael L. Gillette

Bodies of Evidence: The Practice of Queer Oral History
Edited by Nan Alamilla Boyd and Horacio N. Roque Ramírez

Soviet Baby Boomers: An Oral History of Russia's Cold War Generation
Donald J. Raleigh

Freedom Flyers: The Tuskegee Airmen of World War II
J. Todd Moye

Habits of Change: An Oral History of American Nuns
Carole Garibaldi Rogers

They Say in Harlan County: An Oral History
Alessandro Portelli

The Wonder of Their Voices: The 1946 Holocaust Interviews of David Boder
Alan Rosen

Launching the War on Poverty: An Oral History, Second Edition
Michael L. Gillette

The Firm: The Inside Story of the Stasi
Gary Bruce

Singing Out: An Oral History of America's Folk Music Revivals
David K. Dunaway and Molly Beer

Approaching an Auschwitz Survivor: Holocaust Testimony and Its Transformations
Edited by Jürgen Matthäus

The Oxford Handbook of Oral History
Edited by Donald A. Ritchie

Index

Since the index has been created to work across multiple formats, indexed terms for which a page range is given (e.g., 52–53, 66–70, etc.) may occasionally appear only on some, but not all of the pages within the range.

Abrashi, Bahtije 31–32
Agani, Fehmi 128–129
Ahmeti, Sevdije 19–22, 32–33, 72, 123, 186
Albania
   Albanian flag 76–79
   Albanian question 21, 234 n.16
   Greater Albania 21–23
   Pan-Albanianism 25
Améry, Jean 148–149, 195–196, 245 n.8, 248 n.8
Amnesty International 3–4, 16–17, 74–75, 232 n.15, 236 n.44, 238 n.97, 241 n.8, 241 n.18, 241 n.23, 242 n.4, 248 n.65, 248 n.67
Ashkali 38–39

Backer, Berit 58, 238 n.10, 239 n.17, 239 nn.25–26, 239 nn.3–6, 240 n.7
Ballist 74–75, 235 n.27, 242 n.43
Bakalli, Mahmut 26–27, 73–74
Bala, Nazlie 32–33, 65–66, 70, 123–124, 155, 163–164, 210, 212, 237 n.71, 245 n.17
Banac, Ivo 234 n.6, 234 n.18, 235 n.28, 235 n.32
Barker, Pat 147–148, 245 n.4
Basholli, Blerta 217–218, 249 nn.9–11
Beckett, Samuel 194–195
Berisha Lushaj, Zyrafete 80, 241 n.25
blood feuds
   kanun 63–64, 213
   reconciliation campaign 9–10, 233 n.34
   women 58, 213
   Yugoslavia 63–64
Bonomy, Lord Ian 170–171, 176
Bosnia and Herzegovina
   Bosnian war 3–4, 29–30, 81–84, 231 n.11
   Dayton Peace Accord 77–78
   sexual violence 1–2, 4–5, 13–15, 32–34, 37–38, 171, 213–214, 233 n.41, 236 n.61

Srebrenica genocide 34–35, 237 n.79
   international justice 169–172, 183–186
Bracewell, Wendy 233 n.42, 236 n.57, 237 n.66, 238 n.94
Brovina, Flora 122–124, 244 n.3
Broz, Josip (Tito) 22–26, 73, 78–79, 235 n.41, 235 n.28
Bujku 93–94, 122

Center for the Promotion of Women's Rights (Drenas) 7–8, 206
Center for the Protection of Women and Children (Pristina) 33, 186–187
Çetta, Anton 238 n.3, 245 n.16, 249 n.27
Çitaku, Vlora 210
Clark, Mary Marshall 11–12, 233 n.38
Clark, Gen. Wesley 95–97, 123, 242 n.2, 244 n.6
Council for the Defense of Human Rights and Freedom (KMLDNJ) 32–33
Croatia 21–22, 26, 28–30, 38, 81–84, 123–124
Cvijić, Jovan 20–21, 234 n.14

Dačić, Ivica 224–225, 250 n.33
Das, Veena 225, 233 n.31, 250 n.21, 250 n.37
Del Ponte, Carla 156, 169–170
Delbo, Charlotte 190–191, 248 n.2
Dida, Nadire 66–68, 240 n.23
Djordijević, Vlastimir 170–171
Dobruna, Vjosa 32–33, 52–53, 81, 84–87, 123, 125–126, 237 n.73
Drakulić, Slavenka 171, 246 n.12
Drenica 99–100
   KLA early operations 94–96
   poverty 40–41, 95, 238 n.3
   Prekaz massacre 95–98, 123
   Second World War 22–23, 76, 235 n.26
   Serbian counterinsurgency 93–96, 98–99, 107
   solidarity with 123–124
Dreshaj, Myrvete 79–80

Dugolli, Enver 78–79, 241 nn.21–23
Dukagjin 10–11, 40–41, 98–99, 208
 The Code of Lekë Dukagjin, see *kanun*
Dushi, Arbnora 83, 235 n.30, 241 n.31

education
 Albanians' literacy 22, 24–25, 51–52
 class distinctions 65–68
 distance of schools from home 46–48
 "education agreement" 77–78
 education of girls 15–16, 45–55, 71–72
 kanun 48–50
 fear of assimilation 51
 girls' movement for education 52
 parallel schools 28–30, 87–90
 poisoning of Albanian students 88–89
 schools as detention places 109–110, 132–133
 schools as sites of protest 76–79
 schools as shelters 101, 139–140
 women's literacy 51–52
Egyptians 38–39
Emini-Mira, Hyrë 210–211
ethnic cleansing
 forced displacement 1–2, 16–17, 36–37, 105–106, 142, 149–150, 164, 173–174
 Kosovo war 1–4, 15–16, 107–108, 211–212
 intent 36–37, 169–170, 181–182, 216
 sexual violence, *see* sexual violence as a weapon of war
European Union Rule of Law Mission, EULEX 4–5, 186–187

Fishta, Gjergj 63–64, 66–67, 239 n.15, 240 n.15
Fussell, Paul 147–148, 245 n.2

Gashi, Shukrije 79–80
Geci, Halit 93–94, 242 n.46
Gjergji, dom Lush 9–10, 47–48, 82–83, 233 n.35, 238 n.12, 241 n.28
Gjurgjeala, Jehona 88, 242 n.36
Goffman, Erving 148–149, 209–210, 225–226, 245 n.5, 245 n.20, 246 n.25, 248 n.18, 250 n.41
Gradica, Mehmet 91–92, 242 n.43
Grele, Ronald 5–6, 232 n.26

Haradinaj, Hatmone 76–77, 241 n.11
Haradinaj, Ramush 98–99, 243 n.24, 243 n.25
Hasanaj, Dino 194, 248 n.7
Hasani, Nait 78–79
Hasluck, Margaret 49–50, 57–58, 238 n.10, 239 n.13, 239 n.20, 239 n.2
Hoti, Fahrije 217–218

Hoti, Shaqir 74–75, 241 n.6
Hoxha, Enver 23–26
Hoxha, Fadil 31–32, 235 n.26, 237 n.68, 240 n.22
Human Rights Watch 3–4, 38–39, 98–99, 222–223, 231 n.13, 236 n.51, 237 n.85, 238 n.99, 240 n.21, 241 n.27, 242 nn.3–5, 243 n.33, 244 n.17, 244 n.21, 245 n.19, 247 n.44, 249 n.10
Humanitarian Law Center 35–36, 237 n.83, 242 n.6, 243 n.29
Hyseni, Hydajet 78, 241 n.20

International Criminal Court (ICC) 223–224, 249 n.10
International Criminal Tribunal for Rwanda (ICTR) 223–224
Idrizi, Valdete 88–89
Ilegalja 25–26, 74–75, 78, 235 n.40
International Criminal Tribunal for the Former Yugoslavia (ICTY)
 indictments for sexual violence 169–172, 246 n.4
 verdicts on sexual violence 4–5, 36–39, 181–182, 186–187
 witness testimonies 2, 17–18, 156, 169–172, 176, 179–180
Izeti, Selvi 155–156, 161–164, 198–199, 204–205, 208, 213, 246 n.22, 246 n.21, 248 n.10, 249 n.26

Jahjaga, Atifete 6–7, 210
Jashari, Adem 95–98, 242 n.4
Joachim, Ingebor 176
justice
 domestic 186–187
 international, *see* ICTY
 restorative 8–10, 204–208, 223–224

kaçak 21
Kandić, Nataša 125
kanun
 blood feuds, *see* blood feuds
 Code of Lekë Dukagjin 49, 239 n.15
 definition 48–50
 education, *see* education
 women 49–50, 54–55, 213
Kastrati, Bahrije 73–74
Kelmendi, Aziz 82–83
Kelmendi, Bajram 81–82, 125, 241 n.26
Kelmendi, Migjen 69, 240 n.25
Koha Ditore 6–7, 93–94, 96–97, 122, 214, 242 n.49, 243 nn.9–10, 243 n.16, 244 n.1

INDEX 269

Kosovo, Battle 20–21, 234 nn.10–12
Kosovo Liberation Army (KLA) 1–2, 93–167
  civilian population 116–117, 123–124, 134–138, 172–173
  indictments 4–5, 38–39
  labeled as terrorists 173–174, 178–179, 182–183
  narratives 3–4
  relationship with the Albanian Diaspora 33–34
  women 73–74, 105–106, 210–212, 219
Kosovo Oral History Initiative 10–11, 240 n.14
Kosovo Rehabilitation of Torture Center (KRTC) 7–8, 204–205, 208–209
Kraja, Mehmet 28–29, 74–75, 235 n.42, 236 n.50, 241 n.7
Krasniqi, Lumturije (Lumka) 123–124, 212–213, 244 n.9, 248 n.25
Krasniqi-Goodman, Vasfije 2–3, 186–188, 209–210
Krasniqi-Ladrovci, Xheva 73–74

Ladrovci, Ramiz 206–207
Laub, Dori 222–223, 231 n.4, 233 n.47, 249 n.2, 250 n.26
Leydesdorff, Selma 13–14, 233 n.41
Levi, Primo 225–226, 250 n.40
Lokaj, Xhejrane 50–52, 88–89
Luković, Milorad Ulemek (Legija) 185–186
Lukić, Sreten 170, 181–182

Maksutaj, Mervete 105–106, 210–211, 243 n.27, 248 n.21
Malcolm, Noel 234 nn.7–9, 234 n.10, 234 n.17, 235 n.34, 235 n.35, 235 n.39, 236 n.45, 242 n.39
Maliqi, Shkëlzen 27–28, 235 n.33, 236 n.49
marriage
  arranged 15–16, 50–51, 54–57, 61–62
  nusja 58–59
Marković, Mirjana 169
Martinović, Djordje 30–31
May, Sir Robert 172–175, 179–181
Mead, Margaret 40, 238 n.1
Medica Gjakova 4–11, 39, 205–206, 208–209
Meha, Tahir 76, 241 n.10
Milošević, Slobodan 2–5, 14–18, 27–28, 34–35, 38, 72–73, 76–78, 83, 87–88, 93–99, 107, 156, 162–164, 169–184, 203, 222–223, 233 n.2, 246 n.1
Montenegro 21–22, 40–41, 49, 63–64, 98–99, 146, 150–151, 233 n.5, 240 n.12
Mookherjee, Naynika 7–8, 232 n.29

Mulliqi, Shpresa 212, 248 n.24
Murtezi-Shala 2–3
Musa, Pranvera 126, 244 n.14

NATO
  intervention 1–4, 34–38, 107–108, 116–119, 124–125
  peacekeeping (KFOR) 34–35, 150–152
Nice, Geoffrey 172, 181

Ojdanić, Dragoljub 169–170, 181–182
Organization for the Security and Co-Operation in Europe (OSCE) 3–4, 38–39, 124–125, 155, 231 n.13, 234 n.9, 237 n.85, 238 n.99

Paraćin 82–83
Passerini, Luisa 5–6, 232 n.26
police
  arrests 27–29, 78–79
  checkpoints 16–17, 19, 87, 89–90, 94–95, 122–127, 141, 174, 182–183, 205–206
  detentions 37–38, 76, 79–81, 99, 117–118, 169
  house searches 92–93
  "informative interrogations" 80–81
  torture 1–2, 7–8, 11–12, 16–17, 23–27, 30, 32–33, 79–80
Pavković, Nebojša 97, 170–171, 181–182, 184
Portelli, Alessandro 5–6, 12–14, 232 n.26, 233 n.40, 233 n.39
Prekpalaj, Marta 54–55, 239 n.28

Ranković, Aleksandar 23–24, 78, 235 n.33
Reineck, Janet 40–41, 238 n.10, 238 nn.4–5, 239 n.22, 239 n.21, 239 n.16, 240 nn.9–10
Revelli, Nuto 15–16, 233 n.44
Rilindja 93–94
Rogova, Igballe (Igo) 126–127, 210
Rogova, Safete 68, 123–124, 240 n.24, 244 n.15
Roma
  bystanders 132–133, 135
  civilians killed 34–35, 107
  magjup 111–112, 119–121, 145–146
  perpetrators 145
  RAE 238 n.96
  sexual violence against 3–4, 38–39, 238 nn.96–97, 238 nn.98–99
rrethi
  definition 45–46
  opposition to school 45–46, 54–55
  ostracism 45–47, 147–148
  power over people 52, 160, 164–166
  stigma, *see* stigma, social pressure

Rugova, Ibrahim 29–30, 33, 77–78, 91–94, 119–121
Rushiti, Feride 5–8, 200–205

Sada, Mirlinda (Linda) 205–206
Šainović, Nikola 169–170
Selimaj, Bruno 33–34
Serbia
    Memorandum (SANU) 30–31, 236 n.60
    Orthodox Church 20–21, 30–31, 38, 88–89, 98–99, 150–151, 236 n.59, 245 n.12
    Second World War 21–23, 74–75
sexual violence
    branding 112–114, 136–137, 157, 160–161
    crime against humanity 4–5
    definition 169–170
    perpetrators 3, 36–37, 39, 132–133, 135–136, 148–149, 169–171, 180–187, 205, 216, 222–223, 247 n.59, 250 n.27
    rape-camps 32–33, 190, 213–214, 244 n.1
    rape myths 154–155, 221–222
    Second World War 2
    sexualized propaganda 2–14, 19–20, 29–30
    weapon of war 3–5, 10–11, 14, 16–17, 35–37, 170–183, 186–187, 204–206, 217, 223–224, 231 n.13, 232 n.19, 237 n.85
Shala, Hava 47, 55, 238 n.11
Shala Bujupi, Luljeta (Suljota) 210–211
Sherifi-Maçastena, Naime 76–77, 230, 241 n.12
Sheftel, Anna 11–12, 233 n.37
Shehu, Veprore (Lola) 204–205
silence 1–2, 5–6, 18, 221
    breaking 2–3, 8–9, 17–18, 206–208, 210, 222–223
    definition 17, 148–149
    imposed 1–5, 163–164, 217–218, 221–222
    shock 148–149, 155
    self-imposed 204, 222
Simić, Olivera 4–5, 232 n.21
Skjelsbæk, Inger 13–14, 233 n.41
Slovenia 26, 28–30, 82
Spina, Luigi 221, 249 nn.18–20
Steele, Jonathan 94–95, 231 n.11, 242 n.48
stigma
    guilt, *see* trauma, guilt
    physical marks 132–133
    reaction against 209
    resilience 225–226
    secrecy 8–9, 17
    shame 5–6, 17, 112–113, 147–148, 155, 160, 166–167, 218–219, 221–224, 250 n.23

social pressure 12, 147–148, 160, 163–164, 166–167
stigmatizers 222
Surlić, Stefan 88, 242 n.37
Syla, Ola 67–69, 126, 240 n.21, 244 n.13

Tahiraj, Kadire 3, 5, 9–10, 206, 208, 231 n.10, 233 n.33, 248 n.15
Tahiraj, Shukrije 89–90, 242 n.42
Tahiri, Edita 123, 244 n.5
Tahiri-Sylejmani, Shyrete 2–3
tradition, see *kanun*
    joint family 40–41, 238 n.1
    zadruga, see joint family
    tree of milk 40–41
    tree of blood 40–41
    fis 40–41, 62–63, 153, 163–164
    oda 41, 91, 96–97, 163–164
    nda buka 46–47
trauma
    collective 2–3, 211–212, 215–216
    Complex PTSD 17–18
    dreams and nightmares 17–18, 190–191, 193–194
    forgetting 193
    guilt 161–162, 166–167, 181, 189–191, 198–199
    suicide 194–198
    traumatic memories 192–194, 196–197
Tunaj, Martë 2

Ugresić, Dubravka 30–31, 236 n.62, 236 n.58
United Nations
    United Nations Mission in Kosovo (UNMIK) 38–39, 186–188
    Special Representative for Sexual Violence 4–5, 232 n.18

Van der Kolk, Bessel A. 245 n.8, 249 n.4
Vranić, Seada 13–14, 233 n.41
Vula, Xheraldina 122

Winkler, Cathy 196–197, 248 n.9
Woolf, Virginia 148–149

Xhafa-Mripa, Alketa 1

Yugoslavia
    Constitution of 1974 24–26
    League of Communists 24–29, 73, 83
    Yugoslav gulag, Goli Otok 76